中译翻译文库

北外高翻笔译课

An English-Chinese Translation Course in Beiwai

（英译汉）

李长栓　王苏阳　著

中国出版集团
中译出版社

图书在版编目（CIP）数据

北外高翻笔译课：英译汉 / 李长栓，王苏阳著. -- 北京：中译出版社，2020.5（2022.10重印）
（中译翻译文库）
ISBN 978-7-5001-6264-3

Ⅰ. ①北… Ⅱ. ①李… ②王… Ⅲ. ①英语－翻译 Ⅳ. ①H315.9

中国版本图书馆 CIP 数据核字（2020）第 033135 号

出版发行 /	中译出版社
地　　址 /	北京市西城区新街口外大街 28 号普天德胜大厦主楼 4 层
电　　话 /	（010）68359827（发行部）；68359725（编辑部）
邮　　编 /	100044
传　　真 /	（010）68357870
电子邮箱 /	book@ctph.com.cn
网　　址 /	http://www.ctph.com.cn
出 版 人 /	乔卫兵
总 策 划 /	刘永淳
责任编辑 /	范祥镇　王诗同
封面设计 /	黄　浩
排　　版 /	北京竹页文化传媒有限公司
印　　刷 /	山东华立印务有限公司
经　　销 /	新华书店
规　　格 /	710 毫米×1000 毫米　1/16
印　　张 /	29.25
字　　数 /	420 千字
版　　次 /	2020 年 5 月第一版
印　　次 /	2022 年 10 月第七次

ISBN 978-7-5001-6264-3　　定价：69.00元

版权所有　侵权必究

中　译　出　版　社

中译翻译文库
编 委 会

顾　　问（以姓氏拼音为序）
John Michael Minford（英国著名汉学家、文学翻译家、《红楼梦》英译者）
黄友义（中国外文局）　　　　　　　尹承东（中共中央编译局）

主任编委（以姓氏拼音为序）
Andrew C. Dawrant（AIIC会员，上海外国语大学）　柴明颎（上海外国语大学）
陈宏薇（华中师范大学）　　　　　戴惠萍（AIIC会员，上海外国语大学）
方梦之（《上海翻译》）　　　　　　冯庆华（上海外国语大学）
辜正坤（北京大学）　　　　　　　　郭建中（浙江大学）
黄忠廉（黑龙江大学）　　　　　　　贾兵伟（中译出版社）
李亚舒（《中国科技翻译》）　　　　刘和平（北京语言大学）
刘士聪（南开大学）　　　　　　　　吕和发（北京第二外国语学院）
罗选民（清华大学）　　　　　　　　梅德明（上海外国语大学）
穆　雷（广东外语外贸大学）　　　　谭载喜（香港浸会大学）
王恩冕（对外经济贸易大学）　　　　王继辉（北京大学）
王立弟（北京外国语大学）　　　　　吴　青（北京外国语大学）
谢天振（上海外国语大学）　　　　　许　钧（南京大学）
杨　平（《中国翻译》）　　　　　　张高里（中译出版社）
仲伟合（广东外语外贸大学）

编委委员（以姓氏拼音为序）
Daniel Gile（AIIC会员，巴黎高等翻译学校）　蔡新乐（南京大学）
陈　刚（浙江大学）　　　　　　　　陈　菁（厦门大学）
陈德鸿（香港岭南大学）　　　　　　陈　琳（同济大学）
傅勇林（西南交通大学）　　　　　　傅敬民（上海大学）
高　伟（四川外国语大学）　　　　　顾铁军（中国传媒大学）
郭著章（武汉大学）　　　　　　　　何其莘（中国人民大学）
胡开宝（上海交通大学）　　　　　　黄杨勋（福州大学）
贾文波（中南大学）　　　　　　　　江　红（AIIC会员，香港理工大学）
焦鹏帅（西南民族大学）　　　　　　金圣华（香港中文大学）
柯　平（南京大学）　　　　　　　　李均洋（首都师范大学）
李正栓（河北师范大学）　　　　　　廖七一（四川外国语大学）
林超伦（英国KL传播有限公司）　　　林大津（福建师范大学）
林克难（天津外国语大学）　　　　　刘树森（北京大学）

吕　俊（南京师范大学）
马士奎（中央民族大学）
孟凡君（西南大学）
潘文国（华东师范大学）
彭　萍（北京外国语大学）
秦潞山（AIIC 会员，Chin Communications）
任　文（四川大学）
申　丹（北京大学）
石平萍（解放军外国语大学）
孙会军（上海外国语大学）
陶丽霞（四川外国语大学）
王建国（华东理工大学）
王克非（北京外国语大学）
文　军（北京航空航天大学）
温建平（上海对外经贸大学）
闫素伟（国际关系学院）
杨全红（四川外国语大学）
张春柏（华东师范大学）
张美芳（澳门大学）
张秀仿（河北工程大学）
赵　刚（华东师范大学）
朱纯深（香港城市大学）

马会娟（北京外国语大学）
门顺德（大连外国语大学）
牛云平（河北大学）
潘志高（解放军外国语大学）
彭发胜（合肥工业大学）
屈文生（华东政法大学）
邵　炜（AIIC 会员，北京外国语大学）
石　坚（四川大学）
宋亚菲（广西大学）
孙迎春（山东大学）
王　宏（苏州大学）
王　宁（清华大学）
王振华（河南大学）
文　旭（西南大学）
肖维青（上海外国语大学）
杨　柳（南京大学）
姚桂桂（江汉大学）
张德禄（山东大学、同济大学）
张其帆（AIIC 会员，香港理工大学）
章　艳（上海外国语大学）
郑海凌（北京师范大学）
朱振武（上海师范大学）

特约编审（以姓氏拼音为序）
Andrew C. Dawrant（AIIC 会员，上海外国语大学）
戴惠萍（AIIC 会员，上海外国语大学）
高　伟（四川外国语大学）
黄国文（中山大学）
李长栓（北京外国语大学）
李亚舒（《中国科技翻译》）
罗新璋（中国社会科学院）
孟凡君（西南大学）
屠国元（中南大学）
王立弟（北京外国语大学）
谢天振（上海外国语大学）
杨　平（《中国翻译》）
杨士焯（厦门大学）
俞利军（对外经济贸易大学）
张　鹏（四川外国语大学）
祝朝伟（四川外国语大学）

柴明颎（上海外国语大学）
冯庆华（上海外国语大学）
胡安江（四川外国语大学）
黄忠廉（黑龙江大学）
李凌鸿（重庆法语联盟）
刘军平（武汉大学）
梅德明（上海外国语大学）
苗　菊（南开大学）
王东风（中山大学）
王明树（四川外国语大学）
徐　珺（对外经济贸易大学）
杨全红（四川外国语大学）
杨晓荣（《外语研究》）
张　健（上海外国语大学）
赵学文（吉林大学）

前言

翻译可以是谋生的工具,职场升职必备技能,跨文化沟通的桥梁,也可以是一种生活的态度。对于翻译的理解,影响译者在翻译中的追求,也影响学习翻译的方法。

本书向大家呈现的是北京外国语大学高级翻译学院的笔译教学框架。北外高翻笔译课共两个学期,第一学期教学循序渐进、逐一推进各项子能力;第二学期培养学生在各专业领域综合运用各项子能力,引导学生向翻译职业化、市场化、专业化方向发展。

为展现真实教学情况,本书精选了2017—2019学年英汉笔译教学材料和附带详细注释的参考译文。译文的注释包括初稿制作过程查找的资料、译者的思考、多轮修订中补充的材料和修订过程中的对话,反映了北外高翻人对翻译的理解和追求,希望给广大翻译爱好者、教育工作者、研究者带来启示,让大家在这个急功近利的时代,重新理解翻译、界定翻译、爱上翻译。

2005年以来,在两位翻译实践专家李长栓和周蕴仪老师的带领下,北外高翻学院建立了一套独特的笔译教学体系,包括学生译文加注和提交修订稿、参考译文加注、学生互审、批改全覆盖、双师教学、补充专业知识等环节。2017年,王苏阳、曾佳宁、冯爱苏(Ursula Friedman)老师加入了北外高翻的教学团队,传承了这一教学方法。同时,在王苏阳老师的倡议下,教学团队对这一教学模式进行了理论梳理,让翻译教学更加系统化、渐进式、关注学生发展。

在构建高翻教学模式的过程中，教学团队借鉴了西班牙巴塞罗那大学 PACTE 研究团队的翻译能力框架。PACTE 为巴塞罗那大学的一个"翻译能力习得过程与评估"小组，自 1997 年成立以来，一直致力于翻译能力习得研究（仝亚辉，2010:88）。1988 年，PACTE 团队第一次提出了六项相互关联、层层递进的翻译能力要素，分别为语言交际能力、言外能力、工具—职业能力、生理和心理能力、转换能力、策略能力（PACTE, 2017）。PACTE 于 2002 年和 2003 年分别对翻译能力模型进行修改（PACTE, 2017）。重新界定后的六项翻译能力包括双语能力、语言外能力、翻译知识能力、工具能力、策略能力，以及最后的心理和生理要素（2017）。

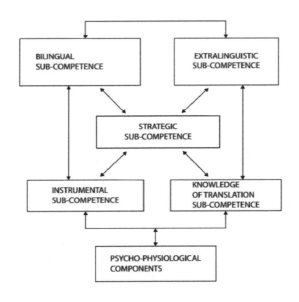

图 1　PACTE 的翻译能力模型

受此启发，团队在北外高翻多年教学实践的基础上，从翻译教学角度提出具有高翻特色的笔译核心能力，包括职业伦理、全局意识、语言能力、跨文化能力、逻辑思维能力、查证能力六项子能力。

职业伦理侧重翻译的基本职业素养，包括职业操守、译文规范、客户沟通等；全局意识是指译者的宏观思维能力，包括从宏观上把握原文、了解作者和写作背景，并根据翻译情景决定翻译策略，形成符合用途的译文；语言能力是指学生的语法知识、欧化中文／中式英文意识、中英文差异敏感度等和语言相关的能力；跨文化沟通能力是指译者能够理解并有效转换具有文化特色的表达方式；逻辑思维能力是指在原文逻辑不通或含混的情况下，译者可以打破原文重建译文，以清楚的逻辑传达作者意图；查证能力是增强上述各项能力的工具，翻译中遇到的各种问题，都可以通过查证加以解决。

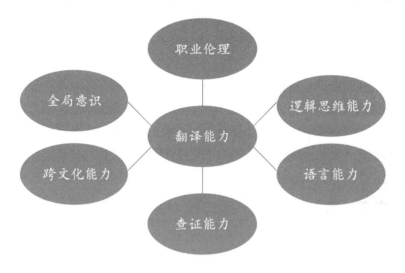

图 2　北外高翻的能力培养模式

这些子能力和 PACTE 翻译能力模型有重合，也有创新。高翻模型中的翻译职业伦理，属于 PACTE 翻译知识能力的一部分。团队认为，从教学角度讲，学生适合接触翻译初期了解翻译的基本做法和职业素养，这是做好一切翻译的基础；翻译模型中的全局意识能力，虽属于 PACTE 双语能力中语篇和语用学的范畴，但对这种超语言、超文本的程序性知识（procedural knowledge）（仝亚辉：89）强调不够，也不具有教学的渐进性启示作用。因此，高翻在模型中推出的全局意识能力就是我们的创新。和 PACTE 模型中双语能力相比，全局意识更强调学生对整个原文产生背景和翻译情境的把握；高翻模型中的语言能力，相当于 PACTE 模型中的双语知识能力，强调学生对语言结构的理解和运用问题；高翻模型中的跨文化沟通能力和逻辑思维能力是对 PACTE 语言外能力这种陈述性知识（declarative knowledge）

的继续推进，特别是在逻辑思维能力中，高翻模型强调在对原文充分尊重的情况下，对原文进行逻辑思维解构与重建，使学生翻译出逻辑通顺的译文；高翻模型中的查证能力相当于 PACTE 模型中的工具能力，然而高翻的查证能力并非仅仅是对工具的运用，还强调对工具的选取，对材料的思考和论证，整体意义大于运用工具本身；最后，PACTE 翻译能力模型中的生理和心理因素虽在我们的能力模型中没有体现，但这些重要因素应贯穿于教学过程始终，因此没有在教学中将其单列为一项重点能力。

总之，两个模型不能完全对应，这是因为高翻模型的最终目标是辅助教学。高翻的模型是理论内核、实践驱动、教学先行。

上述六种基本能力，放在第一学期分别进行；第二学期，笔译教学侧重培养学生对各项翻译能力的综合运用，也就是 PACTE 翻译能力框架中的核心要素"策略能力"（PACTE，2017）。这一阶段旨在让学生译员朝翻译职业化、市场化、专业化发展。诚然，学术上可能存在职业化与专业化之辩，但是，我们的培养目标不是让学生立即成为各领域的专才，而是让他们广泛涉猎，为未来的职业和专业发展打下基础。鉴于此，学生在第二学期会接触各领域的专业文本。

教学材料的选取，遵循循序渐进的原则。第一学期注重基本翻译能力培养，每次以一个主要能力为培养目标，然后挑选特别有利于培养这种能力的材料；第二学期则侧重培养学生对各项翻译能力的综合运用，以专业领域材料为主，包括但不限于政治（联合国文件）、法律、金融财会、信息技术和文化艺术类稿件。每年选材的方向根据市场需求适时变化。

笔译课每学期布置六七次英汉作业（汉英数量相同）；学生独立完成，全部提交，老师抽样批改后统一讲解，然后学生分别修改，再次提交，老师和助教再逐一批改。每次作业 300-700 单词不等，但会把文章全文发给学生。学生完成作业时，需要通读全文。提交的作业包括针对原文理解撰写的原文尾注、译文本身和针对译文表达撰写的译文尾注。

据了解，学生常常为了一份作业熬上几个晚上，精心查证、润色译文。一篇作业原文的字数可能不到 300 字，但学生交上来的作业可能有三四十页。听完老师讲解后，还需要修订译文，提交二稿。也许，区区几百字，机器翻译几秒钟就完成了，但是笔译团队、全体学生在它上面倾注的时间和

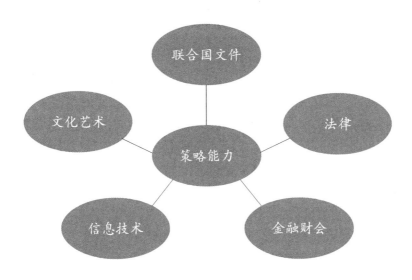

图 3　第二学期选材

精力，是不可估量的。

为了给学生提供具有较高参考价值的译文，笔译团队每次都会竭尽全力，共同修改润色参考译文。与传统参考译文要树立的理念不同，北外高翻的参考译文不讲求树立教师的权威。参考译文先由助教制作一稿，然后由任课教师和助教反复修改，再由李长栓老师修改审定。李老师审定过程中，会和任课教师和助教反复沟通。

助教批改作业的过程中如果发现参考译文有问题，可以提出来完善；参考译文发给学生后，鼓励学生继续挑毛病。无论是谁的见解，只要正确，都会被参考译文吸收，并在注释中说明贡献者。在这样的氛围中，我们创造了教学的共同体、共生体、共促体，培养力臻完美的匠人之心。

从这一角度看，参考译文的目的和作用已经升华。它不再是树立权威的模板，而是教师与学生沟通的桥梁，打破了传统上的师道尊严。不错，模板还在，权威尚存，但这份权威，是众人智慧的结晶，是译者为翻译质量尽善尽美所树立的标杆。

本书并非仅仅是一本教材。它不仅是翻译爱好者的良师益友，也可以为翻译教育者、研究者提供教学和研究参考。

对于翻译学习者、爱好者来说，可以按照每章提出的训练目的和方式，逐渐掌握各项翻译能力，迈向翻译的职业化和专业化。对于翻译教师来说，本书可以作为设置笔译课教学框架、草拟教学大纲的参考。对于翻译研究者来说，本书是研究翻译能力构建的素材，因为从海量的注释材料中，还可能发现更多需要关注的元素。

也许有人会质疑，在这样一个翻译需求倍增，人工智能、大数据技术快速发展的时代，学生需要学习的是快速翻译的能力，教师需要教给学生快速完成任务的诀窍。然而，人们往往忽略了人工智能与人最大的区别。至少从目前来看，人有本心、有初心、有情感、有投入，而这些都是机器暂时（或永远）做不到的。在乱象丛生的翻译市场面前，市场最需要的是高端翻译人才，高质量的翻译才是千金难买的。

如果想要快速产出译文，可以选择机器翻译——原文规范、意思简单的情景下，机器翻译甚至可以让人了解大意。然而，重要文件的翻译、文化经典的译介，需要字斟句酌，这不是机器能完成的。在这样一个以快取胜的时代，我们希望年轻人学会慢下来，不急功近利、急于求成，而是怀着敬畏之情、匠人之心，去追求完美的品质。

最后，我们要感谢助教团队以及2017级全体学生对参考译文的制作的贡献。助教团队是一群热爱高翻、乐于奉献的高翻校友，他们在繁忙的翻译一线，仍不忘回馈高翻，默默地帮我们批改作业。这些校友包括费晨、陈西金燕、李天竹、宋俊阳、彭施龙、杨昉、傅天伊、王文煌、陈佳鑫、李月莎、秦宇池、贾明慧、周亚楠、王雅芹、王雅琪、谢芮、李琦、蔡越、王群、梁修涵、李淑华、马尚、叶俊文。还要感谢参与参考译文制作的助教老师，他们是叶俊文、谢芮、李宋乐颖、王佳楠、侯灵钰、彭博、王文煌、马尚、谢瑞、杨珊、李月莎、于语白、费晨。我们还要特别感谢贾明慧、李稀傲等校友对译文修改提出的宝贵建议。高翻的教学成果并非一人之功劳，而是众多智慧的结晶，由此可见一斑。

最后，特别感谢分别为制作第11单元和12单元参考译文提供专业支持的李延雷和周蕴仪老师。

感谢本书背后众多的无名英雄。

北外高翻笔译教学团队
2019年1月7日

目 录

第 一 单 元	全局意识	1
第 二 单 元	查证能力	42
第 三 单 元	辩证看待欧化中文	63
第 四 单 元	中英语言差异	97
第 五 单 元	跨文化沟通意识	136
第 六 单 元	思辨能力	173
第 七 单 元	联合国文件	204
第 八 单 元	法律	241
第 九 单 元	科学技术	287
第 十 单 元	建筑设计	314
第十一单元	舞蹈艺术	355
第十二单元	金融财会	395

第一单元　全局意识

Exercise 1　Fingerprint Words

翻译情景

平时的翻译练习，往往是为了形成一篇和原文在意思和语言风格上对等的译文；而现实中的翻译工作，往往发生在特定翻译情景下（翻译委托人、翻译用途、翻译对象、翻译目的等），服务于特定需求和目的；生成与原文对等的译文，仅仅是一种可能。译者需要根据翻译的情景，决定翻译的灵活度，即译文在多大程度上和原文对等：是字面意思对等，还是体现作者意图；是否需要超脱原文，达到功能上对等；甚至对原文进行编辑，实现翻译的整体目的。

以下段落摘自 Slate 杂志的一篇文章 Fingerprint Words，共 594 词。假定 Slate 杂志要出中文版，编辑部请你将原文翻译成中文。翻译时需要考虑该杂志的翻译情景，以决定翻译的灵活度。

专项能力

本篇旨在训练译者的全局意识（Act local, think global）。全局意识是指译者在理解原文（"理解"）、形成译文（"表达"）和决定翻译灵活程度（"变通"）时能够从宏观上思考问题，避免只见树木不见森林。

理解方面，译者需要了解原文的性质，即 Who is talking to whom? About what? When, where and why? And how? 简称宏观思维的 6W1H。6W1H 指的是发言者是谁、何时何地针对什么问题发言，说了什么，读者是谁，讲话方式如何。只有回答了这些问题，才能够从宏观上把握原文，掌握原文的宏观结构和意思重点，避免方向性错误。

表达方面，同样需要了解 6W1H，也就是译文读者是谁、对作者是否熟悉、对作者所谈的问题是否了解、什么时候、在什么场合、为了什么目的进行翻译，是否需要反映原文的语言特点。了解这些背景，有助于作出语言使用方面（语域、语体、语气）的选择：是正式，还是口语；是古雅，还是通俗；是严谨，还是活泼；也有助于作出变通决定。

变通是表达的特殊情况。直译行不通，想办法绕道走；有时甚至还需要对原文进行加工改造，形成符合翻译目的（fit-for-purpose）的译文。译者需要根据原文的性质（6W1H）和翻译情景（翻译委托人、翻译用途、翻译对象、翻译目的等），来决定是不说（省译）、少说（简化）、多说（增译）、还是变个说法。同样一个成语，在一篇普通讲话中甚至可以省略不译，或仅仅译出主要意思；但如果是专门向外国人介绍这个成语，就需要逐字逐句解释翻译，这就是策略不同。

这篇文章对于考验译者在理解、表达、变通方面的全局观（宏观思维能力）非常有价值。译者需要瞻前顾后，才能够理解原文，并通过适当变通，做到意思前后连贯，风格与原文一致。司马迁《史记·高祖本纪》所述"运筹帷幄之中，决胜千里之外"。只有宏观、全面地把握了作者背景、写作背景、翻译情景，才能将译文了然于心，准确、自然、恰到好处地翻译出来。

训练难点

原文中的斜体字是翻译的重点。译者应该思考斜体字该不该翻译、如何翻译？在斟酌斜体字翻译策略的过程中，希望译者可以渐渐理解翻译全局意识的重要性，在翻译之前，如何从全局入手，宏观把握原文的背景和语言特色，以连贯、统一的方式产出译文。

训练方式

本单元练习分原文、翻译提示、参考译文、译者注四部分。请先尝试自己翻译原文。做完以后再参看翻译提示,并自行修改、润色,形成第二稿。形成二稿之后,再看参考译文和译者注。翻译能力是在实践过程中不断提升的,希望你可以充分利用每一单元教材,一步步取得翻译能力上的飞跃!

原文[1]

Fingerprint Words

Not too long ago, I was forced to come to grips with[2] something terrible about myself. I use the word *iteration*[3] a lot. More than any human being should. If I had to ballpark[4] it, I'd set the over/under[5] on daily utterances at five.

I'm not proud of this. I'd prefer to be a guy who can refer to a *version* or *edition* or plain old *instance* of something[6], and who doesn't go around saying *iteration* over and over again. Alas, that is not me. And I found out about my *iteration* malady in the most jarring way possible. I had just started a new job. One day, a few weeks in, I heard three different colleagues with whom I interact often use the word iteration independent of one another. When the third of these, a woman I knew prior to taking the job, said it, I stopped her mid-sentence. "Wait, did you just say *iteration*? Why is everyone saying that word here?" Her response hit me like an unabridged thesaurus to the dome[7]. "You should be psyched[8]," she shot back. "That's one of *your* words."

After a fit of denial, and some back-and-forth[9], I went home after work and asked my wife if there were any weird, fingerprint-type words I used often.

"You mean like *iteration*?" she said, without the slightest pause. Then the floodgates opened. "You also say *tangential* all the time. Oh, *antiquated*, too! And you're always talking about *the extent to which* someone did this or that."

She kept going. Turns out I have an affinity for *anachronism* and maintain a close connection with *cognizant*.

By the time I returned to work the next day, I had begrudgingly accepted that I overuse a bunch of goofy words, and that everyone around me knew it. But I also noticed a change in how I spoke to my colleagues at the office. I was just as apt as ever to pepper a sentence with *antiquated*, or to throw in an *extent to which* here and there, but I actively and consciously stopped using *iteration*. That was my word, even though I hadn't realized it until the day before. Now everyone was saying it. I didn't want to appear a mere imitator when I used this noun that now seemed to belong to me.

…

But I also won't become one of those people who go around stealing the fingerprint words of others. How lazy! How unoriginal! How lame! How long after writing those last few sentences was it before I could think of a time I engaged in the exact sort of behavior that so infuriated me when it happened at the office? About four seconds.

I did it a few months ago. One of my closest friends uses the word *tremendous* often in emails. I'll send him a link to some especially outstanding baseball catch or a stupid screaming goat video, and he'll reply, succinctly, "That is tremendous." Or he'll email me an article prefaced with, "This is a tremendous story." It works for him. It really does. And, without knowing it, I've snatched that word from him like nobody's business[10].

I didn't realize this until July, when a different friend responded to one of my own emails by giving me props for my unusual word choice. "Also, great use of *tremendous*," she wrote near the end of her correspondence. This prompted a review of my sent box folder, which confirmed that the word is now pervasive in my outgoing emails. "What an old-school term," she added. "Let's bring that back!"

翻译提示

1. **全局意识**
   本篇的 6W1H，可以重点调查作者的身份、写作风格、创作动因、翻译目的等。

2. **短语理解**
   这个词的理解很关键，建议查询英英词典来理解它的意思。或者可以直接在谷歌当中输入"come to grips with"查找释义。

3. **全局意识：斜体字**
   请译者从语言风格连贯的角度思考以下几个问题：斜体字是否需要翻译？斜体字之间是否有逻辑联系？如果不翻译斜体字可以吗？

4. **词语理解**
   ballpark 这个词一般用作名词，但是这个语境下，注意它的词性和意思，特别注意美语口语中 ballpark 的动作释义。

5. **比喻义**
   over/under 从字面意思上看，就是上／下的意思，那么如果把这个短语放在语境中是什么意思呢？

6. **全局意识：语篇衔接**
   iteration 如果大家查字典，可以查到是"反复"和"迭代"的意思。这个词是这篇文章里面最难的部分。从全局意识来考虑，建议这个词和下面几个斜体词结合起来理解，看看它们之间有什么逻辑联系，如何能让语言和逻辑读起来连贯衔接。

7. **词语／短语理解**
   unabridged 在英汉词典中为"未删减"的意思，那么译者可以思考一下"未删减的词典"是什么样的呢？

8. **短语理解**
   you should be psyched 是美国常用的口头表达，出现在很多的美剧表达中，译者可在网上搜索 you should be psyched 的释义，并联系上下文，理解这个短语的意思。

9 词语理解 / 短语理解

some back-and-forth 到底是和同事的争辩，还是自己心里的状态？要找到答案，不妨把两种情况都放在交际的情景中理解，思考一下，自己会不会和同事吵架争辩？

10 短语理解

like nobody's business 在英英词典中有很多释义，译者需要选取最符合语境的意思。

参考译文[1]

口头禅[2]

不久前，我被迫正视[3]自己的一个坏毛病：我太爱用"番[4]"这个字了，用得比一般人都多。[5]如果非要我估计[6]一下的话，大概[7]每天讲五次吧。

这没什么可骄傲的。[8]我宁愿像别人那样，说"次""回"，或者更土气的"遭"，也不愿意一遍遍念叨"番"字。[9]唉！如果是这样，那就不是我了。说来我还是在极为尴尬的情况下，发现自己爱"番"来"番"去的。[10]那时，我刚换了份新工作。几周后的一天，我听到三位经常打交道的同事都先后使用了"番"这个字。第三位同事（我工作之前就认识的一位女士）还没说完，我就忍不住打断了她："等等，你刚才说'番'？怎么这里每个人都说'番'？"[11]她的回答犹如当头一棒。[12]"你应该高兴才是呀！"她顶了回来，"这可是你的口头禅！"[13]

起初我极力否认，后来又半信半疑。[14]下班回家后，我问妻子有没有听到我经常用一些奇怪的口头禅。[15]

"你说'番'字吗？"妻子不假思索地回答。然后，她便打开了话匣子，"你还老说'牵强附会[16]'。哦，还有'古调不弹'！还有谁谁谁做事'之程度'。"[17]

她说个不停。事实证明，我不仅对"陈词滥调"情有独钟，还和"具结悔过"亲密无间。[18]

到第二天上班时，我已经勉强接受了一个事实：自己老是故作高深，而且身边的人都知道。[19] 但是我也注意到了一个新变化。在办公室和同事说话时，我还是会冒出几个"古调不弹"，甩出几个"之程度"，但是我刻意不说"番"字了。[20] 这可是我的口头禅，尽管我前一天才意识到。现在大家都在用，我可不想在说自己的口头禅时，反倒像是在模仿谁。[21]……

但我也不会跟他们似的，到处用别人的口头禅。太懒！太没创意！太差劲！[22] 这几句话刚写完，也就过了四秒吧，我便想起来，办公室同事这种令我如此恼火的事，自己也干过。[23]

那是几个月前的事了。我一个密友经常在邮件中用"甚佳"这个词。[24] 有时看到超精彩的棒球接球，或者山羊傻叫的视频，我会把链接发给他，他则会简洁地回复道："甚佳。"[25] 有时他也会给我发一篇文章，并附言："此故事甚佳"。这个词很适合他，真的很适合，而我却在浑然未知的情况下，把这个词据为己有了。[26]

意识到这件事时已经是七月份了。当时，另一个朋友在回复我邮件时，夸奖我别具一格的选词。[27] 她在回信末尾写道："还有，'甚佳'用得妙。"[28] 于是，我连忙检查了发件箱，结果发现这个词无处不在。[29] 她补充道："多老派的词啊！我们重新启用吧！"[30]

译者注

1 全局意识 / 语篇连贯：
Slate 杂志语言风格

王：本文选自 Slate 杂志（链接：http://www.slate.com/articles/life/the_good_word/2014/09/fingerprint_words_verbal_tics_that_define_us_and_how_they_spread_to_others.html）

通过 Wikipedia 的介绍可知，Slate 杂志语言风格机智、诙谐、幽默，为大众提供解读世界的新视角。一些见解通常自由、开放、新颖，被一些读者认为是 left of center perspective。在译前规划阶段，可以通过杂志类型、作品性质、语言风格选择合适的翻译风格。英文介绍：

Slate, which is updated throughout the day, covers politics, arts and culture, sports, and news. According to Turner, the magazine is "not fundamentally a breaking news source," but rather aimed at helping readers to "analyze and understand and interpret the world" with witty and entertaining writing. As of mid-2015, it publishes about 1,500 stories per month.

Slate is also known (and sometimes criticized) for adopting self-described "left of center" and contrarian views, giving rise to the term "Slate Pitches." It is ad-supported and has been available to read free of charge since 1999, but restricted access for non-US readers via a metered paywall in 2015.

https://en.wikipedia.org/wiki/Slate_(magazine)

翻译这篇文章的原则和改写（re-writing）比较类似。值得注意的是，仅仅看懂这篇文章的意思还不够。读过这篇文章的同学应该能感觉到，作者经常自觉不自觉地使用一些比较古雅、低频的词，而他自己却没有注意到。也是根据这一经历，作者写下了这篇文章。所以，译文行文应该是通俗的，但是遇到斜体词，就需要使用古雅、低频的词。

Who is talking

李：作者之所以使用低频词，甚至"法言法语"，与作者的身份有关：他原来是学法律的。作者简历：Matthew J.X. Malady is a writer, editor, and attorney living in Berkeley. ... Between 2008 and 2014, he served as the editor of *Columbia Law School Magazine*, where he managed the magazine staff and oversaw all editorial elements of the publication. He remains a contributing editor at the magazine. Before joining the staff at Columbia Law School Magazine, Matthew spent four years as the editor of *AVENUE*, New York City's oldest, most distinguished, and most widely read society magazine. ...He is a summa cum laude graduate of Syracuse University's S.I. Newhouse journalism school and a cum laude graduate of the *University of Michigan Law School.*

https://www.linkedin.com/in/matthew-j-x-malady-9965697

2　关于标题的翻译

王：fingerprint words 就是像指纹一样富有个人特征的词。虽然"指纹词"有创意，但是不易于中国人理解。所以在翻译这个词的时候，就需要决定是采取异化还是归化的方法翻译。毕竟翻译这样的文章，不需要像科研报告那样一板一眼。"个人专属词"和"个人标志词"并不是最佳的译法，因为中文里完全可以用"口头禅"代替。试想在日常对话中，如果你问你的朋友："我的个人专属词是什么？"恐怕人家会丈二和尚摸不着头脑。但是如果你问："我的口头禅是什么？"你的朋友就很容易理解你的意思了。那么问题就在于，"口头禅"这个词是否可以表达 fingerprint words 这个词的意思？几位老师讨论后认为是可以的，理由如下：

口头禅定义：口头禅意指一个人习惯在有意或无意间时常讲的说话语句。口头禅可算是一个人的其中一个标志，亦影响其他人对他的形象与观感。口头禅可以是心理的一种反射，可反应出说口头禅者的心理状态。

根据字典释义，我们认为"口头禅"不仅更地道，而且更能精准反映原文意思。

乐颖：另外，"口头禅"的译法也可以从本文副标题中推断出：The verbal tics that make up who we are—and how they spread to others. (http://www.slate.com/articles/life/the_good_word/2014/09/fingerprint_words_verbal_tics_that_define_us_and_how_they_spread_to_others.html)

Verbal tics 的例子有 Umm、like、you know 等，这些就是英语里的口头禅。

https://www.publicationcoach.com/verbal-tics/

黄：关于标题 Fingerprint words 的译法，我有另外一种理解，想和您探讨一下。您说过，直接译成"指纹词"可能只译出了表层含义，深层含义其实没有表达出来。我在改二稿时，又去原文的网站上看了看，找到原文的配图，是一串串作者在文中举例的词组成的"指纹"。我想象，译成中文排版以后，配图肯定也会保留，读者看到配图是不是也能猜出标题"指纹词"的意思呢？而且这样译比较新颖，能勾起读者的阅读兴趣，若是译成口头禅，就比较平淡无奇了。所以我最后还是想译成"指纹词"，并给指纹加上双引号，暗示有特殊含义。

http://www.slate.com/authors.matthew_jx_malady.html

不知道老师有没有想过配图这层，所以想向老师请教一下，非常感谢！

王：谢谢你提供的这个视角，我觉得你的分析很有道理。从汉语表达和读者接受角度，我想"指纹词"确实可能不是优先选择。但是，你提醒我翻译并不是一项孤立的文字性工作，还涉及文字以外的声音、图像、感官等的集合。如果从配图角度讲，我想处理成"指纹词"也未尝不可。加上引号会更好，这样可以向读者暗示这是一个特殊的词，是作者或者译者有意为之。如果你对这个问题感兴趣，想要再继续深入研究，也可以看看多模态翻译，或者是 PACTE 模型中有关心理和感官因素对翻译过程起到的作用。

李：这确实是个有意义的问题。使用加引号的"指纹词"，括注"口头禅"，也许可以解决文图不符的问题。

3 短语理解

come to grips with 根据下文的释义，可以理解为正视、面对之意：

1. *(idiomatic)* To confront or deal with directly; to commence a confrontation.

*Until she **comes to grips with** her mother's death, she has no hope of put-*

ting it behind her.

值得注意的是，come to grips 可作及物动词短语和不及物动词短语使用，请看例句：

1. *Until she **comes to grips with** her mother's death, she has no hope of putting it behind her.*

2. *It was not until five years after graduation that she finally **came to grips** and began a career.*

https://www.yourdictionary.com/come-to-grips-with

4　全局意识 / 语篇连贯：
斜体字

王：如果理解了本文的语言风格和作者的真正逻辑，就知道这些斜体字是必须要翻译出来的，而翻译这些斜体字，恰恰是本文的难点，也是体现译者理解、表达、变通能力的地方。通过语言风格的分析，同学们应该可以明白，例如 tremendous 这类词并不是所谓的"双关词"，而是语域高、使用频率低的古雅词。所以，怎样不失作者诙谐、幽默、自然的语言风格，又体现斜体字的高语域，是翻译难点。试想，如果不翻译这些斜体字，那么中国读者能看懂吗？我想完全不懂英语的人，甚至懂一点英语的人，都看不懂。这就是为什么我们要在翻译中有读者意识，要理解原文的内涵和逻辑。换句话说，如果同学们把这些斜体字翻译成现今比较常用的词，逻辑上就不对了。遇到斜体词，大家就该想想日常用语中的一些 unusual words, goofy words 或者 weird words。比如，原文中类似 tangential 和 anachronism 的词，都需要选一个古色古香的译法。

5

> 原文：Not too long ago, I was forced to come to grips with something terrible about myself. I use the word iteration a lot. More than any human being should.
>
> 原译：不久之前，我不得不直面一件关于自己的烦心事：我太爱用"变体"这个词了，比任何正常人用的都多。（乐颖）

乐颖：查 The Free Dictionary 可以发现 version、edition 和 instance 都是同义词：

version: A particular form or variation of an earlier or original type.

edition: A version of an earlier publication having substantial changes or additions.

instance（借鉴了刘宁宁同学的查证）。见下：

刘宁宁：原文第二段提到 version，edition 和 instance 几个词，我认为值得思考。作者为何要拿这几个词和 iteration 进行对比呢？如果这几个词和 iteration 在意思上毫无关联，未免在逻辑上有些说不过去。另外，我注意到，version 和 edition 两个词本身就是近义词，那么 instance 一词是否也有类似的含义呢？于是，我做了进一步调查。

In my understanding, a version is a specific instance of a file and an iteration is a period of time. It may be that your site chooses to assign version numbers that coincide with iteration numbers but that would be a distinction made by your own company policies.

https://stackoverflow.com/questions/5803800/whats-the-difference-between-version-and-iteration-on-jira

可见，version 实际上就是指具体的"版本"。而且相对 iteration 来说，日常使用频率更高。再结合句意可以推断，iteration 应与这三个词意思相近，所以 iteration 此处取下面这个释义：A form, adaption, or version of something: *the latest iteration of a popular app*. 我觉得此处若能保留原文的意思，是最好的。

> **改译 1**：不久前，我被迫正视自己的一个坏毛病：我太爱用"刻本"这个词了，使用频率简直超乎常人。（梅畅）

王：我非常同意刘宁宁的意见，iteration, version, edition 和 instance 在译文当中必须要有连续性，体现语域从高到低的变化，符合作者整体文章脉络与逻辑结果。我们可以继续查阅古汉语词典，看是否有其他更好的词。

> **改译 2**：不久前，我被迫正视自己的一个坏毛病：我太爱用"本"这个词了，使用频率简直超乎常人。（乐颖）

乐颖：我继续去查古汉语词典，发现"本"这个字本身就能表示"版本"的意思：

⑿〈名〉版本；底本。《活板》："已后典籍皆为板本。"

http://wyw.hwxnet.com/view/hwxE6hwx9ChwxAC.html

"版本"一词在百度百科里的解释如下：

一种书籍经过多次传抄、刻印或以其他方式而形成的各种不同本子。

"版"是简牍时代以木制作的书籍的一种形制，印刷术发明后，用以印刷书籍的木版也称版。书称"本"，始于西汉刘向父子校理国家藏书。刘向《别录》云："一人读书，校其上下，得谬误，曰校。一人持本，一人读书，若怨家相对，曰雠。"这里的本，即指一书的不同本子。最初写于竹、木简上，后用缣帛与纸写书，雕版印刷术发明后，书籍多以印刷形式流传，版本一词，大多指书籍的雕版印本。

从以上解释部分可以看出，"本"可以表示"一书的不同本子"，而"版本"其实是"本"的下义词，最初专指雕版印本，其实"本"还可以写于竹、木简等材料。

清代叶得辉《书林清话》（卷一）："自雕版盛行，于是版本二字合为一名。"至宋代，版刻大行，名义遂定。版本二字最早见于文献的记载，有宋代叶梦得《石林燕语》（卷八）："五代冯道始奏请官镂六经版印行，国朝淳化中，复以《史记》《前后汉》付有司摹印，自是书籍刊镂者益多，士大夫不复以藏书为意，学者易于得书，其诵读亦因灭裂，然版本初不是正，不无讹误，世既一以版本为正，而藏本日亡，其讹谬者遂不可正，甚可惜也。"

https://baike.baidu.com/item/版本/505574

从上文可以看出，雕版印书盛行之后，版本二字才合二为一，所以就出现时间早晚而言，"本"是最早出现的，而且"本"的含义也最广。因此我建议此处改译为"本"。"本"相比"本子"，在韵律上也更佳，更有古典韵味。

但是修改过全文之后，我还是觉得"本"因为是独字词，还是略显单薄，感觉仍然不是最佳译法。

> **改译3**：不久前，我被迫正视自己的一个坏毛病：我太爱用"刻本"这个词了，使用频率简直超乎常人。（王）

王：此处我还是坚持原译，即梅畅同学的译法。"本"这个词的意思没有问题，但是正如你所说，汉语音节上略有欠缺，查了一下"刻本"的意思，也是指版本类型：

也就是版本类型。亦称刊本、椠本、镌本。均指雕版印刷而成的书本。中国雕版印刷术发明很早。唐代已经有雕版印刷的书籍流行。五代已由政府指令国子监校刻"九经"。至宋代，雕版印刷的书籍大盛。旁及辽、金、西夏，直至元、明、清，前后盛行1000余年。

乐颖：苏阳老师好，我有一个疑问，不知道是否多余。"使用频率简直超乎常人"，这不是很口语化的用词，我们平时说话也不怎么会说使用某词的"频率"是怎样的，一般就说"喜欢说/爱说/用得多"。使用"频率"这个词，（我感觉）一下子语域就提高了。而就 I'm not proud of this 这句话来说，您的改译"这没什么可骄傲的"又十分口语化。我个人是觉得有点语域不统一之嫌，不知您怎么看？

王：同意你提出的问题，请看看这样修改如何。

> **改译4**：不久前，我被迫正视自己的一个坏毛病：我太爱用"刻本"这个词了，用得比一般人都多。（王）

李：建议脱离 iteration 这个词的意思来翻译，另起炉灶，重建一组古今说法分明的同义词。跟"version"意思相关的，更好；不相关，也没关系。毕竟作者的深层含义是"一组有古今区别的同意思"。

李：比如，番、次、回、遭。还有更好的词替换"遭"吗？这几个字的缺点是单音节，不知道你们还有无更好的想法。

王：目前觉得李老师的几个选词不错，也许同学们中有更好的想法。

王：iteration 确实是有版本的意思，而且是比较少用、古雅的词。后面的 version、edition 和 instance 都有版本的意思。如果用文到白的顺序排列这几个词，应该是 iteration>edition>version>instance。词义上讲，这几个词都是指版本没错。因此，学生翻译成类似版本的意思是可以的，但希望学生可以体现出这种"法言法语"到大白话的反差感。此外，从语篇角度分析，这里的形式意义大于词语意义，即这几个词更强调反差感，进一步指代作者喜爱拽词的特点。此处，李老师修改为"番"，也是取形式意义大于实质意义的内涵，从语篇角度，也是连贯的。当然，我们不排斥其他的译法。如果同学们既可以译出词语意思，又体现出"法言法语"、文白相间的落差感，是值得鼓励的。

> **建议译法**：不久前，我被迫正视自己的一个坏毛病：我太爱用"番"这个字了，用得比一般人都多。（李）

6 短语理解

乐颖：ballpark 原本为名词，相关释义如下：

2. *Slang* The approximately proper range, as of possibilities or alternatives: *Your estimate is high, but still in the ballpark*。

<https://www.thefreedictionary.com/ballpark>

此处根据上下文推测用作动词，意思不变，也有据可循：

Ballpark

一般年龄稍大的北美大叔会用这个词来表示"大概""估摸着"。可以当名词，甚至动词！

<https://www.zhihu.com/question/32071242/answer/59683158>

王：课上我们和爱苏老师沟通过这个问题，有同学提出 ballpark 在语法层面不能用作动词。爱苏老师说在日常交际语中，因为语法比较灵活随意，所以经常会这样说。在美语中，ballpark=eyeball。

7　乐颖：over/under 指一种类似竞彩的活动：

An over-under or over/under (O/U) bet is a wager in which a sportsbook will predict a number for a statistic in a given game (usually the combined score of the two teams), and bettors wager that the actual number in the game will be either higher or lower than that number.

https://en.wikipedia.org/wiki/Over-under

中文解释更直观地说明了 over/under：

1. 大小球（over under）

预定球赛中两队的入球总数为大或小。全场总入球若大于「设定球数」为大；全场总入球若少于「设定球数」为小。

「设定球数」为博彩公司设定，会因应每场不同球赛而调节，球赛开始受注后「设定球数」将维持不变。

入球大小的"设定球数"单位与亚洲让球数一样，可为整数（0，1，2），或小数（0.5，0.75，0.25）。

https://zhuanlan.zhihu.com/p/25431732

可知原文的 set the over/under 可理解为"估摸着／估计"之意。

乐颖：苏阳老师好，检查的时候，我有点纠结这里的比喻义要不要译出呢？比如 set the over/under。

王：综合思考了一下，我觉得不必译出。看了你的查证，over/under 有关博彩业。当然中、西方都有博彩文化，但是相较西方，这种文化在中国还并未被广泛接受（合法化问题）。由于中西方文化差异，如果把喻体直接翻译出来，可能会让读者瞬间跳出语境，不利于读者理解。文化词语的翻译，有的时候我们采取替换喻体的方式翻译，比如：He will be as close as an oyster. 他将对此守口如瓶。

李：此处 over/under 其实无关博彩业，就是简单的字面意思"上下"，意思是"左右"！

8

> 原文：I'm not proud of this.
> 原译：我并不以此为荣。（乐颖）
> 建议译法：这没什么可骄傲的。（王）

王：语言可以更自然。这个作者比较喜欢拽词，所以在修改时，我有时候也很纠结：有些口语化的地方，语域是否应该高一些？但是综合考虑杂志风格，以及文章当中一些斜体的古雅词，为了突出对比，我觉得大部分语言表达还是应该自然、口语化一些。作者还是以一种比较戏谑的方式在说自己的经历，也是变相地在批判自己的一些 language snobbery。Slate 杂志的风格和作者的语言特色应该是比较轻松、诙谐、幽默的。

9 全局意识 / 语篇衔接

> 原文：I'd prefer to be a guy who can refer to a *version* or *edition* or plain old *instance* of something, and who doesn't go around saying *iteration* over and over again.
> 原译：我宁愿说"版本""版"，或者简单地说某物的"第几版"，而不是一遍又一遍地重复"变体"。（乐颖）
> 改译1：我宁愿说"版本""版"，或者更直白的"某个"，也不愿意一遍又一遍地重复"刻本"。（王）

王：在翻译的时候，要尽量把这几个词联系起来，让斜体字的用词看起来法言法语，而其他几个词语域稍低，阳春白雪，下里巴人，有所区分。

> 改译2：我宁愿像别人那样，说"次""回"，或者更土气的"遭"，也不愿意一遍又一遍地重复"番"。（李）

贾明慧：读着稍微有点奇怪，一遍又一遍地说不就是重复的意思吗？"一遍又一遍地重复"会不会有点语义重复了？另外也可以考虑译为：……也不愿意走到哪儿都"番"来复去的。（不知道是不是我笑点太低，我觉得这么翻还挺好笑的。）

李：可改为"也不愿意一遍遍念叨'番'"字。"'番'来复去"也很好。

> **建议译法**：我宁愿像别人那样，说"次""回"，或者更土气的"遭"，也不愿意一遍遍念叨"番"字 。（李）

10

> **原文**：Alas, that is not me. And I found out about my iteration malady in the most jarring way possible. I had just started a new job.
> **原译**：唉，但那就不是我了。我以一种极为令人不快的方式发现了自己的"变体"毛病，那时我刚开始新工作。（乐颖）

> **改译1**：唉！我怎么会这样呢？说来我还是在极为尴尬的情况下发现自己有使用"刻本"的毛病的。那时，我刚换了份新工作。（王）
> **改译2**：唉，但那就不是我了。说来我还是在极为尴尬的情况下发现自己有使用"本"的毛病。那时，我刚换了份新工作。（乐颖）

乐颖：关于 that is not me 这一句。我原译为"但那就不是我了"，强调的是如果不说 iteration，而改说其他的词，那就不是我了。苏阳老师改译为"我怎么会这样呢？"，强调的是坚持说 iteration 而不说别的词这件事。此处我的理解是，如果作者这里想埋怨自己为什么老爱说 iteration 这个奇怪的词，那么 that is not me 这句话的语气应该更强烈一点，比如标点符号可用感叹号。但是此处原文仅仅是 Alas, that is not me. 给我的感觉更像是一种无可奈何的感觉：我也想改啊，可是我真的做不到。因此我还是觉得应该保留原译。

王：同意你的分析。如果加强语气，alas 可以变为感叹号，如何？

> **改译3**：唉！但那就不是我了。说来我还是在极为尴尬的情况下发现自己有使用"本"的毛病。那时，我刚换了份新工作。（王）

王：再读原文，这里还是反映出作者的一种 language snobbery。他虽然知道自己有这样拽词的毛病，但戏谑口吻背后，还是有点沾沾自喜，略带小骄傲的。所以，作者的逻辑是，如果我不那样说了，那还是我吗？！

李：可以改为"番"来"番"去。

> **建议译法**：唉！如果是这样，那就不是我了。说来我还是在极为尴尬的情况下，发现自己爱"番"来"番"去的。（李）

11

> **原文**：One day, a few weeks in, I heard three different colleagues with whom I interact often use the word iteration independent of one another. When the third of these, a woman I knew prior to taking the job, said it, I stopped her mid-sentence. "Wait, did you just say *iteration*? Why is everyone saying that word here?"
>
> **原译**：入职几星期之后的一天，我听到三位同事在聊天。与他们单独交流的时候，我经常说"变体"。其中有一位女士，我在接受这份工作之前就认识她了。当她说出"变体"这个词时，我打断了她的话。"等等，你刚刚是说了'变体'吗？为什么大家在这儿都说这个词？"（乐颖）

王：我觉得"入职"一词没有必要增译，根据上下文可以判断是开始新工作以后发生的事。这里理解错误了。不是三位同事在聊天，而是和我经常打交道的几位同事分别使用了 iteration 这个词，原文有 independent of one another。

乐颖：同意修改，我把从句断错句了。

> **改译1**：几周后的一天，我听到三位经常打交道的同事都先后使用了"刻本"这个词。当第三位同事（我工作之前就认识的一位女士）说这个词的时候，我打断了她："等等，你刚才说'刻本'？怎么这里每个人都说这个词？"（王）

改译 2：几周后的一天，我听到三位经常打交道的同事都先后使用了"番"这个字。到了第三位同事（我工作之前就认识的一位女士）说这个字的时候，我打断了她："等等，你刚才说'番'？怎么这里每个人都说'番'？"（李）

贾明慧："先后"应该是"都"的子集，两个留一个就可以了。

贾："到了"这个变化稍微有点大，我是觉得前文已经把条件摆得很清楚了。有三位同事都用了"番"字，那么"第三位同事"肯定是其中之一，不可能是其他情况，也就没有必要重复"说这个字的时候"了。

王：我认为"都"也有加强语气的意思。

李："到了"第三位，隐含前面是两位。可是，前面已经说了"三位"，所以，"到了"也不合适。但原译确实啰唆。可以改为：第三位同事（我工作之前就认识的一位女士）还没说完，我就忍不住打断了她。

建议译法：几周后的一天，我听到三位经常打交道的同事都先后使用了"番"这个字。第三位同事（我工作之前就认识的一位女士）还没说完，我就忍不住打断了她："等等，你刚才说'番'？怎么这里每个人都说'番'？"（李）

12 词语 / 短语理解

乐颖：此处 unabridged 意为"未删减的"：

Containing the original content; not condensed. Used of books, articles, and documents.

https://www.thefreedictionary.com/unabridged

若是未删减的 thesaurus（分类词典），那么一定是一本很厚的书。而 dome 虽有"穹顶之意"，俚语中也有"人的头部"之意。结合上下文，我认为此处的 like an unabridged thesaurus to the dome 是一个比喻，形容作者当时的震惊。

王：也就是犹如"当头一棒"的感觉。

李：是的，不过是拿一本词典砸在脑袋上。或者"犹如一本辞海砸到脑门上。"

13

> 原文：Her response hit me like an unabridged thesaurus to the dome. "You should be psyched," she shot back. "That's one of *your* words."
>
> 原译：她回敬道："你应该高兴才是呀，这是属于你的词"。她的回答让我大脑一片空白。（乐颖）

> 改译1：她的回答有如当头一棒："你应该高兴才是呀，这可是*你的*口头禅"。（王）

冯爱苏：you should be psyched 是美国的常用短语，意即："你应该高兴才是啊！"

王：汉语一般表示强调不用斜体字，用楷体。这里可以先保留，问问李老师的建议。

乐颖：查了中国的标点符号用法，此处应用着重号。

> 4.12 着重号
>
> 4.12.1 定义
>
> 标号的一种，标示语段中某些重要的或需要指明的文字。
>
> 4.12.2 形式
>
> 着重号的形式是"．"标注在相应文字的下方。

http://www.moe.gov.cn/ewebeditor/uploadfile/2015/01/13/20150113091548267.pdf

斜体是英文的强调方式。

王：以上是乐颖的查证结果，此处我认为可以加着重号。请李老师定夺。

李：应该加着重号。

> 改译3：她的回答犹如当头一棒。"你应该高兴才是呀！"她怼了回来，"这可是你的口头禅！"（李）

王：我觉得"怼"这个词不太合适。这个词目前已经变成网络的一种流行语，放在这里不太符合语境：

　　怼是一个汉语字，拼音为 duì，基本意思是会意字，说文，心部，从对声。对，相持也，意为互相对峙，底下加"心"，表示心里抵触，对抗。引申为怨恨，故而怼，怨也。

　　北方方言中表达"用手推撞"或者"用语言拒斥反驳"的意思并且读音为"duǐ"的字，应当为"㨃"。大众媒体中使用"怼"来表达该含义和读音是一种错误。

　　2017年12月12日下午，《咬文嚼字》评出了2017年度十大流行语，"怼"字位列其中。

　　2017年12月18日，"怼"入选"2017年度十大网络用语"。

　　　　　　https://baike.baidu.com/item/%E6%80%BC/4505099?fr=aladdin

从意思上看，同事心里应该也没有抵触的意思。我倾向改译2：她的回答有如当头一棒："你应该高兴才是呀，这可是你的口头禅"。（乐颖）

李：如果不用方言，可以改为"顶"。shoot back 是快速还击。需要翻译出来。

乐颖：我也同意王苏阳老师的看法，不建议用"怼"。"怼"意为怨恨。在日常生活中，"怼"的使用情境一般是：A 说了一些惹怒 B 或者让 B 不舒服、不愉快的话，A 有些"恼羞成怒"，于是"怼"回来。我觉得原文更像是开玩笑，不至于到了"怨恨"的程度。

王：查证 shoot back 的意思如下第一个，意为"还嘴""顶嘴"的意思：

shoot back

定义 | 西班牙语 | 法语 | 英语同义词 | NEW! 共轭 | 上下文 | 图像

WordReference English-Chinese Dictionary © 2018:

主要翻译

英语		中文
shoot back *vi phrasal*	*informal, figurative* (retort)	反击，还嘴
	"I didn't steal her purse!", the street kid shot back.	
shoot back *vi phrasal*	(object: return)	（如回飞镖）飞回来，返回来
	He tossed the boomerang, which shot right back to him.	
shoot [sth] back, shoot back [sth] *vtr phrasal sep*	(reply: send)	（生气地）回复（邮件等）
	I read Ken's email, then shot back an angry reply.	

http://www.wordreference.com/enzh/shoot%20back

改译 4：她的回答犹如当头一棒。"你应该高兴才是呀！"她顶了回来，"这可是你的口头禅！"（李、王、乐颖）

贾：如果原文再放肆一点，或许可以用"怼回来"。但无论放肆与否，"顶回来"都不太成立，如果是取"顶嘴"的意思，那两个人的身份就有高低之分了，建议用"回敬"。

王：这样就没有完全体现出 shot back 的意思了。倾向维持原译。"顶"了回来也可以表示对作者内心的打击。

李："回敬"是反语，"回击"的意思。但问话人并没有"攻击"行为。所以，还是原译更准确一些。

建议译法：她的回答犹如当头一棒。"你应该高兴才是呀！"她顶了回来，"这可是你的口头禅！"（李）

14　短语理解 + 交际情境

冯：some back-and-forth 形容作者的心理状态，some back-and-forth 是作者心里半信半疑的状态，而并不是描述两个人在互相辩论。

乐颖：我同意这种理解，其实就是作者内心"拉拉扯扯"，不涉及其他人。

王：确实也有 argument/discussion 的意思，但这个意思较为具体，要看在具体文义中的适用情况，比如《破产姐妹》里面 back and forth 就是两人来来回回的拉锯战：

那么句子中的意思怎么理解呢？我们从语法角度看看：

> **原文**：After a fit of denial, and some back-and-forth, I went home after work and asked my wife if there were any weird, fingerprint-type words I used often.

这句话是一个状语从句引导的并列结构。此句中，前一个分句是由 After 引导的状语从句。After 作介词用，后接名词，补齐语法结构就是 after a fit of denial in my heart。In my heart 省略了，是因为这是不言自明的。后面的 and some back-and-forth 也省略了 in my heart。有没有可能是和同事的争辩呢？我认为这样理解从语法角度讲是不严谨的。如果所谓"争论"对象是同事，那么这个状语从句就相当于变换了对象。在这种情况下，以英语严谨表达结构的特点，一般会补齐说明对象，而非使用省略（ellipsis）的方式（如果真的是这样就会说 and some back and forth with my colleagues）。因此，两种情况相互比较，作者内心的自我挣扎和斟酌更为可靠。另外，从交际的角度讲，现实生活中，没有必要和同事去争论这个问题（工作了会体会比较深刻），也或者，我们可以说作者和同事也根本没熟悉到这个程度。如果同学们可以把两种情况放到真实的交际情境中去考虑，我想可能会选择解释成作者内心的挣扎。

15

> **原文**：After a fit of denial, and some back-and-forth, I went home after work and asked my wife if there were any weird, fingerprint-type words I used often.
> **原译**：我内心几番抗拒，半信半疑。下班回家后，我问妻子我有没有常用的怪异口头禅。（乐颖）

> **改译1**：起初我极力否认，后来又半信半疑。下班回家后，我问妻子我有没有什么常用的、怪异的口头禅。（王）
> **改译2**：起初我极力否认，后来又半信半疑。下班回家后，我问妻子我有没有经常用一些奇怪的口头禅。（李）

贾：一个不知道可不可行的建议，不少同学译文容易跟着原文走，一段里用了好多个"我""她""你"。人称代词在中文里出现的频率远不及英文，用多了反而会给读者一种"异物感"。要想消除这种异物感，我能想到最好的方法就是把它变成句子的合理成分。比如"我问妻子我有没有经常用一些"就可以顺一下，变成"我问妻子是否常听我用一些"。这个例子可能不是很明显，但我觉得一定可以找到一个相对折中的办法，让人称代词在句子里显得不那么突兀。

王：这个建议我觉得很好。

> **建议译法**：起初我极力否认，后来又半信半疑。下班回家后，我问妻子有没有听到我经常用一些奇怪的口头禅。（李、贾）

16 词义

tangential 的相关释义为：

adj.

1. Of, relating to, or moving along or in the direction of a tangent.
2. Merely touching or slightly connected.
3. Only superficially relevant; divergent: *a tangential remark*.

https://www.thefreedictionary.com/tangential

17

原文："You mean like *iteration*?" she said, without the slightest pause. Then the floodgates opened. "You also say *tangential* all the time. Oh, *antiquated*, too! And you're always talking about *the extent to which* someone did this or that."

原译："你是说像'变体'这样的词？"妻子不假思索地说。她的话匣子就此打开。"你也总是说'牵强附会的'。哦，还有'古旧的'！而且你总是谈论某人'以何程度'做了什么事。"（乐颖）

王："是"字可以去掉。

改译1："你说'刻本'吗？"妻子不假思索地说。然后，她打开了话匣子，"你还说'牵强附会'。哦，还有'古调不弹'！你也老说某人做什么的'程度'如何如何。"（王）

改译2："你说'本'吗？"妻子不假思索地说。然后，她便打开了话匣子，"你还说'牵强附会'。哦，还有'古调不弹'！你还老是说某人做什么的'程度'如何如何。"（乐颖）

改译3："你说'刻本'吗？"妻子不假思索地说。然后，她便打开了话匣子，"你还说'牵强附会'。哦，还有'古调不弹'！你还老说某人做什么的'程度'如何如何。"（乐颖）

乐颖：补充查证，我感觉"古调不弹"这个词见过的人不多。

"古调不弹"意为：

陈调不再弹。比喻过时的东西不受欢迎。

http://cd.hwxnet.com/view/nipegdcpoebfldim.html

而 antiquated 意为：

Too old to be fashionable, suitable, or useful; outmoded.

https://www.thefreedictionary.com/antiquated

> **改译 4**："你说'番'字吗？"妻子不假思索地回答。然后，她便打开了话匣子，"你还老说'牵强附会'。哦，还有'迂腐不堪'！还有谁谁谁做事'之程度'"。（李）

王：这个"字"是否可以删去？

李：我也是考虑再三加上去的。为了配够两个音节。

王："牵强附会"这个词本身并不少见。全文中反映了一种 language snobbery 的意识，有意使用一些高级、生僻的词与他人区别开，显示出自己的与众不同，学富五车。这里我建议使用原词"古调不弹"。这个词和 tangential 的意思相近，而且无论字面还是口语，都很少有人使用。

乐颖：我觉得"迂腐不堪"的情感太强烈了。在中文语料库以及百度上搜这个词，感觉都是非常负面的描述，所以我觉得用"迂腐不堪"有过重之嫌。

李：可以用"古调不弹"。也可以再想想有没有其他罕见成语，表示"过时"，毕竟古调不弹是感慨古风不在，意思有点差距。尸居余气？

王：上文已经查证过，"古调不弹"是过时不再受欢迎的意思，与 antiquated 的 too old to be fashionable 意思是相近的。因此我建议保留之前的译法。"尸居余气"是指像尸体一样但还有一口气，指人将要死亡。也比喻人暮气沉沉，无所作为。放在这里应该不合适。

> **建议译法**："你说'番'字吗？"妻子不假思索地回答。然后，她便打开了话匣子，"你还老说'牵强附会'。哦，还有'古调不弹'！还有谁谁谁做事'之程度'"。（王）

18

> **原文**：She kept going. Turns out I have an affinity for *anachronism* and maintain a close connection with *cognizant*.
> **原译**：她一直说个不停。事实证明，我还喜欢说"落伍之物"和"悟"。（乐颖）

乐颖：此处我把 have an affinity for 和 maintain a close connection with 都译为了"喜欢说"，我感觉没问题。没必要两个词组都一板一眼地译出来。

> **改译 1**：她一直说个不停。事实证明，我不仅对"落伍之物"情有独钟，还和"心领神悟"亲密无间。（王）

词义

cognizant 的释义为：

adj.

Fully informed; conscious.

https://www.thefreedictionary.com/cognizant

王：还是应该保留，不然文字的妙处没有了，当然这也可能是见仁见智。这里找了两个拟人化的表达，增加语言的神采和诙谐感。请看看是否合适。

乐颖：同意苏阳老师的修改，这样译文不仅更加美，而且还有一种自我戏谑的意味。"亲密无间"一开始我觉得有点不太符合中文表达，后来一想这里是拟人表达，也就不觉得有什么奇怪了，也还可以用像"爱不释手""形影不离"等词。

王：我和乐颖讨论过，需要把 have an affinity 和 maintain a close connection 都要翻译出来。我们觉得还是需要把那种传神色彩翻译出来，体现语言的生动。这里我们选择了比较拟人化的表达，请李老师看看是否合适。

李：挺好。换两个词。

> **改译 2**：她说个不停。事实证明，我不仅对"陈词滥调"情有独钟，还和"思想认知"亲密无间。（李）

28

王：李老师，同意您对第一个词的修改。我觉得这里的"思想认知"还不够罕见，我们一般的表达里也会这么说。根据 cognizant 的释意，我觉得改译 1 的"心领神悟"可以。

李："心领神悟"也比较常见。"具结悔过"（recognizance 的翻译）如何？作者是个律师，也许可以换用一个法律术语。recognizance 和 cognizant 看起来还沾边。

王：李老师这个观点很好。cognizant 确实在法律当中也有特殊意义（"有司法管辖权的"）。"具结悔过"虽然不能完全概括这层意思，但我同意这里的语言风格大于实际意义。所以同意修改为"具结悔过"。当然，不排除有同学译出更贴切、更传神的译法。

建议译法：她说个不停。事实证明，我不仅对"陈词滥调"情有独钟，还和"具结悔过"亲密无间。（李）

19

原文：By the time I returned to work the next day, I had begrudgingly accepted that I overuse a bunch of goofy words, and that everyone around me knew it.

原译：到第二天上班时，我勉强接受了一个事实：我滥用了一大堆愚蠢的词语，而且我身边的人都知道这一点。（乐颖）

词义

Goofy 的相关释义为：

Informal

adj. goof·i·er, goof·i·est

1. Silly; ridiculous: *a goofy hat*.

2. Having the right foot forward when riding a board such as a skateboard or snowboard: *a goofy stance*.

https://www.thefreedictionary.com/goofy

> **改译 1**：到第二天上班时，我已经勉强接受了一个事实：自己老是喜欢拽词，而且身边的人都知道。（王）

王：此处是借用了袁梦琪同学的表达，又稍做修改。

> **改译 2**：到第二天上班时，我已经勉强接受了一个事实：自己老是喜欢咬文嚼字，而且身边的人都知道。（乐颖）

乐颖：即使我是 90 后，"拽"出现在这种并非完全是 informal 的文章中，乍看还是觉得有点别扭。"拽"一般是极其口语的用词，而且有种不屑的意味。我觉得在这里使用有些不妥。我在网上查了"拽"的出处：

河南、湖北、西安、四川、安徽等地人把神气、骄傲、张扬、富有的样子叫作"拽"。正确的写法为"跩"。安徽方言 zhuai 发音第三声。

例如：(1) 这小丫头好拽啊！（意思是很神气，套用现代词与"很有范"相近。非贬义词）

(2) 你拽什么拽？（意思为：你狂什么狂）

(3) 这个字很有意思啊，手脚并用，把日头都拽下来了。（拽：拉）

"拽"的人，通常"眼睛都长在头顶"，不知天高地厚，恃才傲物，或者恃财傲物。反正就是刺头一个，因为有本钱，所以根本看不见身边还有旁人。

https://baike.baidu.com/item/ 拽 /5129723

我又去查找了"跩"：

1.［东北方言］调侃人说话咬文嚼字，口语用书面语言、文言——挺能跩呀！"鸭子尚有三跩，何况人乎？"

2.［近年山西俚语］装腔作势、端架子——跩啥呀！那人够跩的。

https://baike.baidu.com/item/ 跩

最终发现，"拽"其实源自"跩"，可以形容人说话咬文嚼字。我个人也比较倾向使用咬文嚼字。因为"拽词"给人的感觉是这人为了显摆而用各种各样古雅的词，但是仔细揣摩原文 I had begrudgingly accepted that I overuse a bunch of goofy words，其实作者之前并不知道自己的行为是在故意炫技，是在"拽词"，他甚至觉得有点无辜。他可能仅仅是用词比较讲究罢了，并没有显摆的意思。因此我建议此处改为稍微中性一点的"咬文嚼字"。

王：咬文嚼字的释义：咬、嚼指反复地念诵、钻研。一般将"咬文嚼字"当作"过分地斟酌字句"，看作贬义词，用于讽刺那些专门死抠字眼而不去领会精神实质的人，也讽刺那些讲话时爱卖弄自己学识的人。

https://baike.baidu.com/item/%E5%92%AC%E6%96%87%E5%9A%BC%E5%AD%97/3272

我第一印象感觉"咬文嚼字"是指反复钻研、抠字眼的意思。我这里还是比较倾向原意。这里请李老师定夺吧。

李：咬文嚼字是有意识选择一些词来用，但这里明显是不自觉脱口而出。

> **改译 3**：到第二天上班时，我已经勉强接受了一个事实：自己呆头呆脑滥用词语，而且身边的人都知道。（李）

王：我觉得 goofy 在这里不是作者呆头呆脑地在滥用词语，而是他用的词比较生僻，不常见，这也是全文中反映的一种 language snobbery。goofy 在口语里我觉得还有奇怪的意思。

> **改议 4**：到第二天上班时，我已经勉强接受了一个事实：自己老是喜欢拽词，而且身边的人都知道。

乐颖：我也觉得"呆头呆脑"不妥，原文没有提到作者用这些词时的窘状，仅仅是说这些词很"囧"，很奇怪。

李：自己喜欢故作高深？

王：同意李老师的修改。这里暂且放上两种不同译法，供同学们参考。这里突然提到作者如何如何有点怪。

> **建议译法 1**：到第二天上班时，我已经勉强接受了一个事实：自己老是故作高深，而且身边的人都知道。（李）
> **建议译法 2**：到第二天上班时，我已经勉强接受了一个事实：自己老是喜欢拽词，而且身边的人都知道。（王）

20

原　文：But I also noticed a change in how I spoke to my colleagues at the office. I was just as apt as ever to pepper a sentence with *antiquated*, or to throw in an *extent to which* here and there, but I actively and consciously stopped using *iteration*.

原　译：但是我也注意到，我在办公室不再像以前那样对同事说话了。我还是一如既往地喜欢在句子中夹杂"古旧的"，或是不时地蹦出一个"以何程度"，但是我有意识地不再说"变体"。（乐颖）

王：这句译文有歧义。原作者说的是一个小变化，而不是所有说话的方式都改变了。从紧接着的后一句可以看出来。

改译1：但是我也注意到了一个新变化。在办公室和同事说话时，我还是一如既往地喜欢在句子中夹杂"古调不弹"，或是不时地冒出一句"以何种程度"，但是我刻意不说"本"了。（王）

改译2：但是我也注意到了一个新变化。在办公室和同事说话时，我还是会冒出几个"迂腐不堪"，甩出几个"之程度"，但是我刻意不说"番"字了。（李）

建议译法：但是我也注意到了一个新变化。在办公室和同事说话时，我还是会冒出几个"古调不弹"，甩出几个"之程度"，但是我刻意不说"番"字了。（王）

21

原　文：That was my word, even though I hadn't realized it until the day before. Now everyone was saying it. I didn't want to appear a mere imitator when I used this noun that now seemed to belong to me.

原　译："变体"是我的词语，尽管直到前一天我才意识到；但是现在，大家都在说这个词。我不想再说"变体"，这个似乎属于我的词语时，看起来像一个拙劣的模仿者。（乐颖）

改译 1：虽然我直到前一天才意识到,"刻本"是我的口头禅,但现在每个人都在用这个词。我可不想在说我的口头禅时,反倒像是在模仿谁。(王)

王：此处借用了袁梦琪同学的表达,又稍做修改。

改译 2：这个字属于我。尽管我前一天才意识到。现在大家都在用,我可不想在说自己的口头禅时,反倒像是在模仿谁。(李)

王：这里是否可以表达得更自然一些?

改译 3：这可是我的口头禅,尽管我前一天才意识到。现在大家都在用,我可不想在说自己的口头禅时,反倒像是在模仿谁。

改译 4：尽管我前一天才意识到,但这可是我的字啊。现在大家都在用,我可不想在说自己的口头禅时,反倒像是在模仿谁。

李：可以改为改译 3。

建议译法：这可是我的口头禅,尽管我前一天才意识到。现在大家都在用,我可不想在说自己的口头禅时,反倒像是在模仿谁。(王)

22

原文：But I also won't become one of those people who go around stealing the fingerprint words of others. How lazy! How unoriginal! How lame!

原译：但是我也不会到处盗用别人的口头禅。真是太懒惰,太没个性,太笨拙蹩脚了!(乐颖)

建议译法：但我也不会跟他们似的,到处用别人的口头禅。太懒!太没创意!太差劲!(王)

23

> **原文**：How long after writing those last few sentences was it before I could think of a time I engaged in the exact sort of behavior that so infuriated me when it happened at the office? About four seconds.
>
> **原译**：在写下上一句话后不久，我想起我也做出过这种令自己十分愤怒的行为，当时是在办公室。我大概花了多久想起来这件事呢？大约四秒钟吧。（乐颖）

王：原文是 last few sentences.

> **改译1**：在写完最后几句话没多久，也就四秒钟吧，我便想起自己在办公室也干过这种令我恼火的事。（王）
>
> **改译2**：在写完前几句话没多久，也就四秒钟吧，我便想起自己在办公室也干过这种令我恼火的事。

乐颖："最后几句话"？哪里的最后几句话？我还是倾向于这里的 those last few sentences 指 How lazy! How unoriginal! How lame! 而非段落或文章的"最后几句话"。

李：the last few sentences 就是指 But I also won't become one of those people who go around stealing the fingerprint words of others. How lazy! How unoriginal! How lame!

> **改译3**：这几句话刚写完，也就过了四秒吧，我便想起自己也干过办公室同事让我如此恼火的事。（李）

李：when it happened at the office 不是修饰 engage，而是修饰 infuriated。因为他自己的模仿行为不是在办公室，是和好友之间。

王：同意李老师前半句分析。这句话后半句似乎不通。

> **改译4**：这几句话刚写完，也就过了四秒吧，我便想起来，办公室同事这种令我如此恼火的事，自己也干过。（王）

王：同意李老师对于前半句的分析。改译3的后半句似乎不通。

建议译法：这几句话刚写完，也就过了四秒吧，我便想起来，办公室同事这种令我如此恼火的事，自己也干过。

李：同意你的译法。

24

原文：I did it a few months ago. One of my closest friends uses the word *tremendous* often in emails.

原译：那是几个月之前的事情了。我最亲密的朋友之一经常在邮件中使用"甚佳"这个词。（乐颖）

词义

此处 tremendous 结合上下文，应取下面的释义2：

adj.

1. a. Extremely large in amount, extent, or size; enormous: *a tremendous sum of money.* See Synonyms at **enormous**. b. Very great in scope or importance: *tremendous influence.*

2. Remarkable; outstanding: *What a tremendous example you have set.*

3. *Archaic* Capable of making one tremble; terrible.

https://www.thefreedictionary.com/tremendous

王：还是有些欧化的感觉。

改译1：那是几个月前的事了。我一个密友经常在邮件中用"甚佳"这个词。（王）

改译2：那是几个月前的事了。我一个密友经常在邮件中用"精彩绝伦"这个词。（李）

王：我觉得乐颖原译的"甚佳"蛮不错的。比较古雅、低频。"精彩绝伦"现在用得也不少见。我还是建议改回"甚佳"。

李：同意改回。

> **建议译法**：那是几个月前的事了。我一个密友经常在邮件中用"甚佳"这个词。（乐颖）

25

> **原文**：I'll send him a link to some especially outstanding baseball catch or a stupid screaming goat video, and he'll reply, succinctly, "That is tremendous."
> **原译**：我有时会给他发一些特别精彩的棒球接球或者蠢山羊尖叫的视频链接，他则会简洁地回复道："甚佳。"（乐颖）

查证视频

可以从 youtube 上看出，stupid screaming goat vedio 是一类搞笑视频：

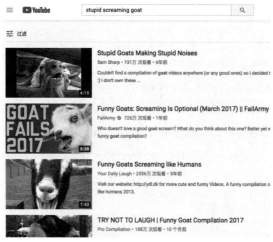

https://www.youtube.com/results?search_query=stupid+screaming+goat+&pbjreload=10

> **改译 1**：有时看到超精彩的棒球接球，或者山羊傻叫，我会把视频链接发给他，他则会简洁地回复道："甚佳。"（王）

王：此处借用了袁梦琪同学的表达，又稍做修改。

> **改译 2**：有时看到超精彩的棒球接球，或者山羊傻叫的视频，我会把链接发给他，他则会简洁地回复道："甚佳。"（乐颖）
>
> **改译 3**：有时看到棒球比赛超级棒，或者山羊傻叫的视频，我会把链接发给他，他则会简洁地回复道："甚佳。"（李）

王：李老师，这里我有两点疑问。首先 baseball catch 应该不完全等同于 baseball match。比赛强调延续性，接球一刻强调瞬时性。baseball catch 定义为：

In **baseball**, a **catch** occurs when a fielder gains secure possession of a batted ball in flight, and maintains possession until he voluntarily or intentionally releases the ball。

https://en.wikipedia.org/wiki/Catch_(baseball)

因此 baseball catch 我还是倾向翻译为"棒球接球"。

此外，这句话的改译从对仗角度看，前面的棒球部分是名词加形容词做补语，后面的山羊部分是以名词结尾。此处我还是倾向改译 2。

李：同意改回。

> **建议译法**：有时看到超精彩的棒球接球，或者山羊傻叫的视频，我会把链接发给他，他则会简洁地回复道："甚佳。"（乐颖）

26

> **原文**：Or he'll email me an article prefaced with, "This is a tremendous story." It works for him. It really does. And, without knowing it, I've snatched that word from him like nobody's business.
>
> **原译**：有时他也会给我发一些文章，邮件开头写着："此故事甚佳"。这个词很适合他，真的很适合。而且不知不觉地，我很快就从他那夺走了这个词。（乐颖）

Like nobody's business 意为：
INFORMAL

1. If someone or something is doing something **like nobody's business**, they are doing it very fast, in large amounts or to a great extent.

The people with this disease are dying off like nobody's business. I'm enjoying myself like nobody's business.

2. If someone or something does something **like nobody's business**, they do it very well. *He sings like Sinatra, dances like Sammy Davis, plays piano like nobody's business, and lays on the charm like an old pro.*

See also: **business, like**

https://idioms.thefreedictionary.com/like+nobody%27s+business

> **改译 1：**有时他也会给我发一篇文章，并附言："此故事甚佳"。这个词很适合他，真的很适合。而且不知不觉地，我很快就把这个词占为己有了。（王）
>
> **改译 2：**有时他也会给我发一篇文章，并附言："此故事甚佳"。他用得得心应手。真的。而我很快就把这个词占为己有了。自己都不知道。（李）

王：这里的疑问是，"得心应手"比喻技艺娴熟，心手相应。但是这里作者意在表明这个词很适合他。另外，这里句号是否用得有些频繁呢？我还是比较倾向改译 1。

李："不知不觉"和"很快"意思有冲突。不知不觉是连快慢都不知道。

> **改译 3：**有时他也会给我发一篇文章，并附言："此故事甚佳。"这个词很适合他，真的很适合。不知不觉地，我就把这个词顺手牵羊了。（李）

王：李老师，我查了一下汉语语料库，"顺手牵羊"似乎后面还会接动词。当然，汉语使用方式并不固定。但"顺手牵羊"指顺手把人家的羊牵走。比喻趁势将敌手捉住或乘机利用别人。现比喻乘机拿走别人的东西。这个"趁势"是否和 without knowing it 矛盾呢？

> 1　罗惠忘不了十年内乱,那个月黑风凄之夜:造反派冲进了她的家,吆喝她外公低头认罪,她和外婆被驱到阳台一隅,翻箱倒柜,戳破沙发,衣物撒落一地……最后还顺手牵羊提走一只新式的皮箱,这是外公特地托人从广州买来,准备送给罗惠将来上大学的礼物。
> #语料来源 [样本名称]:《人生没有单行道》[作者]:林志刚 [写作时间]:N/A [出版时间]:1985-5-1 [书刊名称]:文化与生活 [编著者]:N/A [出版社]:上海文化出版社
>
> 2　这时,大家顺手牵羊每人拿一个,却也听不到什么意见了。
> #语料来源 [样本名称]:N/A [作者]:N/A [写作时间]:N/A [出版时间]:1988-1-3 [书刊名称]:经济日报 [编著者]:N/A [出版社]:经济日报社
>
> 3　她想起丈夫的手,那一双手曾因"顺手牵羊"而使他不得不远走他乡,并给她和孩子们带来羞辱。
> #语料来源 [样本名称]:《邓肯欢鸣乐》节录 [作者]:徐JU [写作时间]:N/A [出版时间]:1982-5-1 [书刊名称]:四川文学 [编著者]:N/A [出版社]:四川人民出版社

http://corpus.zhonghuayuwen.org/CnCindex.aspx

snatch 本身有抢夺之意。因此,我的建议为:

> **建议译法:** 有时他也会给我发一篇文章,并附言:"此故事甚佳。"这个词很适合他,真的很适合,而我却在浑然未知的情况下,把这个词据为己有了。

李:可以。

27

> **原文:** I didn't realize this until July, when a different friend responded to one of my own emails by giving me props for my unusual word choice.
> **原译:** 直到七月份,我才意识到这一点。当时另外一个朋友在回复我写的邮件时,赞赏了我别具一格的选词。(乐颖)

give props 意为:

To praise and show one respect. *Thank you, but I have to give props to Jeanne, who organized this entire event for us.*

https://idioms.thefreedictionary.com/give+props+to

> **改译 1:** 意识到这一点时已经是七月份了。当时,另一个朋友在回复我邮件时,夸奖我别具一格的选词。(王)
> **改译 2:** 意识到这一点时已经是七月份了。当时,另一个朋友在回复我邮件时,夸奖了我别具一格的选词。(乐颖)

改译 3：意识到这件事时已经是七月份了。当时，另一个朋友在回复我邮件时，夸奖我别具一格的选词。（李）

28

原文："Also, great use of *tremendous*," she wrote near the end of her correspondence.
原译：她在回信的末尾写道："另外，你的'甚佳'用得很妙。"（乐颖）
改译 1：她在回信末尾写道："还有，'甚佳'用得妙。"（王）
改译 2：她在回信末尾写道："还有，'精彩绝伦'用得妙。"（李）

王："精彩绝伦"已经根据上文的修订改回"甚佳"。

建议译法：她在回信末尾写道："还有，'甚佳'用得妙。"（王）

29

原文：This prompted a review of my sentbox folder, which confirmed that the word is now pervasive in my outgoing emails.
原译：她的话促使我检查了一下我的发件箱，结果发现我现在发出的邮件里确实充斥着"甚佳"这个词。（乐颖）
改译 1：于是，我连忙检查了发件箱，结果发现这个词已经充斥在我的发件箱里了。（王）

改译 2：于是，我连忙检查了发件箱，结果发现这个词已经充斥我的发件箱了。（乐颖）

贾：两个逻辑连词接得有点近。"结果"就是一个逻辑交代，有了它"于是"就显得有点没必要了。

王：我觉得都可以，请李老师定夺一下吧。觉得加了"于是"，可以更好地承接上文。

李：感觉都可以。保留"结果"吧。

> **建议译法**：于是，我连忙检查了发件箱，结果发现这个词无处不在。（李）

30

> **原文**："What an old-school term," she added. "Let's bring that back!"
> **原译**：我的朋友还说："这个词可真老派啊！我们一起复活它吧！"（乐颖）
> **建议译法**：她补充道："多老派的词啊！我们重新启用吧！"（王）

第二单元　查证能力

Exercise 2　A Letter Brief

翻译情景

本次练习选自选美国谷歌 Waymo 公司和美国 Uber 公司之间的知识产权诉讼文书，仅 162 个单词。假定你是原告 Waymo 公司的专职译员，需要把诉讼文书翻译为汉语。

法律翻译不同于文学翻译、广告翻译、标识翻译等灵活性较大的翻译。法律翻译必须忠实于原文，做到双语文本的绝对对等。因此，译者需要对原文有极为透彻的理解，然后以精确的语言传递理解的意思，变通的余地非常小。

专项能力

本单元旨在训练大家的查证能力。何为"查证"？从字面意思来理解，"查证"分为"查"和"证"两部分。这个过程不仅是一个查找的过程，也是一个论证的过程。翻译的过程，就是发现和再现真相的过程。译者不断发现问题、寻找答案、消除疑问、解决问题。这个过程不仅训练译者利用工具和资源查找答案的能力，还训练译者辨别、批判、选择答案的批判性思维能力。科技发展日新月异，新事物层出不穷，译者不可能成为"活字典""百事通"，必须学会利用技术工具和资源，通过调查研究，弥补自己知识储备的不足；必要时还需要与专业人士沟通。当然，在查找资料的过程中，译者也应该是积极、开放、批判、辩证的"研究者"，学会选取、利用、构架资源，而不是被海量的信息淹没，不知所措。

做非文学类翻译（法律、文件、报告等），要避免闭门造车。必须利用字典、网络、语料库等一切手段获得理解和表达的证据，作出知情判断。关于查找资料的具体方法，可以参照李长栓《非文学翻译理论与实践》（第二版）第五章和第六章；本章在涉及具体例子时，也会作具体说明。

查证能力和态度应该贯穿在翻译教育的始终。对于翻译教育工作者来说，可以有意识地训练学生查找信息、证明观点、解决问题的能力。即使让学生学习机辅翻译，教育者应关注机器解决不了的问题，而非仅仅把翻译教育停留在技术操作层面。查证的能力具有通识性，养成了查证习惯，不仅可以解决翻译问题，专业地翻译出各类文本，还有助于解决将来工作中的一切问题。

在当今追求"速度"的时代，我们希望翻译学习爱好者和教育者能够具备"匠人"精神，知其然，知其所以然，通过查证和思辨，对译文精雕细琢，让译文趋于完美。

训练难点

译者一直都在平衡 know something of everything 和 know everything of something，有时也会因此而苦恼。很多情况下，译者不可能掌握所需的全部专业知识，只能现学现卖，调动各种工具、资源，查找、理解相应知识点，再找到的专业术语所表达的意思。本单元的难点在于，专业领域的一些常识性的概念，网上甚至找不到专门的解释，译者必须通过上下文，来推断这些概念的含义，甚至需要请教专家。当然，如果在律所作专职译员，这样的专家比比皆是。本次练习字数虽少，却是冰山一角。要想破解这"一角"，可能需要破解水下的整座冰山。具体而言，虽然这份诉讼文书仅涉及民事诉讼中的"证据开示"，但背后却是美国整个民事诉讼制度。要想真正理解这一制度，需要对整个诉讼制度有大致了解。为了给大家的查证工作提供一个基础，

训练方式

本单元练习分为原文、翻译提示、参考译文、译者注四部分。在尝试翻译原文前，可以先尝试破解一下整座冰山。可先了解 Uber 和 Waymo 的知识产权诉讼案，包括相关报道和往来诉讼文书，再大致了解一下美国的民事诉讼制度。为了帮助梳理材料，可以画一个"思维导图"，根据自己的理解，将核心事件和关键事件联系起来；或者，可以尝试梳理一个时间轴，标注事件发生的时间、主要内容和相应文件。由此，译者训练的不仅仅是查找资料的能力，更是系统梳理资料、重点选取资料、论证翻译决定的能力。这次作业难度不小，希望大家迎难而上，通过充分查证，出色地完成翻译任务！

原文[1]

Dear Judge Alsup:[2]

Plaintiff Waymo respectfully submits this discovery letter brief[3] in response to[4] the Court's Order Setting Hearing[5] Re Discovery Letter Dated April 11, 2017 (Dkt[6]. 211) and Defendants' April 11 Discovery Letter (Dkt. 210). Uber attempts to blame Waymo for its inability to comply with the Court's most recent order, but its difficulties are of its own making. They reflect Uber's continued failure to comply with the Court's original expedited discovery order[7] to find all "uses" of Waymo's confidential information. (Dkt. 61.) Uber violated that order and continues to do so. Uber has now doubled down on its "head in the sand[8]" approach to locating Waymo's trade secret information, leveraging only "fuzzy hashes[9]" generated by its forensic[10] vendor (which are insufficient to find files that have been changed) and raw search terms (which are insufficient to find evidence of use of Waymo's schematics). As Waymo has repeatedly explained, this approach does not comply with the Court's order.

翻译提示

1　全局意识

本书第一单元强调的全局意识将贯穿翻译学习始终。请大家针对原文和译文，分别回答 Who is talking to whom? About what? When, where and why? And how? 然后再开始翻译。

2　全局意识：翻译风格

法律文本的翻译要准确、通顺、正式，变通处理的情况较少。国外的法律概念，可能与中国的概念不对等，无法找到唯一的译法，因此，只要意思正确都可以接受。

3　法律知识 / 专业表述

discovery letter brief 是本段查证的一个难点。目前传统的词典大多已经电子化，推荐大家在阅读英文原文时，先去查看英英词典，例如：

　　Cambridge dictionary：https://dictionary.cambridge.org/

　　Collins dictionary：https://www.collinsdictionary.com/dictionary/english

　　The free dictionary：https://www.thefreedictionary.com/

　　在谷歌搜索框中输入单词和 definition，就会查到这些词典的解释。

　　翻译初学者遇到不懂的句子时，可能会逐一查证每个单词，然后把每个单词的意思拼凑在一起。这样做与机器翻译无异。译者需要做的是将词语放入语境中理解。目前谷歌（https://www.google.com/）和百度（http://www.baidu.com）是使用较为普遍的搜索引擎，尤其在搜索英文资料方面，谷歌无可替代。利用谷歌和百度查找资料，一般在网页中输入关键词，即可找到相关文本。具体的方法可以参见《非文学翻译理论与实践》第五章第 94 页。就此处的查证来说，我们可以输入关键词 "discovery letter brief"，分别在谷歌和百度上查找。我们马上会发现，即使是谷歌，对 discovery letter brief 也没有直接的释义。法律当中的表述固然严谨，但是理解表述背后的含义，才能让译者在严谨之下更游刃有余。这时可以分开来查查看，首先查一下 brief 这个词在法律当中是什么意思，再查证 discovery 程序本身。说不定开示（discovery）程序的解释中，会有详细的解释和对应说法。最后，检查自己是否省略了某个词的翻译？ letter 和 brief 的意思是否相同？

4 **修饰关系**

in response to 后接的这句话，不仅是语法关系的难点，也是法律知识查证的难点。在修改二稿的过程中，译者需要思考以下几个问题：

1） in response to 是后接一个宾语，还是两个宾语？

2） Re 是什么意思？ Dkt.210 是 Re 的修饰成分吗？

5 **法律知识 / 专业表述**

order setting hearing 的意思可以按照译者注 3 所说的查证方式在谷歌或百度中找到答案。

6 **法律知识 / 专业说法**

通过查证，我们可以得知 Dkt. 是 docket 的简写。docket 这个词的用法非常灵活，也不太好处理。要翻译 docket，还是要理解这个词在原文中是什么意思。

7 **法律知识 / 专业说法**

查找资料时不应盲目查找，而是应该带着问题查证。此处译者应该通过运用网络资源、询问专家等方式理解 expedited discovery 的意思，包括它的主要作用等。

8 **短语理解**

这个短语起到比喻义的作用。译者可以更进一步思考这个比喻义和 Uber 做法之间的关系。

9 **专业知识**

fuzzy hashes 这个词想必大家通过查找平行文本，可以确认译法。但 hashes 在这里指的是算法，还是具体数值呢？

10. 专业表述

forensic 是我们在美剧里会经常看到的词。一般有"法医"的意思。那么，在这篇文章中，forensic 是不是解剖尸体的"法医"呢？不做人体解剖的"法医"，是否有别的叫法？

参考译文

尊敬的阿尔苏普法官：

原告 Waymo[1] 谨此呈交本开示意见书[2]，回应法院就 2017 年 4 月 11 日开示函（Dkt.[3] 211 号）发布的听证安排指令以及被告 4 月 11 日的开示函（Dkt. 210 号）[4]。Uber 试图把自己未能遵守法院最新指令的行为归咎于 Waymo，但其面临的困难是自己一手造成的[5]。Uber 的困难反映出，它一直未能遵从法院最初的加速开示令（Dkt. 61 号）[6]，查明其对 Waymo 保密信息的所有"使用"。[7] Uber 已经并继续违反该指令[8]。现在，Uber 以更加自欺欺人的方式[9]来查找对 Waymo 商业机密的使用，因为它的查找方式仅仅是法证公司生成的"模糊哈希值[10]"（这不足以找到被篡改的文件），以及原始搜索关键词（这不足以找到使用 Waymo 示意图的证据）[11]。Waymo 已经多次说明，Uber 这一查找方式不符合法院指令[12]。

译者注

1　全局意识 / 背景知识

王：从网上资料可知，诉讼文书涉及美国谷歌旗下的 Waymo 公司和美国 Uber 公司之间的知识产权诉讼。原告是 Waymo，被告是 Uber。2017 年 2 月，Waymo 向旧金山联邦地区法院提起诉讼，称 Uber 侵犯了自家专利且涉嫌盗窃商业机密，多项指控指向创办 Otto 的 Waymo 前任硬件工程师、Uber 现任副总裁——安东尼·莱万多夫斯基（Anthony Levandowski）。同年 3 月，因为得不到 Uber 的法律回应，Waymo 向法院申请立即执行临时禁令。2017 年 4 月 11 日，Uber 坚持在他们的服务器上，从未拥有、使用过莱万多夫斯基从 Waymo 窃取的任何信息。另外，Uber 还强调，两家公司使用的激光雷达技术，存在本质上的不同。此外，Uber 还补充道，为什么 Waymo 在发现邮件之后，整整过了 5 个月后才向法院提起诉讼？这暗示着 Waymo 的动机不纯。随后，不善罢甘休的 Waymo 回应道，Uber 这是在绕圈子，虽然在 Uber 的服务器上没有被窃取的信息，但是不代表在莱万的电脑上也没有。只是，至今双方都没有拿出有说服力的证据，本节选是 Waymo 在 4 月份针对 Uber 的回应。具体案件介绍请看以下链接：https://caselaw.findlaw.com/us-federal-circuit/1873720.html。整个案件的 docket 在这里：https://www.docketbird.com/court-cases/Waymo-LLC-v-Uber-Technologies-Inc-et-al/cand-3:2017-cv-00939。为了帮助大家理解节选的背景和时间脉络，以下是一些重大事件的发展脉络：

Dkt 23 • 2017.3.10：FIRST AMENDED COMPLAINT

Dkt 61 • 2017.3.17：ORDER RE EXPEDITED DISCOVERY AND RELATED MATTERS

Dkt 135 • 2017.4.3：Inform the Court of Defendants' ("Uber") willful violation of the Court's March 16 Expedited Discovery Order.

Dkt 210 • 2017.4.11：Requesting relief related to this Court's April 6 Order After Hearing Re Discovery Letter Dated April 3, 2017.

Dkt 211 • 2017.4.11：Plaintiff Waymo LLC shall respond to defendants' discovery letter brief dated April 11 (Dkt. No. 210) by 5:00 P.M. TODAY.

Dkt 217 • 2017.4.11：Plaintiff Waymo respectfully submits this discovery letter brief in response to the Court's Order Setting Hearing Re Discovery Letter Dated April 11, 2017 (Dkt. 211) and Defendants' April 11 Discovery Letter (Dkt. 210).（作业选文）

叶俊文：Waymo 的译法，译者最终选择保留英文，不译公司名称。Waymo 是 Alphabet 旗下负责无人驾驶业务的独立公司，原先无人驾驶业务仅仅是 Google X 实验室的一个项目，目前尚未推出产品，在中国的知名度不高。本文涉及的是美国境内发生的 Waymo 诉 Uber 窃用商业秘密案件，应该沿用其在美国的称呼，音译的意义不大。Uber 的译名"优步"虽然在中国为人熟知，若译成"优步"，一是与 Waymo 的翻译策略不一致，二是可能会让人有优步（中国）窃用 Waymo 商业秘密的歧义，而优步（中国）已与滴滴合并。

2 discovery letter brief 和 discovery letter

胡洪（中国律师）：对于该词的理解应当区分两个层次："discovery letter"与"brief"

brief

brief 在实践中有比较明确的界定，即当事人在诉前、诉中、诉后向法院就某个法律问题所提交的**法律意见 / 文书**：

> brief
> 1) n. a written legal argument, usually in a format prescribed by the courts, stating the legal reasons for the suit based on statutes, regulations, case precedents, legal texts, and reasoning applied to facts in the particular situation. A brief is submitted to lay out the argument for various petitions and motions before the court (sometimes called "points and authorities"), to counter the arguments of opposing lawyers, and to provide the judge or judges with reasons to rule in favor of the party represented by the brief writer. Occasionally on minor or follow-up legal issues, the judge will specify that a letter

http://legal-dictionary.thefreedictionary.com/brief

各法院往往对提交的 brief 有固定的形式要求，以美国联邦巡回上诉法院（该法院是唯一一家具有知识产权案件上诉管辖权的法院）为例，它对 brief 的类型、具体应当包括的内容，甚至是字数都有规定。具体请参考下述链接：

- http://www.cafc.uscourts.gov/sites/default/files/cmecf/QuickReference-FormalBrief Requirements.pdf
- http://www.cafc.uscourts.gov/sites/default/files/rules-of-practice/forms/form19.pdf
- http://www.cafc.uscourts.gov/announcements/new-rules-practice-federal-circuit-beginning-december-1-2016
- https://www.mindingyourbusinesslitigation.com/2016/06/new-word-limits-for-federal-appellate-briefs-how-low-is-too-low/

discovery Letter

胡：discovery letter 并无明确界定，实践中也有与"discovery letter brief"混用的情形，譬如本案中就出现了两者不做区分的情形，本案 Docket No.135 文件本身名称为："Discovery Letter Brief re Defendants' Violation of the

Court's March 16 Expedited Discovery Order filed by Waymo LLC."

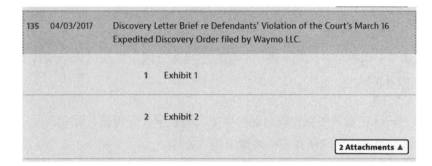

https://www.docketbird.com/court-cases/Waymo-LLC-v-Uber-Technologies-Inc-et-al/cand-3:2017-cv-00939

而在法官基于上述法律意见所做出的 order 中又把该文件称为"discovery letter":

> As stated on the record at the hearing yesterday concerning plaintiff Waymo LLC's discovery letter dated April 3, 2017 (Dkt. No. 135), defendants shall use Waymo's 15 search

（摘自：ORDER AFTER HEARING RE DISCOVERY LETTER DATED APRIL 3,2017）

与此同时，我还在网上找到将诉讼当事人之间就 Discovery 程序进行沟通的文件命名为"discovery letter"。具体请参考以下链接：

- Sample Discovery Letter
- https://www.justice.gov/sites/default/files/usao/pages/attachments/2015/04/01/ct_discovery_policy.pdf

基于上述原因，我倾向于将 discovery letter brief 译为"开示函法律意见"，即指与开示函相关的法律意见：

- 对 discovery letter 做模糊化处理，译为"开示函"；
- brief 理解为"法律意见"，而不将 brief 和 letter 视为同一事物。

李：discovery letter 和 discovery letter brief 是两种不同的诉讼文书。letter brief 直接写给法院；discovery letter 写给对方当事人，要求对方回答问题或出示证据。

1. Letter Brief. letter brief 应当理解为一个单位：This is Plaintiffs' *letter brief*, with attached discovery requests, in support of Plaintiffs' motion to overrule defendants' objections to discovery and require responses（https://www.jdsupra.com/legalnews/plaintiffs-letter-brief-in-support-of-m-15409/）

2. Petition for Certification. The petition for certification is *a formal brief – or a letter brief* – four copies of which must be filed with the Clerk's Office within thirty days of the filing date of the decision of the Appellate Division. Two copies must be served on your adversary. There are special requirements for a petition for certification that make it different from the brief you filed in the Appellate Division.（https://njcourts.gov/forms/10538.pdf）

分别查找 discovery letter、discovery letter brief、letter brief 并阅读样本发现，discovery letter 是写给对方（律师）的，请求对方开示证据（注意里面的 To opposing counsel）：

CHAPTER 6
Written Discovery Letters 121
   A. To Opposing Counsel – Requesting 122
      1. Discovery Letter – Discovery Requests 122
      2. Discovery Letter – Service on Counsel 123
      3. Discovery Letter – Overdue (Perfunctory) 124
      4. Discovery Letters – Overdue (Detailed) 125
      5. Discovery Letter – Incomplete 126
      6. Discovery Letter – Incomplete/Refused – General 128
      7. Discovery letter – Incomplete/Refused – Specific 129
      8. Discovery Letter – Follow-up to Document Request 132
      9. Discovery Letter – Follow-up to Interrogatory 133
     10. Discovery Letter – Supplement Request 134
     11. Discovery Letter – Follow-up 135
   B. To Opposing Counsel – Responding 136
      1. Discovery Letter – General Purpose 136
      2. Discovery Letter – Document Production 137
      3. Discovery Letter – Document Production Supplement ... 138
      4. Discovery Letter – Responses 139

Letter brief 是律师写给法院的一封信（A letter brief is used to persuade the court and provide case law to substantiate one's position.）开头无一例外是 Dear Judge…，同时也抄送对方（A letter brief is simply a letter filed with the court and served on all parties.）用来说服法院做一件事，不妨暂时翻译为"意见"。a discovery letter brief 也叫作 LETTER BRIEF REGARDING DISCOVERY ISSUES（https://www.justice.gov/atr/case-document/letter-brief-regarding-discovery-issues-and-replying-defendants-letter-brief），是在律师要求对方开示证据时，对方没有开示或没达到要求，或双方对开示有争议，律师请求法院干预。此处建议补充 discovery letter 的意思。

ORDER SETTING HEARING DATE

It is ORDERED that a hearing on the petition for expunction of criminal records filed in the above-captioned cause will be held on _____, 20____ at _____ o'clock ___.m. in the courtroom of the district court for the _____ Judicial District of Texas in Houston, Texas.

SIGNED this _____ day of _____, 20____.

因此，discovery letter 和 discovery letter brief 是两种不同的诉讼文书，可以分别翻译为"开示函"和"开示意见（书）"。因为 letter brief 是一个整体，翻译为"意见"，看似译文丢掉了一个"letter"，实际上没有省略。我问了耶鲁大学和纽约大学的美国和中国法律学者，对话如下：

李：高原（纽约大学美国亚洲法研究所），请问民事诉讼中 discovery letter 和 discovery letter brief 有什么区别？

高：不好意思啊李老师，我也没学过民事诉讼法，也不是特别清楚……不过我在网上查了一下，有一个大致的感觉，不知道对不对。就是 discovery letter 看起来像是一个纯粹请求证据开示的文件，比如按照哪条法律，我要求对方提供一下几种证据，比如各种报告、书籍、证人撰写的报告、证人作证的基本内容等等。discovery letter brief 看起来像是用于一方当事人对证据开示的内容或者形式有争议的情况下向法庭提交的请求对方特定证据的文书，比如一方当事人可能向法庭提出，对方当事人没有按照我方请求开示某个证据，而我方按照法律规定或者约定是有权利得到这个证据的，请求法院要求对方提供或者因此判定对方承担不利后果。不过还是建议您找一个更熟悉民事诉讼的人再核实一下，我也不是特别有把握……

李：谢谢。通常开示函是直接写给对方律师，还是通过法庭转交，还是直接给对方，抄送法院？

高：我觉得一般是第三种，但联邦民事诉讼规则里面好像说这几种都可以。

李：那我大致明白了。谢谢。

李：刘超（纽约大学美国亚洲法研究所），请问民事诉讼中 discovery letter 和 discovery letter brief 有什么区别？通常开示函是直接写给对方律师，还是通过法庭转交，还是直接给对方，抄送法院？Letter brief 应该读在一起，好像是写给法院的。

刘：discovery letter 可以直接给对方的；如果过程中有一些问题需要法官来解决，那就写个 brief 给法院。

李：Jeremy Daum（唐哲，耶鲁大学北京中心，懂中文），通常开示函是直接写给对方律师，还是通过法庭转交，还是直接给对方，抄送法院？letter brief 应该读在一起，好像是写给法院的。

唐：Discovery letter is usually to the other party, and can be a request for production of documents, answers to questions, or requests for admissions. A brief is always a legal argument, so should be aimed at the court, usually dealing with a contention, arguing over motion related to discovery etc.

李：志琛（Jake Clark，孔志琛，耶鲁大学北京中心，懂中文），请教民事诉讼中 discovery letter 和 discovery letter brief 有什么区别？letter brief 好像是一种诉讼文书类型，写给法院的。另外，请问 discovery letter 是直接写给对方律师，还是通过法庭转交，还是直接给对方，抄送法院？

孔：对的，letter brief 是一种诉讼文件类型，如果一个 discovery request 被对方挑战，写给法院一个 letter brief 支持你的立场。Discovery letter 是一种提交 discovery request 的文件，要求对方答问题或 produce evidence。在民事诉讼中就直接给对方，然后应该就要抄送法院，但是不要直接交给法院。

> **建议译法**：discovery letter："开示函"
> discovery letter brief："开示意见（书）"（李）

3　Dkt.

胡：Dkt. 是 docket 的简写，docket 的用法非常灵活，在本案中它主要用来表示诉讼事件号码，譬如这里的 Dkt. 210 就是指诉讼事件 210。Defendants' April 11 Discovery Letter (Dkt. 210) 就可以理解为诉讼事件 210 中所涉及的文件 210，详见附件 4，尤其是下面截图部分：

> Case 3:17-cv-00939-WHA　Document 210　Filed 04/11/17　Page 1 of 3
>
> **MORRISON | FOERSTER**　425 MARKET STREET
> SAN FRANCISCO
> CALIFORNIA 94105-2482
>
> MORRISON & FOERSTER LLP
> BEIJING, BERLIN, BRUSSELS,
> DENVER, HONG KONG, LONDON,
> LOS ANGELES, NEW YORK,
> NORTHERN VIRGINIA, PALO ALTO

同时，docket 也可以被用作动词，表示"立案或者受理"的含义，譬如"case docketed on or after"。

> **NEW RULES OF PRACTICE FOR THE FEDERAL CIRCUIT BEGINNING DECEMBER 1, 2016**
> The Federal Circuit has revised its local rules and hereby provides those revisions along with amendments to the Federal Rules of Appellate Procedure (FRAP). Those rules, which are applicable to cases docketed on or after December 1, 2016, are available 📄 here.
>
> http://www.cafc.uscourts.gov/rules-of-practice/notices）

李：从网上给出的文件图片看，就是案件大事记（可以说"案件目录"），但此处原文用的缩写，用意是尽量简洁，不妨简单译为"编号"，或者干脆保留 Dkt.。网上很多资料显示，Docket No. 似乎就是案卷编号（Case No.），一个案件只有一个 Docket No.。但本文所用 Docket No.，每处编号都不同，说明不是通常所说的 Docket No.。这个词，我 20 年前就开始试图理解，到现在都不明白。它的意思好像不止一个。换句话说，docket 的用法很混乱，有时是整个案卷的编号，具有唯一性；有时是案件诉讼过程中的"大事记"

表，里面摘要登记发生了什么事，每件事一个编号。

胡：我赞成您的说法。docket 的用法非常灵活。这个案子里面 docket 就被用来表示诉讼事件，所以才会有 Dkt.61, 210, 211 等的区分。

王：docket 指诉讼事件，诉讼事件里包括一系列诉讼文件（其中就有文件 210 等），所以 Dkt. 210 不能翻译为诉讼文件，而是诉讼事件，此处也可以不翻译。

4　法律知识 / 专业表述

> **原文**：Plaintiff Waymo respectfully submits this discovery letter brief in response to the Court's Order Setting Hearing Re Discovery Letter Dated April 11, 2017 (Dkt. 211) and Defendants' April 11 Discovery Letter (Dkt. 210).
>
> **原译**：原告 Waymo 谨此呈交本证据开示 信函，回应法院关于 2017 年 4 月 11 日的证据开示信函确定听证会的命令，以及回应被告 4 月 11 日的证据开示信函。（叶）

王：order setting hearing 的意思可以按照翻译提示 3 所说的查证方式在谷歌或百度中找到答案。

王：这里指的是关于听证安排的法院指令，包括听证（hearing）的时间、地点等。Order Setting Hearing 的查证可见以下链接：

http://www.houstontx.gov/police/expunction/forms/Expunction_Petition_(ProSe)_MUNICIPAL.pdf

> **改译 1**：原告 Waymo 谨此呈交本证据开示信函，回应法院既定听证命令，答复 2017 年 4 月 11 日的证据开示信函（案件目录 211），以及被告 4 月 11 日的证据开示信函（案件目录 210）。（王）
>
> **改译 2**：原告 Waymo 谨此呈交本证据开示函摘要，回应法院就 2017 年 4 月 11 日证据开示函（编号 211）以及被告 4 月 11 日证据开示函（编号 210）发布的听证安排令。（李）

> **改译 3**：原告 Waymo 谨此呈交本证据开示争议说明，回应法院就 2017 年 4 月 11 日开示争议说明发布的听证安排令（Dkt. 211 号）以及被告 4 月 11 日的开示争议说明（Dkt. 210 号）。（李）

王：Plaintiff Waymo respectfully submits this discovery letter brief in response to [the Court's Order Setting Hearing Re Discovery Letter Dated April 11, 2017 (Dkt. 211)] and [Defendants' April 11 Discovery Letter (Dkt. 210)]. 这句话要注意一下修饰成分。我用方括号划出了句子的修饰成分。首先，用核心句分析的方法，这句话可以把动词提炼出来并简化为 Plaintiff Waymo submits this discovery letter brief. 但是，这里关键的问题在于 in response to 是管一个宾语 Court' Order Setting Hearing Re Discovery Letter Dated April 11, 2017 (Dkt. 211)，还是管两个宾语（加上后面的 Defendants' April 11 Discovery Letter (Dkt. 210)）。从语法角度，两种理解都可以说得清，所以这里是需要查证的。经查证，首先，Court's Order Setting Hearing Re Discovery Letter Dated April 11, 2017 不能分开，因为 Dkt. 211 是指 Order Setting Hearing Re 2011 Discovery Letter Dated April 11, 2017，后者才是 title。见下：

April 11, 2017 00:00
Order Set Motion and Deadlines/Hearings
Document: 211
ORDER SETTING HEARING RE 210 DISCOVERY LETTER DATED APRIL 11, 2017. Signed by Judge Alsup on 4/11/2017. Responses due by 4/11/2017. Motion Hearing set for 4/12/2017 11:30 AM in Courtroom 8, 19th Floor, San Francisco before Hon. William Alsup. (whalc2, COURT STAFF) (Filed on 4/11/2017)

其次，从以上 211 的具体内容可知，这个 to 管两个宾语：211+210。210 不是"Re"的宾语。

基于这样的分析，to 管两个宾语，Order Setting Hearing Re Discovery Letter Dated April 11，2017（Dkt. 211）是一部分，Defendants' April 11 Discovery Letter（Dkt. 210）是另外一部分。这句话的后半部分重心应该落在 Court's Order Setting Hearing，也就是听证安排的法院指令，而不是开示函。后面的 Re 是它的修饰成分。所以，如果同学们把 Court's Order Setting Hearing 变为 Discovery Letter 的修饰成分就不对了。此外，如果有同学看到 Court's Order Setting Hearing 就加了书名号，这样也不是不可以，但是即

使加书名号,也要处理为《关于〈2017 年公示…〉…法院指令》,重心不可以错。

> **改译 4**:原告 Waymo 谨此呈交本开示函法律意见,回应 2017 年 4 月 11 日开示函听证安排的法院指令(Dkt 211 号)以及被告 4 月 11 日的开示函(Dkt. 210 号)。(胡)

李:基于前面关于 discovery letter、discovery letter brief、letter brief 的调查,进一步修改如下:

> **建议译法**:原告 Waymo 谨此呈交本开示意见书,回应法院就 2017 年 4 月 11 日开示函(Dkt. 211 号)发布的听证安排指令以及被告 4 月 11 日的开示函(Dkt. 210 号)。(李)

5

> **原文**:Uber attempts to blame Waymo for its inability to comply with the Court's most recent order, but its difficulties are of its own making.
> **原译**:Uber 没能遵循法院最新的命令而试图归咎于 Waymo,但 Uber 面临的困境是自己造成的。(叶)
> **改译**:Uber 试图把未能遵守法院最新命令的行为归咎于 Waymo,但实则是自取其咎。(王)

李:咎指灾祸。没这么厉害。

> **建议译法**:Uber 试图把未能遵守法院最新指令的行为归咎于 Waymo,但其面临的困难是自己一手造成的。(李)

6 法律知识 / 专业说法

王:根据与胡洪(律师)的讨论,expedited discovery order 指的是"加速开示令"。

李:证据开示,是指在法庭审理之前,原被告交换证据,做到知己知彼,以

57

便在法庭上专门针对争议之处进行辩论。证据交换之后，对于没有争议的证据，就不需要到法庭辩论了。

王：从 Docket 61 可以看出，诉讼程序是有时间限制的，如：

The deadline for defendants to oppose plaintiff's motion for preliminary injunction is continued from March 24 to APRIL 7.

Plaintiff may depose the declarants who submit declarations in opposition to the motion for preliminary injunction. In addition, plaintiff may depose three additional officers, directors or employees of defendants. Defendants must make the deponents available upon 48 hours' notice. Plaintiff may have a total of 18 hours of deposition time (not counting breaks) to be allocated as it wishes. All depositions to be taken by plaintiff shall occur after defendants' opposition.

7.

原文：They reflect Uber's continued failure to comply with the Court's original expedited discovery order to find all "uses" of Waymo's confidential information. (Dkt. 61.)

原译：且反映出 Uber 依然没能遵循法院最初颁布的加速证据开示的命令，即查明 Waymo 机密信息的所有"用途"。（叶）

改译 1：Uber 面临的困境反映出，它依然未能遵从法院原有的加速证据开示命令，协助查明 Waymo 机密信息的所有"用途"。（案件目录 61）（王）

李：所谓"开示"，就是要求对方出具自己掌握的证据，包括对自己不利的证据。

改译 2：Uber 的困难反映出，它一直未能遵从法院最初的加速开示令，查明其对 Waymo 保密信息的所有"使用"。（编号 61）（李）

李："编号 61"应该放在"加速开示令"后面，不是句子末尾。证据如下：

61	03/16/2017	ORDER RE 26 28 EXPEDITED DISCOVERY AND RELATED MATTERS by Judge Alsup. (whalc2, COURT STAFF)
	03/16/2017	Set/Reset Deadlines as to 24 MOTION for Preliminary Injunction. Responses due by 4/7/2017. Replies due by 4/21/2017. Motion Hearing set for 5/4/2017 08:00 AM in Courtroom 8, 19th Floor, San Francisco before Hon. William Alsup. (whalc2, COURT STAFF) (Text entry; no document attached.)

建议译法： Uber 的困难反映出，它一直未能遵从法院最初的加速开示令（Dkt.61号），查明其对 Waymo 保密信息的所有"使用"。（李）

8

原文： Uber violated that order and continues to do so.
原译： Uber 已经并继续违背该命令。（叶）
建议译法： Uber 已经并继续违反该命令。（王）

9 短语理解

叶：bury (one's) head in the sand

To avoid, or try to avoid, a particular situation by pretending that it does not exist. The phrase refers to the common but mistaken belief that ostriches bury their heads in the sand when frightened, so as to avoid being seen. *Lou, you can't bury your head in the sand about your health — please, make an appointment with your doctor and get that rash checked out! A: "How has Peter been handling the break-up?" B: "Oh, just burying his head in the sand and ignoring his feelings."*

http://idioms.thefreedictionary.com/bury

另见 bury one's head in the sand 的解释：

The story also relies on the supposed stupidity of ostriches, and of birds in general. In fact, there's little to support that either as birds have a significantly larger brain to weight ratio than many other species of animal. <u>The notion is that the supposedly dumb ostrich believes that if it can't see its attacker then the attacker can't see it.</u> This was nicely reformed as a joke on Douglas Adams' 'Hitchhiker's Guide to the Galaxy', in which the 'Ravenous Bugblatter Beast of Traal' was described as 'so mind-bogglingly stupid that it assumes that if you can't see it, then it can't see you.'

http://www.phrases.org.uk/meanings/80800.html

结合上面的解释，bury one's head in the sand 颇有"掩耳盗铃"的意味。

10

叶：fuzzy hashing 是用来识别相似文件的算法，其特点是能够识别文件是否经过修改：

> Fuzzy hashing is a suitable approach where similarity of content can be recognized through similarity of the raw byte sequences contained in files. This holds especially for text files like HTML and XML files, source code files, or configuration files (.conf, .ini, etc.). Fuzzy hashing is also suitable for compiled software, for example in the form of binary executables or Java class files (bytecode). Compressed file
>
> https://books.google.com/books?id=xBjWBgAAQBAJ&pg=PA246&lpg=PA246&dq=fuzzy+hashing+definition&source=bl&ots=8bowovxh9H&sig=Fx0BtVivCoiEWWyA_LFEcbB-jPY&hl=en&sa=X&ved=0ahUKEwikxsau19vVAhWljVQKHXnIDUY4ChDoAQhaMAk#v=onepage&q&f=false

简单来说，哈希算法就是将一个任意大的数据项（如计算机文件）映射为固定长度（比原数据短得多）的二进制位串，也就是哈希值。就目前而言，哈希算法依然能够确保它是原始数据的唯一标识，就像人的指纹可以唯一地标识一个人，因此哈希算法还具有精确匹配的特性。

http://blog.csdn.net/mznewfacer/article/details/7642305

李：hashing 是抽象表达，可以译为算法。此处 hashes 用复数，可能是指 hash values，因为这个算法算出来的东西，应当是一个数值。建议译为"哈希值"。

11 语法逻辑

原文：Uber has now doubled down on its "head in the sand" approach to locating Waymo's trade secret information, leveraging only "fuzzy hashes" generated by its forensic vendor (which are insufficient to find files that have been changed) and raw search terms (which are insufficient to find evidence of use of Waymo's schematics).

> **原译**：现在，Uber 变本加厉地贯彻其"鸵鸟政策"，查找 Waymo 商业秘密信息时，仅使用由其鉴识软件公司 计算的"模糊哈希值"（而这不足以找到被修改的文件）和原始搜索关键词（而这不足以找到使用 Waymo 图表的证据）。（叶）

> **改译 1**：现在，Uber 更是变本加厉，继续"掩耳盗铃"。在查找 Waymo 商业机密信息时，仅使用由其鉴识软件公司生成的"模糊哈希算法"（这不足以找到被篡改的文件），以及原始搜索关键词（不足以找到使用 Waymo 图表的证据）。（王）

李：按逻辑，这个 locating 是指上一句的 find all uses。

> **改译 2**：现在，Uber 以更加自欺欺人的方式查找 Waymo 商业机密的去处，因为它仅仅利用法证公司生成的"模糊哈希值"（这不足以找到被篡改的文件），以及原始搜索关键词（这不足以找到使用 Waymo 示意图 的证据）。（李）

李：forensic 过去经常翻译为"法医"，现在多译为"法证"，如 forensic science 法证科学。

胡：这个词实践中有两种用法，第一个就是你所提及的"法证科学"意义上的法医鉴定相关：

https://baike.baidu.com/item/%E6%B3%95%E8%AF%81%E7%A7%91%E5%AD%A6/10663773?fr=aladdin）

另外一种则是将更广泛意义上的科学知识（而不限于法医学）用于解决司法问题，这点也可以从韦氏词典的解释得以印证："relating to or dealing with the application of scientific knowledge to legal problems"。

从表述上来看，"forensic vendor"是来指为 Uber 在本案中提供专业证据筛查技术服务的服务商。

建议译法：现在，Uber 以更加自欺欺人的方式来查找对 Waymo 商业机密的使用，因为它的查找方式仅仅是法证公司生成的"模糊哈希值"（这不足以找到被篡改的文件），以及原始搜索关键词（这不足以找到使用 Waymo 示意图 的证据）。（李）

李：forensic 这个词来源于 forum，由于法院是解决司法问题的 forum，与 forum 相关的 forensic，便成了"法医""法证"。

22

原文：As Waymo has repeatedly explained, this approach does not comply with the Court's order.
原译：Waymo 已经多次说明，Uber 这一做法没有遵循法院的命令。（叶）
改译：Waymo 已经多次说明，Uber 这一做法没有遵循法院命令。（王）
建议译法：Waymo 已经多次说明，Uber 这一查找方式不符合法院指令。（李）

第三单元　辩证看待欧化中文

Exercise 3　Blockchain

翻译情景

区块链是当今热门的话题之一。以下段落摘自 Blockchain: *Ultimate guide to understanding blockchain, bitcoin, cryptocurrencies, smart contracts and the future of money* 一书[1]，作者 Mark Gates。本书是对 Blockchain 的全面介绍，属于科普文章。假定译文用途不发生变化，作为科普读物在中国出版，请翻译以下节选（共 520 字）。

专项能力

本次练习旨在训练大家的中文表达能力，确保译文符合中文表达习惯。说到中文表达能力，就不得不谈到欧化中文在翻译当中的特殊角色。当代白话文是综合了文言文、古代白话、新文化运动之后的白话、以及外文而形成的，尤其受五四运动影响很深[2]。五四运动以后，以鲁迅为代表的一批文人希望以欧式表达改变国人思考方式，强调"欧化文化的侵入中国

1　Gates M. Blockchain: *Ultimate guide to understanding blockchain, bitcoin, cryptocurrencies, smart contracts and the future of money* [M]. California: CreateSpace Independent Publishing Platform, 2017.
2　郝志景．反思文白之争与欧式中文 [J]．浙江社会科学，2012(11)：131-134.

白话的大原因,并非因为好奇,乃是为了必要。"[1] 但余光中先生认为:

"精确"固然是翻译的一大美德,但牺牲"通顺"去追求,代价就太大了。

在坚守"精确"的原则下,译者应常常自问:"中国人会这么说吗?"如果中国人不这样说,译者至少应该追问自己:"我这样说,一般中国人,一般不懂外文的中国人,能不能理解?"如果两个答案都是否定的,译者就必须另谋出路了。

译者追求"精确",原意是要译文更接近原文,可是不"通顺"的译文令人根本读不下去,怎能接近原文呢?不"通顺"的"精确",在文法和修辞上已经是一种病态。要用病态的译文来表达常态的原文,是不可能的。

理论上来说,好的译文给译文读者的感受,应该像原文给原文读者的感觉。如果原文是清畅的,则不够清畅的译文,无论译得多么"精确",对原文来说仍是"不忠",而"不忠"与"精确"恰恰相反。[2]

我们对此表示赞同。我们认为,翻译应当尽量摆脱原文句法的影响,在理解作者意图的基础上,尽量按照汉语语法造句,把翻译当成一种写作,尽管不是表达自己的思想,但遵循汉语写作当中的所有遣词造句规则。

另一方面,完全摆脱原文的影响,不是在所有情况下都能做到,因此,大家读到的译作,往往会有一些翻译的痕迹,但只要不带来理解上的障碍,我们对此也持一种宽容的态度。

训练难点

原文所使用语言和汉语的结构差距甚大,所描述的事物("区块链"),也是源自国外的概念。译者需要在翻译中想办法将这些"舶来品"转化为地道的中文表达。在翻译过程中,要尽量避免亦步亦趋,套用英文的表达方式。要像余光中先生说的一样,时刻问问自己:中国人会这样说吗?

---

[1] 转引自董娟娟. 论汉语第三人称代词的欧化现象[J]. 云南师范大学学报(对外汉语教学与研究版), 2010, v.8; No.42(1): 68-73.
[2] 本段节选自余光中先生为思果先生新书《翻译研究》作的序。思果先生的翻译思想与余光中先生一脉相承,非常注重译文的通顺表达,反对中文文法的欧化现象。思果先生的《翻译研究》具体请参见:思果. 翻译研究[M]. 北京:中国对外翻译出版公司, 2001.

训练方式

本单元练习分原文、翻译提示、参考译文、译者注四部分。建议在翻译之前，读读余光中先生的《怎样改进英式中文？——论中文的常态与变态》，然后再开始翻译，翻译时不要看翻译提示。审改自己的二稿时，可参看翻译提示，并注意译文的表达是否符合中文的表达习惯。修改二稿以后，可参看译文和译者注，进一步理解并润色表达。需要提醒的是，虽然语言表达很重要，但一切表达的基础是理解。很多理解问题解决了，表达问题可能就迎刃而解！

原文[1]

…

Blockchain is one of the underlying technologies of Bitcoin[2]. There is[3] a misunderstanding that the blockchain is the only technology behind Bitcoin. However, Bitcoin has been created using a range of other[4] cryptographic technologies combined with the blockchain.

Bitcoin is a digital currency, primarily used for payments. Bitcoin uses a one-way[5] blockchain technology； however, the blockchain can be used to record and transfer anything of value, not just financial transactions[6].

Blockchain-based systems are being used for a wide range of applications across different industries, including digital identities, social networks, voting, cloud storage, decentralized applications and more covered later in the book. There are seemingly endless possibilities for blockchain-based systems that companies and governments are currently developing.

Bitcoin, on the other hand, is still only being used for digital payments. While Bitcoin is gaining in popularity with its price continually hitting record highs, it is designed primarily as a method of payment[7].

…

Key Points:

- In order for a transaction to be processed and considered valid, it is grouped with other transactions and added to a new block.
- This new block is added "on top" of the previous block in the blockchain. Each block refers to the previous block number, linking them together like a chain, which is where the name "blockchain" comes from.[8]
- The chain of blocks in the blockchain links all the way back to the first block on the chain known as the "genesis block."
- With a decentralized blockchain, each block of transactions on the blockchain is validated by the network. Everybody on the network receives information about transactions on the network; it is not controlled by a centralized database owned by one company or institution.
- Once a block of transactions has been added to the blockchain, it is difficult to reverse. Every block added on top is a confirmation that the transaction won't be reversed. The more blocks on top, the harder it is to reverse until it is unfeasible. On the Bitcoin network, 6 blocks are accepted as confirmation the transaction won't be reversed.
- With distributed consensus, the majority of computers on the network need to agree that a transaction is valid before it is accepted on the blockchain.
- Double spending is where someone on the network attempts to duplicate transactions. This is generally done by sending transactions more than once before one of them is confirmed and accepted onto the blockchain.
- A double spending attack is where a user controls more than 50% of the computers on the network. This allows the user to double spend transactions by controlling which transactions are accepted and rejected.
- Mining is the process of validating transactions and adding new blocks to the blockchain. Small rewards are given for each new block added to

the blockchain, like mining a small reward out of a big block.
- Proof of work involves solving a computer puzzle to add a new block to the blockchain. It is difficult to solve but easy to prove, like a combination lock. It provides evidence that computing power and resources were used and contributed to the network.

翻译提示

1 **全局意识**
请大家针对原文和译文，分别回答 Who is talking to whom? About what? When, where and why? And how? 然后再开始翻译。

2 **语言能力：欧化句式**
one of the 很容易译为"……之一"，这是英文表达习惯的自然迁移，说明我们对英文的句型结构已经了然于心。但是，想要作出地道的译文，译者的语言差别意识和中文素养就尤为重要。译者需要问问自己：中文里面有没有类似的表述？中国人会这样说话吗？在审视二稿时，可以不断问自己这些问题，警惕因为按英语结构转换，导致中文表达翻译腔过重。

3 **语言能力：欧化句式**
there be 句型是英文句式的常见结构。如果按照原英文结构翻译成"有"，则译文会缺少主语，显得和原文亦步亦趋，较为欧化。在处理 there be 句型时不妨思考给译文加上主语。

4 **语言能力：欧化表达**
思考一下 a range of other 是否需要按照原文表达翻译成"一系列其他"？修改时要时不时问问自己：中国人会这样说吗？

5 **语言能力 / 查证能力**
one-way 中文可以直译为"单向"。为了避免亦步亦趋地翻译原文，译者需要知道所谓的"单向"技术到底指的是什么？这时，译者就需要运用第二单元的查证能力，找找看"单向"的意思。当然，在最后确定译文的时候，译者要平衡查证资料和原文表达之间微妙的关系，既要避免亦步亦趋，也要避免因为查证资料而对译文进行过度解读。

6　逻辑问题

这段话的逻辑并不是特别清楚。如果在原文逻辑不清楚的情况下，译者可以考虑打破重建原文逻辑，做到尽量贴近原文作者的逻辑思路。

7　逻辑问题

这句话逻辑上是否存在问题？不是所有作者都能通顺连贯地表达自己的意思。如果原文的逻辑出现问题，或者没有逻辑，根据翻译情景，译者或可打破原文束缚，重建译文逻辑；实在没办法，则尽力而为，因为如果原文作者的逻辑太过混乱，达到无可救药的地步，译者再大本事，也无能为力。译者毕竟不能把自己的意思强加给作者。

8　查证能力

翻译时可能需要查证 block number 指的是什么。为缩小检索范围，可以在搜索框中搜索：blockchain "block number"。注意用引号，否则搜出来的 block 和 number 可能不在一起。加上 blockchain 是为了限定搜索范围。否则，内容可能是关于"街区"的 block。在网上搜索，可以找到有关 block number 的很多中英文资料。

参考译文[1]

区块链是比特币的一项底层技术。[2]有人误以为，区块链是比特币背后唯一的技术。但实际上，比特币还使用了其他加密技术。[3]

比特币是一种数字货币，使用单向加密技术，主要用于支付，但区块链用于记录和转让任何有价值的东西，不仅仅是金融交易。[4]

基于区块链的系统在不同行业有各种应用，包括数字身份证、社交网络、投票、云存储、去中心化应用，以及本书后文面提及的更多应用。[5] 利用区块链技术似乎可以开发出无穷无尽的系统，这也是各国政府和众多企业正在努力的方向。[6]

而比特币仍然仅仅用于电子支付。[7] 虽然比特币价格不断刷新，日渐受到人们宠爱，但其设计的初衷，主要是作为一种支付手段。[8]

……

要点总结：

- 为了处理并验证一项交易，该交易会与其他交易打包，一同添加到新的数据块。[9]
- 新数据块被添加在数据块链条上最后一个数据块之上。[10] 每个数据块指向上一个数据块编号，各个数据块像链条一样紧密相连，由此产生"区块链"名称。[11]
- 在区块链中，各数据块首尾相连，可以一直链接到第一个数据块，也就是"创始数据块"。[12]
- 区块链没有管理中心。链条上每个交易数据块都由整个网络验证。[13] 网络上人人都能收到该网络上产生的交易信息，这些信息不受任何公司或机构的中央数据库控制。[14]
- 交易数据块一旦添加到数据块链条中，就很难撤销。[15] 每添加一个数据块，就是再次确认交易不可逆。[16] 叠加在上面的数据块越多，数据块就越难撤销，直到交易"不可逆"或无法撤销。[17] 在比特币网络中，一般认为6个数据块就能够确认交易不可逆。[18]
- 在分布式共识模式下，只有网络中的大多数计算机一致同意某交易有效，该交易才会被区块链接受。[19]
- "一币双花"（另译"双重支付"）是指网络中有人企图重复交易。通常是在交易得到确认并添加到区块链之前，某人多次发送交易数据造成的。[20]
- "一币双花攻击"是指用户控制交易网络中超过半数的算力，

以操纵系统接受或拒绝哪些交易,达到一次交易"花"(使用)两次的目的。[21]
- "挖矿"是验证交易并把新数据块添加到区块链上的过程。每添加一个新数据块,"矿工"都会获得小小的奖励,这就像挖矿一样,从大块矿藏中挖出一小块,就得到一点酬劳。[22]
- 矿工的工作量证明,就是他通过解决一个计算机难题,将新的数据块添加到了区块链上。破解难题就像解密码锁。找到密码很难,验证密码很容易。破解谜题证明矿工花费了算力和资源,并由此为网络作出贡献。[23]

译者注

1 全局意识 / 风格

王:原文具有科普性,语言风格是 non-technical, informative and easy to understand,原书引言部分(Introduction)对此有清楚说明:

This book is written for people new to blockchain technology looking for a non-technical understanding of the technology. There are some technical aspects covered towards the end of the book; however, the technical details of the blockchain are not the focus of the book.

When first learning about blockchain technology, I found there was a lot of technical information about blockchain technology scattered and poorly structured, but no clear guide starting from a non-technical basis.

I have written this book as it is the book I wanted to read when first learning about and trying to understand the blockchain.

I hope you enjoy reading this book and find it useful, educational, and insightful in your understanding of blockchain technology.

因为译文面向同样的读者,所以也应具备科普写作的特点,语言尽量简洁、易懂,符合中文表达习惯。可以把翻译视为写作,以译入语的写作规范要求译文。

2

> 原文：Blockchain is one of the underlying technologies of Bitcoin.
> 原译：区块链是比特币的核心技术之一。（王佳楠）
> 改译：区块链是比特币的一项核心技术。（王苏阳）

王：改译避免了"之一"的说法。余光中先生对"之一"等各种欧化现象深恶痛绝。虽然翻译中完全避免欧化是不可能的，但我们需要保持警惕，尽量采用更具符合中文习惯的表达方法。此处也可以不改，因为此种说法已经司空见惯。

余先生关于"之一"的相关论述：

「……之一」虽然是单数，但是背景的意识却是多数。和其他欧洲语言一样，英文也爱说 one of my favorite actresses, one of those who believe…, one of the most active promoters。中文原无「……之一」的句法，现在我们说「观众之一」实在是不得已。至于这样的句子：

刘伶是竹林七贤之一。

作为竹林七贤之一的刘伶……

目前已经非常流行。前一句虽然西化，但不算冗赘。后一句却恶性西化的畸婴，不但「作为」二字纯然多余，「之一的」也文白夹杂，读来破碎，把主词「刘伶」压在底下，更是扭捏作态。其实，后一句的意思跟前一句完全一样，却把英文的语法 as one of the Seven Worthies of Bamboo Grove, Liu Ling... 生吞活剥地搬到中文里来。

所以，与其说「作为竹林七贤之一的刘伶以嗜酒闻名」，何不平平实实地说「刘伶是竹林七贤之一，以嗜酒闻名」？其实前一句也尽有办法不说「之一」。中文本来可以说「刘伶乃竹林七贤之同俦」；「刘伶列于竹林七贤」；「刘伶跻身竹林七贤」；「刘伶是竹林七贤的同人」。

「竹林七贤之一」也好，「文房四宝之一」也好，情况都不严重，因为七和四范围明确，同时逻辑上也不能径说「刘伶是竹林七贤」，「砚乃文房四宝」。目前的不良趋势，是下列这样的句子：

红楼梦是中国文学的名著之一。

李广乃汉朝名将之一。

两句之中。「之一」都是蛇足。世间万事万物都有其同俦同类，每次提到其一，都要照顾到其他，也未免太周到了。中国文学名著当然不止一部，汉朝名将当然也不会只有一人，不加上这死心眼的「之一」，绝对没有人会误会你孤陋寡闻，或者挂一漏万。一旦养成了这种恶习，只怕笔下的句子都要写成「小张是我的好朋友之一」，「我不过是您的平庸的学生之一」，「他的嗜好之一是收集茶壶」了。

「之一」之病到了香港，更变本加厉，成为「其中之一」。在香港的报刊上，早已流行「我是听王家的兄弟其中之一说的」或者「戴维连一直以来都是我最喜欢的导演其中之一」这类怪句。英文复数观念为害中文之深，由此可见。

这就说到「最……之一」的语法来了。英文最喜欢说「他是当代最伟大的思想家之一」，好像真是精确极了，其实未必。「最伟大的」是抬到至高，「之一」却稍加低抑，结果只是抬高，并未真正抬到至高。你并不知道「最伟大的思想家」究竟是几位，四位吗，还是七位，所以弹性颇大。兜了一个大圈子回来，并无多大不同。所以，只要说「他是一个大名人」或「他是赫赫有名的人物」就够了，不必迂而回之，说什么「他是最有名气的人物之一」吧。

——余光中《怎样改进英式中文？——论中文的常态与变态》

李：虽然说"核心技术"也不算错，但查找 underlying 在区块链中的意思发现，技术专家有更加贴切的说法，直接来自英文："简单来说，比特币是一种区块链，区块链就是比特币的底层技术。"这个说法，以前很少听到。但这个新颖的说法可以顾名思义，又很贴切，建议采用。可以输入"区块链 技术 比特币"三个关键词来查找。遇到不熟悉的说法，看看专家是否已经给出了答案。不要闭门造车。

王：同意。

建议译法： 区块链是比特币的一项底层技术。（李）

3

> 原文：There is a misunderstanding that the blockchain is the only technology behind Bitcoin. However, Bitcoin has been created using a range of other cryptographic technologies combined with the blockchain.
> 原译：有人误解区块链是比特币背后唯一的技术。其实比特币是依靠区块链技术和其他许多密码技术而产生的。（王佳楠）

王佳楠：There be 句型我处理成了"有人"，不知是否严谨。另外，However 是转折关系，个人感觉读者语气偏向"举出一个错误观点后，用事实澄清这个观点"，所以用了"其实"。

王：我觉得没有问题。There is 句型本来就是典型的欧式句式，如果不用"有人"作主语，译文中就会出现"有"字，会让译文更加欧化。这里我换个说法，让读者更加从容。

> 改译 1：有人误解区块链是比特币背后唯一的技术。其实，比特币的出现不仅结合了区块链技术，还使用了其他加密技术。（王苏阳）

李：这两句话更是说明，区块链技术不一定是核心，而仅仅是一种底层技术。鉴于这是一部科普读物（act local, think global），不是联合国文件，所以译者的自由度较大，可以以译入语最简洁的方式来表达。因此可以改为："但实际上，区块链还融合了（或结合使用了）其他一系列加密技术。"这样，省略了冗余信息，使逻辑关系更为紧密。原译变换了一次主语，使读者失去逻辑的连贯性，必须重新寻找这句话和上句话之间的联系。等找到了，却发现前半句（"比特币的出现不仅结合了区块链技术"）是无用的，仅仅是重复上句话的意思，很恼火。

> 改译 2：有人误以为，区块链是比特币背后唯一的技术。但实际上，区块链还结合使用了其他一系列加密技术。（李）

王佳楠：Bitcoin has been created using a range of other cryptographic technologies combined with the blockchain 可以翻成"区块链还结合使用了其他一系列加密技术"吗?我觉得是"比特币还融合使用了一系列其他加密技术"。我觉得按照李老师的思维,不如把前一句话的主语改成比特币,前一句话说的也是比特币。"比特币背后的技术不只是区块链,还融合了一系列其他加密技术"。

陈佳鑫:原文前半句说的是区块链技术用于记录和转让有价值的东西,而非比特币。

王:作者的表述前后变化了主语。这时,可以试着变换主语,让前后逻辑统一。如果变换主语行不通,就按照原文字面主语顺序翻译,也是译者的无奈之举。"一系列"和"其他"重复。从语义出发,去掉"一系列"即可。不影响原文意思。

> **建议译法**:有人误以为,区块链是比特币背后唯一的技术。但实际上,比特币还使用了其他加密技术。(李)

4

> **原文**:Bitcoin is a digital currency, primarily used for payments. Bitcoin uses a one-way blockchain technology; however, the blockchain can be used to record and transfer anything of value, not just financial transactions.
>
> **原译**:比特币是主要用于支付的数字货币;它是区块链技术的一种应用。然而,区块链可以用于记录和转让任何有价值的东西,不仅限于金融交易。(王佳楠)
>
> **改译1**:比特币是一种数字货币,主要用于支付。比特币使用单向区块链技术;然而,区块链可以记录和转移任何有价值的东西,不仅仅是金融交易。(王苏阳)

李:我个人理解,区块链技术本身就是单向的,没有双向的区块链技术。否则,区块链就被破解了。因此,原文 one-way 按说后面还应该有个逗号。把"单向区块链技术"改为"单向的区块链技术",可以减轻被误解的倾向。

实际上,所谓"单向",就是本文所讲的"不可逆"(只能朝一个方向走)。

林昕頔: 在互联网上是搜索不到单向区块链技术这种说法的,也就是说这里不能直译为单向区块链技术,那么单向的是什么呢?

Hashing is a method of cryptography that converts any form of data into a unique string of text. Any piece of data can be hashed, no matter its size or type. In traditional hashing, regardless of the data's size, type, or length, the hash that any data produces is always the same length. <u>A hash is designed to act as a one-way function — you can put data into a hashing algorithm and get a unique string, but if you come upon a new hash, you cannot decipher the input data it represents.</u> A unique piece of data will always produce the same hash.

Well, the distributed nature of a blockchain database means that it's harder for hackers to attack it — they would have to get access to every copy of the database simultaneously to be successful. It also keeps data secure and private because <u>the hash cannot be converted back into the original data — it's a one-way process.</u>

可以看出 one-way 是用来形容哈希算法的,那么我们再来看一下哈希算法的介绍:

哈希算法有个显著的特点:单向加密、不可逆,它的实现原理往往是通过丢掉一部分信息来实现的。比如:给出一串数字12345,你对它进行平方,去掉前三位,再除以固定的数字比如678,取整数。

1. 12345×12345=152399025
2. 去掉前三位就是 399025
3. 399025/678=588.532448
4. 取整数为 558

可以看到,通过固定的计算公式,可以由 12345 得出 558 的结果,但仅仅提供 558 这个数字,尽管把算法公开,你也几乎不可能再推导出它计算前的数字。

这种丢掉一部分信息的加密方式被称为"单向加密",即哈希算法。

我们可以搜索"单向加密"以再次验证这样的说法是否存在:

加密算法一般有两种，即单向加密算法和双向加密算法。双向加密是加密算法中最常用的，它将可以直接理解的明文数据加密为不可直接理解的密文数据，在需要的时候，又可以使用一定的算法将这些加密以后的密文数据解密为原来的明文数据。双向加密适合于隐秘通讯，比如，在网络上注册用户或者购买商品时，提交的真实姓名、身份证号码、银行账号、信用卡密码等信息，应当通过双向加密算法加密以后，再在网络上传输，这样，可以有效地防止黑客"偷听"，保证数据的安全，同时，网站接收到我们的数据以后，可以通过解密算法来获得准确的信息。双向加密既可以加密，又可以解密。而单向加密则刚好相反，它只能对明文数据进行加密，而不能把加密了的密文数据再解密成原来的明文数据。可能读者会认为，不能解密的加密算法有什么作用呢？在实际应用中，对软件系统数据库中的系统用户信息（如用户密码）加密，就是一个典型的例子。当用户注册一个新的账号时，其用户密码信息不是直接保存到数据库，而是经过单向加密后再保存，这样，即使这些账号信息被泄露，别人也不能得到相应的用户密码，当然也就达不到盗窃账号的目的。也许，有的读者会想，既然单向加密无法解密，那用户一旦忘记了密码，几乎没有办法找回原来的密码，又该怎么办呢？这确实是一个比较麻烦的问题，如果是一个功能简单的软件系统，也许真的只能删除忘记密码的账号信息，然后再重新注册来解决。但是比较完善的软件系统，一般都可以让用户提供一些其他的注册信息，如出生地址、父母妻子的职业等，如果正确，则直接给用户提供修改密码的功能，然后用新密码替换掉数据库中的旧密码，这样，用户只要记住新的用户密码就可以了。

MD5、SHA 算法就是单向加密的加密算法。

所以我们现在可以得出结论，这里的 one-way 应该译为单向加密技术或算法，而不是单向区块链技术。

李：这个调查很好。在我们确信的情况下，可以说得更清楚。但也可以像原文那样说"单向的区块链技术"。"单向的"用于强调区块链的特性，而不是限定。

改译 2：比特币是一种数字货币，使用单向加密技术，主要用于支付，但区块链可用于记录和转让任何有价值的东西，不仅仅是金融交易。（李）

王：第二个"用于"是否可以删去？

"转让"和"转移"还是有区别的：

1. 转移，在《国际收支手册》第五版中，将转移分为经常转移和资本转移，资本转移计入国际收支平衡表中的资本和金融账户，从而使得国际收支口径和国民经济核算体系一致。

2. 转让就是把自己的东西或合法利益或权利让给他人，有产权、债权、资产、股权、营业、著作权、知识产权转让、经营权、租赁权等等。

https://zhidao.baidu.com/question/1820379431504662708.html

李：不必去掉第二个"用于"。主要用于……也用于……，前后关联。转让隐含着有对价，转移是位置的移动。网上的交易，是转让，不是转移。

这段话的逻辑凌乱。可以整段打乱重来。Again，这不是联合国决议。译者有权按照最理想的方式来改造。建议改为：比特币是一种数字货币，使用单向的区块链技术，主要用于支付，但也可用于记录和转让任何有价值的东西，不仅仅是金融交易。

建议译法：比特币是一种数字货币，使用单向加密技术，主要用于支付，但区块链可用于记录和转让任何有价值的东西，不仅仅是金融交易。（李、王）

5

原文：Blockchain-based systems are being used for a wide range of applications across different industries, including digital identities, social networks, voting, cloud storage, decentralized applications and more covered later in the book.

原译：以区块链为基础的系统在不同产业应用非常广泛，包括数字身份、社交网络、投票、云储存、去中心化应用等等，更多将在之后章节讨论。（王佳楠）

改译 1：基于区块链的系统在不同行业应用广泛，包括数字身份、社交网络、投票、云储存、去中心化应用，以及本书后面提及的更多应用。（王苏阳）

王：blockchain-based systems 的翻译我有些疑虑的。按照目前的改译来看，是有欧化痕迹的。但是为了和下一句中的 blockchain-based systems 保持一致，体现其专有名词短语属性，我还是按照欧化的形式处理了。我们要辩证看待欧化，取长补短。当然，并不是说此为最佳译法。如果可以在原语和形式之间找到最佳取舍，那再好不过了。

改译 2：基于区块链的系统在不同行业有各种应用，包括数字身份证、社交网络、投票、云存储、去中心化应用，以及本书后面提及的更多应用。（李）

李：这样一改，"包括"所指就是"应用"，否则会被认为是在指"行业"。

关于数字身份证的资料：数字身份证是身份标识方式的一种，是一对"钥匙"，其中一个只有他本人知道（即密钥），另一个是公开的（公钥）。把数字身份证比喻成一个证件，那么数字证书就是身份认证机构盖在数字身份证上的一个章或印（或者说加在数字身份证上的一个签名），表示身份认证机构已认定这个人的这个数字身份证并为这个人的这个数字身份证背书。没有任何背书/印/加签/数字证书的数字身份证是没有什么实际意义的。

或者改为"区块链身份认证/识别"。例如（资料）："基于区块链技术的身份识别。""如今，若将基于区块链的识别机制引入到网络安全问题中，可能会提供一个有趣的解决方案。"单说"数字身份"意思不清楚。

建议译法：基于区块链的系统在不同行业有各种应用，包括数字身份证、社交网络、投票、云存储、去中心化应用，以及本书后面提及的更多应用。（李）

6

> 原文:There are seemingly endless possibilities for blockchain-based systems that companies and governments are currently developing.
> 原译:区块链机制似乎有无限可能,公司和政府正在开发这种系统。(王佳楠)

王苏阳:我觉得这句译文的重心有些偏移。这句话强调的是 endless possibilities,而非 that 后面的从句。

> 改译1:公司和政府正在开发基于区块链的这种系统,似乎有无限可能。(王苏阳)
> 改译2:公司和政府正在开发基于区块链的系统,似乎有无限可能。(王佳楠)

李:前半句会被误以为是个完整句子,从而使下半句没有主语。

> 建议译法:利用区块链技术似乎可以开发出无穷无尽的系统,这也是各国政府和众多企业正在努力的方向。(李)

7

> 原文:Bitcoin, on the other hand, is still only being used for digital payments.
> 原译:另一方面,比特币仍用于电子支付(王佳楠)
> 改译:而比特币仍然只用于电子支付。(王苏阳)

王:多数同学查到了"数字支付"这一说法,但是相较"电子支付"还是用得较少。此处采纳"电子支付"的说法。

  on the other hand 从欧化的角度衡量,大多处理为"另一方面"。这种译法无可厚非,然而,译者要时刻提醒自己,看看是否有更符合中文表达习惯的译法。从句子的连贯性看,改为"而"意思更紧密。

> **建议译法：** 而比特币仍然仅仅用于电子支付。（李）

8

> **原文：** While Bitcoin is gaining in popularity with its price continually hitting record highs, it is designed primarily as a method of payment.
> **原译：** 尽管比特币方兴未艾、价格不断创下新高，它设计的初衷主要用于支付。（王佳楠）

李：原文逻辑问题。作者的逻辑性很差。这两部分之间没有转折关系。

王苏阳：我认为这两部分还是有转折关系的，只是作者表述不清楚。他的逻辑应该是比特币只用于数字支付，无论它现在多受欢迎、价格多高，它还只是一种支付手段。

李：这个逻辑我认为说不通。这两段的逻辑似乎是：区块链用途多，比特币只是个支付手段。后者现在炒得很热，其实不值那么多钱。无论如何，可以保留原文的逻辑，不是译者的问题。

王：原文逻辑很混乱，如果连打破重来都不可以，就只好保留原文逻辑，但我们要注意译文的可读性。

李：原文这样的逻辑混乱，译者无能为力，只能复制原文错误。[1]

> **建议译法：** 虽然比特币价格不断刷新，日渐受到人们宠爱，但其设计的初衷，主要是作为一种支付手段。（王苏阳）

9

> **原文：** In order for a transaction to be processed and considered valid, it is grouped with other transactions and added to a new block.
> **原译：** 为了一个交易能够进行并确认有效，该交易和其他交易一起打包，添加到新的区块。（王佳楠）

---

[1] 本书首次出版印刷后，读者陈某指出，这句话逻辑没有问题。我再读觉得确实如此。遂修改参考译文。

王佳楠：中文读下来能够理解，但是这句话主语不明确，"谁"打包交易？虽然理解上没有问题，还是觉得中文不够严谨，找不到更好的方法。

王苏阳：这句话的主语不需要明确。英文之所以有被动语态，就是要弱化施动者，增强表达的科学性。比如，一项化学实验，试验结果不需要报告是大科学家做的，还是年轻科学家做的，数据质量更重要。比特币的验证过程，本身就是由多人参与的。因此，不必强调主语。

王力《中国现代语法》（p.97）里也有详细说明不用"被"字的情形。

1. 主事者无说出的必要，或说不出主事者为何人，则不用关系位，同时也不用"被"字。

2. 主语为无生之物，无所谓不如意或不企望的事，则"被"字必不能用，关系位也因此用不着了。

这句话的被动语态，为了更符合中文表达，可以使用强势动词。"打包"和"一起"意思相近，有些重复。我稍做调整。

> **改译**：为了处理并验证一项交易，该交易会与其他交易打包，一同添加到新的区块。（王苏阳）

李：区块链根本就是个错误的命名。正确的命名应该是数块链。因为 block 是指 blocks of data: May 6, 2018 — A blockchain is a digital concept to store data. This data comes in blocks, so imagine blocks of digital data. These blocks are chained together... 英文的 block 没有"区"的含义，只有"块"的意思；译者是为了配成双音节词，而添加的"区"。但却因为不求甚解，添加错误。既然是数据块，不妨简称为"数块链"。然而，既然业界已经接受"区块链"，我们可能无法扭转。不过，在叙述过程中，仍然可以用"数据块"的概念。

> **建议译法**：为了处理并验证一项交易，该交易会与其他交易打包，一同添加到新的数据块。（李）

10

> 原文：This new block is added "on top" of the previous block in the block-chain.
> 原译：这一新区块在区块链中加在前一个区块"之上"。（王佳楠）

王佳楠：用"之上"是因为英文的表达是一个区块 builds on top of the previous one，中文是否可以用"之后"呢？不过"之上"也符合中文表达习惯。

王苏阳：也可以。但是，如果翻译为"之后"，其实就不需要加引号了，而且原文的语言特色也有些流失了。

> 改译：在数据块链中，这一新数据块是在前一区块"之上"添加的。（王苏阳）

李：in the blockchain 的修饰关系搞错了，导致"在数据块链条上，这一新数据块……"逻辑错误：新数据块在添加之前不在区块链中。previous block 其实就是指最后一块。

> 建议译法：新的数据块叠加在数据块链条中最后一个数据块之上。（李）

11

> 原文：Each block refers to the previous block number, linking them together like a chain, which is where the name "blockchain" comes from.

王佳楠：（资料）每个区块都必须要指向前一个区块，否则无法通过验证。
https://yq.aliyun.com/articles/118203

> 原译：每个区块指向上一个区块号，从而使各个区块连接成链，这即是"区块链"名称的由来。（王佳楠）

王苏阳：linking them together like a chain 并不是显义的动作，是描述相连的状态。

> **改译 1**：每个区块指向上一个区块号，就像链条一样紧密相连，这就是"区块链"名称的由来。（王苏阳）

许芳玲：审校指出这里"Each block refers to the previous block number"指每个区块中都包含着上一区块的内的数字指纹。我在最初看到这个句子时也有这样的想法，因为老师发的阅读材料中明确指出："区块至少包含以下信息：前一个区块的数字指纹 + 固定信息 + 收到的交易记录 + 一个随机数"。但数字指纹是区块链中一个非常复杂的概念，而原文作者 Mark Gates 在开篇说，本文是为从未了解过区块链的人编写的非技术性介绍文档，且在 Each block refers to the previous block number 这句话之前，作者也并未对数字指纹进行过讲解和介绍，为何会在这里突兀地提出一个很难理解的技术概念？带着这个疑问，我以"block number"为关键词进行了检索，从检索结果来看，block number 的含义远没有我们想象的那么复杂，它其实就是指每个区块的编号而已。原文中作者针对"Each block refers to the previous block number"的进一步论述也证明了这一点。

> The Block number is not *inherently* unique. The Block number is the measure of blocks starting from the block in question to the first block (the genesis block).
> It might be simple to assume that the direction of counting the blocks is an unnecessary clarification but this gains some ambiguity when dealing with **hard forks**.
> In the case of a blockchain with hard forks, if you were to count the blocks from the bottom up, you would reach two (*or more!*) different blocks based on which path of the fork you chose to track and how many total forks there were.
>
> https://ethereum.stackexchange.com/questions/46784/is-a-block-number-unique-or-does-it-change-if-the-block-becomes-uncle-does-the

王：许芳玲同学的分析很有借鉴意义。这次作业有一个普遍问题，就是许多同学把过多的查证结果补充到译文中，尽力译出原文的所指含义，而非字面含义，这种情况叫作"过度翻译"（over-translation）。大家查证精神是可取的，但注意分寸，不需要补充的内容，不必补充，更不要把简单的东西复杂化。

> **改译 2**：每个数据块指向上一个数据块编号，就这样像链条一样紧密相连，这就是"区块链"名称的由来。（王）

李："每个数据块指向上一个数据块编号，就这样像链条一样紧密相连"简化后是："每个数据块相连"。"相连"的主语只能是"各个数据块"。"每个"强调个体，一个东西没法相连。

> **建议译法**：每个数据块指向上一个数据块编号，各个数据块像链条一样紧密相连，由此产生"区块链"名称。（李）

李：本来应该说"由此产生'数块链'的名称"，但胳膊扭不过大腿。"区块链"的说法铺天盖地，改名还没有形成共识，译文为迁就现有名称，导致逻辑上稍有不顺，也无可奈何。

李：另外，原文 Each block …linking them together like a chain 也经不起语法分析。them 显然是指 blocks。但 each block links blocks like a chain 是说不通的。但意思清楚，我们按照汉语的习惯造句即可。

12

> **原文**：The chain of blocks in the blockchain links all the way back to the first block on the chain known as the "genesis block."
> **原译**：区块链中连接成链的区块能一直追溯到第一个区块，即"创世区块"。（王佳楠）

王佳楠：译文有点重复，但是原文也是绕口令的感觉，不知这样贴近原文的翻译是否妥当。

王苏阳：看似有些重复，我认为侧重点不同。The chain of blocks 强调链条的连续性，但并没有忽略单个 block 的存在。所以这里稍微变换了一下表达方式，让侧重点和语气有些变化。

> **改译1：** 在区块链中，链条般的区块可以一直追溯到第一个区块，也就是"创世区块"。（王苏阳）

李：什么"创世"？就是"创始"。genesis 的本意是 the origin or coming into being of something: the process or mode of origin。词源意义就是"产生"。第一位译者，只是在词典上看到"创世纪"的译法，就自作聪明翻译为"创世"。你创造了哪个世界？跟"区块"的翻译错误如出一辙。太多不懂翻译的人在做翻译。

> **改译2：** 在区块链中，各个数据块可以一直链接到第一个数据块，也就是"创始数据块"。（李）

王：感觉还是表达不够自然。不妨再大胆一些，links all the way back to 可作更形象化的处理。

> **建议译法：** 在区块链中，各数据块首尾相连，可以一直链接到第一个数据块，也就是"创始数据块"。（王）

13

> **原文：** With a decentralized blockchain, each block of transactions on the blockchain is validated by the network.
> **原译：** 由于区块链去中心化，每个区块中的交易都由网络验证。（王佳楠）

王佳楠：这里指的是特定的交易网络。以区块链技术为基础的各个交易平台有各自的交易网络。

http://www.blockchainbrother.com/article/154

王苏阳：由上文"打包"可知，区块链中的每一个区块中，都有很多笔交易。这一点也可以通过查证得知：

产生一笔新交易

一笔新交易产生时，会先被广播到区块链网络中的其他参与节点，各节点将数笔新交易放进区块，每个节点会将数笔未验证的交易 Hash 值收集到区块中，每个区块可以包含数百笔或上千笔交易。

https://blog.csdn.net/love_Aym/article/details/80867456

此外，我在后面添加了"整个"，意在与"去中心化"形成对比。

> **改译**：在去中心化的区块链中，每个交易块都由整个网络验证。（王苏阳）

李：区块链本身就是去中心化的。"block of transactions"是交易数据块，如你们查到的资料所述，里边包含很多次交易。

> **建议译法**：区块链没有管理中心。链条上每个交易数据块都由整个网络验证。（李）

14

> **原文**：Everybody on the network receives information about transactions on the network; it is not controlled by a centralized database owned by one company or institution.
>
> **原译**：交易网络中人人都能收到网络中的交易信息，这一网络不受某个公司或机构的中心化数据库控制。（王佳楠）

王佳楠："交易"是我添加的，因为原文 the network 是指向某一个交易网络，节点需先加入那个网络社群才能进行交易。

王苏阳：我觉得不添加也可以。这里强调的是 everybody，而非网络，不添加也不会引起混淆。

王佳楠：这个 network 也在原文中出现很多次了，可能是为了强调，也可能是为了初学者考虑。在原书中，相同的概念作者也在不同章节解释多次，甚至有一些表达的重复，这也是这本书的一些亚马逊书评打低分的原因。也许译文可以保留这些重复，帮助读者理解。

王苏阳：我们要区分是内容上的重复还是语言上的重复。本书被打低分，可能是内容上重复较多。这里的语言重复，第一个 network 是修饰 everybody，第二个是修饰 transactions。it 根据上下文应该指的是"交易信息"。

> **改译1**：网络上人人都能收到网络交易信息，交易不受任何公司或机构集中数据库的控制。（王苏阳）
> **改译2**：网络上人人都能收到网络交易信息，交易不受任何公司或机构的集中数据库控制。（王佳楠）

李：it 指代不明，根据逻辑，是指"交易信息"（不能省略"信息"）。因为正常的记账方法，都是把信息交给会计（所谓"中心"）。区块链没有会计。

> **建议译法**：网络上人人都能收到该网络上产生的交易信息，这些信息不受任何公司或机构的中央数据库控制。（李）

14

> **原文**：Once a block of transactions has been added to the blockchain, it is difficult to reverse.
> **原译**：一旦含有交易信息的一个区块加到区块链中，就很难回滚。（王佳楠）

王佳楠：reverse 业内的表达统一都为"回滚"，虽然对外行比较难理解，但是为了保持一致还是不作修改。

王苏阳：这里要考虑作者写这本书的目的。本书是给外行人写的。作为外行人，我是不会明白"回滚"是什么意思的。翻译成"回滚"有一种可能，就是作者在本章正文具体解释了什么叫 reverse in a technical sense。不然，我们就只能按通俗处理。

> **改译**：交易块一旦添加到新区块中，就很难篡改。（王苏阳）

李："篡改"也不错。"撤销"更接近原意。

> **建议译法**：交易数据块一旦添加到数据块链条中，就很难撤销。（李）

16

> **原文**：Every block added on top is a confirmation that the transaction won't be reversed.
> **原译**：每增加一个区块都是一次确认，确认交易不可逆。（王佳楠）
> **改译1**：在原有区块上每添加一个区块，就更证明交易不可逆。（王苏阳）

王佳楠：这里的"确认"和本段最后一句的"确认"相呼应，英文为confir-mation。

> **改译2**：在原有区块上每添加一个区块，就更确认交易不可逆。（王佳楠）

李：可以更简洁。

> **建议译法**：每添加一个数据块，就是再次确认交易不可逆。（李）

17

> 原文:The more blocks on top, the harder it is to reverse until it is unfeasible.
>
> 原译:新增的区块越多,就越难回滚,直到不可能实现。(王佳楠)
>
> 改译1:上面的区块越多,就越难篡改,直到不可逆。(王苏阳)
>
> 改译2:叠加在上面的数据块越多,数据块就越难撤销,直到撤销行为不太现实。(李)
>
> 改译3:叠加在上面的数据块越多,数据块就越难撤销,直到撤销不可逆。(李)

王佳楠、陈佳鑫:这里是不是说,"直到无法撤销"或者"直到交易不可逆",而不是"撤销不可逆"?

李:王/陈说得对,是交易不可逆。这个交易,就是数据块链背后的一个个商业交易。交易"不可逆",就是"无法撤销",不妨把"不可逆"加上引号,说明这是区块链中常见的说法,然后补充"不可撤销"作为解释。

资料:Can my transaction be canceled or reversed?

No, we're unable to cancel or reverse your transaction.

Even many advanced cryptocurrency users can recall an incident when they failed to double-check their transaction details and they accidentally sent funds to the wrong recipient, or sent the wrong amount. As unfortunate as it is, cryptocurrency transactions on the Bitcoin, Ethereum, and Bitcoin Cash networks are designed to be irreversible and we have no control over them.

Knowing this, it's extremely important to make sure your transaction details are correct before you click send.

> **建议译法**:叠加在上面的数据块越多,数据块就越难撤销,直到交易不可逆或无法撤销。(王佳楠、陈佳鑫)

18

原文：On the Bitcoin network, 6 blocks are accepted as confirmation the transaction won't be reversed.

原译：在比特币网络中，一般认为6个区块能够确认相关交易不可逆。（王佳楠）

改译1：在比特币网络中，一般认为6个区块能够确认交易不可逆。（王苏阳）

改译2：在比特币网络中，一般认为6个数据块就能够确认交易不可逆。（李）

19

原文：With distributed consensus, the majority of computers on the network need to agree that a transaction is valid before it is accepted on the blockchain.

原译：通过分布式共识，交易网络中的大多数计算机需要在区块被接受到链上之前同意交易是有效的。（王佳楠）

王苏阳：before it is accepted on the blockchain 可提前作条件状语。

改译1：通过分布式共识，在区块链接受交易之前，网络中大多数计算机需要同意交易有效。（王苏阳）

改译2：在分布式共识模式下，网络中的大多数计算机必须一致同意某交易有效，该交易才会被区块链接受。（李）

建议译法：在分布式共识模式下，只有网络中的大多数计算机一致同意某交易有效，该交易才会被区块链接受。（王苏阳）

20

原文：Double spending is where someone on the network attempts to duplicate transactions. This is generally done by sending transactions more than once before one of them is confirmed and accepted onto the blockchain.

> **原译**：双重支付是交易网络中的某人企图复制交易。通常由某人在其中一次交易确认并添加到区块链之前，多次发送交易造成。（王佳楠）
>
> **改译1**：双重支付是指网络中有人企图复制交易。通常由某人在交易确认并添加到区块链之前，多次发送交易造成。（王苏阳）
>
> **改译2**："一币双花"是指网络中有人企图复制交易。通常由某人在交易得到确认并被添加到区块链之前，多次发送交易造成。（李）
>
> **改译3**："一币双花"（或译"双重支付"）是指网络中有人企图复制交易。通常由某人在交易得到确认并被添加到区块链之前，多次发送交易造成。（李）

李："双重支付"加个引号，便于识别为一个术语。此外，加括号让译者现身，以纠正误译。

王：这里想请教李老师为什么要让译者现身？

李：主要是为了告诉大家，如果看到"双重支付"，就是"一币双花"（一分钱花两次），借以纠正"双重支付"这个不够达意的译法。后文讲到，这些记账的人就像矿工，挖到一点矿，才得到一些奖赏。但有些矿工投机取巧，挖到一车矿，报了两次账。

> **改译4**："一币双花"（有人译为"双重支付"）是指网络中有人企图复制交易。通常由某人在交易得到确认并被添加到区块链之前，多次发送交易造成。（李）

陈佳鑫：这里是不是说"重复交易"好一些？我看网上解释"一币双花"时常用"重复交易"，也就是重复使用同一比特币，"复制交易"可能会有歧义。

> **改译5**："一币双花"（有人译为"双重支付"）是指网络中有人企图重复交易。通常由某人在交易得到确认并被添加到区块链之前，多次发送交易造成。（陈）

建议译法："一币双花"（另译为"双重支付"）是指网络中有人企图重复交易。通常由某人在交易得到确认并被添加到区块链之前，某人多次发送交易数据造成的。

21

原文：A double spending attack is where a user controls more than 50% of the computers on the network. This allows the user to double spend transactions by controlling which transactions are accepted and rejected.
原译：双重支付攻击是某个用户控制交易网络中超过半数的计算机。该用户控制接受或拒绝一些交易来进行双重支付。（王佳楠）

王苏阳："控制接受"搭配有些奇怪，暂时想不到更好的译法。尝试过"决定哪些交易被接受或被拒绝"，似乎被动又太多。

改译1：双重支付攻击是指用户控制交易网络中超过半数的计算机，操纵接受或拒绝哪些交易，从而实现双重支付。（王苏阳）
改译2："一币双花攻击"是指用户控制交易网络中超过半数的计算机，从而可以操纵系统接受或拒绝哪些交易，达到一次交易"花"（使用）两次的目的。（李）

王："从而可以"略显欧化。

改译3："一币双花攻击"是指用户控制交易网络中超过半数的计算机，以操纵系统接受或拒绝哪些交易，达到一次交易"花"（使用）两次的目的。（王）

同学分析：受审校同学译文的启发，究竟是取得超过半数的计算机还是算力的控制才能进行双花攻击呢？经查证应该是算力即 computing power。

This is a double-spend attack. It is commonly referred to as a 51% attack because the malicious miner will require more **hashing power** than the rest of the network combined (thus 51% of the hashing power) in order to add blocks to his version of the blockchain faster, eventually allowing him to build a longer chain.

https://medium.com/coinmonks/what-is-a-51-attack-or-double-spend-attack-aa108db63474

算力并不等于计算机数量,而应该是其运算能力。

Hash rate, or hash power as some call it, is the unit of measurement for the amount of computing power the Bitcoin network is consuming in order to be continuously operational.

https://www.quora.com/What-does-Bitcoin-hash-rate-mean

算力,在通过「挖矿」得到比特币的过程中,<u>一个节点每秒钟能做多少次计算</u>,就是其「算力」的代表,单位写成 hash/s,简写为 h/s。1 h/s 表示 1 秒钟能做 1 次 hash 碰撞。

https://www.chainnews.com/articles/079393830402.htm

因此,此处应该是原文表述出现错误。

> **建议译法**:"一币双花攻击"是指用户控制交易网络中超过半数的算力,以操纵接受或拒绝哪些交易,达到一次交易"花"(使用)两次的目的。(佚名)

李:自己经过充分调查,发现原文不严谨之处,只要觉得作者不会反对,就可以自行予以纠正。因此,此处把"计算机"换为"算力"没问题。维持原文不当之处,也没问题。毕竟译者没有义务纠正原文错误。

22

> **原文**: Mining is the process of validating transactions and adding new blocks to the blockchain. Small rewards are given for each new block added to the blockchain, like mining a small reward out of a big block.
>
> **原译**:挖矿是验证交易并添加新区块到区块链上的过程。每添加一个新区块到区块链上,节点都会获得小笔奖励,就像从大块中挖掘出小奖励。(佚名)

王佳楠：老师，我这里又遇到了主语问题："区块链上每增加一个区块就会发放奖励"——以区块链系统为主语，还是"每添加一个区块到区块链上，记账人就能获得奖励"？可是似乎主语（"记账人"）不能随意决定、添加。

王苏阳：从这句话的语境可知，作者是在探讨 mining，即挖矿的过程。主语不确定的时候，我先想到在原作中寻找答案，找到表述如下（第 85 页）：

A number known as a "nonce" (Number used Once) will also be included. The nonce is the answer to the puzzle that miners must solve to add a valid block to the blockchain and earn rewards.

可见，挖矿的主语是挖矿的人，即 miners。这个专有名词怎么称呼呢？我们查证一下：

实行"区块头优先挖矿"（head first mining）：在网络上尽可能快地传播新的 80 字节的区块头，一旦矿工们得悉区块头，就可以给他们机会去开始挖取一个空块。

https://www.8btc.com/article/83372

类似的表达在很多其他文章中也可见到。因此，我将主语推断为"矿工"。获得奖励的并不是"节点"，而是矿工。

资料：我们本次开发的区块链，从原理上是模仿比特币的模式的。每当有矿工挖矿成功的时候，我们都要给出一定的奖励，这也是区块链中数字币的来源。有了这些数字币，区块链中的各个交易才得以流通起来，那么从代码上我们应该怎么实现矿工奖励呢？

https://www.tongpankt.com/4483

因此，此处主语我处理为"矿工"。

王佳楠：这个感觉非常奇怪。而且觉得原文比喻好像没什么必要。

王苏阳：这句话确实有点问题，没看出比喻用得多巧妙。经过你的查证可知，作者是田纳西大学的实验研究员，学术能力应该不差，但是从这句话可以看出，作者文学表达能力还是比较有限的。我们只能试着在原语言表达上稍做修改。

改译1：挖矿是验证交易并添加新区块到区块链上的过程。每添加一个新区块到区块链上，矿工都会获得小奖励，这就像挖矿一样，从大块里面挖出一个个小奖励。（王）

改译2："挖矿"是验证交易并把新数据块添加到区块链上的过程。每添加一个新数据块到区块链上，矿工都会获得小小的奖励，这就像挖矿一样，从大块矿石里面挖出一小块酬劳。（李）

王：矿石和酬劳并不对应，"酬劳"明显有比喻义。

李：其实一个矿工就是一个计算机节点，不过没有必要引入"节点"概念，把问题复杂化。

原文比喻措辞不当，根据我们对矿工工作的了解（他受雇于人，挖到矿也是别人的，自己挣点辛苦钱），可以稍做诠释。本书作为科普读物，不是什么重要的法律或政府文件，译者灵活性较大。在不偏离核心意思的前提下，可以相当灵活，不需要征得作者同意。此处的比喻，就可以重新拟定（还可以简化一点）。

建议译法："挖矿"是验证交易并把新数据块添加到区块链上的过程。每添加一个新数据块，"矿工"都会获得小小的奖励，这就像挖矿一样，从大块矿藏中挖出一小块，就得到一点酬劳。（李）

31

原文：Proof of work involves solving a computer puzzle to add a new block to the blockchain. It is difficult to solve but easy to prove, like a combination lock. It provides evidence that computing power and resources were used and contributed to the network.

原译：工作量证明涉及解决计算机难题以添加一个新区块到区块链中。难题不易解但易证，就像密码锁。工作量证明证实了算力和资源消耗并投入到交易网络中。（王佳楠）

王佳楠：Puzzle suggests a problem or matter that is difficult to solve or interpret or that puts one at a loss.

https://odict.net/puzzlel

网络上现存和区块链相关的翻译有：难题、谜题、解题、解谜、问题。"谜题"让人联想到"猜谜"，"难题"能呼应难度（difficulty），这里我选择的是"难题"。

http://www.blockchainbrother.com/article/255
https://zhuanlan.zhihu.com/p/32739785

李：根据搭配的动词（solve），it 应当是指 a computer puzzle。

> **改译 1**：矿工的工作量证明，就是他通过解决一个计算机难题，将新的数据块添加到了区块链上。难题就像密码锁，很难破解，但是容易证明密码对不对。破解谜题证明了矿工花费并为网络贡献了算力和资源。（李）

李：这个译法把矿工解决难题视为"已然"（已完成），但我倾向于把这句话应理解为"未然"。

> **改译 2**：矿工为证明自己的工作量，需要通过解决一个计算机难题，将新的数据块添加到区块链上。难题就像密码锁，很难破解，但是容易证明密码对不对。解题过程证明了矿工为网络贡献了算力和资源。（李）
>
> **改译 3**：矿工的工作量证明，他通过解决一个计算机难题，将新的数据块添加到了区块链上。难题就像密码锁，很难破解，但容易证明。破解谜题证明了矿工花费并为网络贡献了算力和资源。（王）

李："矿工的工作量证明"和"他通过"之间缺乏衔接。"证明密码锁"搭配不当。

> **建议译法**：矿工的工作量证明，就是他通过解决一个计算机难题，将新的数据块添加到了区块链上。破解难题就像解密码锁。找到密码很难，验证密码很容易。破解谜题证明矿工花费了算力和资源，并由此为网络作出贡献。（李）

第四单元　中英语言差异

Exercise 4　Art of the In-between

翻译情景

本单元练习摘自大英博物馆馆长、纽约大都会艺术博物馆服装研究所首席策展人 Andrew Bolton 的专著 *Rei Kawakubo/Comme des Garçons: Art of the In-Between*，其中包含 Bolton 对 Kawakubo 的采访，练习即出自这一部分，共 518 词。假定你接受中国某出版社委托翻译此书。值得注意的是，这篇练习是访谈录，因此语言要尽量自然、得体、口语化，同时也要符合说话人的知识背景与风格特点。另外，访谈录是自然对话的记录，由于人在说话时思维可能比较跳跃，有些表达也未必非常清晰明确，因此，译者必须通过上下文、作者身份、写作背景等信息，判断作者的逻辑。也有个别情况下确实无法确知作者的意图。

专项能力

此篇作业旨在训练大家对中英文差异的敏感性。莫言的翻译葛浩文曾经说过，他翻译大多是凭灵感，越想理论，就会越觉得对语言无从把握。但是翻译学家刘宓庆也说过，"翻译思维必须具有高度的选择性、批判性、审美性……对中国语言学家来说，既要研究语言的同质性，又要研究语言的异质性,而且应该更加关注汉语的异质性。"译者作为语言文字工作者,必须熟悉语言之间的差异,才能做到无缝转换。关于中英文差异,国内不乏经典著作,比如连淑能的《英汉对比研究》[1]、刘宓庆的《新编汉英对比与翻译》、潘文国的《汉英语对比纲要》[2]、思果的《翻译新究》[3]、王文斌的《汉语流水句的空间性特质》[4]、王文斌的《论英语的时间性特质与汉语的空间性特质》[5],大家可选择阅读。

虽然翻译时不可能时刻思考中英文差异理论,而多半是凭语感作出判断,但如果对中英文的特点有所了解,可以增强自己对译文的信心。

在了解中英文语言差异的同时,译者也应该对语言的差异保持开放甚至怀疑态度。著名哲学家戈特弗里德·威廉·莱布尼茨(Gottfried Wilhelm Leibniz)曾经说过:"世界上没有两片完全相同的树叶",这也从侧面证明了差异的普遍性。因此,译者也可以经常问问自己:"中英文之间真的存在差异吗?这个差异具有普遍性还是特殊性?中英文之间有没有相同点?"

训练难点

本单元的训练重点是中英文差异。这篇练习涉及很多中英文差异之处,包括主语地位的差异、中英文数量词的差异、中英文时态语序上的差异,以及中英文语流和节奏的差异等。译者在翻译过程中,要对英文特有的表达形式保持敏感。虽然训练重点是锻炼译者对中英文差异的敏感度,但难点还是对原文的理解。理解问题解决了,表达问题就迎刃而解。

训练方式

本单元分为原文、翻译提示、参考译文、译者注四部分。建议在翻译过程中,避免按照原文结构亦步亦趋。特别注意英文中的人称代词、被

---

[1] 连淑能. 英汉对比研究 [M]. 北京:高等教育出版社,1993.
[2] 潘文国. 汉英语对比纲要 [M]. 北京:北京语言大学出版社,1997.
[3] 思果. 翻译研究 [M]. 北京:中国对外翻译出版公司,2001.
[4] 王文斌,赵朝永. 汉语流水句的空间性特质 [J]. 外语研究,2016(4):17-21.
[5] 王文斌. 论英语的时间性特质与汉语的空间性特质 [J]. 外语教学与研究,2013(2):163-173.

动语态、主谓结构、语流节奏等特色表达方式的处理。在修改二稿时，可以参看翻译提示，加深理解，修正表达；修改二稿之后，再看译者注中的讨论。

原文

[KAWAKUBO/BOLTON[1]:
A CONVERSATION

Andrew Bolton[2] conducted this conversation with Rei Kawakubo via simultaneous translation in Tokyo in November 2016.]

…

RK: There is method behind your madness.[3]

AB: That's a nice segue[4] into talking about the curation.[5]

RK: It was a battle. Are you going to write that we fought? [6]

AB: Yes, of course. From the outset, you were resolute that the exhibition not be a retrospective.

RK: No[7], I did not want a retrospective, but you've turned it into one.

AB: I haven't. The show does not present a historical overview of your work, nor is it organized chronologically. Those traditionally are the defining characteristics of a retrospective. Why were you so opposed to a retrospective?

RK: Looking back at clothes I made forty years ago—or even five years ago—is very difficult for me. I think all artists don't like looking back at their work.

AB: I think most of them don't, yes. In your case, it must be especially difficult. Since early in your career, when you made your much-quoted claims to "start from zero" and to "do things that have not been done before,"[8] you've remained steadfast in your attempts never to look back, only forward. Given your denial of the past, I can see why a retrospective would be unthinkable.

RK: I see the value of a retrospective of an artist's work, particularly for an institution like The Metropolitan Museum of Art, but for me it's an impossibility. In terms of my work, the only way forward is not to look back. For me, there are many clothes I've made that I regret or that I would have done differently.

AB: Differently?

RK: Yes, if I'd had more time. It always comes down to time.

…

AB: You've spoken candidly about how your collections are often personal expressions of your inner feelings and sentiments—your fears, hopes, doubts, and desires. You've said, "Nothing new can come out of a situation without suffering" and "There is very little creation without despair." The fact that your clothes serve a kind of diaristic function must only compound your anxieties about reflecting on your previous collections.

RK: I can only compare my feelings to those of a man or woman late in life ruminating on his or her past mistakes. Surely, with hindsight, we would all make different choices, different decisions. We can't turn back the clock.

AB: Time has a tendency to normalize fashions that were once not only provocative and transgressive but also genuinely revolutionary and transformative.[9] We become blind to what our eyes initially viewed as radically different. Innovations have a tendency to become invisible over the years; they become assimilated into the everyday language of fashion. But many visitors to the exhibition will be seeing your clothes for the first time. Most will find them as daring and as shocking as audiences did originally.

RK: But I've moved on. You must appreciate that I'm speaking from a purely personal perspective. I have no desire to look back. I only want to look ahead, to create clothes that no one has seen before.

翻译提示

1. **全局意识**

   请大家针对原文和译文，分别回答 Who is talking to whom? About what? When, where and why? And how? 然后再开始翻译。

2. **全局意识：翻译情景**

   准确、通顺翻译的前提，是了解全局意识中所提及的 6Ws（Who is talking to whom? About what? When, where and why?）。译者在翻译前，还是要调动自己的查证能力，了解原文的风格、说话人的身份、背景、性格、立场等。此外，在这篇文章中，全局意识还要求译者考虑翻译的媒介，即对话人是通过什么样的媒介进行交流的，这样的媒介对语言的产出和理解有什么样的影响。

3. **全局意识：上下文**

   第一单元的全局意识中强调过译者一定要 act local, think global，从语篇的连贯和衔接角度理解原文内涵。此处的 There is method behind your madness 与上文有着非常密切的联系，因此翻译时译者需要参考上文内容；此外，在了解上文所指以后，还需要考虑如何与下文 That's a nice segue into talking about the curation 逻辑上连贯。

   语言能力

   这里是英文中的 there be 句型。将 there be 句型转换为中文时，译者要考虑中英文语言的差异性。译者可以重点思考中英文主语的差异性，问问自己 there be 句型转换成中文是否需要加主语？是否所有的句子都需要加主语？

4. **词义 / 逻辑构建**

   seuge 这个词的意思，可以通过查询英英词典找到释义。理解这个词的关键，还是要把词义放在上下文中去理解，具备全局意识，思考 madness、seuge 逻辑上有什么关系，在逻辑上对话人为什么要这样说，对话逻辑与他们的观点立场有什么关系。

5. **语言能力：中英文语言差异**

   这句话既存在逻辑理解上的难点，也有语言表达上的难点。在处理这句话的时候，译者要注意理解是表达的前提。因此，译者应首先联系上下文，梳理逻辑，这是解决表达的关键；在解决逻辑理解问题以后，译者需要做的是"脱壳"，也就是用理解的话将译文以符合译入语习惯的方式表达出来。译者不妨把自己置身在访谈对话情景中，或者干脆拉一个朋友来念念自己的译文稿，看看是否符合译入语表达习惯。

6. **语言能力 / 全局意识**

   原文中的 battle 涉及隐喻的处理方式。译者需要思考是把 battle 直译出来，还是进行简单的转化？如何将后半句 Are you going to write that we fought 自然衔接起来？

7. **语言能力**

   译者在修改二稿时需要思考 No 是否需要翻译出来。从中英文表达的差异上看，中文更注重意思上的连贯与衔接。

8. **标点符号**

   此处可能有同学会指出，原文的引号点错了地方，应该置于逗号里。如果你发现了这个问题，不妨再去查查看，认证一下引号的位置是否有错。

9. **语言能力**

   川久保玲说话自带艺术气质，因此想要将这句话翻译出行云流水的感觉并不简单。汉语中的诗词歌赋通常有极强的韵律感，这是汉语独特的魅力与特点。译者在修改二稿时，不妨参看参考译文尾注中王文斌对汉语流水句特点的分析，再思考如何把汉语的这种特点运用在译文的表达上。

参考译文[1]

川久保玲／博尔顿：一场对话[2]

2016年11月，安德鲁·博尔顿在东京借助同声传译与川久保玲对话[3]。
……

川[4]：这么说，疯狂背后还别有深意。[5]

博：说到这里，我们正好可以谈谈策展。[6]

川：那是一场鏖战。你要写这段吗？[7]

博：当然。一开始你就坚决不办回顾展。[8]

川：我不想办回顾展，但你还是办了。[9]

博：其实并没有。这次展览既不是对你作品的历史盘点，也没有按时间顺序陈列，何来回顾展一说？你为什么如此抵触回顾展？[10]

川：要回顾自己四十年前设计的衣服，哪怕是五年前的，对我来说都太难了。我觉得艺术家都不喜欢回顾自己的作品。[11]

博：大部分艺术家应该不喜欢。对你来说，肯定格外困难。你在职业生涯早期，就说过"从零开始"[12]"敢为人先"[13]这样的名句。从那时起，你一直坚持永不回头，勇往直前。想到你如此抵触过去，我就能明白你为什么坚决不办回顾展了。[14]

川：办回顾展是有价值的，尤其是对大都会艺术博物馆这样的机构来说，但是，我不可能办回顾展。我做设计，要想前进，就不能回顾过去。我对很多衣服都抱有缺憾，或者说本来可以做得不一样。[15]

博：不一样？

川：没错，要是时间更充裕，就会做得不一样。说到底，总是时间的问题。[16]
……

博：你曾经坦率地说，你的设计通常是内心感受和情感的表达，表达恐惧、希望、怀疑和欲望。你说"没有痛苦，就难以创新""没有绝望，就没有创造"。你的服装像是一本日记，只会加剧你回顾过去时的焦虑。[17]

川：我的感觉就像人在晚年时反思过去的错误。当然，以现在的眼光看待过去，我们都希望当初作出不同的选择、不同的决定。但是时间不会倒流。[18]

博：曾经离经叛道、革风易俗的时尚，在时间的洗礼下往往变得稀松平常。过去看起来标新立异，现在却平淡无奇。随着时间的推移，新观念趋于无形，逐渐成为日常时尚语言的一部分。但是，很多参观者是第一次看到你的设计。大多数人会和最初的观众一样，认为你的设计大胆而令人震撼[19]。

川：但我已经和过去了断。你应该明白这纯粹是我的个人观点。我不愿回头看，只想向前看，创造从未有人见过的服装。[20]

译者注

1 全局意识：翻译情景

对话人身份背景

王：要准确、到位地传达访谈者与受访者的思想，必须了解两者的身份、关系、知识和专业背景。访谈者为 Andrew Bolton。根据维基百科（https://en.wikipedia.org/wiki/Andrew_Bolton_(curator)），他是大英博物馆馆长，纽约大都会艺术博物馆服装研究所的现任首席策展人，举办过很多大型展览。Bolton 毕业于东英吉利大学，获得人类学学士学位和非西方艺术硕士学位。2017 年，他被任命为皇家艺术学院荣誉院士。从以上资料可知，Bolton 对艺术、展览非常熟悉，具备一定的艺术修养和语言表达魅力，因此语言要有艺术修养，也要自然流畅。

受访者为川久保玲，日本设计师，非设计科班出身，创立了自己的品牌 Comme des Garçons（"像男孩一样"）。从多方的资料来看，川久保玲是一个比较内向、气场强大、说话简单精辟的人。因此，译文语言要简洁、深刻，不宜过于华丽。川久保玲非常热爱服装设计事业，但不擅于交际。从

Guardian 上的访谈内容上看（见下方链接），川久保玲很少接受采访，她的丈夫是 Comme des Garçons 的总裁 Adrian Joffe，经常为川久保玲做英文和日文之间的翻译。

https://en.wikipedia.org/wiki/Rei_Kawakubo
https://www.mings-fashion.com/rei-kawakubo-comme-des-garcons-%E5%B7%9D%E4%B9%85%E4%BF%9D%E7%8E%B2-45857/

对话人风格、立场

侯：从二人对话交流上看，二人是老熟人，中间有很多沟通甚至争执。对话一开始，川久保玲就表示自己"厌恶采访"，认为把"采访"说成"对话"只是文字游戏：

> REI KAWAKUBO: I hate interviews.
> ANDREW BOLTON: I know, but this is more of a conversation.
> RK: That's just a matter of semantics.

从这一来一回中可以看出川久保玲的语言风格很直接，而且二人之间也比较熟悉。

翻译媒介

王：另外，值得注意的是，在本次访谈中，博尔顿和川久保玲是借助同声传译对话的，一些逻辑或文法问题，也可能是同传引起，翻译时需要考虑如何处理。

2

> 原文: KAWAKUBO/BOLTON: A CONVERSATION
> 原译: 对话：川久保玲与博尔顿（侯）

李：原译不太符合汉语习惯。

> 改译 1: 川久保玲与博尔顿的对话（李）

王：我更倾向原译。我认为，如果是文内语言，的确改译1是更符合汉语习惯的。但是这里是标题，原译的冒号可能更能起到提示主题的作用。中文标题中，有很多这样的用法。比如：

资深导游曝潜规则：国内游客分九等
　　　　http://www.jiaodong.net/travel/system/2010/06/03/010857966.shtml
视频：人体动作实验反映身体健康状况
　　　　　　http://blog.sina.com.cn/s/blog_6630a8310100j1t4.html
白岩松：命案必破规定等刑讯逼供动力尚未全消除
　　　　　http://news.sina.com.cn/c/sd/2010-06-01/012720382595.shtml

以上三个例子中，冒号虽然分离了句子结构，但却起到提纲挈领的作用，提示文章性质或方向与重点内容。因此我更倾向原译。

> **改译2**：对话：川久保玲与博尔顿。（侯、王）

李：我还是感觉不对。这三个例子，都符合冒号的一般用法，即冒号前后的内容隐含为同一关系：潜规则内容＝国内游客分九等，视频内容＝人体动作实验反映身体健康状况，白岩松讲话内容＝命案必破规定等刑讯逼供动力尚未全消除。关于标点符号用法的国家标准GB/T 15834-2011（代替GB/T 15834-1995）中列举的用例，也可归入前后同一的关系。但此处对话的内容≠川久保玲与博尔顿。两个人是对话的主体。英文原文是KAWAKUBO/BOLTON: A CONVERSATION，其中的斜线，表示"和"。在国标《标点符号用法》（GB/T 15834-2011）中，分隔号（"/"）也有类似用法：

分隔组成一对的两项，表示"和"。
示例1：13/14次特别快车
示例2：羽毛球女双决赛中国组合杜婧/于洋两局完胜韩国名将李孝贞/李敬元。

不妨遵循原文表达方式，译为"川久保玲/博尔顿：一场对话"。加上量词"一场"，一是为了加强节奏感，二是表示这是专门安排的一次活动。

这个译法，也解决了冒号前后的关系问题：川久保玲与博尔顿之间，隐含着一场对话。

建议译法： 川久保玲/博尔顿：一场对话（李）

3

原文： Andrew Bolton conducted this conversation with Rei Kawakubo via simultaneous translation in Tokyo in November 2016.

原译： 二〇一六年十一月，安德鲁·博尔顿在东京借助同声传译与川久保玲对话。（侯）

李： 关于数字的用法，见 http://www.moe.gov.cn/ewebeditor/uploadfile/2015/01/13/20150113091154536.pdf。尽量使用阿拉伯数字，除非是特别正式的文本。

改译： 2016年11月，安德鲁·博尔顿在东京借助同声传译与川久保玲举行对话。（李）

李： "举行""进行"不滥用，但也不避讳。此处不用，压不住阵脚。

王： 虽然同意您的分析，但我还是不建议此处加"举行"。这里本身是两个人的对话，二人也比较熟悉，所以使用"举行"一词反倒破坏了谈话的氛围和译文的语域。中文语料库中，"举行"一般搭配会议、仪式、重大事件等：

1. 第25届奥运会运动员村今日第一次举行了升旗仪式。

1992-7-20，中国青年报社

2. 我国老将许海峰、王义夫多次在奥运会和世锦赛上取得好成绩，在4月底举行的巴塞罗那热身赛上许海峰获得冠军，说明他们还有夺取奖牌的实力，关键要看临场发挥了。

1992-7-20，中国青年报社

3. 中国音乐学院业余音乐学校北京通县分校日前举行了成立大会。

1992-7-20，中国青年报社

http://corpus.zhonghuayuwen.org/CnCindex.aspx

建议译法： 2016年11月，安德鲁·博尔顿在东京借助同声传译与川久保玲对话。（侯、王）

4

原文： RK/AB
原译： 川久保玲/博尔顿（侯）

侯： 英文原文将人名简写为两个字母主要是因为英文长，缩写成字母省空间。但是中文三四个字的名字本身也很常见，没有必要简略成一个字。将二人简略成"川""博"反而不利于中文读者分辨谁是采访者，谁是被访者。

李： 我认为还是分别简化为"川"和"博"好一些。作为参考，川久保玲的姓为"川久保"（Kawakubo），名字为"玲"（Rei）。

建议译法： 川/博（李）

王： 学生作业中大致有以下几种译法。第一种是侯老师的译法，用中文译出全名，而后均保持全名写法；第二种采用缩写加注释的方式，即全篇使用RK或AB，但是在开篇第一次使用时在注释中写明RK、AB分别代表谁；第三种译法是采用姓或名中文译法的第一个字。目前出版刊物中，采用缩写的方式比较多。我认为，姓名的译法，无论是译出全称、缩写，还是姓或者名，保持统一即可。

5

原文： There is method behind your madness.
原译： 你的疯狂有迹可循。（侯）

王： 这句话源自《哈姆雷特》中的一句话 Though this be madness, yet there is method in't。黄琳同学从功能对等的角度，想到唐伯虎《桃花庵歌》中的那句"别人笑我太疯癫，我笑他人看不穿。"这是非常巧妙的译法，但是拍案叫绝的同时，也要考虑川久保玲的说话风格。

李：没有一点文化素养（像我这样），恐怕既看不出这句话的出处，也想不到唐伯虎。但是，唐伯虎说"他人看不穿"，但此处川久保玲恰恰是理解了博尔顿的安排。所以，也不能因辞害意。

> **改译 1**：你的布局看似混乱，背后却颇有章法。（李）
> **改译 2**：你真是乱中有序啊！（李）

李：There is method behind your madness 是对上一段的评论，所以必须结合前面几段来理解。要 act local, think global。前面几段的内容是：

　　AB: I hope visitors experience the exhibition as a tourney, as a voyage of discovery.

　　RK: But do you think the space is disorienting? Do you think people will get lost in the exhibition?

　　AB: The exhibition provides an immersive experience, and getting lost is part of that experience. In terms of the curation, there is a definite path through the exhibition, and there will be clear signage. But people will also be given maps when they enter the space and they will be free—in fact, encouraged—to forge their own paths and to make their own discoveries. While the specific themes all relate to the overarching curatorial narrative, they also stand alone and can be read separately, like distinct, discrete chapters of a book. So, in effect, it does not matter which route you take through the exhibition.

侯：这句话和后面"那是一场战斗。你打算把我们打架的事情写下来吗？"的翻译策略不一致：改译 1 尽可能译出了背后的含义，而"打架"（battle）则只保留了字面意思。

　　但是考虑到这是选文的第一句，如果不补充上文，则需要把话说得清楚一点，否则读者莫名其妙，不知道为什么说到这里就可以谈策展（"布局"）。所以，不补充前文的情况下，我同意这句话点出"布局"。

整个展览的布局如下：

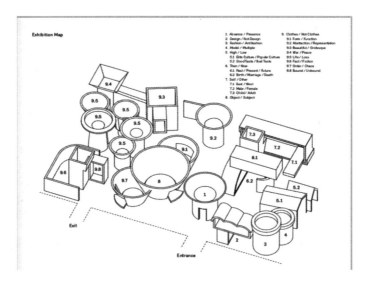

https://www.metmuseum.org/-/media/files/exhibitions/2017/rei-kawakubo-guide.pdf

参考本句的上文：

The exhibition provides an immersive experience, and getting lost is part of that experience. In terms of the curation, there's a definite path through the exhibition, and there will be clear signage. But people will also be given maps when they enter the space and they will be free—in fact, encouraged—to forge their own paths and to make their own discoveries. While the specific themes all relate to the overarching curatorial narrative, they also stand alone and can be read separately, like distinct, discrete chapters of a book. So, in effect, it does not matter which route you take through the exhibition.

madness 指 getting lost 以及 stand alone and can be read separately。看图片，展厅确实"乱"。这些展厅之间的联系在于它们展示的都是 art of the in-between，即上文所说的 the specific themes all relate to the overarching curatorial narrative。换言之，原文所说的 method，是展览的宏观思路/大主题。"章法"和"乱中有序"的"序"，都是"规则/秩序"的含义，背后的思路/主题应该不能说是一种"秩序"。

王：我同意侯灵钰的分析。我本人更倾向不点出布局。原因主要有两点：

1. 译文要符合说话人的特性。川久保玲本身就是个不爱解释的人，说话妙语连珠，一语中的。她语言的妙处，就在于让读者、听众有无限的遐想和解读。这句话李老师的译文是把实际的意思翻译出来了，很忠实于原文，但我觉得川久保玲并不会这样说话。因此，我更倾向原译。所谓的"疯狂"读者可以自行体会，无论是布局、还是自我突破。"有迹可循"暗指疯狂背后的规律，意思上并非不忠，也没有脱离与上文的关系。

2. 语篇连贯。从行文风格上，我觉得译文现在整体有些语言风格不一致。时而比较口语化、时而比较书面化。

王：两位老师译文中的 you 都采取了"你"的译法。经过课上讨论，我们发现同学们还有三种不同意见。第一种意见认为应该把 you 全部翻译为"您"，因为考虑到川久保玲和博尔顿都是时尚界的大人物，彼此应该以尊称相称；第二种意见认为可以把"你"和"您"搭配使用。尤其是朱丹阳同学的查证后认为：

川久保 1942 年出生，博尔顿 1966 年出生，川久保比博尔顿大二十多岁。另外，读完两人的对话，再结合网上的一些资料，译者发现川久保的性格比较"拽"，和常人大不相同。所以译者把川久保称呼博尔顿的"you"翻成了"你"，博尔顿称呼川久保的"you"翻成了"您"。

第三种意见则认为是否翻译出 you 应视情况而定，可省略主语。王宏锐同学查证论文《论访谈类文本中人称指示语用等效翻译》后认为，此句中的 you 可以省略，因为从语境和中文特点角度讲，you 的指代已经非常清楚。就此处的译文来说，可以考虑省略。

王：再深入一下，这三种观点反映出了中英文语言差异的主语特点。在英译中时，如何处理里面的主语问题？是否所有主语都需要翻译出来？刘宓庆（2006: 84）曾经说过，汉语中多无主句，英语中的主语却具有不可或缺性。此外，汉语主语具有模糊性，可以多个主语或隐或现并常出现跨句段指认（王文斌，2016）。也就是说，汉语的主语有时候是可有可无的，而且汉语的形式也是多种多样的（刘宓庆，2006: 87）。学了很多年外语的同学，很容易把英语表达习惯进行再迁移。因此，在英译汉时，很可能不考虑英汉语言差异性，就按照英文的句子结构机械地翻译出来，这也是造成译文欧化的原因之一。因此，了解中英文语言的差异性，包括主语的差异性问题，是非常重要的。

> **建议译法：** 这么说，疯狂背后还别有深意。（王）

李： 这个译法可以接受。但明确把意思传达出来也未尝不可；这是仁智之见，非对错之分。但"你的疯狂有迹可循"意思就错了，因为"有迹可循"的意思是可以看到蛛丝马迹，即：有证据表明你是疯狂的。可是，这句话的意思是：你看起来疯狂，但背后还是有条理的。参照 methodical 的意思：done in a careful and logical way: a methodical approach / study；(of a person) doing things in a careful and logical way.

关于侯灵钰支持我的前提："如果不补充上文，则需要把话说得清楚一点，否则读者莫名其妙"，其实，我们仅仅是做一次练习，现实生活中，必定是把整个对话都翻译出来。即使翻译整个对话，存在上文，仍然可以明确翻译出这句话的意思。当然也可以像王老师那样处理。

关于 you 如何翻译，我认为同学们的第二种和第三种意见都比较可取。

6

> **原文：** That's a nice segue into talking about the curation.
> **原译：** 这个说法还挺适合描述这次策展的。（侯）

侯： seuge 是指无缝衔接，过渡到下一阶段，正好引出下面的内容。

noun

an uninterrupted transition made between one musical section or composition and another.

any smooth, uninterrupted transition from one thing to another.

https://www.dictionary.com/browse/segue

张旭： 译者感觉这句话的处理非常有难度。难点主要有两个：第一，信息上，要与上下文吻合；第二，形式上也要和上下文吻合。解决第一个难题，需要译者从宏观上理解整个对话的信息流。在谈话的一开始，两位讲话人不断在策展的问题上拉拉扯扯。而本句其实是一个过渡，之后就开始讨论回顾展形式是否合适。在信息上，要把这种过渡体现出来。第二个难题在于形式，用一种什么样的形式才能自然、顺畅地过渡？译者冥思苦想很久，认为首先要deverbalize，取得"过渡"这一重要信息点之后，要用一个口语化、符合中文习惯的形式来表现。想清楚这一点之后，译者就用一个比较灵活的方法来处理：正好，我们谈谈策展吧！

李：这个译法很好。

王：刘宓庆（2006）曾经提及汉语语序的时序律（the Principle of Temporal Sequence，简称PTS）。也就是说，汉语的时序不一定以显性为表现特征，有时可以隐去。有些情况下，按照事情的发展顺序，即使汉语时态不翻译出来，时态和时序也会非常明确。这对英译汉是有非常大的启示。

李：从上文可知，madness是指空间布局像迷宫（疯子才这样布置）。这样就跟下一句联系起来：你既然说到布局，咱正好可以过渡到布局（策展）。

建议译法：说到这里，我们正好可以谈谈策展（或：展品布局）。（李）

7

原文：It was a battle. Are you going to write that we fought?
原译：那是一场妥协之战。你打算写这一段吗？（侯）

侯：此处battle指的不是具体的某次争执，而是更偏向理念上的冲突。如川久保玲过去多年来都不希望办展，不希望"回头看"，而办展本身不可避免地要回顾过去。再如川久保玲不喜欢解释自己的作品，也不喜欢别人来解释，但是从策展的角度来看，难免要做介绍。最终办成展览是两方妥协的结果。

"She's always trying to start from zero. But by definition, looking back... means there's baggage," he explained. "She was always saying the person that did those things in the '80s and '90s is not the person she is now." She would rather, she told Joffe, that any exhibition of her designs happen[s] after she was gone.

https://fashionista.com/2017/05/met-museum-costume-
institute-rei-kaw-akubo-timestalks-series

Bolton's job as curator, however, is expressly to interpret her work for visitors. The resulting theme of the exhibit feels like a compromise between Kawakubo and Bolton, a push and pull between opposing forces, which is also how the Met ended up framing things.

https://qz.com/963629/what-are-clothes-anyway/

改译 1：那是一场战斗。你打算把我们打架的事情写下来吗？（李）

李：不必点出"妥协",两人都知道是什么意思。看来此次采访,就是为了写书,在书中回顾策展过程。但还是不知道采访发生在展览期间还是之后。也许知道与否不影响翻译。

侯：川、博二人虽明白 battle 是什么,但是突然说"策展是战斗",读者不一定明白。

李：现实的翻译活动中,不可能只翻译其中几段,很可能是翻译全书。译文读者看了上文,会清楚是什么意思。当然,如果用户真的只要我们翻译部分段落,就可能需要补充隐含的信息。

侯：fight 处理为"打架"可能真的会让人以为两个人动手了。

fight:

6. verb

If one person fights with another, or fights them, the two people hit or kick each other because they want to hurt each other. You can also say that two people fight.

7. verb

If one person fights with another, or fights them, they have an angry disagreement or quarrel. You can also say that two people fight.

https://www.collinsdictionary.com/dictionary/english/fight

此处意思应为 have an angry disagreement or quarrel，而非真的"打架"。博、川二人对如何策展有争议，但是不至于真的大打出手。

王：这里涉及英语隐喻的处理问题。英语隐喻的处理有很多种方式。"战斗""打架"在中文里都会让人联想到战争或动手，这里的意思就是说两人意见分歧。此处经与李老师讨论，后参考黄琳同学的译法，决定改为"鏖战"。这样修改是考虑到川久保玲说话的风格。川久保玲说话一语中的、妙语连珠，不乏金句，却又不显矫揉造作之感。当然，也许会有同学认为"鏖战"用词过于华丽。无论如何，译者要尽力揣测说话人的语言风格，尽力与说话人产生思想共鸣。

改译 2：那是一场鏖战。你要写这一段吗？（黄琳）

王：这里还涉及中英文差异中的量词问题。王文斌（2013）曾经提到现代汉语中量词不可或缺，如果少了量词，大部分的句意会发生变化。我的建议是，量词的使用要视语境而定。比如，妻子会问刚下班的丈夫，"你吃饭不？"这和"你吃碗饭不？"意思是一致的。在英译汉时，汉语的数词可以适当省略，有些情况下，不必把数词全部译出。比如，这里的修改"你要写这一段吗？"可以继续改为"你要写这段吗？"可能更为简洁、符合口语化的表达。

建议译法：那是一场鏖战。你要写这段吗？（黄琳、王苏阳）

8

原文：AB: Yes, of course. From the outset, you were resolute that the exhibition not be a retrospective.

原译：博尔顿：当然了。一开始你就很坚决，坚持不能办成回顾展。（侯）

王：这里我把意思稍微合并了一下。

> **改译1**：博尔顿：当然了。一开始你就坚决不办回顾展。（王）
> **改译2**：博尔顿：是的。当然要写下来。一开始你就坚决不办回顾展。（李）

侯：yes 是否有必要译出"是"这个字眼？中文口头表示肯定时，"是的"听起来有点书面（甚至西化），"没错""对"之类的词显得更口语一些。

王：我同意侯灵钰的分析。如果从上下句衔接的角度看，这里不翻译出"是的"比较好。上文如果翻译成"那是一场妥协之战。你打算写这一段吗？"这里直接回答"当然"即可。

王：到此为止，有必要对前四句话的语篇衔接进行梳理。请看以下分析：

RK: There is method behind your madness [in the spatial arrangement].

AB: That's a nice segue [transition] into talking about the curation. [Since you mentioned the spatial arrangement, let's talk about that (curation = spatial arrangement).]

RK: It [the curation] was a battle. Are you going to write that we fought?

AB: Yes, of course [I will write about our fight]. From the outset, you were resolute that the exhibition not be a retrospective.

这四句话的逻辑是，川久保玲在听完博尔顿的解释后，评论说，看来这空间设计的背后，还是别有深意的。博尔顿说到，既然你谈到了策展（空间设计），我们就正好来说说策展吧。川久保玲接下来说，这策展策划过程就像打仗一样，你要写这段？博尔顿说，当然要写这段。

> **建议译法**：博尔顿：当然。一开始你就坚决不办回顾展。（王）

9

> **原文**：I did not want a retrospective, but you've turned it into one.
> **建议译法**：我不想办回顾展，但是你还是办了。（侯）

侯：川久保玲希望展览自己近期的作品，而最终的展览选择了各个时期的作品，所以她认为这是 retrospective。中文报道中有不少使用了"回顾展"一词：

其实这并非 Met Gala 第一次以设计师为主题的创新之举，早在1983年，Met Gala 就以设计师伊夫·圣·洛朗（Yves Saint Laurent）为主题。同时在舞会过后，纽约大都会艺术博物（The Met）还会举办名为《Rei Kawakubo/Comme des Garçons: Art of the In-Between》的回顾展，并在5月4日也就是今天正式开放！

http://life.haibao.com/article/2468514.htm

10

原文：I haven't. The show does not present a historical overview of your work, nor is it organized chronologically. Those traditionally are the defining characteristics of a retrospective. Why were you so opposed to a retrospective?

原译：我没有。这次展览既不是对你作品的历史盘点，也没有按时间顺序陈列。这才是人们眼中回顾展的核心特点。你为什么如此抵触回顾展？（侯）

改译1：我没有。这次展览既不是对你作品的历史盘点，也没有按时间顺序陈列。这才是人们眼中回顾展的特征。你为什么这么抵触回顾展呢？（王）

改译2：我没有。这次展览不是对你作品的历史盘点，也没有按时间顺序陈列。传统上，人们认为这两点是回顾展的特征。你为什么这么抵触回顾展呢？（李）

王：这里是否需要翻译出"传统"呢？traditionally 指的是一直以来人们的想法都是如此。"传统"在中文当中也容易和"风俗传统"等同。但作者的意思可能只是想说人们一贯的想法是如此。我更倾向原译，又在原译上稍做修改。

建议译法 1：我没有。这次展览既不是对你作品的历史盘点，也没有按时间顺序陈列，而这些才是人们眼中回顾展的一贯特点。你为什么如此抵触回顾展？（王）

王宏锐：如果直译"我没有"则对抗性太强，安德鲁·波顿作为访谈的主持人还是要注意语言的礼貌和克制，所以采取委婉的说法。

建议译法 2：其实并没有。这次展览既不是对你作品的历史盘点，也没有按时间顺序陈列，何来回顾展一说呢？你为什么如此抵触回顾展？（王、侯）

李：以上各种译法都可以接受，都是仁智之见，没有对错之分。

11

原文：Looking back at clothes I made forty years ago—or even five years ago—is very difficult for me. I think all artists don't like looking back at their work.

原译：回顾自己四十年前设计的衣服对我来说太难了，我甚至没办法再看自己五年前的设计。我觉得艺术家都不喜欢回顾自己的作品。（侯）

改译 1：要回顾自己四十年前设计的衣服，甚至是五年前的，对我来说都太难了。我觉得艺术家都不喜欢回顾自己的作品。（王）

王：原译意思上没有问题，不过这里我更倾向再口语化一些，甚至稍微按照顺句驱动的原则表达，因为他们的对话本身是借助同声传译进行的。这样也更符合对话语体。当然这是个见仁见智的问题。英语的表达一般是主语＋谓语，而汉语的表达一般是主题＋评论（刘宓庆，2006）。我们回看原文，发现川久保玲说话的英语句式结构与中文的主题＋评论句式非常类似。据了解，这可能是受日语句式的影响。这样，按照主题＋评论的方式翻译，正好符合中文的表达方式。

思果先生在《翻译新究》中写道：

我试验了无数次，发现许多句子都可以照英文的词序翻译；办法是把连接词和一部分虚字改变，或者补充一些无关紧要的字词。这种保持原文词序译法的最大好处是译文自然易读，而且译来也很省事。反过来，如果保留原文的连接词意义，把其他的词序更动，既极其辛苦，译出来的文字又一点也不自然，有时一改再改，还是改不好。

按照思果先生的意思，我们如果按照原文顺序可以清楚翻译，就没必要舍近求远。

> **改译2**：要回顾自己四十年前设计的衣服，哪怕是五年前的，对我来说都太难了。我觉得艺术家都不喜欢回顾自己的作品。（侯）

侯："甚至"的递进感比较强：

【甚至】shènzhì 连 强调突出的事例（有更进一层的意思）：参加晚会的人很多，～不少平常不出门的老年人也来了。

中国社会科学院语言研究所词典编辑室. 现代汉语词典（第7版）. 北京：商务印书馆，2016。

但是此处是"四十年"和"五年"的对比，虽然从语意来看，确实可以理解为从"四十"到"五"是递进，但是中文中，难免会觉得数字从少到多才是递进。因此，这里说"甚至"会有一种违和感。

"哪怕"可以表示"即使"，有退一步的感觉：

【哪怕】nǎpà 连 表示姑且承认某种事实；即使：～他是三头六臂，一个人也顶不了事｜衣服只要干净就行，～是旧点儿。

中国社会科学院语言研究所词典编辑室. 现代汉语词典（第7版）. 北京：商务印书馆，2016。

李：此处用"甚至"和"哪怕"，我的感觉区别不大。另外，严格说来，all artists don't like looking back at their work 表示部分否定：不是所有艺术家都喜欢……。但日语原文也有可能是全部否定，只是同传译员不小心用了表达部分否定的英语句式。从下一句可以看出，博尔顿本人听到这句话，都不敢确信自己理解正确。所以，现在的译法也可能是符合作者意图的。我试图找到这场对话的日语版本，但没有找到。

王：经与李老师讨论，这句话到底是部分否定还是全部否定，由于我们无法与作者沟通，也找不到当时的对话录音，所以无法确信。但从回答来看，理解为全部否定可能更有道理。所以，维持改译2。

12　标点符号

两组引号之间是否需要用顿号？

"标有引号的并列成分、标有书名号的并列成分之间通常不用顿号。若有其他成分插在并列的引号之间或并列的书名号之间（如引语或书名号之后还有括注），宜用顿号。"《标点符号用法》（GB/T 15834-2011）因此，此处两组引号之间不用顿号。

13　标点符号

李：关于"英文逗号是否应该放入引号中"，查到：

The most common question people ask about quotation marks is whether periods and commas go inside or outside, and the answer depends on where your audience lives because in American English we always put periods and commas inside quotation marks, but in British English periods and commas can go inside or outside (kind of like the American rules for question marks and exclamation points). I use this memory trick: Inside the US, inside the quotation marks. Here are some examples:

"Don't underestimate me," she said with a disarmingly friendly smile.

I can never remember how to spell "bureaucracy."

Don't get confused when you see this handled differently in *The Economist* or on the BBC website; just remember that it's different in those publications because the British do it differently.

https://www.quickanddirtytips.com/education/grammar/
how-to-use-quotation-marks

Here is a quick chart of the differences:

Style issue	American Style	British Style
To enclose a quotation, use…	Double quotation marks	Single quotation marks
To enclose a quotation within a quotation, use…	Single quotation marks	Double quotation marks
Place periods and commas…	Inside quotation marks	Outside quotation marks
Place other punctuation (colons, semi-colons, question marks, etc.)…	Outside quotation marks*	Outside quotation marks*

https://blog.apastyle.org/apastyle/2011/08/punctuating-around-quotation-marks.html

结论：美式用法中，逗号或句号需要放在引号内；英式用法中，需要放在引号外。

但无论英语用法如何，译为汉语需要遵守汉语引号使用规则：

1. 引语被当作完整独立的话语来用，句末标点应放在引号里面。

例如：

古人曰："多行不义必自毙。"

引语被作为作者的话的组成部分，句末标点应放在引号外面。

例如：

大革命虽然失败了，但火种犹存。共产党人"从地下爬起来，揩干净身上的血迹，掩埋好同伴的尸首，他们又继续战斗了"。

2. 横排和竖排的引号都要外双内单，即引号里面还有引号时，外面一层用双引号，里面一层用单引号。

全国报纸编校质量评委会，报纸编校质量评比差错认定细则，原载1997年4月9日《新闻出版报》第3版。

转引自"知乎"（https://www.zhihu.com/question/19593375/answer/12761089），作者李晓诚。

14

> 原文：I think most of them don't, yes. In your case, it must be especially difficult. Since early in your career, when you made your much-quoted claims to "start from zero" and to "do things that have not been done before," you've remained steadfast in you attempts never to look back, only forward. Given your denial of the past, I can see why a retrospective would be unthinkable.
>
> 原译：我想大部分艺术家确实不喜欢。对你来说，回顾过去肯定格外困难。你在职业生涯早期就立志要"从零开始"，"做前人没有从没的事"，这些说法流传甚广。从那时起，你一直坚持永不回头，只向前看。想到你如此抵触过去，我就能明白为什么不可能办回顾展。（侯）

侯：第一句的语序应该是：Yes, I think most of them don't。其中，yes 放在句尾，可能是口语采访时颠倒了语序。但是考虑到已经整理为文字稿，且全篇都没有出现太过口语的内容，所以也可能是有意强调。中文译文中用"确实"来表示强调。

> 改译1：我想大部分艺术家确实不喜欢。对你来说，肯定格外困难。你在职业生涯早期就立志要"从零开始"，"做前人从没做过的事"，这些说法广为流传。从那时起，你一直坚持永不回头，只向前看。想到你如此抵触过去，我就能明白你为什么不办回顾展了。（王）

王："甚"字在原译中有些过于书面了，因此去掉。查了语料库里面甚的用法，都出现在较为正式和古早的说法中：

  1. 在这一点上，道佛差别甚大，佛教认为人的身体是"臭皮囊"，人若想进"西方极乐世界"，非得抛却肉身的存在不可，因此，佛教所谓的"涅盘"，同时也就意味着人的死亡。

  郑晓江；1990-9-20；知识窗；江西科学技术出版社

  2. 民间传流甚广的"八仙"：铁拐李、汉钟离、张果老、何仙姑、蓝采和、吕洞宾、韩湘子、曹国舅给中国民众以多少奇思遐想。

  《道教纵横》节录；郑晓江；1990-9-20；知识窗；江西科学技术出版社

3. 他说:"谭氏仁学之说,拉杂失伦,有同梦呓";"余怪其杂糅,不甚许也"。

《辛亥革命前章太炎的封建意识试析》节录;
罗耀九;1962-6-10;学术月刊;上海人民出版社
http://corpus.zhonghuayuwen.org/CnCindex.aspx

> **改译 2**:大部分艺术家不喜欢。是的。对你来说,肯定格外困难。你在职业生涯早期就立志要"从零开始","做前人从没做过的事",这些说法广为流传。从那时起,你一直坚持永不回头,只向前看。想到你如此抵触过去,我就能明白你为什么坚决不办回顾展了。(李)

李:博尔顿先说"I think most of them don't",可能是为了向川某确认自己的理解。如果川某是这个意思,自己就同意(yes)。毕竟全部否定,太绝对了。不要忘记,交流是通过同传进行的。如果同传的意思不符合常识,听众通常会怀疑同传不准确,此处就是一例。把问话翻译为全部否定,可能不符合这个句型的语法意义,却可能是川某用日语表达的意思("语不惊人死不休")。另外,改译 2 去掉"我想"(I think),以便和问句对得上。加上"我想",则有可能理解为两人在分别表明立场,与 yes 表示附和存在矛盾。

侯:"大部分艺术家不喜欢"对应原文"I think most of them don't, yes."
不确定李老师加上"是的"是翻译了这个 yes,认为 I think most of them don't 和 yes 是两个部分,还是为了语意而增加的。单看中文,"是的"后置且独立成句,可能会让人觉得翻译的痕迹有点重。

王:我同意侯灵钰的分析。我认为此处博尔顿再重复一遍川久保玲的话,已经起到确认的作用,是不是没有必要加上这个"是的"呢?

王:综合考虑李老师的建议,后与李老师讨论,将此句改为:"大部分艺术家应该不喜欢。对你来说,肯定格外困难。你在职业生涯早期,就说过'从零开始''敢为人先'这样的名句。从那时起,你一直坚持永不回头,勇往直前。想到你如此抵触过去,我就能明白你为什么坚决不办回顾展了"。李老师认为,也可以改为:"我同意,大部分艺术家都不喜欢"。既表示附和,也表明了自己的观点。

> **建议译法**：大部分艺术家应该不喜欢。对你来说，肯定格外困难。你在职业生涯早期，就说过"从零开始""敢为人先"这样的名句。从那时起，你一直坚持永不回头，勇往直前。想到你如此抵触过去，我就能明白你为什么坚决不办回顾展了。

王：此译法是受到了很多同学版本的启发，因此没有标记最后的译者。

15

> **原文**：I see the value of a retrospective of an artist's work, particularly for an institution like The Metropolitan Museum of Art, but for me it's an impossibility. In terms of my work, the only way forward is not to look back. For me, there are many clothes I've made that I regret or that I would have done differently.
>
> **原译**：我了解艺术家作品回顾展的价值所在，回顾展对大都会艺术博物馆这样的机构尤有价值，但是我不可能办回顾展。我做设计，要想前进，只能拒绝回顾过去。我设计过不少让自己后悔的衣服，还有一些可以设计得不一样。（侯）

侯：原文最后一句用 or 连接了两种情况，分别是 clothes I've made that I regret 和 clothes I've made that I would have done differently if I'd had more time。

If you regret something that you have done, you wish that you had not done it.

https://www.collinsdictionary.com/dictionary/english/regret

regret 是指"希望从没做过这个设计"，而 would have done differently 是说"应该还能做得不一样"，or 前后的两部分意思不同。所以此处可以理解为：做过的衣服中，有一些衣服"让我后悔了"，还有一些衣服"可以做得不同"。

王：第一句我稍微修改了一下，保证前后主语一致，但表达更简洁了一些。

> **改译1**：办艺术家作品回顾展是有价值的，尤其是对大都会艺术博物馆这样的机构来说，但是我不可能办回顾展。我做设计，要想前进，就不能回顾过去。我设计过不少让自己后悔的衣服，还有一些可以设计得不一样。（王）
>
> **改译2**：办艺术家作品回顾展是有价值的，尤其是对大都会艺术博物馆这样的机构，但是我不可能办回顾展。我做设计，要想前进，就不能回顾过去。我设计过不少让自己后悔的衣服，还有一些可以设计得不一样。（侯）

李：关于or，我的理解是"换个说法"，即前后表示同一个意思。因为对于设计师来说，本职工作就是设计，光后悔，不改进，是不符合设计师的职业要求的。

> **改译3**：办回顾展是有价值的，尤其是对大都会艺术博物馆这样的机构来说；但对我来说，不可能办回顾展。我做设计，要想前进，就不能回顾过去。有很多衣服，让我感到后悔，或者说本来可以做得不一样。（李）
>
> **建议译法**：办回顾展是有价值的，尤其是对大都会艺术博物馆这样的机构来说，但是，我不可能办回顾展。我做设计，要想前进，就不能回顾过去。我对很多衣服都抱有缺憾，或者说本来可以做得不一样。（王）

16

> **原文**：Yes, if I'd had more time. It always comes down to time.
>
> **原译**：没错，要是时间更充裕，就会不一样。说到底，还是时间的问题。（侯）

侯：根据对原文的分析，第一句完整句为：I would have done [these clothes] differently if I'd had more time。

此处，如果只翻译 if I'd had more time（"如果我有更多时间"/"如果时间更充裕"/"时间更充裕的话"等）：

川：我设计过不少让自己后悔的衣服，还有一些可以设计得不一样。
博：不一样？
川：没错，时间更充裕的话。

这样不仅让人觉得中文话说一半就断了，语言欧化严重，而且会造成句意不连贯，可能需要反应一会儿才能看懂，所以此处补全中文。

王：同意分析。稍做修改。

建议译法： 没错，要是时间更充裕，就会做得不一样。说到底，总是时间的问题。（李）

17

原文： You've spoken candidly about how your collections are often personal expressions of your inner feelings and sentiments—your fears, hopes, doubts, and desires. You've said, "Nothing new can come out of a situation without suffering" and "There is very little creation without despair." The fact that your clothes serve a kind of diaristic function must only compound your anxieties about reflecting on your previous collections.

原译： 你曾经坦率地说你的设计通常是内心感受和情感的个人表达，表达你的恐惧、希望、怀疑与欲望。你说"唯有经历痛苦，才有新事物诞生"，"唯有绝望，才有创造"。事实上，你设计的服装像是日记，只会加剧你回顾以往设计时的焦虑。（侯）

王：第一句稍微断下句更好。

改译1： 你曾经坦率地说，你的设计通常是自己内心感受和情感的表达，表达你的恐惧、希望、怀疑与欲望。你说"唯有经历痛苦，才有新事物诞生"，"唯有绝望，才有创造"。事实上，你设计的服装像是日记，只会加剧你回顾以往设计时的焦虑。（王）

李:"唯有经历痛苦,才有新事物诞生"两小句的逻辑主语不同,逻辑不顺。两个引用,均可改为与原文同义的反面表达。最后一句,可以再简洁一些,哪怕丢掉不言自喻的信息。

> **改译 2:** 你曾经坦率地说,你的设计通常是内心感受和情感的表达,包括你的恐惧、希望、怀疑和欲望。你说"没有痛苦的经历,就没有创新创造","没有绝望,就没有创造"。你的服装像是一本日记,这种日记功能,肯定只会加剧你回顾过去时的焦虑。(李)

王:建议改为动词驱动形式,如"没有经历痛苦,就没有创新创造"。

王:李老师,我不建议翻译出 diaristic function。个人认为偏文学性的访谈稿不必字字都翻译出来。是否删去比较连贯?考虑到语言风格和连贯性,这句话建议修改为:

> **改译 3:** 你曾经坦率地说,你的设计通常是你内心感受和情感的表达,表达你的恐惧、希望、怀疑和欲望。你说"没有痛苦,就难以创新","没有绝望,就没有创造"。你的服装像是一本日记,只会加剧你回顾过去时的焦虑。(王)

侯:中文往往省略人称代词,第一句话一句之内有四个"你",读起来非常啰唆。

王:我同意侯灵钰的建议。

> **建议译法:** 你曾经坦率地说,你的设计通常是内心感受和情感的表达,表达恐惧、希望、怀疑和欲望。你说"没有痛苦,就难以创新","没有绝望,就没有创造"。你的服装像是一本日记,只会加剧你回顾过去时的焦虑。(侯)

李:同意你们的改法。

18

原文：I can only compare my feelings to those of a man or woman late in life ruminating on his or her past mistakes. Surely, with hindsight, we would all make difference choices, different decisions. We can't turn back the clock.

原译：我的感觉就像人在晚年时反思过去的错误。回顾过去时，我们当然都能做出不同的选择、不同的决定。但是时间不会倒流。（侯）

改译1：我的感觉就像人在晚年时反思过去的错误一样。回顾过去，我们当然都能做出不同的选择、不同的决定。但是时间不会倒流。（王）

with hindsight 是"事后诸葛亮"的意思，但不宜这样翻译。would all make 是虚拟语气，"会作出"，不是"能做出"。或者说"希望当初做出"。

改译2：我的感觉就像人在晚年时反复回想过去的错误一样。当然，以现在的眼光看待过去，我们都希望当初作出不同的选择、不同的决定。但是时间不会倒流。（或者：但我们不会让时钟倒转）（李）

王：有部分同学把 man or woman 直译出来了，因为川久保是有女权主义思想的人。这样处理也未尝不可。

建议译法：我的感觉就像人在晚年时反思过去的错误。当然，以现在的眼光看待过去，我们都希望当初作出不同的选择、不同的决定。但是时间不会倒流。（李）

19

原文：Time has a tendency to normalize fashions that were once not only provocative and transgressive but also genuinely revolutionary and transformative. We become blind to what our eyes initially viewed as radically different. Innovations have a tendency to become invisible over the years; they become assimilated into the everyday language of fashion. But many visitors to the exhibition will be seeing your clothes for the first time. Most will find them as daring and as shocking as audiences did originally.

> **原译：** 曾经引人思索、离经叛道、真正革命性和变革性的时尚，在时间的洗礼下往往变得稀松平常。我们会对最初认为完全不同的事物习以为常。创新随着时间的推移逐渐隐形，化为了日常的时尚用语。但是，很多参观者是第一次欣赏你的设计。大多数人会和最初的观众一样，认为你的设计大胆而令人震惊。（侯）
>
> **改译 1：** 曾经离经叛道、革风易俗的时尚，在时间的洗礼下往往变得稀松平常。面对最初眼中迥然不同的事物，我们会变得盲目。创新随着时间的推移趋于无形，化为日常时尚用语。但是，很多参观者还是第一次看到你的设计。大多数人会和最初的观众一样，认为你的设计大胆而震撼。（王）

王： 原译对 provocative 的意思处理得不太准确，provocative 和 transgressive 有点离经叛道、反其道而行之的意思。它并非"挑逗"的意思。

1. 形容词

If you describe something as **provocative**, you mean that it is intended to make people react angrily or argue against it.

He has made a string of outspoken and sometimes provocative speeches in recent years.

His behavior was called provocative and antisocial.

同义词：offensive, provoking, insulting, challenging

provocatively 副词 [usually ADVERB with verb]

The soldiers fired into the air when the demonstrators behaved provocatively.

https://www.collinsdictionary.com/zh/dictionary/english/provocative

"革命性"和"变革性"的意思差别不大，这里我们是否可以再大胆一些：曾经离经叛道、革风易俗的时尚，在时间的洗礼下往往变得稀松平常。

李： 借用汉语成语的优势，对原文简化浓缩是可取的。但不排斥与原文文字上更接近的其他译法。

> **改译 2**：曾经离经叛道、革风易俗的时尚，在时间的洗礼下往往变得稀松平常。面对最初眼中迥然不同的事物，我们会变得视而不见。创新随着时间的推移趋于无形，化为日常时尚用语。但是，很多参观者还是第一次看到你的设计。大多数人会和最初的观众一样，认为你的设计大胆而震撼。（侯）

侯：原文中的 blind 含义如下：

If you say that someone is blind to a fact or a situation, you mean that they ignore it or are unaware of it, although you think that they should take notice of it or be aware of it.

https://www.collinsdictionary.com/dictionary/english/blind

而"盲目"意思不同，"盲目"现在多用比喻义，而比喻义已经不表示 ignore 或 unaware of：

盲目：眼睛看不见东西。比喻认识不清；考虑不慎重；目标不明确：～行动｜～崇拜｜～乐观｜这样做也太～了。

视而不见：尽管睁着眼睛看，却什么也没看见，指不重视或不注意。

熟视无睹：虽然经常看见，还跟没看见一样，指对应该关心的事物漠不关心。

视若无睹：虽然看了却像没有看见一样，形容对所看到的事物漠不关心。

中国社会科学院语言研究所词典编辑室. 现代汉语词典（第 7 版）. 北京：商务印书馆，2016。

可见，"视而不见"更符合原文意思。

李：invisible，意思是"不显眼"，引申为"不再新颖"。"创新变成用语"搭配不当。

> **改译 3**：曾经离经叛道、革风易俗的时尚，在时间长河的洗礼下往往变得稀松平常。最初看起来很辣眼的事物，慢慢会让人视而不见。过去的创新，随着时间的推移而不再新颖；新概念会变成日常时尚用语。但是，很多参观者是第一次看到你的设计。大多数人会和最初的观众一样，认为你的设计大胆而震撼。（李）

王：李老师，我认为川久保玲不会这样说话，建议去掉"长河"。

侯：不同意此处"辣眼"的改法。"辣眼"来自"辣眼睛"，是网络用语：

> 多用于形容看到不该看、不好看的东西。具有不忍直视、惨不忍睹、看了长针眼等潜在含义。属于新兴网络流行语，多见于微博、豆瓣、贴吧、各大论坛。
>
> 2017年7月18日，教育部、国家语委在北京发布《中国语言生活状况报告（2017）》，辣眼睛入选2016年度十大网络用语。
>
> 总的来说是个讽刺性用语，当然讽刺的程度要视上下文环境而定，在开玩笑和骂人中都经常出现"辣眼睛"一词，可见要理解该词，必须结合具体语境。
>
> https://baike.baidu.com/item/辣眼睛/19865868?fr=aladdin

此处有两个问题。一是语意问题。原文说 radically different，radically 形容的是程度：

> Radical changes and differences are very important and great in degree.
>
> radically *adverb*
>
> https://www.collinsdictionary.com/dictionary/english/radical

因此原文字面说的就是"很不同"，different 是比较中性的词，而"辣眼"显然是个贬义词。川的设计就属于 radically different，博对于川是欣赏和推崇的，从他口中说出"（川的设计）不忍直视、惨不忍睹、看了长针眼"这么强烈的贬低，而且是当面贬低，显然不该。

二是语域问题。博是受过高等教育的人。本段内，用词都处理得比较文雅，多成语，如"离经叛道""移风易俗""稀松平常""视而不见"，还有"时间长河""随着时间的推移"，而没有说"不一样""风俗变了""没什么特别""看不见""时间"或"时间长了"。或者至少是我们给博定了这样的语言风格，这个时候突然冒出一个网络流行语"辣眼"，和说话人身份、整体语域不符。

另外，"视而不见"的习惯用法是"对/对于……视而不见"，不说"让人视而不见"：

2. 他时而沉思,时而和我讨论,对周围景色似乎视而不见。

> 1980-4-3;中国青年报;中国青年报社

3. 否则,政府官员就会面临一种困境:要么强迫公民去实现他们不可能实现的事情,从而构成十分不公正的行为;要么对公民的违法行为视而不见,从而削弱对法的尊重。

> 《当代西方法学思潮》第 1,4,6,10,13,16 章节录;张文显;1988-8-1;
> 当代西方法学思潮;辽宁人民出版社

4. 如果我们手中只有一个阶级观点作武器,就会对大量值得研究的历史现象视而不见,或者便只能对之不恰当地贴上阶级的标签。

> 《历史学的发展趋势》节录;白钢等;1989-11-1;
> 历史学的发展趋势;辽宁教育出版社
> http://corpus.zhonghuayuwen.org/CnCindex.aspx

所以这句话应改为人作主语。

王:我同意侯灵钰的分析。另外,您说"创新"和"用语"搭配不当,所以我这里稍做修改。

改译 4:曾经离经叛道、革风易俗的时尚,在时间的洗礼下往往变得稀松平常。最初眼中迥然不同的事物,慢慢会让人视而不见。随着时间的推移,创新趋于无形,融入日常时尚用语。但是,很多参观者是第一次看到你的设计。大多数人会和最初的观众一样,认为你的设计大胆而震撼。(王)

侯:这段开始几句是一个意思反复说。什么东西"迥然不同"、谁"视而不见"其实上下文都很清楚。这句话总是读不通,原因之一在于主语宾语一直来回换。有同学处理时直接去掉了主语和宾语,读起来更通顺:

一开始认为非同寻常,渐渐却视而不见。(黄琳)

过去觉得标新立异,现在已经熟视无睹。(朱安琪)

> **改译 5:** 曾经离经叛道、革风易俗的时尚，在时间的洗礼下往往变得稀松平常。过去觉得标新立异，现在却视而不见。随着时间的推移，新事物趋于无形，融入日常时尚用语。但是，很多参观者是第一次看到你的设计。大多数人会和最初的观众一样，认为你的设计大胆而震撼。（侯、黄琳、朱安琪）

李：与其说是主语一致性问题，不如说是两个成语对立关系不强。但几种改译仍然没有理顺。建议译法 1 是过去看起来标新立异，现在却平淡无奇。建议译法 2 是一开始让人眼前一亮，渐渐却熟视无睹。

可分别找出这几个成语的反义词，组成一对表达。

王：在授课的过程中，我们发现两种不同风格的译文：

> **同学译文 1:** 时光总会磨平棱角，一些时尚潮流无论曾经多么引发争议、大胆出格、颠覆正统、开拓创新，历经岁月，也会泯然众物。
>
> **同学译文 2:** 对于那些惊天动地，离经叛道的时尚，时间能将之变得普通。那些我们曾经认为十分破格的时尚，现在看了却觉得没什么。

课堂上，大部分的同学是更倾向第一种译文的。这还涉及中英文的差异问题。为什么大家更倾向第一种译文呢？王文斌（2013）认为，汉语是具有块状结构的，这种名词性结构在非文学中表现得淋漓尽致。此外，汉语是具有流水线特点的（王文斌 & 赵朝永，2017）。换句话说，汉语像行云流水一样，倾泻而下，气势蓬勃（王建国 & 周冰洁，2017）。这对我们翻译非文学作品有很大的启示。多使用名词性结构、工整对仗，可以让译文更加优美。

> **改译 6:** 曾经离经叛道、革风易俗的时尚，在时间的洗礼下往往变得稀松平常。过去看起来标新立异，现在却平淡无奇。随着时间的推移，新事物趋于无形，融入日常时尚用语。但是，很多参观者是第一次看到你的设计。大多数人会和最初的观众一样，认为你的设计大胆而令人震撼。（李、侯、黄琳、朱安琪）

李：关于 Innovations have a tendency to become invisible over the years; they become assimilated into the everyday language of fashion，还是觉得"新事物融入……时尚用语"搭配有问题。"新观念……成为日常时尚语言的一部分"才是正确搭配。时尚的创新，源于观念创新，所以，innovations 理解为"新观念"应该没问题。另外，The Language of Fashion 还是一本书，把时尚比作语言（https://rosswolfe.files.wordpress.com/2015/04/roland-barthes-the-language-of-fashion.pdf），丢掉这个比喻比较可惜。

> **建议译法：** 曾经离经叛道、革风易俗的时尚，在时间的洗礼下往往变得稀松平常。过去看起来标新立异，现在却平淡无奇。随着时间的推移，新观念趋于无形，逐渐成为日常时尚语言的一部分。但是，很多参观者是第一次看到你的设计。大多数人会和最初的观众一样，认为你的设计大胆而令人震撼。（李）

20

> **原文：** But I've moved on. You must appreciate that I'm speaking from a purely personal perspective. I have no desire to look back. I only want to look ahead, to create clothes that no one has seen before.
>
> **原译：** 但是我已经变了。你应该明白这纯粹是我的个人观点。我对回头看毫无兴趣。我只想向前看，创造人人都未曾见过的服装。（侯）

王："变了"这个意思不明确。让意思更明确，我改成了"向前看了"。

> **改译 1：** 但是我已经向前看了。你应该明白这纯粹是我的个人观点。我不想回头看。我只想向前看，创造从未有人见过的服装。（王）
>
> **改译 2：** 但是我已经向前走了。你应该理解这纯粹是我的个人观点。我不想回头看。我只想向前看，创造从未有人见过的服装。（李）

改译 3： 但我已经放下了。你应该明白这纯粹是我的个人观点。我不愿回头看，只想向前看，创造从未有人见过的服装。（王）

李："放下了"似乎不明确。不如改为"但我已经和过去了断"意思更清楚。

建议译法： 但我已经和过去了断。你应该明白这纯粹是我的个人观点。我不愿回头看，只想向前看，创造从未有人见过的服装。（李）

第五单元　跨文化沟通意识

Exercise 5　A Gardener's Education

翻译情景

本单元摘自 Michael Pollan 的 *Second Nature: A Gardener's Education*，共 438 词。这本书是 Michael Pollan 的第一本书，也是有关园艺的一本书，曾被推选为美国园艺学会 75 本伟大的美国园艺书籍之一。在这本书中，Michael Pollan 从园艺的视角探讨了人与自然的哲学关系，语言风趣幽默，又不乏哲思。假定某出版社委托你翻译这本书，在中国出版。

专项能力

这篇作业旨在训练大家的跨文化沟通意识。跨文化沟通是来自不同文化背景的人之间传递信息、交流情感、相互理解的过程。从事翻译和任何其他跨文化交流活动，都必须具备跨文化沟通意识。

余光中曾经在思果新书《翻译研究》[1] 导读中提到，"翻译如婚姻，是一种两相妥协的艺术"。解构学派翻译理论代表家劳伦斯·韦努蒂（Lawrence Venuti）首次在《译者的隐身》(*The Translator's Invisibility*)[2] 中提到异化和

---

[1] 思果. 翻译研究 [M]. 北京：中国对外翻译出版公司，2001.
[2] Venuti L. *The Translator's Invisibility: A History of Translation* [J]. London: Routledge, 1995.

归化的翻译策略。异化指尽量让读者向作者靠拢，以期传达原汁原味的文化意象和语言表达；归化指的是尽量向读者靠拢，让译文烙上本土语言文化的印记。

我们认为，跨文化意识不应当沦落为"策略"（归化异化），而应当是最高层面的思维方法，就像全局意识一样。这种观点也和文化学派翻译理论有异曲同工之妙。例如，这一学派的代表人物苏姗·巴斯奈特（Susan Bassnett）曾经在《文化研究的翻译转向》（*The Translation Turn in Cultural Studies*）[1]一书中指出，翻译已经"超越了形式主义阶段，开始考虑有关语境、历史和传统的更广泛问题"。实际上，我们的全局意识已经包括了跨文化意识，因为要根据翻译的情景决定策略。

训练难点

西方园艺术语中，有很多在中国没有直接对应的概念。翻译时，需要你调动全局意识，思考所谓的 6Ws。就这篇选文来讲，你的翻译目的、翻译对象就尤为重要了。明确了这个问题，才能更好地使用异化和归化的策略。喜欢园艺吗？一起来一场美妙的园艺之旅！

训练方式

本次练习分原文、翻译提示、参考译文、译者注四部分。请先尝试独立翻译，做完以后再看原文尾注，并根据翻译提示，自行修改、润色，形成第二稿。之后再看参考译文和参考译文尾注。只有不断实践，才能提升翻译能力。希望你充分利用每一单元，一步一个脚印地向上攀登！

1　Bassnett S. *The Translation Turn in Cultural Studies* [J]. Constructing Cultures: Essays on Literary Translation, 1998: 123-140.

原文[1]

A Gardener's Education[2]

They might very well sweat, too, at the sight of one of the winter squashes[3] I discovered in my garden this October.[4] I didn't fully appreciate the magnitude of it until then, after the mass of foliage beneath which it spent the summer fattening itself had shriveled. Without a doubt the biggest thing I've ever grown, this squash tipped the scales at close to thirty pounds. Its seed I had obtained last winter from a firm in Idaho that specializes in "heirloom" vegetables—old varieties no longer grown commercially.[5] Called 'Sibley[6]', my squash is said to be an American Indian[7] cultivar that was passed on to the early settlers. The reason it fell from commercial grace, I'd guess now that I've laid eyes on one, probably has to do with its looks, which are definitely on the homely side. A[8] Sibley is a big warty thing[9] with the washed out, blue-green color of dirty ice; it might be a chunk of glacier. Its form, however, is pleasing, sort of pinched at both ends and bulging at the waist, it looks like a gondola, or a Viking ship, listing under a fat cargo. Or like a crescent moon with the belly of a Buddha[10].

Where did this thing, this great quantity of squash flesh, come from? The earth, we say, but not really; there's no less earth here now than there was in May when I planted it; none's been used up in its making. By all rights creating something this fat should require so great an expense of matter that you'd expect to find Sibley squashes perched on the lips of fresh craters. That they're not, it seems to me, should be counted something of a miracle.

翻译提示

1 **全局意识：语篇**

想要翻好本选段，需要具备宏观意识。Act local, think global。请宏观思考原文的 6W1H，包括了解作者背景、写作背景、作品结构、思想逻辑、写作风格等信息。

2　**全局意识：标题含义**
请大家在这本书中搜索 education，确定 a gardener's education 是指作者教育别人，还是作者受到的教育？受到谁的教育？
关于本书及作业介绍，详细参见：https://en.wikipedia.org/wiki/Second_Nature_(book)

3　**文化沟通 / 可视化**
什么是 winter squashes？可以按照以下思路查找：
1) 用谷歌图片搜索 winter squash；
2) 猜测中文译法，比如 "冬瓜" "冬南瓜" "笋瓜"，在谷歌网页和图片中搜索；
3) 确定哪个译法正确；
4) 译文中需要精确译出，还是使用上义词即可？为什么？

4　**全局意识：上下文**
要翻译好这句话，还是要有全局意识，也就是李老师所说的 act local, think global。请联系上下文，思考一下 They might very well sweat too —— 其中的代词 they 具体指什么？

5　**理解原文**
什么是 no longer grown commercially？记得避免按照字面意思生硬翻译，要清楚它的意思。no longer 暗指什么？

6　**文化意象**
对 Sibley 的翻译，需要考虑以下几个问题：
1) 什么是 Sibley？
2) Sibley 长什么样？
3) Sibley 与 Winter squashes 的关系？
4) Sibley 是不是 heirloom vegetables？
5) Sibley 名称的起源是什么？

6) 音译还是意译？

7) 是否可以借助《人名大辞典》翻译？

7 **译文准确性**

如何处理 American Indian？请检查一下你的译文，是否准确翻译了 American Indian，是否可以处理成"印第安人""原住民"？

8 **冠词**

从这个冠词看，是一类南瓜的通用名，而不是作者给某个南瓜起的专用名（像给小狗起名那样）。用 Sibley 加上 winter squash pumpkin 查，得知：Sibley – also known as Pike's Peak. (Maxima) Heirloom America 1837。再查相关图片，得知是一类南瓜。

9 **译文准确性 / 可视化**

a big warty thing 是什么样子，可以通过谷歌图片检索。可以尝试在谷歌中搜索"Sibley warty thing"。有了直观感受，翻译起来也就更形象。

10 **文化意象 / 可视化**

Gondola, Viking ship 和 belly of a Buddha 都带有文化意象，翻译的时候需要考虑以下几个问题：

1) 是否可以通过图片了解这些文化意象？

2) 这些意象和瓜的形状有什么关系？

参考译文[1][2]

　　根据梭罗的研究，老普林尼曾经说过，苹果是所有东西中最重的，牛仅仅是看到一车苹果，还没上套，就会吓得冒汗。[3]

　　今年十月我在菜园里发现的大南瓜，[4]牛要是看见，很可能也会冒汗。[5]整个夏天，南瓜都躲在大片绿叶[6]下养膘，直到叶子枯萎了，我才看清楚它原来这么大！[7]这南瓜差不多三十磅重，[8]毫无疑问，是我种出来的最大的东西了。[9]南瓜种子是我去年冬天在爱达荷州的一家公司买的。这家公司专营"传家宝"蔬菜，都是些不再大规模种植的老品种。[10]我买的种子叫西布利，[11]据说是美洲印第安人[12]栽培的品种，[13]后传给早期的欧洲定居者。[14]我以前没见过这个品种，今天一睹芳容，猜想它在市场上"失宠"的原因，可能与此有关。这家伙确实其貌不扬[15]：浑身疙疙瘩瘩，[16]呈泛白的青绿色，像个脏兮兮的冰坨子。[17]它的体形倒是讨人喜欢：两头尖，中间鼓，跟装满了货物的贡多拉或维京船似的，又像是弯弯新月挺着弥勒肚。[18]

　　这一大坨子南瓜肉从哪里来？从土里来？恐怕也不尽然。比起五月播种的时候，这里的土量没有减少；长南瓜没有用什么土。[19]按理说，长出这么大的东西应该消耗不少物质，在旁边留下一个坑才对，但事实并非如此。这，在我看来，应该算作奇迹。[20]

译者注

1　全局意识：标题含义

李：调查可知，a gardener's education 是指作者在尝试园艺的过程中受到的教育。

2　全局意识：语篇

王：这篇文章的作者是 Michael Pollan。Pollan 于 1977 年获得贝宁坦大学（Bennington College）的学士学位。他于哥伦比亚大学继续深造，并于 1988 年获得该校英文硕士学位。

https://zh.wikipedia.org/wiki/ 迈克尔·波伦

　　节选出自作者的第一本书 Second Nature: A Gardener's Education。译者需要浏览全书，掌握全书脉络，从宏观的角度，理解选段细节。笔者通读全书以后，获得三个关键词：

　　关键词一：nature

For I soon came to the realization that I would not learn to garden very well before I'd also learned about a few other things: about my proper place in nature (was I within my rights to murder the woodchuck that had been sacking my vegetable garden all spring?); about the somewhat peculiar attitudes toward the land that an American is born with (why is it the neighbors have taken such a keen interest in the state of my lawn?); about the troubled borders between nature and culture; and about the experience of place, the moral implications of landscape design, and several other questions that the wish to harvest a few decent tomatoes had not prepared me for.

关键词二：consciousness

Michael Pollan 的大部分思想源自梭罗，Pollan 对自然的见解蕴藏着很多哲学思考。

Like most Americans out-of-doors, I was a child of Thoreau. But the ways of seeing nature I'd inherited from him, and the whole tradition of nature writing he inspired, seemed not to fit my experiences.

Now it is true that there are countless volumes of practical advice available to the perplexed gardener, but I felt the need for some philosophical guidance as well.

虽然 Pollan 承认自己受到梭罗的影响，但是他并非机械接受梭罗的观点，而是通过与梭罗"隔空对话"，呈现自己的观点。这也是社会哲学的魅力所在。没有绝对的真理，而是在不断辩论中追求真理：

I find I spend a lot of time arguing with Thoreau. Many of these arguments don't get settled; this book is an exercise in discovery rather than truth telling. It is, as I say, the story of an education, and, as will be clear from the high incidence of folly in these pages, I remain more pupil than teacher. I know more at the end of my narrative than I did at the beginning, . . .

关键词三：culture

本书的精华是从哲学角度看待自然，并将自然与人类社会文化有机融合在一起：

For one thing, we need, and now more than ever, to learn how to use nature without damaging it. That probably can't be done as long as we continue to think of nature and culture simply as antagonists. So how do we begin to find some middle ground between the two? To provide for our needs and desires without diminishing nature? The premise of this book is that the place to look for some of the answers to these questions may not be in the woods, but in the garden.

王：无论是通过阅读作品，还是听作者在 TED 上的演讲，都感到作者是一个幽默风趣的人。本书时不时透露出作者幽默的文风。仅举两例：

I liked Jimmy because, compared to me, he was bold and fearless; he liked me because, compared to him, I had a brain. We made a good team.

I usually set the agenda, explaining to Jimmy where we were going to dig or what we were going to plant that day, citing my grandfather whenever I needed to bolster my authority.

因此，文章风格诙谐幽默、生动形象，译文也不宜僵硬。另外，作者是一个知识分子，充满对园艺的好奇，所以才有戏剧性的矛盾情节出现，比如认为"西布利"这种南瓜可能会消耗很多土。因此，请注意把握语言，既不要过于随意，也要尽量幽默生动。注意作者讲话的语气。

3

王：根据李老师的建议，为了更好地翻译选段第一句话，最好把上文最后一句也翻译出来。这一句的翻译和修改的过程如下：

> 原文：…Pliny said *that* apples were the heaviest of all things, according to Thoreau, and *that* oxen start to sweat at the mere sight of a cartload of them.
> 原译：……根据梭罗的研究，老普林尼曾经说过，苹果是所有东西中最重的，牛要是看到一车苹果，还没上套就开始冒汗了。（李）

王：我觉得"上套"一词不合适。一般这个词都用于诈骗等语境中，比如：不法分子还会在现场扮成取款人唆使持卡人"上套"。在插卡口上做手脚。不法分子在插卡口将颜色、形状、大小相近的……

http://bcc.blcu.edu.cn/zh/search/2/ 上套

> **改译**：……根据梭罗的研究，老普林尼曾经说过，苹果是所有东西中最重的，牛要是看到一车的苹果，没准会吓得冒汗。（王）

李：start to sweat 是肯定的说法，不是"没准"，是"一定"！mere 这个词也很重要。这句话是说，牛只要一看到（言外之意是还没被套上车），就会冒汗。牛为什么会冒汗？因为牛根据经验，知道苹果比别的东西都要重，害怕拉这种东西。"上套"的本义就是把牲口套在车上，后来才引申为"被套牢""脱不开身""陷入圈套"的意思。看来在乡村生活的经验，对翻译也有帮助！另外注意，两个 that 都是 said 的宾语。资料：

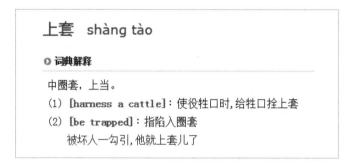

> **建议译法**：根据梭罗的研究，老普林尼曾经说过，苹果是所有东西中最重的，牛仅仅是看到一车苹果，还没上套，就会吓得冒汗。（李）

4

王：要理解 winter squashes，不妨搜索谷歌图片：

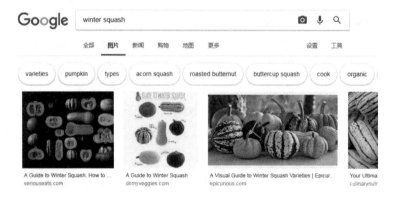

前面三条结果都是 a guide to winter squash，可以点开仔细查看 winter squash 的种类。虽然作者强调的是一个南瓜，但原文用的是复数，有必要了解一下各种南瓜。在搜索多个 reference guide 之后，发现下面的这个解释最全面：

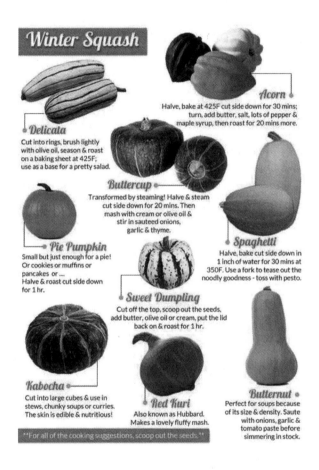

https://www.pinterest.com/pin/249386898095782630

大致了解英文之后，可以假设中文译法，然后核查中英文说法是否是同一事物。比如，有些同学翻译成了"笋瓜"，但如果在百度等网站搜索图片，会发现笋瓜类似于西葫芦（左图为笋瓜，右图为西葫芦）：

但是根据文中的描述，A Sibley is a big warty thing with the washed out, blue-green color of dirty ice。从颜色和形状上判断 Sibley 应该表面不那么光滑，和光滑的"笋瓜"应该不同。因此翻译成笋瓜肯定不对。

还有的同学翻译成了"冬瓜"，但一对比图片就会发现不对：

因表面光滑，也和文中所说的 Sibley（winter squashes 的一种）不符。此外，通过查证可知，冬瓜属于葫芦科冬瓜属植物，和南瓜的葫芦科南瓜属植物也不相符。因此，也不能翻译成"冬瓜"。

那么这个 winter squash 到底如何翻译呢？我认为难点在于，中国没有完全对应的概念。这就涉及如何进行文化的译入和传播问题。如果是翻译成学名词，不仅破坏了原文的语言风格，也可能让中国读者摸不着头脑。查到这份资料：

What else makes winter squash different from summer squash?

Have you ever had a zucchini or crookneck squash that tasted (and smelled!) especially squash-y? It probably had large seeds and thick skin too. Summer squash and winter squash are from the same family of vegetables; the difference is that summer squash tastes best when harvested young and winter squash tastes best when harvested at full maturity. That's why a zucchini or crookneck squash left to grow too large isn't as tasty as one that's picked when it's still small.

由此可见，winter squash 和 summer squash 是相对应的，由此猜想是否可以翻译成"冬南瓜"呢？我们带着这个思路搜索"冬南瓜"，结果如下：

blog.sina.com.cn/yydy1970

菜地里结了很多的瓜。有一种叫作 Butternut squash，就是图中那个枕头一样的家伙。查了一下，中文叫作冬南瓜，也是南瓜家族中的一员。冬南瓜非常容易种植，结下的瓜至少有 3-5 磅，大的甚至 10 磅左右。

http://blog.sina.com.cn/s/blog_64ac7bed010169c6.html

这份资料来自博客，使用"磅"表示重量，应该是翻译过来的材料。还见到英汉对照的材料：

Butternut squash is a member of the Cucurbitaceae family, which also includes cucumber, melon, and pumpkin. Since it has seeds, it's basically a fruit.

冬南瓜属葫芦科，其他成员还包括黄瓜、甜瓜和大南瓜。因为有籽，固归为水果类。

http://www.sohu.com/a/245248518_100234488

在谷歌网页上搜索"冬南瓜"，也有很多相关内容。因此，虽然"冬南瓜"不一定是正式称呼，但已经有一定接受度，所以我译为"冬南瓜"。

王：结合课上的讨论情况，winter squashes 主要有四种译法：冬南瓜、南瓜、老南瓜、晚熟南瓜。

这几种译法的区别主要是视角不同。翻译为"冬南瓜"和"晚熟南瓜"的同学，更多是从成熟时节上考虑的；翻译成"老南瓜"的同学更多是从口感上谈的。非常幸运的是，这节课有一位河南农村的学生来旁听。她说，课件中展示的南瓜她都见过。她到讲台上分享了农业知识。这名同学的名字叫 Jane。Jane 说南瓜都是在夏季长成的，只不过所谓的"冬南瓜"，需要多放一段时间，放到冬天口感会好一些。所以，翻译成"冬南瓜""夏南瓜"，无论从成熟时节还是口感上来讲，区别都不太大。Jane 认为，从口感上区别更好一些，翻译成"老南瓜"，农民们一下子就会知道是什么意思。

李老师认为，翻译成"大南瓜"即可。本文虽然讲的是园艺，但并非精讲蔬菜花卉品种。此处提到 winter squash，唯一的目的就是说，这个东西个头大。具体是什么瓜无所谓。因此，不必纠结于名称的准确性。是个南瓜就行。如果是翻译种子手册，建议翻译为"冬南瓜"。虽然美国的"冬南瓜"需要成熟了再吃，和我们的老南瓜一样，但可能不是同一品种，"归化"我们熟悉的说法（"南瓜""老南瓜""晚熟南瓜"），可能妨碍引进一种新的作物。

王：综上所述，遇到对方文化中不存在的概念，比如 winter squashes，需要根据翻译情景决定如何翻译。可能需要创造一个新名词（如"冬南瓜"），也可能不需要太精确，找一个大致相当的说法即可（如"南瓜"）。作出决定时，译者需要考虑语篇的性质、这个词在语篇中的作用、读者的理解能力、表述的方便性等因素。李老师的意见非常可取。处理成"大南瓜"，牛看到大南瓜吓得冒汗也就顺理成章了。

5

> 原文：They might very well sweat, too, at the sight of one of the winter squashes I discovered in my garden this October.
>
> 原译：牛要是看到今年十月我在菜园里发现的东南瓜，没准也会吓得汗流浃背。

Apples especially seem vested with the season's extravagant gravity. Pliny said that apples were the heaviest of all things, according to Thoreau, and that oxen start to sweat at the mere sight of a cartload of them.

They might very well sweat, too, at the sight of one of the winter squashes I discovered in my garden this October. I didn't fully appreciate

王：理解这句话要联系上下文。上文有这样一段话：Pliny said that apples were the heaviest of all things, according to Thoreau, and that oxen start to sweat at the mere sight of a cartload of them。原文出自梭罗的典故，感兴趣的同学可以自行查看。

从衔接的角度看，"汗流浃背"是一个表持续性过程的动词，不能和"看到"这个瞬时动词搭配。换句话说，牛不可能看到南瓜，就汗流浃背。联系后文的 magnitude，就不难理解，因为这个冬南瓜很大，看起来很重，所以连大力气的公牛，看到也会吓得冒汗（sweat），怕自己拉不动。

王：在语言结构的处理上，如果把 winter squashes in my garden this October

处理成定语，可能会导致定语过长，影响句子的节奏；另外这篇文章的语言风格幽默、生动，是偏文学性的语言风格，因此我对译文做适当增补，点出冬南瓜很"大"，这样更容易理解。

> **改译 1**：今年十月，我在菜园里发现了一个冬南瓜，要是牛看到这么大的南瓜，没准也会吓得冒汗。（王）

李：不翻译上段最后一句话，改译 1 就没问题。加上那句话，这里可能就要修改。必须亲眼看到上句话怎么说，才知道这里如何衔接。

王：我非常赞同翻译出上一句。最后一段的结尾是说牛紧张得冒汗，如果以"今年十月"开启段落，相当于变换了中文的主语／主题，读者可能要迟疑一下才能理解。此外，综合考虑李老师在上个注释中的建议，这里修改为"大南瓜"，略去南瓜的属性。我继续修改为：

> **改译 2**：牛要是看见今年十月我在菜园里发现的大南瓜，也得吓得冒汗。（王）

王：有同学把 oxen 译为"公牛"，也是给牛增加了不必要的属性。作者并没有强调公牛比母牛劲儿大。所有的牛，劲儿都不小。只是因为英语中没有不表示性别的"牛"，作者才用了 ox。因此，译文不必说"公牛"。

李：改译 2 的定语略显长一些。改译 1 中，没准＝可能；改译 2 中，也得＝肯定会；might very well＝很可能。改译如下：

> **改译 3**：［根据梭罗的研究，老普林尼曾经说过，苹果是所有东西中最重的，牛仅仅是看到一车苹果，还没上套，就会吓得冒汗。］今年十月我在菜园里发现的大南瓜，牛要是看见，很可能也会冒汗。

6　**彭**：尽管文中这里只说了 foliage，但搜索 foliage winter squash 时可以发现，foliage 均为绿叶，故此处译为绿叶。

https://harvesttotable.com/squash_squash_growing_success/

7

原文：I didn't fully appreciate the magnitude of it until then, after the mass of foliage beneath which it spent the summer fattening itself had shriveled.

原译：长南瓜在一大片绿叶下，花了一个夏天的时间把自己养肥。直到绿叶干枯时，我才充分意识到它到底有多大。（彭）

王：原译的意思非常准确，没有问题。在语言风格上，为了突出作者幽默、生动的语言风格，我将句末的句号变为叹号，且使用一些活泼的表达，如"乘凉""养膘"等。另外，我选取了两个时间点（一是summer，二是had shriveled）进行对比，这样更能突出南瓜大小的变化，请看看是否合适。

改译1：整个夏天，冬南瓜都躲在大片绿叶下乘凉养膘，直到叶子枯萎了，我才知道它原来这么大！（王）

李：用"看清楚"会更具体，隐含原来被绿叶遮挡，看不到全貌。

改译2：整个夏天，南瓜都躲在大片绿叶下养膘，直到叶子枯萎了，我才看清楚原来这么大（或：看清楚它的体量）！（李）

8 译文准确性

> 原文: tipped the scales at close to thirty pounds

李: tipping the scales 说明作者称过这个南瓜,注意表达的准确性。

王: thirty pounds: "磅"是外来概念,也涉及文化意象的问题。课堂上同学们针对 thirty pounds 的"异化""归化",展开了讨论。以下是支持归化的见解:

李军:原文为 close to thirty pounds。外国通常以"磅"为计量单位,而中文通常用"斤"。英译中,受众成了中国人,因此此处采取归化的译法。1 磅约等于 0.91 斤,因此 30 磅约等于 27.3 斤,最终翻译成"近 30 斤"。

李骏达:原文"this squash tipped the scales at close to thirty pounds"很有动感,可以看到天平往一边倾斜的样子,实实在在地感受到这个南瓜的分量;但是即便如实翻出"天平倾斜"这层意思,中文读者也未必能够体会那种"沉甸甸"的分量感,而且中国较少用天平去称量蔬菜,所以不如适当地归化,再加上一点创造,翻译成"足足快有 30 斤重,都快把秤杆给压折了"。审校觉得"把秤压折"过度翻译了,确实是发挥过头了。但是译者还是觉得读到 tip the scale 脑海里就有天平猛地朝一侧倾斜的画面,所以就把原译改为"把秤压弯",稍微没那么夸张。

> 30 pounds =
> 13.6077711 公斤

此外,30 磅大概是 27、8 斤吧。考虑到原文不是科技文本,这里列举的数字也是个概数,所以不是特别重要;而中文里整十的数字往往更有力量,所以不如直接四舍五入,翻译成"30 斤"(open to discussion)。

> **原译**: 这家伙绝对是我种过的最大的作物,接近 30 斤的重量都快把秤杆压弯了。

Jane: 这个译法有点太夸张了,在我们老家,那个秤能称上百斤的东西,怎么可能30斤的东西就把秤压折了呢？

王：虽然有些夸张，但这篇文章是偏文学的纪实体小说，"压弯秤砣"也是夸张幽默的写法，这倒不足为怪。

李：此处是否归化都可以讲出道理。受西方文化影响这么多年，30磅是多少，读者也应该清楚。即使不清楚，上下文的叙述方式也足以让读者认识到分量不轻。

但即使归化，也不能说外行话。现在的学生真是缺乏生活常识。大家没有用过天平、没有用过杆秤，所以，不太清楚是怎么回事。"把秤砣压弯"可能是笔误：秤砣是个铁疙瘩，怎么会压弯！秤杆也压不弯，更压不折：那上面仅仅挂了个最多一两斤重的秤砣。杆秤运用的是杠杆原理。东西挂在秤钩上或放在托盘里，滑动秤砣，达到平衡，秤砣所在刻度就是重量。东西太重的话，可能把上面那根绳子拉断；超出杆秤最大称重范围的话，秤杆会向上挑起，秤砣滑到拉绳处。秤杆是根坚硬的木头，不承受多大重量，既不会弯，也不会断。

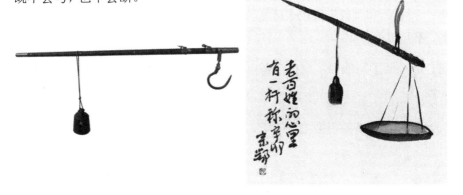

9

> **原文**：Without a doubt the biggest thing I've ever grown, this squash tipped the scales at close to thirty pounds.
> **原译**：毫无疑问，这是我种过最大的植物，近三十磅之重。（彭）

彭：这里本来想直接译为"东西"，但感觉不够妥当，根据上下文，plant的一定是植物，故这里译为winter squash的上义词"植物"。

王：我不建议处理成"植物"。"植物"是下面这些东西：

另外，原文的语言比较生动、活泼，所以我认为处理为"东西"没问题。

> **改译1：** 这南瓜得有三十磅重，肯定是我种过最大的东西了。（王）

李："得有"和"肯定"都表示猜测。这里作者显然拿天平称过，是确切判断，不是猜测。

王：昨天听了您的课，觉得是否可以处理成：毫无疑问是我种出来最大的东西了。

> **改译2：** 这南瓜差不多三十磅重，毫无疑问是我种出来最大的东西了。（王）

李：加一个"的"字。

> **改译3：** 这南瓜差不多三十磅重，毫无疑问是我种出来的最大的东西了。

李：我很不愿意在一个句子中用两个"的"字，但也想不出好办法。曾想改为"毫无疑问，这是我个头最大的物产了"，但"物产"不是很常用。

> **建议译法：** 这南瓜差不多三十磅重，毫无疑问，是我种出来的最大的东西了。（李）

10

> **原文**: Its seed I had obtained last winter from a firm in Idaho that specializes in "heirloom" vegetables—old varieties no longer grown commercially.
>
> **原译**: 去年冬天，我在爱达荷的一家公司买到了长南瓜种，这家公司专门售卖"祖传"蔬菜，也就是不再大规模种植的老品种。（彭）

彭：grow commercially 的意思是不再商业化生产，也就是不再大面积种植的意思。

> commercially: produced or used in large quantities as a business

> com·mer·cial·ly /-ʃəli/ adv.
> commercially produced/grown/developed 商业化生产的／种植的／开发的 The product is not yet commercially available. 这种产品还没有上市。His invention was not commercially successful. 他的发明从营利角度看并不成功。

no longer 暗指以前有商业种植（大面积种植），因此，译文在生动幽默的同时，也要准确。

王：意思上我觉得没有问题，只是与上文衔接不够紧密。我调换了时间状语和主语的位置，看是否好些。

> **改译1**：南瓜种子是我去年冬天在爱达荷州的一家公司买的。这家公司专营"传家宝"蔬菜，也就是不再大规模种植的老品种。（王）

李："祖传""传家宝"都很好，还可以说"地方传统蔬菜品种"，去掉引号。或者说"不再大规模种植的老品种"也可直译为"不再商业化种植的品种"。

王：看过几十份同学作业，同学们的译法可以归结如下：

> **同学译文1**：瓜种是去年冬天我从爱达荷州的一家公司得来的，该公司专卖那些"古董"类蔬菜，就是那些不再进行商业化种植的古老品种。

同学译文2：这个南瓜种子是我去年冬天在爱达荷州一个公司那里买的，那家公司专卖"祖传"蔬菜，也就是不再大规模种植的古老品种。

同学译文3：去年冬天，我从爱达荷州一家公司买了这个南瓜种子，这家公司专门卖珍稀蔬菜——已经不再商业化种植的老品种蔬菜。

课堂讨论认为，这几种译法都可以接受。但是，在采用"古董"或者"祖传"这类词的时候，注意加引号，因为此处和平时的意思不太一样。heirloom 就是比较珍稀的蔬菜品种。

改译2：南瓜种子是我去年冬天在爱达荷州的一家公司买的。这家公司专营"传家宝"蔬菜，也就是不再大规模种植的老品种。（王）

李：可以把"也就是"改为"都是些"。毕竟"传家宝"并不当然意味着"不再大规模种植"。

11

王：关于 Sibley 的译法，如果查一下名字起源，可以发现它是由 Hiram Sibley Company of Rochester 大面积推广的。虽然这是一个公司名称，但 Hiram Sibley 是个人名，不妨在人名大辞典里查一下它的音译。查询确认 Sibley 音译为"西布利"。

另外,在课堂分享中,意外发现江子豪同学译为"西不理",可媲美"狗不理",暗指这种瓜其貌不扬,谁都不爱搭理它。这种幽默风趣的译法,值得肯定。

12

彭:根据对原文的查证,American Indian 指的就是 Native American,即美洲原住民——印第安人:

美洲原住民,是对美洲所有原住民的总称。美洲原住民中的绝大多数为印第安人,剩下的则是主要位于北美洲北部的因纽特人。

https://zh.wikipedia.org/wiki/ 美洲原住民

13

王:cultivar 指的是栽培品种,具体参见维基百科:

栽培品种(英语:Cultivar)是指经由人工栽培之后产生的植物种类,也称为品种或变种,不过后两个字有其他不同意义。栽培种根据特征,有一个专有的命名,以和其他同种植物有所区隔。而命名方式,则是由《国际栽培植物命名法规》(*ICNCP*)来规范。

https://zh.wikipedia.org/wiki/ 栽培品种

关于 cultivar(栽培种)和 variety(品种 / 变种)的关系,这里有清楚说明:Varieties often occur in nature and most varieties are *true to type*(不变异 /

下一代性状与原系相同）。That means the seedlings grown from a variety will also have the same unique characteristic of the parent plant. For example, there is a white flowering redbud that was found in nature. Its scientific name is *Cercis canadensis* var. *alba*. The varietal term "alba" means white. If you were to germinate seed from this variety, most, if not all would also be white flowering。

  Cultivars are not necessarily true to type. In fact cultivar means "cultivated variety." Therefore, a cultivar was selected and cultivated by humans. Some cultivars originate as sports or mutations on plants. Other cultivars could be hybrids of two plants. To propagate true-to-type clones, many cultivars must be *propagated vegetatively*（营养繁殖/无性繁殖）through cuttings, grafting, and even tissue culture. Propagation by seed usually produces something different than the parent plant.

https://hortnews.extension.iastate.edu/2008/2-6/CultivarOrVariety.html

  简而言之，天然品种（variety）性状稳定，不易变异；栽培品种（cultivar）性状不稳定，可能发生变异，因此通常不通过种子繁殖。

14

> **原文**：Called 'Sibley', my squash is said to be an American Indian cultivar that was passed on to the early settlers.
>
> **原译**：我的长南瓜名叫西布利，据说是传给早期定居者的印第安品种。（彭）
>
> **改译**：我买的种子叫西布利，据说是美洲印第安人栽培的品种，后传给早期定居者。（王）

李："定居者"对于中国人来说，意思不是不言自喻。应补充一点背景。

> **建议译法**：我买的种子叫西布利，据说是美印第安人栽培的品种，后传给早期的欧洲定居者。（李）

15

> 原文：The reason it fell from commercial grace, I'd guess now that I've laid eyes on one, probably has to do with its looks, which are definitely on the homely side.
> 原译：我见过这种瓜，所以我猜它在市场上"失宠"可能与其外观有关，这瓜确实其貌不扬。（彭）
> 改译：我见过这种瓜，想来它在市场上"失宠"可能和长相有关，这瓜确实其貌不扬。（王）

李：作者以前没见过，种出来才见到，所以说 now that……

> 建议译法：我以前没见过这个品种，今天一睹芳容，猜想它在市场上"失宠"的原因，可能与此有关。这家伙确实其貌不扬……（李）

16

彭：wart 本来指的是疣、肉赘等，但这里如果直译，可能会让读者有些不大好的联想，汉语中表示相同概念时，一般会说：表面有疙瘩的南瓜，如：

> 南瓜"保留了，大家摘下十几个南瓜。她们的生活经验都比我丰富，说表皮有疙瘩的南瓜面，说涩刀的南瓜甜，有人教我怎么做南瓜饼，有人教我怎么做南瓜干，还有人说，放在屋角，只要不沾水，放半年也不会坏。
> 　　再三动员。只有两个同事带走了南瓜，大大小小的南瓜摆满了厨房桌子档。想到大家帮我收获，免费进行南瓜烹调辅导，我也投桃报李，找了个浑身鼓起许多疙瘩的老南瓜，砍了煮熟，和了面粉，放了白糖，捏了圆球，拍扁了放在油锅里炸好，带到办公室共享。甜甜的南瓜饼，每人只吃一两只，但分享的快乐，是吃独食体验不到的好滋味。

books.google.co.jp

故这里结合目的语习惯，译为"疙瘩"。

王：谷歌上图片搜索 warty sibley，确认可以处理为"疙瘩"。由下图可知，这些南瓜确实像长了疙瘩一样，表面不光滑。

http://www.realseeds.co.uk/wintersquash.html

17

原文：A Sibley is a big warty thing with the washed out, blue-green color of dirty ice; it might be a chunk of glacier.

原译：西布利是个长疙瘩的大南瓜，呈褪色的蓝绿脏冰色，好像一块冰川。（彭）

彭：这里我看了上下文，也不大明白为什么作者要说它像 a chunk of glacier。

王：还是要查找图片帮助理解，谷歌里面搜索 Sibley winter squash，结果如下：

看到图片，不难理解，Sibley 这种瓜的外表颜色确实像脏冰一样，呈渐褪的蓝绿色。

改译1：浑身长疙瘩，颜色也像裹着脏冰一样，呈渐褪的蓝绿色，看着就像一块冰坨子。（王）

李：植物瓜果的颜色不说蓝色，说青色。这句话写颜色，下句话写形状。

改译2：这家伙确实其貌不扬：浑身上下长满疙瘩，说青不青，说绿不绿，就像衣服洗过百遍，或者说脏水结冰后的颜色。（李）

王：原文并没有出现衣服的意象，这样处理觉得不太合适。

费晨：blue 可以是青色，但青绿色就太绿了，蓝绿色是接近蓝灰色吧。

改译3：这家伙确实其貌不扬：浑身疙疙瘩瘩，呈泛白的蓝绿色，像个脏兮兮的冰坨子。（费）

李：赤、橙、黄、绿、青、紫颜色的瓜果都有，就是蓝色的十分罕见。还是改为"青绿色"符合常理。

建议译法：这家伙确实其貌不扬：浑身疙疙瘩瘩，呈泛白的青绿色，像个脏兮兮的冰坨子。（费）

18

原文：Its form, however, is pleasing, sort of pinched at both ends and bulging at the waist, it looks like a gondola, or a Viking ship, listing under a fat cargo. Or like a crescent moon with the belly of a Buddha.

原译：但它的"体形"却很招人爱，两头有些"清瘦"，"腰部"圆鼓鼓的，看起来像载有重物向一侧倾斜的凤尾船或维京船，或是一弯长着啤酒肚的新月。（彭）

彭：under 本来应该是"在……之下"，但这个语境中，我觉得应该指的是船上载有重物，受这些 fat cargo 影响，船才会往一侧倾斜。

下文中作者用了很多拟人的表达，如 pinched (If someone's face is pinched, it looks thin and pale, usually because they are ill or old), waist，故这里将 form 拟人化，译为体形，凸显作者生动的表达。

王：如果拟人化，不妨再彻底一下，干脆把引号去掉。另外，这个"啤酒肚"处理得确实很生动，但是如果处理成"啤酒肚"，原文的 Buddha 意象是否流失了？虽然"弥勒肚"和"啤酒肚"这两种译法在帮助读者形成意象的作用上基本一致，但思来想去，我还是改成了"弥勒肚"，以便更贴近原文。另外，如你的查证所示，啤酒肚多为 beer stomach。

> **改译 1**：它的体形倒是讨喜，两头窄，腰身粗，跟装满了货物的贡多拉或维京船似的，又像是弯弯新月上长了个弥勒肚。（王）

对于文化意象，同学们有以下几种处理方式：

> **同学译文 1**：但它的形状还挺讨人喜欢，两头尖、中间胖，就像艘头尾窄、货仓宽的贡多拉或维京船，又像一轮新月，月牙中部隆起，如同佛陀的肚皮。
>
> **同学译文 2**：不过它的形状倒是讨喜：两头窄，中间宽，像一艘威尼斯共渡乐或维京海盗船，船身不堪货物重负，朝一侧倾斜……
>
> **同学译文 3**：不过形状还蛮可爱的，两头尖中间鼓，像载满货物的扁舟和海盗船，因为太重向一边倾斜；也像一轮新月，鼓着弥勒佛的大肚子。

这几种译法不是"异化"，就是"归化"，各有其道理。比如李骏达同学认为：

- 贡多拉（意大利语：Gondola），又译刚朵拉、共渡乐，是意大利威尼斯特有的和最具代表性的传统划船，船身全漆黑色，由一船夫站在船尾划动。

https://zh.wikipedia.org/wiki/%E8%B4%A1%E5%A4%9A%E6%8B%89

- 冰心曾经把gondola翻译成"共渡乐",相当有诗意,而且"渡"字也提示了gondola的功能,可谓是形和、意合兼具。不过呢,平心而论,初看这个译法要理解到"gondola"的含义还是有点困难的,所以译者在"共渡乐"前添加了"威尼斯"这一解释性成分,一说"威尼斯"就很容易想到水上漂着的弯弯的小船了。

冰心《再寄小读者》通讯六

- 亲爱的小朋友:

  四月十二日,我们在微雨中到达意大利东海岸的威尼斯。

  威尼斯是世界闻名的水上城市,常有人把它比作中国的苏州。但是苏州基本上是陆地上的城市,不过城里有许多河道和桥梁。威尼斯却是由一百多个小岛组成的,一条较宽的曲折的水道,就算是大街,其余许许多多纵横交织的小水道,就算是小巷。三四百座大大小小的桥,将这些小岛上的一簇一簇的楼屋,穿连了起来。这里没有车马,只有往来如织的大小汽艇,代替了公共汽车和小卧车;此外还有黑色的、两端翘起、轻巧可爱的小游船,**叫做Ｇｏｎｄｏｌａ,译作"共渡乐"**,也还可以谐音会意。

1900—1999

李军同学对 belly of a Buddha 采取不译的策略:

考虑到受众可能是信仰不同宗教的群体,因此为了避免产生不必要的麻烦,此处译者选择了去象化的处理方式。

处理方式:但是,锡布利的形状很有趣,两头窄中间宽,看起来就像是贡多拉或是维京船,满载货物;又像是一轮新月,大腹便便。

采取哪一种方式都有道理。重要的是具备跨文化沟通的意识,想办法帮助读者克服文化障碍,达到顺利沟通的目的。

李:"宽"和"窄"相对,是一个平面概念,而南瓜是立体概念,所以用宽窄不妥当。在谷歌中查证可知,pinched at both ends 是两头尖的意思。如图:

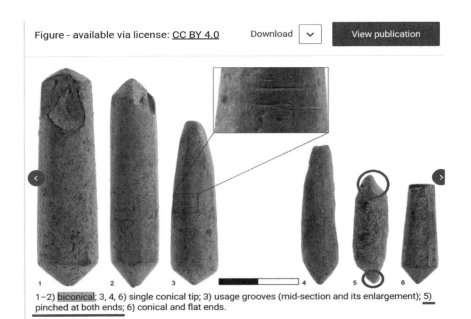

> **改译 2**：体形倒是讨人喜欢：两头尖，中间鼓，跟装满了货物的贡多拉或维京船似的，又像是弯弯新月上长的佛陀肚。（李）

王：李老师认为弯弯新月本来就有个大肚子，即弯月的外围。这个问题我跟佳宁老师交流了一下，我们认为：

1) 从原文结构看，这两部分前后修饰位置是一致的。Listing under a fat cargo 是为了说明船上载满了货物，不是表伴随；而后半部分也是说新月上长了个肚子，不是新月本身有肚子。
2) 从形状上看。西不利瓜是立体图形。佳宁老师认为，新月是二维图形，里侧加上大肚子，才和瓜的形状类似。
3) 另外，这里应该不能处理成"佛陀肚"，因为不是所有的佛都是大肚子的。为了避免宗教文化等不必要的麻烦，建议处理为大肚子。

综上，我还是坚持新月上长了一个大肚子的解释。

费：弯弯新月挺着弥勒肚。

李：恐怕讨论难以形成共识，但这不妨碍翻译。费晨的这个译法，有一定的模糊性，怎么解释都可以。

建议译法： 它的体形倒是讨人喜欢：两头尖，中间鼓，跟装满了货物的贡多拉或维京船似的，又像是弯弯新月挺着弥勒肚。（费）

19

原文： Where did this thing, this great quantity of squash flesh, come from? The earth, we say, but not really; there's no less earth here now than there was in May when I planted it; none's been used up in its making.

原译： 这么多南瓜果肉到底从何而来？从土地中来？恐怕不是。比起五月种瓜的时候，这里的土壤并没有减少，在这个过程中，没有任何东西被耗尽。（彭）

改译： 这瓜怎么长这么大？因为土壤肥沃？恐怕不是。比起五月种瓜的时候，这里的土量既没减少，又没消耗什么资源。（王）

李：none 是指 none of the earth，不是其他资源或物质。原文分号前后是同义反复，不是指两种物质的消耗。

建议译法： 这一大坨子南瓜肉从哪里来？从土里来？恐怕也不尽然。比起五月播种的时候，这里的土量没有减少；长南瓜没有用什么土。（李）

20

原文： By all rights creating something this fat should require so great an expense of matter that you'd expect to find Sibley squashes perched on the lips of fresh craters. That they're not, it seems to me, should be counted something of a miracle.

彭：根据对原文的查证，"by all rights" is used to describe what should happen if things are done fairly or correctly，结合上下文语境，这里译为"按理说"。

create 本该译为"创造"，但在上下文的这个语境中，"创造"感觉有些蹩脚，故改为"长出"。

> **原译：** 按理说，长出这么大的瓜应该需要巨大代价，你可能期待在新形成的火山坑边上发现西布利瓜。但它们确实不在火山坑边上，对我来说，这应该算是奇迹。（彭）
>
> **改译 1：** 按理说，长出来个这么大的瓜应该代价不小，怎么说也该长在土壤肥沃的新火山坑边才对。但它确实不在火山坑边上，在我看来，简直是个奇迹。（王）

李：火山口的土地应该非常肥沃。资料称"火山喷发物和熔岩风化物富含磷、钾等营养物质，土壤极为肥沃，宜于林木生长"，因此这么理解有道理。

王：我看了几十份同学的译文，对这句话的理解有两派意见：

> **同学译文 1：** 按理来说，长出这么大的东西应该需要汲取很多养分，有人还觉得西伯力南瓜长出来之后周围的土地都会凹陷下去。
>
> **同学译文 2：** 按理说，这么大的南瓜应该耗费大量养料，长在新的火山口边上才合理。
>
> **目前的参考译文：** 按理说，长出来个这么大的东西应该消耗的物质不少，怎么说也该长在肥沃的新火山口才对。

最开始，我的理解与同学 2 类似，就是要从土壤中汲取很多养分，因此长在土壤肥沃的火山口才是合理的。但是，在看了很多第一种同学译文的分析以后，我觉得这种理解不对，原因有三点：

1. 从 perched 这个词上来看，应该指"砸落感"，强调 to be in a position of something：

English: Aerial view of the perched lava lake in Puù `Ō `ō crater. Small fluctuations in the lava lake level lead to frequent overflows. These serve to build the levee around the lake even higher, amplifying the perched appearance.

2. fresh crater：如果在谷歌图片上搜索 fresh crater，一般出现的并不是刚喷发的火山坑，而是一些陨石坑。虽然很多同学都查到，火山爆发后的土壤肥沃，但是这个材料中也显示，这种肥沃的土壤是随着时间推移（第一行）形成的，而非刚爆发的火山就有肥沃土壤。

> 火山爆发后下陷形成大坑，随着时间的推移，坑口内部分岩石风化成土，火山灰成了树木的极好养料，在火山口陡直幽深的环境中，长成了郁郁葱葱的参天大树，时间的更迭化作生生不息的生命轮回，谁也不曾知道，在一百万年时间的隧道中，这里的一草一木发生过怎样的故事，如今，这片地下森林犹如宝库一般呈现在世人的眼前，绿波滚滚，物种繁多。这里有红松、黄花松、鱼鳞松、臭松、落叶松等针阔叶混交林。

这个问题我跟爱苏老师、佳宁老师讨论了一下，爱苏老师觉得歧义出现在这个 fresh 上，也就是说，两派同学的分歧可能是对 fresh 的理解不同。对此，我查了一些（爆发后的）火山的图片，确实是光秃秃的，没有什么植被。

3. 从语篇衔接的角度看，我最终认为，土壤是否肥沃不等于土量的增减。我开始百思不得其解，但后来我结合上下文，发现作者一直在说土量没有减少：

> 原文：Where did this thing, this great quantity of squash flesh, come from? The earth, we say, but not really; there's no less earth here now than there was in May when I planted it; none's been used up in its making. <u>By all rights creating something this fat should require so great an expense of matter that you'd expect to find Sibley squashes perched on the lips of fresh craters.</u> That they're not, it seems to me, should be counted something of a miracle.
>
> 原译：按理说，长出来个这么大的东西应该消耗的物质不少，怎么说也该长在肥沃的新火山口才对。

从语篇衔接和连贯的角度看，我觉得这里我想多了：并不是土壤是否富含微量元素、是否肥沃的问题，作者在文中就是说南瓜很大，需要吸收很多物质，吸收完了，这个地方应该留下个坑才对。

另外，crater 也并不一定指火山，我看了国家地理杂志的解释，crater 分为 impact crater、explosion crater 和 volcanic crater。这里要强调的并非火山坑，而是这个瓜 suck up all the soil nutrients，以至于这个地方出

现了个大坑。

因此，我建议进一步修改参考译文。

> **改译 1**：按理说，长这么大个东西，应该消耗不少，怎么说也该耗尽周围土壤，留下一个深坑才对。（王）

李：你的分析很有道理。我完全赞同。我当初想都没想，就相信了原来的译法。可见先入为主（火山灰营养丰富）危害有多大！原文作者的逻辑主线确实是物质数量的减少，与土壤肥力没有关系。请在课堂上表扬查对的同学，提醒同学老师也会出错。但改译 1 中的"周围"不对，容后再改。

李：关于 perch，你说的"砸落感"我不太理解。以下是 perch 的含义：

```
Random House Webster's Unabridged Dictionary

perch¹
  —perchable, adj.
  /perrch/, n.
    1. a pole or rod, usually horizontal, serving as a roost for birds.
    2. any place or object, as a sill, fence, branch, or twig, for a bird, animal, or person to alight or rest upon.
    3. a high or elevated position, resting place, or the like.
    4. a small, elevated seat for the driver of any of certain vehicles.
    5. a pole connecting the fore and hind running parts of a spring carriage or other vehicle.
    6. a post set up as a navigational aid on a navigational hazard or on a buoy.
    7. Brit.
        a. a linear or square rod.
        b. a measure of volume for stone, about 24 cubic feet (0.7 cubic meters).
    8. Textiles. an apparatus consisting of two vertical posts and a horizontal roller, used for inspecting cloth after it leaves the loom.
    9. Obs. any pole, rod, or the like.
  v.i.
    10. to alight or rest upon a perch.
    11. to settle or rest in some elevated position, as if on a perch.
  v.t.
    12. to set or place on or as if on a perch.
    13. to inspect (cloth) for defects and blemishes after it has been taken from the loom and placed upon a perch.
  [1250-1300; ME perche < OF < L pertica pole, staff, measuring rod]

perch²
  /perrch/, n., pl. (esp. collectively) perch, (esp. referring to two or more kinds or species) perches.
    1. any spiny-finned, freshwater food fish of the genus Perca, as P. flavescens (yellow perch), of the U.S., or P. fluviatilis, of Europe.
    2. any of various other related, spiny-finned fishes.
    3. any of several embiotocid fishes, as Hysterocarpus traski (tule perch) of California.
  [1350-1400; ME perche < MF < L perca < Gk pérkē]

Roget's II: The New Thesaurus 英语同义词词典
```

总结 perch 的意思，就是供（鸟类等）栖息的横木、枝杈、窗台、篱笆；凸起的位置。你查的资料中有句话：These serve to build the levee（堤岸）around the lake even higher, amplifying the perched appearance. 其中的

perched appearance,就是指高出地面的台地。

所以,文中说南瓜躺在坑边上(不是坑里面),和 perch 的本义还是相通的:坑的边缘是相对较高的台地,南瓜躺在旁边就像小鸟站在树枝或窗台上。

王:思考了很久,并请教了爱苏老师,终于理出了头绪。perch 本身是像小鸟栖于枝头一样。作者此处用 perch 形容南瓜,也是夸张、幽默的写法。请看下图:

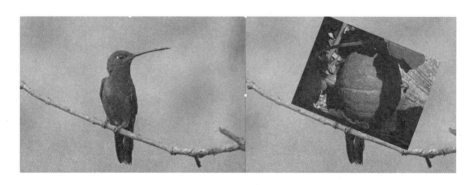

其次,原来理解的"砸落感"确实不对。想了很久,症结在于自己不知道南瓜是怎么长的(可怜的城里人)。这里引用李老师的解答:

"你仔细想想:南瓜本身不会吸养料,要靠南瓜秧的根系来吸。根系分布的范围很广,但很可能达不到长南瓜的那个地方(瓜藤很长)。而且越靠近主根,根系越发达,吸收的能力越强。

假如真的是靠吸收地里的物质长成瓜，那么这个坑，就是以南瓜主根为中心的一个平缓的大坑。南瓜长在爬到远处的瓜秧上，位置一定是坑的边缘（内侧或外侧，取决于根系是否到达南瓜所在处），而不是卧在坑的中央。但上述情况是不可能发生的，这是作者在开玩笑。作者完全清楚，南瓜（通过根）吸收的主要是水分，不是土里的物质。"

根据李老师的解释，假如瓜果生长真的要留下坑，这个坑应该是在植株主根周围，而不是南瓜周围。因此，更符合作者描述的情景的不是第1个圆圈的位置，而是第2个，这也是 perch 的本义。

课后有同学提出，圈1的情况有没有可能？答案是两种情况均无可能。但如果把作者的玩笑当真，那么苹果树就属于第一种情况：结那么多苹果，那要吸收多少物质？不下沉才怪，最后长在大坑里！

总之，我没有看过南瓜地，如果大家能亲自到地里走走，种种菜，再来翻译这段可能会有更深的体会。这也说明，笔译不是孤立的文字工作，译者也要对实际生活有切身体会才行。

另一方面，译者有的时候想得太多，思想反倒会脱轨。作者可能没有考虑那么多，只是本能地觉得，这么大个南瓜，应该把土地吸出个坑才对。

> **改译 2**：按理说，长出这么大的东西应该消耗不少物质，在旁边留下一个坑才对，但事实并非如此。这，在我看来，应该算作奇迹。（李）

李:"这"字后面加一个逗号,是为了强调。

句子不论长短,在主语需要强调时,其后加逗号同谓语分隔。例如:

(6)青,取之于蓝,而青于蓝;冰,水为之,而寒于水。(荀况《劝学》)

(7)她,教了三十年的书,绝不能看着一个人才被埋没。(李心田《永不忘记》)

http://old.pep.com.cn/xiaoyu/jiaoshi/study/jszy/bdfhyf/dh/201012/P020101202732677301026.pdf

第六单元　思辨能力

Exercise 6　Get Out of My Dreams and Into My [Self-Driving] Car

翻译情景

本单元摘自 2017 年有关无人驾驶车的一份研究报告（*The Race to 2021: The State of Autonomous Vehicles and a "Who's Who" of Industry Drivers*，可在网上检索到），共 363 词。假定你受雇于国内汽车行业客户，需要将报告翻译为中文。

专项能力

本单元旨在训练译员的逻辑思维能力。逻辑思维能力指的是分析、联系、总结、批判、论证的能力。学生在学习翻译时，在熟悉了基本的翻译技巧以后，往往会陷入一个翻译误区，在翻译时脱离全局意识，去单一地找单词和句法上的直接对应关系。这在翻译学家丹尼尔·吉尔（Daniel Gile）看来，就是忽视了理解过程的重要作用，没有给逻辑分析留有足够空间（Daniel Gile, 2011 : 93）[1]。

1　Daniel, Gile. 口笔译训练的基本概念与模型 [M]. 上海：上海外语教育出版社, 2011.

对吉尔的这种观点，我们表示同意。我们还认为，逻辑思维贯穿理解、表达、变通的各个环节。通过逻辑思维，可以发现作者论证的思路，理顺原文的逻辑，纠正原文的逻辑瑕疵；确保表达的一致性和连贯性；还可以帮助作出变通取舍的决定。

逻辑思维对人的分辨能力、表达能力、学习能力和创新能力起到决定作用，是译员应当具备的基本能力。翻译训练是提高逻辑思维能力的有效手段，所以，翻译教育也是一种通识教育。

本次练习的重点，是发现原文存在的逻辑瑕疵，并在译文中予以修复。以中文为母语的译者，往往盲目崇拜英文，不敢对英文质量提出质疑。但普通的英文作者与中文作者一样，写作水平不一定很高，许多文字经不起译者推敲，翻译之前需要先行编辑。这篇训练旨在让翻译学习者和教育工作者认识解到，原文往往存在瑕疵，通过严密的逻辑思维就可以发现。译者要敢于质疑，必要时对原文的表述和逻辑进行解构与重建。当然，从职业伦理的角度来看，文责自负，译者不应该对作者的错误负责，但当原文行文不畅、逻辑不通时，直译、死译不仅对读者不公，也无法实现作者的意图。因此，在翻译过程中，译者时刻要根据翻译情景，作出符合各方利益的决定。

训练难点

这篇文章的难点是如何以开放、客观、批判的视角看待原文，判断原文的表达和逻辑问题，并在此基础上以尊重作者、读者以及其他利益相关方的方式，产出符合逻辑的译文。

训练方式

这篇文章的语言质量整体欠佳、逻辑问题层出，是训练逻辑思维的优质素材。本单元分为原文、翻译提示、参考译文、译者注四部分。请先尝试自己独立翻译，然后再参看翻译提示，并自行修改、润色，形成第二稿。之后，再看参考译文和译者注。

原文[1]

Get Out of My Dreams and Into My [Self-Driving] Car[2]

...

Self-driving cars have always stoked our imaginations. From movies, to cartoons, to advertisements, autonomous vehicles portray a life only possible in science fiction or a dream to be realized off in the distant future[3]. Though our "Jetsons" or "Minority Report"[4] moment is still forthcoming, autonomous capabilities are arriving in increments. With each new invention, science fiction is transformed into reality, one chapter at a time. Today, aspects of self-driving cars are making their way into new models, introducing intelligent, driver-assisted features that are slowly bridging the gap between semi- and fully autonomous abilities. This is years in the making of course.

...

State of Autonomous Vehicles: Executive Summary

(p.2)

- Semi-autonomous vehicles are the stepping stone to fully autonomous vehicles, with most car manufacturers and technology companies taking the lead of Tesla[5] and offering features such as self-parking, adaptive cruise control, emergency braking, and semi-hands off driving within highway/interstate conditions. Semi-autonomous features help consumers become comfortable with the idea of robots taking the wheel.

- In addition to data science, social science is also becoming prevalent in autonomous development as companies such as Nissan and Audi take an anthropological approach to teach self-driving cars to act more human in their control and on-road actions (e.g. honking, signaling other people or vehicles, moving closer to lane marketing[6] before switching lanes).

- With the latest round of updates from CES[7], there is more focus on intelligent vehicles (e.g. Toyota, AutoLiv, Ford's concept vision video)[8]. These self-driving cars can think on their own, communicate with other vehicles (V2V) through deep learning and AI. This means that all software that exists may run into compatibility issues when asked to communicate with other systems within a vehicle.[9] This is similar to the interoperability conundrum the industry witnessed around IoT[10]. However, when solved for, V2V opportunities abound in improving traffic experience, reducing accidents, and new value-added in-car design components[11].

• Mapping software has emerged as its own category among technology providers in the autonomous space, as 3D terrain mapping is a critical component to the effectiveness and safety of self-driving cars as they navigate their environments.

翻译提示

1 宏观思维

请大家针对原文和译文,分别回答 Who is talking to whom? About what? When, where and why? And how? 然后再开始翻译。

2 跨文化沟通意识

这句话有没有什么典故?

3 逻辑严谨性

这句话是否严谨?如果不严谨,译文是否可以适当调整?如何让译文逻辑更连贯?

4 逻辑连贯性 / 跨文化沟通意识

这句话有两处需要慎重考虑:

1)作者为何要提到这两部作品?这些作品与自动驾驶车有什么关系?

2)从文化沟通的角度看,中文读者可能不熟悉这两部影视作品,翻译时如何处理，使读者抓住上下文的逻辑？

5 **逻辑重建/批判思维**

这句话要重点理解 taking the lead of，包括是否存在 take the lead of 这一搭配。从篇章逻辑来看，到底是谁领先于谁？如果原文有问题，是否考虑打破原文结构和意思，重新构建原文逻辑？

6 **逻辑重建/批判思维**

如果看不懂，可以用 lane 或 marketing 搜索整个报告，获得灵感，看看原文是否存在问题，译者需要采取什么策略。

7 **查证能力**

这个缩写可能对应很多机构。请先查查报告本身是否有线索；如果有，按照线索在网上做进一步调查。

8 **逻辑主语**

这句话需要弄清楚是谁的 focus，普通百姓还是汽车厂。难道是 CES 发现观看这三家视频的人多了，所以认为自动汽车受到的关注多了？需要查看 CES 的相关报道，观看 Youtube 相关视频。

9 **理解**

自动驾驶涉及车与车之间的关系。这里指的是不同车辆之间各系统相互沟通时，可能出现软件兼容问题，还是一个车辆内部系统出现的软件兼容问题？译者应该忠实于作者的文字，还是作者的意图，抑或是客观事实？

10 **指代关系**

按照逻辑，这个 industry 应当是指哪个行业？汽车行业还是物联网行业？如何确定？翻译中如何取舍？

11 **原文错误**

这个句子有语法问题：solved 是 dangling modifier，它的逻辑主语实际上是前文隔一句的 issues，加 for 似乎没有道理。无论如何，意思是清楚的。译文也需要故意模仿原文的语言瑕疵吗？

参考译文

自动驾驶汽车：从梦想到现实[1]

......

自动驾驶汽车[2]一直在激发着我们的想象力。电影、卡通、广告中描绘的自动汽车，只有在科幻小说中才可能出现，或者说仅仅是遥远的未来才能实现的梦想。[3]尽管科幻动画片《杰森一家》或科幻电影《少数派报告》描绘的时代尚未到来，但自动驾驶的功能正在逐步实现。[4]每一项新发明，都在一步步地把科幻小说变为现实。[5]如今的新车型都或多或少具备自动驾驶功能，比如智能化和驾驶员辅助功能。随着智能化特征增加，半自动功能逐渐向全自动功能转变。[6]当然，这个进程还需要很多年。[7]

自动驾驶汽车现状：行政摘要[8]

- 半自动是走向全自动的过渡。在特斯拉（Tesla）[9]的引领下，[10]多数汽车制造商和科技公司开始推出新功能，如自动泊车、自适应巡航控制、紧急制动以及公路行驶状态[11]下的半"脱手"[12]驾驶功能。[13]半自动驾驶功能可以让消费者逐渐接受机器人驾车的理念。[14]

- 除了数据科学，社会科学也越来越多地应用于自动化进程。日产、奥迪等公司就采用人类学方法，教会自动驾驶汽车以更人性化的方式控制车辆和执行路上动作（例如：鸣笛、向行人或车辆打灯，在变道前先靠近车道线等）。[15]

- 消费电子展（CES[16]）的最新消息显示，汽车制造商更加关注智能汽车的发展（见丰田、美安和福特等的概念车视频）。[17]这些自动驾驶汽车能够独立思考，并通过深度学习和人工智能，[18]与其他汽车交流（即V2V通信）[19]。这意味着不同车辆之间各系统相互沟通时，可能出现软件兼容问题，这和物联网发展过程中面临的互操作难题一样。[20]但是，只要解决这个问题，在改善交通体验、减少事故、提升车内设计组件价值方面，V2V通信将大有可为。[21]

- 在自动驾驶技术中，测绘软件"独树一帜"，因为三维地形测绘对自动驾驶汽车导航的效果和安全至关重要。[22]

译者注

1

> **原文**：Get Out of My Dreams and Into My [Self-Driving] Car
> **原译**：别做梦了，快上（自动驾驶）车吧。（王文煌）
> **改译**：自动驾驶汽车：从梦想到现实。（王文煌）

王文煌：在初次翻译时，本来想紧跟原文的句式结构翻译成"别做梦了，快上（自动驾驶）车吧"，但是总感觉缺了一层意思，没有办法体现自动驾驶汽车正慢慢地从幻想变为现实的这个过程，所以最后的办法是，打破原文的句式结构来处理，希望能照顾到原句各个层面的意思，翻译成："自动驾驶汽车：从梦想到现实"。

王苏阳：经查证，这句话的灵感可能源于一首歌，名为：Get Outta My Dreams, Get into My Car，是英国著名歌手 Billy Ocean 的歌。

查找歌词，其中有一句话 get outta my mind, get into my life 与 get outta my dreams, get into my car 对应。歌手 Billy Ocean 是希望梦想中的女伴成为现实。结合作者这里的意思，应该是让梦想中的无人车成为现实：

[Chorus:]

Get outta my dreams

Get in to my car

Get outta my dreams

Get in the back seat baby

Get in to my car

> Beep beep, yeah
> Get outta my mind
> Get into my life
> Ooh
> Oh I said hey (hey) you (you)
> Get in to my car

王：我们要考虑这层文化背景含义是否需要翻译出来。如果完全脱离原文结构，这层意思可能就丧失了。

煌：这个文化概念翻译出来的话，是否能为中文读者所接受，达到和英文读者阅读相同的效果？中文读者会不会因为文化差异感知不到这一层意思（因为这些"梗"对我们来说非常陌生）？翻出来可能会让读者一头雾水。好难解决。

李：首先，此处的意思并非原译"别做梦了，快上车吧"。根据你们的调查，是演唱者请自己的梦中情人从梦中走出来，上车跟他走（"梦中情人，出来上车"）。如果要反映原来的意思，可以译为"梦中情人，出来上 [自动驾驶] 车"。但中国人对这首歌不一定熟悉，尤其是这首歌可能并无中文版本。因此，即使翻译出来，读者也难以理解。鉴于这个典故对于全文并不重要，可以不保留文化内涵。现在的处理方式我觉得就不错，建议维持。

建议译法：自动驾驶汽车：从梦想到现实（王文煌）

2

原文: self-driving car
原译: 自动驾驶汽车

煌：不确定如何处理 autonomous car，以及是否需要和 self-driving car 的译法区分，所以进行查证。经查，autonomous car, self-driving car 和 driverless car 的意思相同，但是此处考虑到是报告，所以还是在不妨碍通顺表达的前提下，尽量照顾字面。查找平行文本，维基百科上把 self-driving car 处理成

"电脑驾驶汽车",把 autonomous car 处理成"自动驾驶汽车"。

自动驾驶汽车 [编辑]

维基百科,自由的百科全书

自动驾驶汽车,又称**无人驾驶汽车**、**电脑驾驶汽车**或**轮式移动机器人**,为一种运输动力的无人地面载具。作为自动化载具,自动驾驶汽车不需要人类操作即能感测其环境及导航。完全的自动驾驶汽车仍未全面商用化,大多数均为原型机及展示系统,部分可靠技术才下放至量产车型,逐渐成为现实。

自动驾驶汽车能以雷达、光学雷达、GPS及电脑视觉等技术感测其环境[1][2]。先进的控制系统能将感测资料转换成适当的导航道路,以及障碍与相关标志。根据定义,自动驾驶汽车能透过感测输入的资料,更新其地图资讯,让交通工具可以持续追踪其位置。

A **self-driving car**, also known as a **robot car**, **autonomous car**, or **driverless car**,[1][2] is a vehicle that is capable of sensing its environment and moving with little or no human input.[3]

Autonomous cars combine a variety of sensors to perceive their surroundings, such as radar, computer vision, Lidar, sonar, GPS, odometry and inertial measurement units. Advanced control systems interpret sensory information to identify appropriate navigation paths, as well as obstacles and relevant signage.[4][5]

  但是,不确定维基百科的说法是否准确,所以在谷歌上搜索 the difference between autonomous and self-driving cars,结果发现 Economist 上有一篇文章,专门讲二者的区别。文章提到,虽然二者在报纸杂志上经常被混用,但是对于汽车制造商来说,有本质区别。文章中说明,autonomous car 是自动驾驶汽车,目前市面上也普遍存在,仅仅在特定环境下接管司机工作,进行自动驾驶。而 self-driving car "更上一层楼",应该翻译为"无人车"。根据文章第六页的 Five levels of autonomous driving,可以进一步确定 autonomous 和 self-driving 以及 fully autonomous 还是有所区别的。

  The end point of these developments is routinely referred to as self-driving or autonomous cars. The two terms are used interchangeably (even by this newspaper). But carmakers, including the bosses of Volvo and Renault Nissan, are keen to draw a distinction between the two, and with good reasons of self-interest.

  Autonomous cars will look like the vehicles we drive today, according to carmakers, with forward facing seats and a steering wheel. These cars will take over from the driver under certain circumstances. Some elements of autonomy are already available. Self-parking, adaptive cruise control—which adjusts speed to keep a safe distance from cars ahead—and automated braking are available on quite modest machines. In the near future autonomous vehicles might take over driving completely in heavy traffic or on motorways.

Self-driving cars are a stage further on. The steering wheel will disappear completely and the vehicle will do all the driving using the same system of sensors, radar and GPS mapping that autonomous vehicles employ. While some personal cars will remain, a fleet of shared vehicles will likely fill the streets of towns and cities. Call up a car with a mobile device, key in the destination and the vehicle will do all the work.

https://www.economist.com/blogs/economist-explains/2015/07/economist-explains】

李：这段话（Self-driving cars have always stoked our imaginations. From movies, to cartoons, to advertisements, autonomous vehicles portray…）中两种说法显然没区分，否则逻辑上不连贯。既然没有区分，全篇肯定也不区分，否则概念体系就乱了。因此，翻译的时候，不必区分，最好是自始至终使用同一概念，如：自动汽车或自动驾驶汽车。汉语中不怕重复使用同样的说法；不断变换说法反而引起逻辑混乱。

不做区分，即使翻译到下表，也不会产生混乱：

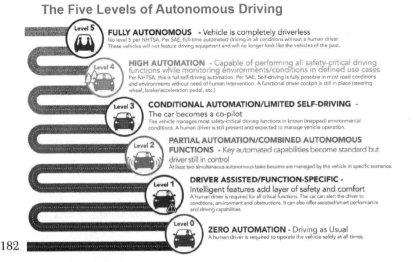

建议译法： 自动驾驶汽车（李）

3

原文： Self-driving cars have always stoked our imaginations. From movies, to cartoons, to advertisements, autonomous vehicles portray a life only possible in science fiction or a dream to be realized off in the distant future.

原译： 自动驾驶汽车总能激起诸多想象。从电影、卡通到商业广告，自动驾驶汽车展现了一种只存在于科幻小说中的生活，一种在遥远的未来才能实现的幻梦。（煌）

王： 我觉得原译还是没有完全脱离英文原文的结构。仔细分析一下中文文法，也似乎有语病，说自动驾驶汽车（主语）展现（谓语）某种生活或者幻梦，也有一点牵强。 我想这句话的意思应该是自动驾驶车只存在于科幻小说，或者遥远的未来。

改译 1： 自动驾驶汽车总能激发我们的想象。无论电影、卡通还是广告中，自动驾驶汽车描述了在科幻小说中才能存在的生活，或者在遥远的未来才能实现的梦。（王）

煌： 是否可以把 portray 省略掉？这样在中文里就完全说通了，而且和英文的意思也一样。

改译 2： 自动驾驶汽车一直在激发我们的想像。无论在电影、卡通，还是广告里，无人驾驶车都只存在于科幻小说描绘的生活中，是一个在遥远未来才能实现的梦。（煌）

王： 其实，我觉得还有一个地方很奇怪：前面的电影、卡通、广告和这个句子的关系是什么？为什么要在三个本来就是虚构成分居多的传媒介质里面再说科幻小说？而且前一句就说了 imagination，后文应该是对 imagination 的解释。可能作者在说这句话的时候并没有很严谨。又读了一下原文。我觉得我们不应该纠结于前面三个传媒介质与后面科幻小说的关系。我想作者本意只是想说自动驾驶汽车展现的生活是不真实的、虚构的，或者是在遥远的未来才能实现的梦。

李：讨论中的问题也是我的疑问。原文似乎不严谨。科技文章不像联合国文件那样咬文嚼字，翻译时灵活性大一些。可以译为：电影、卡通、广告中描绘的自动汽车，只有在科幻小说中才可能出现，或者说仅仅是遥远的未来才能实现的梦想。

李：这样的修改与原文主语保持一致，也更加对称。

王：从这句话的处理来看，当原文语言逻辑不严谨时，译者就需要对原文做适当的编辑加工，力求让译文逻辑通顺、文法通顺，而不拘泥于原文的不当表达。译者忠实的是原文的意思，不是文字。

建议译法：自动驾驶汽车一直在激发着我们的想象。电影、卡通、广告中描绘的自动汽车，只有在科幻小说中才可能出现，或者说仅仅是遥远的未来才能实现的梦想。（李）

4

原文：Though our "Jetsons" or "Minority Report" moment is still forthcoming, autonomous capabilities are arriving in increments.
原译：《杰森一家》或《少数派报告》中展现的高科技未来要走入现实还尚需时日，但自动驾驶已经离我们越来越近。（煌）

王文煌：在维基百科上查询得知，*The Jetsons* 是一部关于未来世界的科幻类动画片，其中提及 robotic contraptions（机器人装置）。这样 our Jetsons is forthcoming 就与上下文联系上了：尽管机器人时代尚未来临，但已经在逐步实现。

The Jetsons is an American animated sitcom produced by Hanna-Barbera, originally airing in primetime from September 23, 1962, to March 17, 1963, then later in syndication, with new episodes in 1985 to 1987 as part of The Funtastic World of Hanna-Barbera block. It was Hanna-Barbera's Space Age counterpart to The Flintstones.

While the Flintstones live in a world with machines powered by birds and dinosaurs, the Jetsons live in a world with elaborate robotic contraptions［奇妙的装置］, aliens, holograms, and whimsical inventions……

https://en.wikipedia.org/wiki/The_Jetsons

Minority Report 同样是一部科幻电影，展现了一个能够预知和预防犯罪发生的未来世界：

Minority Report is a 2002 American science fiction film directed by Steven Spielberg and loosely based on the short story of the same name by Philip K. Dick. It is set primarily in Washington, D.C., and Northern Virginia in the year 2054, where "PreCrime", a specialized police department, apprehends criminals based on foreknowledge provided by three psychics called "precogs".

https://en.wikipedia.org/wiki/Minority_Report_(film)

煌：这句话我在写初稿的时候很纠结，中文读者其实并不熟悉这两个影视作品，在阅读的时候可能达不到英文读者读原文那种效果，是否应该对文本内容稍做解释？

李：适当解释有助于读者理解，你实际上已经做了一些解释。顺便说一下，因为不是重要文件，不必使用注释的形式来解释，直接纳入译文即可。

王：起初不理解这里 arriving in increments 的意思是什么。先查找 increment 的含义：

increment
noun [C] ● US 🔊 UK 🔊 /ˈɪŋ.krə.mənt/

⭐ **one of a series of increases:**
  You will receive annual **salary/pay** increments every September.

理解单词的定义后，做联想性查证，根据报告原文第 7 页中的 The Five Levels of Autonomous Driving 初步判断作者讲的应该是无人车驾驶技术在不断更新发展的状态。

> **改译 2**：尽管我们还没有来到科幻动画片《杰森一家》或科幻电影《少数派报告》中描绘的时代，但自动驾驶的功能正在逐步实现。（李、王）

贾明慧：原文中没有 we，译文也没看出来添加"我们"的必要。

> **建议译法**：尽管科幻动画片《杰森一家》或科幻电影《少数派报告》描绘的时代尚未到来，但自动驾驶的功能正在逐步实现。（贾）

5

> **原文**：With each new invention, science fiction is transformed into reality, one chapter at a time.
> **原译**：相关发明出现的速度快不可当，每来一次就把科幻小说里整整一章的内容变成现实。（煌）
> **改译 1**：每当有新发现，科幻小说里的一章就会成真。（王）

王：原文不强调速度，也不强调"整章"。

> **改译 2**：每一个新的发明，都在把科幻小说变为现实，一次一个章节。（李）

贾：这里是否可以考虑灵活处理？"一次一个章节"放在句尾，有一种重心偏移的感觉，好像作者在强调每次只能是一个章节。原文其实只是说科技将科幻小说一步步变为现实，one chapter at a time 应该只是一种修辞手法，不一定非要放在句尾。

王：同意明慧的建议。

> **改译 3**：每一项新发明，都在一步步地把科幻小说变为现实。（贾、王）

李：这样修改也可以。但原文 one chapter at a time 之前有一个不寻常的逗号，显然是作者为了强调渐进性，所以"一次一个章节"放在后面也可以。

建议译法：每一项新发明，都在一步步地把科幻小说变为现实。（李）

6

原文：Today, aspects of self-driving cars are making their way into new models, introducing intelligent, driver-assisted features that are slowly bridging the gap between semi- and fully autonomous abilities.

原译：今天，自动驾驶汽车的方方面面成功地嵌入了各厂商的新车款中；引入功能如智能化和驾驶员辅助，正慢慢为半自动和全自动之间的鸿沟筑起桥梁。（煌）

王：爱苏老师认为，making their way 在这句话中表强调作用。这句话的意思是，如今很多车型都或多或少具备自动驾驶功能。这里以新车型做主语可能更符合汉语的表达习惯。我结合上下文，加上了"弥补差距"。我想，弥补差距，就是在逐渐实现想象中的无人车。原译分号前后关联性不强。

改译：如今，几乎所有新车型都或多或少具备自动驾驶功能，引入功能如智能化和驾驶员辅助，慢慢弥补半自动和全自动能力之间的差距。（冯爱苏、王苏阳）

贾：非常理解"几乎所有"存在的合理性，确实要考虑到不是所有新车型都具备自动驾驶功能。但这里原文没有讨论范围问题，只是用了 new models，我们是不是也可以模糊处理，减少限定词带来的负担和不必要的误会？

李：同意明慧的分析。苏阳加入"几乎所有"，可能是为了"配重"，因为主语"新车型"太短，压不住。另外，后半句只要意思正确，语言可以灵活一些，让逻辑更加通顺。

建议译法：如今的新车型都或多或少具备自动驾驶功能，比如智能化和驾驶员辅助功能。随着智能化特征增加，半自动功能逐渐向全自动功能转变。（李）

7

> 原文：This is years in the making of course.
> 原译：这还需要很多年。

王：我曾经考虑这个 this 到底指前文的谁。我问了冯爱苏老师，她觉得这里没有一个明确的主语，意思是想要实现这样的无人车，还需要很多年。

煌：我的考虑是，this 很难说清楚指代是谁，可以当成全篇的主题，也可以说是前面的"差距"。那么是否可以模糊化处理？

王：你说的有道理。因为原文也是在做总结，我这里就加入一个范畴词"进程"。

> 建议译法：当然，这个进程还需要很多年。（王）

李：this 就是指 bridging the gap between semi- and fully autonomous abilities。建议译法和前文衔接得很好。

8

> 原文：executive summary
> 原译：执行摘要（煌）

李：尽管不少人用"执行摘要"，我们还是尽量避免。"行政摘要"也不好，但稍微强一点。executive 的意思是行政人员、公司高管。这个摘要是写给领导看的。领导太忙，没时间看报告全文。这个摘要不同于 abstract（摘要）。前者相当详细，后者仅仅提供一个文章框架，甚至看不到结论。

维基百科谈两者的区别：

An executive summary, or management summary, is a short document or section of a document, produced for business purposes, that summarizes a longer report or proposal or a group of related reports in such a way that readers can rapidly become acquainted with a large body of material without having to read it all. It usually contains a brief statement of the problem or proposal covered in the major document(s), background information, concise analysis and main conclusions. It is intended as an aid to decision-making by managers and has been described as the most important part of a business plan.

An executive summary differs from an abstract in that an abstract will usually be shorter and is typically intended as an overview or orientation rather than being a condensed version of the full document. Abstracts are extensively used in academic research where the concept of the executive summary is not in common usage. "An abstract is a brief summarizing statement... read by parties who are trying to decide whether or not to read the main document", while "an executive summary, unlike an abstract, is a document in miniature that may be read in place of the longer document".

建议译法：行政摘要（李）

9

原文：Tesla

李：Tesla 的译法，我鼓励使用中文加注英文。但联合国文件翻译，通常不加注英文概念（仅仅是惯例，不一定合理）。

建议译法：特斯拉（Tesla）

10

原文：taking the lead of Tesla

谢芮：以下是我对原文 taking the lead of Tesla 的理解，还请老师们指正。我觉得这里指的是很多公司早于特斯拉就开发出了一些新的技术。

首先，Tesla 公司是 2003 年成立的。这是一个很年轻的公司，主营业务是新能源汽车，也就是电动汽车。我的感觉是，世界上有那么多的汽车公司，怎么可能会是由一个这么年轻的公司带领呢？其他老牌的汽车公司服气吗……

其次，从技术发展历史来看，我的感觉是 Tesla 的贡献并不是很突出。所以我觉得这里的 take the lead of 指的是很多公司"早于"Tesla，或者说"抢先一步"开发了这些技术。

王：非常感谢谢芮学长提供的说明和资料。这里我的理解还是 Tesla 在众多公司中起到引领作用。

首先从逻辑上分析，公司年轻与否不足以说明它的技术水平。也许 Tesla 不是最新开发出这些技术的，但是从目前的业界水平看，Tesla 应该还是起到引领作用。从逻辑上分析，如果这句话中作者不想强调 Tesla，而是说其他公司抢先于 Tesla，那么这里 Tesla 就多余了，所以反推作者还是要强调 Tesla。

从全文来看，作者引用了大量关于 Tesla 的文献，这是肯定 Tesla 在业界的技术水平。

从整个研究报告内的内容上看，Tesla 也有很多引领作用：

举例 1：GM will introduce Super Cruise in high-end Cadillac models in 2017, initially offering a Tesla-like autonomous experience that allows drivers to commute in a semi-hands off capacity.

举例 2：Similar to Tesla and Mercedes-Benz models, the Civic will feature advanced driver assistance systems (ADAS) which offers lane keeping and changing assistance, automatic braking, and adaptive cruise control.

举例 3：The prototype is said to follow Tesla's lead in that it: will include self-driving capabilities（这句话应该就很清楚说明了 Tesla 的引领地位了）。

李：我没看报告全文，但这句话似乎有毛病，应改为 with Tesla taking the lead。全句改为：Semi-autonomous vehicles are the stepping stone to fully autonomous vehicles. Many car manufacturers and technology companies offer features such as ...with Tesla taking the lead。查资料发现：Semi-autonomous vehicles are the stepping stone to fully autonomous vehicles. Most car manufacturers and technology companies *have taken Tesla's lead* and are offering features like self- parking, adaptive cruise control, emergency braking and semi-hands off driving in highway/interstate conditions. Semi-autonomous features help consumers become comfortable with the idea of robots taking the wheel. 资料意思很清楚，是别的公司学习特斯拉。原文似乎抄自这份参考资料，因此，我们应该按照参考资料明确表达的意思来翻译，即：多数厂商步特斯拉的后尘……根据你们所查资料，特斯拉也是引领企业。苏阳的理解正确。我怀疑 take the lead of 这个用法是否正确；但现在意思很清楚。

王：我没有查到 take the lead of 的用法。只有 take the lead：

take the lead idiom

Definition of *take the lead*

1 : to take a position that is ahead of others : go first
// You *take the lead* and we'll follow right behind you.

2 : to take the winning position in a race or competition
// Her car has taken the lead.
// Our team *took the lead* in the eighth inning.
—often used figuratively
// Their company has *taken the lead* in developing this new technology.

李：原文和参考资料中的 take the lead of 都应该改为 follow the lead of…：

follow someone's lead idiom

Definition of *follow someone's lead*

: to do the same thing that someone else has done
// He *followed her lead* and voted in favor of the proposal.

> **建议译法**：在特斯拉（Tesla）的引领下（李）

11

> **原文**：highway/interstate conditions

李：interstate 是指美国的州际公路，在中国语境下翻译出来无意义，可省略。也可以粗略地归化为"国道""高速公路"。但如果把 interstate 翻译为"高速公路"，就需要把 highway 翻译为"普通公路"，还不如把两个统一译为"公路"。

关于高速公路说法的一些资料，供参考：

A controlled-access highway ［出入管制公路］ is a type of highway which has been designed for high-speed vehicular traffic, with all traffic flow ingress- and egress-regulated. Common English terms are freeway (in Australia, South Africa, United States and Canada), motorway (in the United Kingdom, Pakistan, Ireland, New Zealand and parts of Australia) and expressway (parts of Canada, parts of the United States, and many Asian countries). Other similar terms include *Interstate* and parkway. Some of these may be limited-access highways, although this term can also refer to a class of highway with somewhat less isolation from other traffic.

建议译法：公路行驶状态。（李）

12

原文：semi-hands off driving

李：hands-off 只翻译为"自动"不形象。"脱手"是"自动"的意思，网上有这个说法。

王：我查了一下网上的说法，"脱手"的使用比较少。而且"脱手"还有"转手出让"的意思。我们是不是脱离原文结构，用"半自动"比较好？

李：英文很具体，中文"自动"比较泛。如果觉得"脱手"有别的意思，就加个引号：半"脱手"，引号中没有"半"。用"半自动"也没问题。

建议译法：半"脱手"（李）

13

原文：Semi-autonomous vehicles are the stepping stone to fully autonomous vehicles, with most car manufacturers and technology companies taking the lead of Tesla and offering features such as self-parking, adaptive cruise control, emergency braking, and semi-hands off driving within highway/interstate conditions.

原译：汽车要走向全自动，必须从半自动开始。在特斯拉（Tesla）的引领下，多数汽车制造商和科技公司正在提供诸如自动泊车、自适应巡航控制、紧急制动以及公路／州际条件下半自动驾驶的功能。（煌）

李：后半句前置定语过长。尽量避免前置定语过长，要构建开放的句子架构。另外，不要强调"必须"，是现在技术没达到，不能一步到位，不是必须分步走。如果意思明确，省略几个字没问题。

改译1：半自动是走向全自动的过渡阶段。在特斯拉（Tesla）的引领下，多数汽车制造商和科技公司正在提供新的功能，如自动泊车、自适应巡航控制、紧急制动以及公路行驶状态下的半脱手驾驶功能。（李）

贾：原文的 offering 虽然是进行时，但在句中语法结构属于分词做状语（主动式），而非真正表示进行时态，翻译成"正在"会不会误导学生？

改译2：半自动是走向全自动的过渡阶段。在特斯拉（Tesla）的引领下，多数汽车制造商和科技公司开始推出新功能，如自动泊车、自适应巡航控制、紧急制动以及公路行驶状态下的半"脱手"驾驶功能。（贾）

李：改得很好。还可以把"阶段"去掉。

建议译法：半自动是走向全自动的过渡。在特斯拉（Tesla）的引领下，多数汽车制造商和科技公司开始推出新功能，如自动泊车、自适应巡航控制、紧急制动以及公路行驶状态下的半"脱手"驾驶功能。（李）

14

> 原文：Semi-autonomous features help consumers become comfortable with the idea of robots taking the wheel.
>
> 原译：半自动驾驶功能可以让消费者更易接受由机器操船掌舵的理念。（煌）
>
> 改译1：半自动驾驶功能可以让消费者更易接受由机器人操控方向盘的理念。（王）
>
> 改译2：半自动驾驶功能可以让消费者逐渐接受机器人驾车的理念。（李）

李：毕竟是车，说"操船掌舵"不太合适。王译也很好。我的修改可能简洁一些。

> 建议译法：半自动驾驶功能可以让消费者逐渐接受机器人驾车的理念。（李）

15 逻辑重建 / 批判思维

> 原文：In addition to data science, social science is also becoming prevalent in autonomous development as companies such as Nissan and Audi take an anthropological approach to teach self-driving cars to act more human in their control and on-road actions (e.g. honking, signaling other people or vehicles, moving closer to lane marketing before switching lanes).
>
> 原译：社会科学和数据科学并驾齐驱，在自动化研发中大放光彩。厂商如日产、奥迪，更是采用人类学手段，使自动驾驶汽车的上路表现更人性化（例如：向行人行车鸣笛打灯、变更车道前先靠近标线等）。（煌）
>
> 改译1：除了数据科学，社会科学也越来越多地应用于自动化进程。比如日产、奥迪这些公司，就采用人类学方法，让自动驾驶汽车的上路表现更人性化（例如：向行人或车辆鸣笛打灯，在变更车道前先靠近标线等）。（王）

王：前半句逻辑重心稍稍有点改变。这段强调的是社会科学在无人车中的发展。但是译文读起来更像是两者并驾齐驱。

李：经查 lane marketing 应为 lane marking。参考报告第 15 页：

Similar to Nissan's anthropological approach to making autonomous driving more human, Audi has been teaching its robotic vehicles to drive more like humans in an effort to make them safer on the roads. For example, the car will move closer to lane markings before signaling that it is about to change lanes.

另，lane marking 意为：

Road surface marking is any kind of device or material that is used on a road surface in order to convey official information; they are commonly placed with road marking machines (or road marking equipment, pavement marking equipment). They can also be applied in other facilities used by vehicles to mark parking spaces or designate areas for other uses.

https://en.wikipedia.org/wiki/Road_surface_marking

王：关于 lane marking 的翻译，查到《道路交通标志和标线》规定的交通标志分为七大类：

(1) 警告标志：警告车辆和行人注意危险地点的标志。

(2) 禁令标志：禁止或限制车辆、行人交通行为的标志。

(3) 指示标志：指示车辆、行人行进的标志。

(4) 指路标志：传递道路方向、地点、距离的标志。

(5) 旅游区标志：提供旅游景点方向、距离的标志。

(6) 道路施工安全标志：通告道路施工区通行的标志。

(7) 辅助标志：附设于主标志下起辅助说明作用的标志。

规定的道路交通标线分为三大类：

(1) 指示标线：指示车行道、行车方向、路面边缘、人行道等设施的标线。

(2) 禁止标线：告示道路交通的遵行、禁止、限制等特殊规定，车辆驾驶人员及行人需要严格遵守的标线。

(3) 警告标线：促使车辆驾驶人员及行人了解道路上的特殊情况，提高警觉，准备防范应变措施的标线。

http://www.lawtime.cn/ask/zj_8602/

所以译为"标线"。"分道线"更具体，指如何划分道路，如白色实线、单黄实线、双黄实线、黄色虚实线等。如下图：

贾：建议改为"车道线"。正如王老师资料所示，标线包括三类，其中之一是"指示车行道"，那就是"车道线"或"分道线"。放在原文的语境里考虑，变道之前靠近的那条线，肯定是马路上区分快慢和转向车道的车道线，不太可能是其他道路标线。所以这里翻译成"车道线"应该就够了，"标线"概念有点太宽泛了。原文是 *lane* marking。

李：同意这个处理。

> **改译**：除了数据科学，社会科学也越来越多地应用于自动化进程。日产、奥迪等公司就采用人类学方法，教会自动驾驶汽车以更人性化的方式控制车辆和执行路上动作（例如：鸣笛、向行人或车辆打灯，在变道前先靠近车道线等）。（李）

16　查证能力

> **原文**：CES

李：需要说明为什么就是"消费电子展"，而不是其他名称的缩写。看了 YouTube 视频，发现确实是"消费电子展"：

CES, formerly The International Consumer Electronics Show (International CES®), showcases more than 3,900 exhibiting companies, including manufacturers, developers and suppliers of consumer technology hardware, content, technology delivery systems and more; a conference program with more than 300 conference sessions and more than 170K attendees from 150 countries.

http://www.ces.tech/about-us.aspx

CES 翻译为：消费电子展，参考了：

消费电子展（英语：Consumer Electronics Show，简称：CES）是一个知名国际性电子产品和科技的贸易展览会，每年吸引来自世界各地的主要公司和业界专门人士参加。消费型电子展每年1月于美国内华达州的拉斯维加斯会议中心举行。展览由消费电子协会赞助，并不开放一般民众入场，展览期间通常会举行多场产品预览会和新产品发表会。在2015年5月，亚洲消费电子展（CES Asia）首度于中国上海市举行。2016年时，主办单位将展览名称中原有的"国际"（International）去除，简化名称为"CES"。

https://zh.wikipedia.org/wiki/消費電子展

17　逻辑主语

> **原文**：With the latest round of updates from CES, there is more focus on intelligent vehicles (e.g. Toyota, AutoLiv, Ford's concept vision video).
>
> **原译**：消费电子展（CES）的最新消息显示，汽车制造商更加关注智能汽车的发展（见丰田、美安和福特等的概念车展望视频）。（煌）

李：通过看 YouTube 视频，发现是这些公司在推广概念车，所以 focus 的主语是厂商。明白了是谁的 focus，翻译就可以更加灵活。

王：我批改了很多同学的作业，发现大多数同学把 concept 处理成"概念车"。我思考了一下，觉得 vision 不应该翻译出来，因为概念车本身就包含 vision（展望）的含义。

概念车定义：概念车（Concept Car）可以理解为未来汽车，一种介于设想和现实之间的汽车。汽车设计师利用概念车向人们展示新颖、独特、超前的构思，反映人类对先进汽车的梦想与追求。这种车往往只是处在创意、试验阶段，也许不会投产，主要用于车辆的开发研究和开发试验，可以为探索汽车的造型、采用新的结构、验证新的原理等提供样机。

此外，杨若晨同学的查证也给了我启发，让我觉得原文并不是非常严谨：

杨若晨： 经过查证，我发现原文这里也有问题。福特在CES展会上发布的并不是一款概念车，也没有关于概念车的影片介绍，而是"the next-generation Fusion Hybrid Autonomous Development vehicle"，如下图。这辆新一代自动驾驶汽车根据蒙迪欧混动版改装而成，在展览上首次亮相。鉴于此，我把这句做了修改，望得到批评指正。

Jan 6, 2017

Ford at CES 2017

LAS VEGAS, NV. Jauuary 06,2017--At CES 2017, Ford Motor Company showcases mobility solutions, the next-generation Fusion Hybrid Autonomous Development vehicle, as well as several new connectivity capabilities, including integration with Amazon Alexa and new AppLink apps DriverScore, ExxonMobil Speedpass+ and Sygic. Ford President and CEO Mark Fields delivered the closing CES keynote at the Leaders in Technology Dinner, as well as participated in a SuperSession panel on global innovation. Photo by: Sam VarnHagen

https://media.ford.com/content/fordmedia/fna/us/en/media-kits/2017/ 17ces.html

王： 谢谢若晨的查证，这个问题我在做参考译文的时候也没有注意。我同意你的分析，如果查证无误，那么就是原文表述不严谨，福特没有发布概念车的视频，而是展出了一辆概念车。不过，我又转念一想，可能作者并没有去这个展会，而是看了展会的视频，所以直接把福特展出的概念车实体，表达成了概念车视频。所以，我斟酌了一下，还是尊重原文，保留"视频"二字。

改译： 消费电子展（CES）的最新消息显示，汽车制造商更加关注智能汽车的发展（见丰田、美安和福特等的概念车视频）。（王）

李： 同意你的观点和修改。纠正原文的错误，仅仅限于译者在理解原文或查找表达方式时偶然发现的错误。但即使发现，也不一定纠正。如果是一处小错,修改了皆大欢喜,就顺便改一下;如果拿不准是否修改,可以征求委托人意见;与委托人联系不方便,可以写个注释。如果觉得处理这个错误很麻烦,也可以置之不理,照原文翻译。译者不会为了挑错而挑错。对原文的编辑是译者对作者的恩惠,不是译者的责任。

> **建议译法**:消费电子展(CES)的最新消息显示,汽车制造商更加关注智能汽车的发展(见丰田、美安和福特等的概念车视频)。(李)

18

> **原文**:deep learning and AI

李:"深度学习"和"人工智能"不需要括注英文。专名、不常见说法可以给出英文。

> **建议译法**:深度学习和人工智能(李)

19

> **原文**:communicate with other vehicles (V2V)

煌:V2V 翻译为"V2V 通信",参考了:
V2V 通信(vehicle-to-vehicle communication; V2V communication)
什么是 V2V 通信
V2V 通信是指机动车辆间基于无线的数据传输。
V2V 通信是为了防止事故发生,通过专设的网络发送车辆位置和速度信息给另外的车辆。依靠技术的实现,驾驶员收到警告后就能降低事故的风险或车辆本身就会采取自治措施,像是制动减速。

http://wiki.mbalib.com/wiki/V2V 通信

自动驾驶行业的读者,一定具备基本的自动驾驶知识,熟悉相关概念,所以,一些缩写不用翻译。

> **建议译法**：与其他汽车交流（即 V2V 通信）（李）

20

> **原文**：This means that all software that exists may run into compatibility issues when asked to communicate with other systems within a vehicle. This is similar to the interoperability conundrum the industry witnessed around IoT.
>
> **原译**：这意味着，所有相关软件和其他车载系统交流时，都可能面临兼容问题，就如同物联网行业面临的互操作性难题一样。（煌）

王：我一直不理解，为什么谈汽车之间的交流还要用 compatibility 这个词。究竟这个 compatibility 是指汽车内部系统的兼容问题，还是汽车与汽车之间的兼容问题呢？

李：自动车应当是依靠自己的感知系统与自然界和其他车辆沟通。如果其他车辆的感知系统和这个车不匹配，彼此之间就无法沟通。就好比发射频率和接收频率不一致，就接收不到信号。所以，我还是怀疑不是一辆车之内（within a vehicle）软件不兼容，而是不同车辆的软件不兼容。一辆车之内，厂商肯定能搞定。就好比预装软件的电脑，各软件之间肯定不会发生冲突。但 Windows 作出的文件，在苹果上就是打不开。下一句 This is similar to the interoperability conundrum the industry witnessed around IoT 也间接说明是设备之间的互操作性。

下面这两段话很说明问题：The success of failure of self-driving cars — that's whether you will eventually be able to surf the web, chat with friends, read emails, or even take a nap while your car pilots itself down the road — comes down to code. Every major automaker employs an army of programmers tasked with virtually the same goal: Write the code that keep a car rolling safely down the road to its destination.

The problem is that eventually, they'll all share the same road. Which begs the question: If self-driving systems can't talk to one another, can multiple systems safely navigate roadways without conflict?

https://www.digitaltrends.com/cars/should-autonomous-driving-systems-be-compatible/

也许应该把 This means that all software that exists may run into compatibility issues when asked to communicate with other systems *within a vehicle*. 当中的 within a vehicle 换个地方：This means that all software that exists *within a vehicle* may run into compatibility issues when asked to communicate with other systems.

王：下一个问题是原文中的 industry 指的是什么呢？是汽车行业，还是物联网行业？

彭博：我第一次的时候也觉得 industry 指的就是 Internet of things。但后来我自己只读译文的时候就觉得如果这么理解的话，逻辑的跳脱有点大，为什么作者突然要把系统不兼容的问题和物联网相比较呢？而且如果 industry 确实指 IoT 的话，为什么作者不直接说 interoperability conundrum in IoT，而要用一个定语从句 the industry witnessed around IoT？定语从句中的这个 witness 给我的感觉是 the industry 并不是 IoT。然后我又读了一遍上下文，隐约觉得这个 the industry 指的就是前文一直在说的汽车行业或无人驾驶汽车行业。但是在调查的过程中，也可以证实物联网中互操作性的问题和原文所说的汽车系统间的 incompatibility 很相似，也符合原文的逻辑。但我始终觉得如果真是这样的话，作者没必要兜那么大的圈子用 industry 来指代 IoT。

李：由于本文不严谨之处甚多，此处也可能是另一个例子。理解为汽车行业，显然逻辑不同。汽车行业并不去发展物联网。如果把 industry 改为 we，意思就明确了。译文不妨灵活处理一下："这和物联网发展过程中面临的互操作难题一样。"王文煌的思路是对的。

建议译法：这意味着不同车辆之间各系统相互沟通时，可能出现软件兼容问题，这和物联网发展过程中面临的互操作难题一样。（李）

21

原文：However, when solved for, V2V opportunities abound in improving traffic experience, reducing accidents, and new value-added in-car design components.

原译：解决这些问题之后，V2V 通信一旦成行，将能带来绝佳的驾乘体验并减少事故发生，车内部件设计也能更新颖、更具价值。（煌）

王：原文补齐结构应为：However, when [the interoperability conundrum] is solved for [V2V], V2V opportunities abound in improving traffic experience, reducing accidents, and new value-added in-car design components. 原译略显拖沓，这里我将状语前置，让表达更符合汉语习惯一些。最后那句中的 new 我没有翻译出来，我觉得"提升"附加值本身就含有"新"的意思。

改译 1：但是，只要解决这个问题，在改善交通体验、减少事故、提升车载设计组件附加值方面，V2V 通信将大有可为。（王）

改译 2：但是，只要解决这个问题，在改善交通体验、减少事故、提升车内设计组件价值方面，V2V 通信将大有可为。（李）

建议译法：但是，只要解决这个问题，在改善交通体验、减少事故、提升车内设计组件价值方面，V2V 通信将大有可为 。（李）

22

原文：Mapping software has emerged as its own category among technology providers in the autonomous space, as 3D terrain mapping is a critical component to the effectiveness and safety of self-driving cars as they navigate their environments.

原译：在自动驾驶领域各类技术供应商中，测绘软件作为一个独特类别崭露头角，因为三维地形测绘对自动驾驶汽车导航的效果和安全至关重要。（煌）

李：Has its own category 我理解和 in a class of its own 比较类似。在商业领域，business category 也就是有属于自己的类别和体系；

Choose a business category

Categories are used to describe your business and connect you to customers searching for the services you offer. For example, if your primary category is "Pizza restaurant", Google may show your business in local search results to people who search for "Restaurants", "Italian restaurants", or "Pizza" in their area. Keep in mind that your category is just one of many factors that can affect your local ranking on Google.

Depending on the type of business you operate, your category may also be used to assign a <u>place label</u> to your business.

https://support.google.com/business/answer/7249669?hl=en

所以，我的改译为：在自动驾驶技术中，测绘软件"独树一帜"。这里也部分借鉴了马崧译同学"独树一帜"的处理方式。这里我使用"独树一帜"，而没有选择"自成一家"或者"自成一体"，原因是"独树一帜"不仅突出其技术自成一体，也起到了强调作用，因为作者在后文中也说了测绘软件的重要性。

王：批改到马崧译同学的作业，我开始对 technology providers 有疑问。认为 technology providers 和软件测绘并不属于同一类。technology providers 是我们一般说的技术供应商，也就是 one that provides the technology，是行为主体；而 mapping software 是软件，是产品。所以如果直接说"在自动驾驶领域各类技术供应商中，测绘软件"有些不合适。

李：同意你的分析。从逻辑上看，technology providers 应该改为 technologies。

> 建议译法：在自动驾驶技术中，测绘软件"独树一帜"，因为三维地形测绘对自动驾驶汽车导航的效果和安全至关重要。（李）

第七单元 联合国文件

Exercise 7　Report of the Secretary-General

翻译情景

以下节选来自2017年联合国秘书长关于工作的报告。秘书长每年都会向大会作报告，总结上一年在政治、经济、军事、安全等方面开展的工作并提出工作展望。秘书长报告是了解联合国的窗口，也是训练翻译全局观的优质素材。2017年，安东尼奥·古特雷斯担任第九任联合国秘书长，并于就职典礼上做了工作报告。古特雷斯在就任联合国秘书长之前，曾担任联合国难民事务高级专员长达十年之久，目睹了战争地区生灵涂炭，决心将工作重点放在促进和平、改善人民生活状况上。[1]

假定你是联合国译员，译文将作为联合国的正式文件发布。可在搜索引擎中输入任意片段检索全文。

训练重点

前六单元以专题方式训练了翻译所需的各项能力，从本单元开始，将学习如何综合运用各项能力，翻译不同专业领域的文件。本单元的重点包

1　联合国秘书长简介请参见 https://www.un.org/sg/zh/content/sg/biography

括增强全局意识，提高语言敏感性和查证能力。

训练难点

秘书长的讲话，字斟句酌，具有较高的政治敏感度，需要原原本本地翻译出来，不能随意增删，这一点与翻译文学作品、论文摘要、广告、公共标识等所采取的灵活策略有很大不同，与法律文本倒是有相似之处。

训练方式

本次练习分原文、翻译提示、参考译文、译者注四部分。请先尝试自己翻译原文。做完以后再参看翻译提示，并自行修改、润色，形成第二稿。形成二稿之后，再看参考译文和译者注。翻译能力是在实践中不断提升的，希望你可以充分利用每一单元，一步步取得翻译能力上的飞跃！

原文[1]

Introduction[2]

1. I am deeply honoured and humbled to be at the helm of the United Nations at this critical time[3]. In this annual report on the work of the Organization, which reflects on the first few months of my term and the last few months of my predecessor's term, my aim is to offer a candid view of the world today and a realistic vision of how we can better deliver on the promise of the United Nations.

The world we live in presents a mixed picture of[4] progress, challenges and opportunities

2. The United Nations was established to prevent war and human suffering by binding us together through a common rule-based international order. Today that order is laden with contradictory trends[5], and a clear assessment must be

made if we are going to address these challenges effectively.

3. Hundreds of millions of people have been lifted out of poverty. More children, both boys and girls, are achieving greater levels of education and more women are entering the political world than ever before. This progress represents concentrated efforts by United Nations Member States to work towards these and other development goals. Yet after years of decline, the number of conflicts is on the rise and they are lasting longer, fuelled by the spread of[6] terrorism and violent extremism, transnational criminal networks and deep regional divisions. The threat of famine in several countries, resulting from violence compounded by drought[7], lurks just around the corner[8]. These contradictory trends are exacerbated by international power dynamics that are in flux. As we move towards a multipolar world order composed of multiple and shifting centres of power, there is an added feeling of unpredictability.

4. Now more than ever, multilateral action is needed to find effective solutions to this mix of challenges.

5. While progress on development indicators is moving ahead, the risks to global stability may be[9] accelerating, affecting these hard-earned achievements. Climate change is creating deserts where once there was farmland; it is also generating extreme weather that threatens lives, livelihoods[10] and infrastructure and leads to critical shortages of water. The planet's population will grow to nearly 10 billion people by 2050, two thirds living in cities that could be left unprepared for such rapid growth unless urban leaders grasp this opportunity to prosper by utilizing concentrated habitats to build more efficient infrastructures.

6. People are on the move, to cities and all parts of the world, in search of opportunity and safety. Population displacement and migration on a scale not seen since the Second World War bear witness to enduring challenges grounded in escalating conflicts and systemic[11] inequalities. While some countries have been willing to open their arms to people in need, others

have reacted by succumbing to deep national and international tensions and polarization.

Inequality and exclusion underlie many of today's challenges

7. Inequality and exclusion underlie a great many of today's challenges. Globalization has brought immense gains in the fight against poverty worldwide and has improved living conditions nearly everywhere. But it has been cruelly unfair: as wealth has increased, so too has its asymmetry, leaving millions behind in all parts of the world. Both developed and developing countries, North and South, face greater inequality and marginalization now than they did 20 years ago. Unless we work together, the coming decades are likely to drive poverty more deeply into fragile low-income countries, pushing them even further onto the sidelines, while even larger numbers of people struggling with poverty live in middle-income countries. Furthermore, this sense of exclusion is not limited to the poorest countries but is vividly on the rise in developed countries as well, fuelling trends of nationalism and a lack of trust in national and multilateral institutions. Our hard-won collective progress towards combating poverty and promoting common security is newly at risk.

Countries and institutions are struggling to fully deliver[12]

8. Threats to global stability are frequently rooted in weak infrastructure and failing institutions in fragile States. Where States cannot provide basic protections and services to their people, the likelihood of violence, pandemics or violent extremism increases dramatically. We must collectively invest more to help countries build inclusive institutions and resilient communities capable of thriving in a globalized world.

9. Overwhelmed[13], a significant number of States across the world are struggling to effectively address today's major challenges and deliver the services needed by their populations. Tensions are exacerbated by a lack of opportunities and by a strong sentiment among many peoples[14] — their youth especially — that they are being excluded by the very institutions meant to

serve them. Few countries or institutions appear to have a long-term vision to meet peoples' needs or strategies to manage today's interlinked crises, instead finding themselves entangled in reactive responses[15].

10. The United Nations and many other international institutions deserve credit for their achievements, but may also be perceived as bureaucratic and remote.

翻译提示

1 全局意识

请大家针对原文和译文，分别回答 Who is talking to whom? About what? When, where and why? And how? 然后再开始翻译。

2 全局意识：文章结构

可以通过目录，了解一篇文章的整体结构。可以具体看看原文一共分为几部分，每一部分都是什么主要内容；感兴趣的同学可以把往年的秘书长报告找出来，再看目录作对比，思考秘书长报告每年是否有固定的内容和体例，秘书长报告是否可以反映当今国际形势的变化。此外，同学们还可以把历年的秘书长报告中英文找出来进行对照阅读。对照阅读的目的是了解秘书长报告的风格、措辞，进而找准翻译的原则和策略。这和第一单元强调的译者的全局意识密不可分。

以下这个网站可以检索到联合国文件：http://www.un.org/en/documents/ index.html。

输入联合国文件的文件号（一般在文件首页右上角），就可以找到所需要的文件和对应的六种语言。例如，此份文件的文件号为 A/72/1，找到网站右下角的搜索栏，键入文件号，如图：

```
Search by symbol (e.g. A/63/100)
Document symbol  A/72/1    Search
Research Guide: Document Symbols

Enhanced Search

ODS search page
```

3 **全局意识：文体特征**

除了把握文章结构，译者还需要了解原文的写作风格和使用场合。翻译前译者需要把握原文属于什么语体，是正式还是非正式的？

此外，还要思考一下联合国文件的性质。联合国以《联合国宪章》为原则，旨在维护世界和平与稳定。目前联合国有193个会员国，联合国的工作不以一个国家的意识为转移，因此具有较强的政治中立性特点。由此，译者需要思考翻译联合国文件应该采取什么样的策略。

4 **查证能力**

请利用工具查找这个短语的意思。直接在谷歌搜索框输入要搜索的单词或短语，再加上 definition，就可以看到众多英英词典的解释。也可以直接在以下网站搜索：

剑桥英语词典：https://dictionary.cambridge.org/

牛津英语词典：https://en.oxforddictionaries.com/

不列颠百科全书：https://www.britannica.com/

Free Dictionary：https://www.thefreedictionary.com/

以下两个网站可以检索联合国术语和双语语料：

UNTERM：https://unterm.un.org/UNTERM/portal/welcome

Linguee：https://www.linguee.com/

查找英语词语的含义，尽量用英英词典或英文资源，多看例句，必要时查看词源信息。只有理解词源，才是最深刻的理解。

5 **逻辑思维**

注意此处的 trend 是复数；检查译文逻辑是否成立。

6 **语言能力：修饰关系**

判断 spread of 管几个短语，仅包括 terrorism and violent extremism，还是也包括 transnational criminal networks and deep regional divisions？结构歧义是翻译中经常遇到的问题，需要结合上下文、生活常识、语法/意思搭配等方式加以判断（think global）。翻译中经常遇到的另一个问题是一词多义，解决方式相同。

7 **语言能力：修饰关系**

compounded 是修饰 threat 还是 violence？从语法上看是修饰谁？实际上应该修饰谁？用 drought 搜索报告全文，有什么发现？原文是否存在瑕疵？violence 和 drought 的作用是否相同？哪一个是根源？哪一个是加剧因素？

8 **语言能力：理解和表达**

利用工具查找短语 around the corner 的意思；查找类似 Linguee 的语料库，借鉴他人的译文。

9 **语言能力：情态动词**

要译出谓语动词的情态；注意情态动词的时态。不同情态动词（can、may、must 等）含义全不同，翻译错误会导致意思南辕北辙。

10 **语言能力：词义辨析**

lives 和 livelihood 不可混为一谈；用英英词典查找两个单词的含义。

11 **语言能力：词义辨析**

systemic 和 systematic 是否相同？

12 **全局意识：上下文**

deliver 的对象是什么？用该词搜索全文，有什么发现？

13 **语言能力：词义辨析**

借助英英词典和上下文，确认 overwhelmed 的意思。

14 语言能力：理解和表达

a strong sentiment among many peoples 应当指什么？为什么 people 是复数？用 Linguee 查查 strong sentiment，看看能否给翻译带来启发？

15 全局意识：上下文

此处要结合全文理解 reactive response 的含义。reactive 的反面是什么？什么是 proactive response？

参考译文[1]：

导言[2]

1. 能在此重要时刻执掌联合国，我深感荣幸，又诚惶诚恐。[3]这份关于联合国[4]工作的年度报告，回顾了前任秘书长任期最后几个月和我任期最初几个月的工作，目的是坦陈我对当今世界的看法，并就如何更好地履行联合国的承诺，提出切实可行的构想。[5]

当今世界有喜有忧，进步、挑战与机遇共存。[6]

2. 创立联合国，是为了建立一个遵守规则的共同国际秩序，以此团结全人类，防止战祸和人类苦难。[7]如今，这一秩序呈现出多种相互矛盾的趋势。要有效应对这些挑战，就必须对国际局势进行清晰的评估。[8]

3. 数亿人口已经脱贫。有更多的儿童（包括男童和女童）教育程度提高，步入政坛的妇女也比以往任何时候都多。[9]这一进步是联合国会员国为实现这些和其他发展目标集中努力的结果。[10]然而，由于恐怖主义和暴力极端主义蔓延、跨国犯罪网络扩大和深刻的地区矛盾，冲突的数量经历数年下降之后又重新上升，而且冲突持续的时间也在加长。[11]在一些国家，暴力引发的饥饿威胁因干旱变得更为严峻，饥荒随时都会发生。[12]上述相互矛盾的趋势，因国际权力格局的不断变化而更加严峻。[13]随着权力中心的不断变化和多元化,世界秩序走向多极,我们愈发感到世事难料。[14]

4. 现在比以往任何时候都更需要采取多边行动,寻找应对这些复杂挑战的有效方法。

5. 尽管我们在发展指标上取得了进展,但全球稳定面临的风险可能正在升级,影响着这些来之不易的成就。气候变化正将农田变为荒漠,并引发极端天气,威胁生命、生计[15]和基础设施,导致严重缺水。地球人口到2050年将增至近100亿,其中三分之二生活在城市。如果城市领导者不抓住机遇谋发展,利用集中住区建设更为高效的基础设施,这些城市将无法承受如此快速的人口增长。[16]

6. 人口在不断流动,流向城市,流向世界各地,去寻找机遇和安全的环境。[17]自第二次世界大战以来,流离失所和移民的规模前所未有,见证了冲突不断升级和制度性不平等带给我们的持久挑战。[18]面对需要帮助的人,一些国家愿意敞开怀抱,而另一些国家则屈从于深刻的国内国际矛盾和两极化意见。[19]

今天的许多挑战都源自不平等和社会排斥[20]

7. 当今的许多挑战源于不平等和社会排斥。全球化为世界范围内消除贫困作出了巨大贡献,改善了几乎所有地区的生活条件。[21]然而,全球化带来了残酷的不公[22]:随着财富的增加,财富分配也愈发不平等,在世界所有地方,都有千百万人被甩在后面。[23]无论发达国家还是发展中国家,无论是北方还是南方,不平等和边缘化现象都甚于二十年前。[24]除非我们通力合作,否则在未来几十年里,本就脆弱的低收入国家将更加贫困,进一步陷入边缘化境地,甚至中等收入国家也会出现更多贫困人口。[25]此外,这种被排斥感不限于最贫穷的国家,在发达国家也明显增加,从而助长民族主义,侵蚀人们对国家机构与多边机构的信任。在消除贫困和促进共同安全方面,我们集体取得的进步来之不易,如今却面临新的风险。[26]

一些国家和机构正在通过艰难努力,全面兑现承诺[27]

8. 威胁全球稳定的根源,常常是脆弱国家[28]基础设施薄弱、机构运转失灵。如果国家不能为本国人民提供基本的保护和服务,暴力、流行病或暴力极端主义[29]就有可能急剧增加。我们必须携起手来,加大投入,帮助各国建设能在全球化世界中健康发展的包容性机构[30]和复原力强的社区。[31]

9. 全世界许多国家面对今天的重大挑战和本国人民所需的服务,在苦苦挣扎,艰难应对。[32]许多族群,尤其是其中的青年人,由于缺乏机会,并强烈不满本应为之服务的机构却排斥他们,造成社会矛盾进一步加剧。[33]似乎没有什么国家或机构能够放眼长远,满足人民的需求,或制定战略,管理当今社会各种相互关联的危机;相反,他们陷于被动应对而不能自拔。[34]

10. 联合国和许多其他国际机构取得的成就值得称赞,但这些机构也被认为过于官僚,遥不可及。

译者注

1　全局意识:文章结构

王:通过目录可知,报告包括四部分:导言、联合国的工作、加强联合国和结论。其中,联合国的工作部分包括:促进经济增长和可持续发展、维护国际和平与安全、非洲的发展、促进和保护所有人权、有效协调人道主义援助工作、促进司法和国际法、裁军、毒品管制、预防犯罪和打击国际恐怖主义,是报告的主体部分。本单元选自导言部分(Introduction)。导言部分提纲挈领,对整体把握报告内容十分重要。实际翻译工作中,即使仅负责报告的一部分,至少也要把目录、导言和结论看一下。

全局意识：文体特征

李：本文属于正式语体，语域较高；同时，本文用于大会宣读。因此，译文的表达应类似中国的政府工作报告：虽属正式发言，但也朗朗上口。

全局意识：文件性质

李：联合国文件政治性强，表达字斟句酌，不允许译者自由发挥，基本采用直译的方法。一句之内，各句子成分可以打乱重组，但在句子和段落层面打乱重组的情况几乎不存在。重要的概念，都要译出；不得已时的增词、减词，都要有充分依据。尽管如此，译文也要做到符合中文表达习惯。

2

李：联合国文件翻译的一些基本格式要求：

  a. 文件的正文两端对齐；

  b. 汉字之间不留空格；

  c. 中文句号为圆圈（"。"），不要用英文句号（"."）；

  d. 所有标点，均用中文标点，但括号除外。无论圆括号（"()"）还是方括号（"[]"），均采用英文符号（这一条可以等到成为联合国译员时再遵守）；

  e. 每段序号 123 之后都需要有英文圆点，如："1.""2.""3."；

  f. 凡英文斜体，中文均为楷体（注意不是华文楷体或其他楷体）；有的专门机构要求斜体，有的要求正体；凡英文正常体加粗，中文为黑体字（注意不是加粗）；UNEP 要求黑体字同时加粗。

  g. 字体通常用宋体，字号与英文相同。

王：注意，联合国总部、各办事处以及附属机构之间的要求可能略有不同，与国内标点用法也有差异，译员需要事先了解。

3

原 文：I am deeply honoured and humbled to be at the helm of the United Nations at this critical time.

> **建议译文1**：能在此重要时刻执掌联合国，我深感荣幸，谦恭万分。（马）
> **建议译文2**：能在此重要时刻执掌联合国，我深感荣幸，诚惶诚恐。（程萍）
> **建议译文3**：能在此重要时刻执掌联合国，我深感荣幸，又诚惶诚恐。（李）

李："谦恭""谦虚"用来称赞别人，不能用来夸奖自己。不添加"又"字也没关系。添加是因为 honoured 和 humbled 之间，有一点点转折关系。

4

王：the organisation 译为"本组织"和"联合国"都可以。

5

> **原文**：In this annual report on the work of the Organization, which reflects on the first few months of my term and the last few months of my predecessor's term, my aim is to offer a candid view of the world today and a realistic vision of how we can better deliver on the promise of the United Nations.

马：如果按原文结构直译此句，即为"在［这份反映了我任期最初几个月和前任秘书长任期最后几个月的工作的］［有关本组织工作］的年度报告中，我的目的是在报告中坦陈当今世界形势，为如何更好地实现联合国承诺提供切合实际的愿景。"两组方括号中的长定语让句子头重脚轻，读者负担加重。所以将定语内容提出来，单独成句，使表述更加流畅。

> **原译**：这份关于联合国工作的年度报告，回顾了前任秘书长任期最后几个月和我任期最初几个月的工作。我想借此报告坦陈对当今世界的看法，并就如何更好地履行联合国的承诺提出一个现实的愿景。

王：英文能够搭配的词语，直译为汉语不一定搭配得当，可能需要根据汉语习惯进行调整。这句话中，offer a candid view...and a realistic vision 以及 deliver on the promise 都涉及词语搭配问题。如原译所示，正确搭配为"坦陈……看法／意见""履行……承诺"。

程：关于 realistic，作者的意思是说，既不要搞出一个雄心勃勃但根本实现不了的构想，也别对自己没有高标准严要求。应该说就是"革命尚未成功，同志仍需努力"的意思。

李：view 的意思是"看法""观点"，不是"愿景"。顺便提及，广泛使用"愿景"一词，始于 2005 年中共中央总书记胡锦涛与时任中国国民党主席连战达成并共同发布"两岸和平发展共同愿景"。后来人们以"愿景"对译 vision。但要注意，不是所有情况下都能把 vision 译为"愿景"。

> **建议译法**：这份关于联合国工作的年度报告，回顾了前任秘书长任期最后几个月和我任期最初几个月的工作，目的是坦陈我对当今世界的看法，并就如何更好地履行联合国的承诺，提出切实可行的构想。（李）

6

> **原文**：The world we live in presents a mixed picture of progress, challenges and opportunities.
> **原译**：当今世界错综复杂，进步、挑战与机遇共存。

李：不是形势"错综复杂"，mixed 是指下面所说，既有进步，也有挑战和机遇。"错综复杂"不能用来涵盖"进步、挑战和机遇共存"。原文中，后者是前者的具体化。Think global。

程：a mixed picture of 在这里译为"错综复杂"是有点悲观的气息。但是，"喜忧参半"则有些过于乐观。事实上，尽管联合国几十年辛苦地呼吁宣传努力做工作，整个世界的局势依然十分严峻，很多方面简直是令人气馁，咱先不说失望。如果非要给个百分比，"喜"的方面微乎其微，也许只有 5% 至 10%，而且也是集中在教育、女童接受教育方面。由于国内媒体很多事情不报道，所以我们看不到真正的 picture。但是实际上，这些年来，特别是近年来，国际上战争持续不断，大规模的流离失所，难民人数持续增加，恐怖主义蔓延，甚至连一直享受着相对安稳生活的欧洲各国也未能独善其身。其他方面，如气候变化、经济衰退和就业困难都使各国焦头烂额。秘书长那里可喜的事情实在数不出来几个。因此"喜忧参半"显然是过于乐观了。

李：难处在于，mixed 没说明喜忧的百分比。但即使"喜事"较少，仍旧可以说"有喜"。"喜忧参半"给出了比例，就不恰当。

改译：我们生活的这个世界有喜有忧，进步、挑战和机遇并存。（李）

王：在 The Free Dictionary 上查证得知，a mixed picture 的意思确实为"有喜有忧"：

A portrayal of a situation highlighting both positive and negative aspects of its nature or status.

Despite the government's upbeat remarks, the Federal Reserve today published a report showing a mixed picture of the status of the economy's recovery.

https://idioms.thefreedictionary.com/a+mixed+picture

有同学处理为"形势混杂"也不妥当。

the world we live in 可以简化为"当今世界"，不影响原文意思。

建议译法：当今世界有喜有忧，进步、挑战与机遇共存。（王）

7

原文：The United Nations was established to prevent war and human suffering by binding us together through a common rule-based international order.
原译：创立联合国的初衷，是通过建立一个基于规则的共同国际秩序将全人类团结起来，以避免战祸和人间疾苦。（马）

李：原译加一个逗号，更便于阅读："创立联合国的初衷，是通过建立一个基于规则的共同国际秩序，将全人类团结起来，避免战祸和人间疾苦。"也可以简化一些：

> **改译**：创立联合国，是为了建立共同的法治化国际秩序，以此团结全人类，防止战祸和人类苦难。（李）

程：西方人在讨论 rules，不一定全都是指法律 / 法治，除非说 rule of law。他们平时更多指的是，大家要遵守规则。各个地方、部门、各个领域都有自己的规章制度，大到政府，小到每位公民都需要遵守各自所在地方的 rules。即所谓"国有国法，家有家规"。比如学校里有自己的 rules，联合国有 staff rules，这里更多的是指规则、规章条例。那么具体到秘书长这里的 rules，也是指"规则"，就是说各国都需要遵守规则。如果说法治的话，很多国家不承认别国的法律，甚至在联合国讨论某条国际法时，各国代表们可以吵得天翻地覆。所以这里说"法治化"可能有点牵强。联合国文件还是贴近原文比较妥当。有译者认为，"基于规则"属于完全按照英文走，意思不走样，中文也可以懂，但是咱们中国人一般都说要"遵守规则"。这里我改为"遵守规则"；也可以用"基于规则"。

> **建议译法**：创立联合国，是为了建立一个遵守规则的共同国际秩序，以此团结全人类，防止战祸和人类苦难。（程）

8

> **原文**：Today that order is laden with contradictory trends, and a clear assessment must be made if we are going to address these challenges effectively.
> **原译**：如今，这一秩序充满了各种相互矛盾的趋势。要有效应对这些挑战，就必须对国际局势进行清晰的评估。（马、王）

李："充满趋势"搭配不当。因为"充满"描述状态，"趋势"描述动态，意思上无法搭配。这句话就是指下一段所说：一方面脱贫等取得成就，另一方面冲突在增加。Act local, think global。

建议译法： 如今，国际秩序呈现出多种相互矛盾的趋势。要有效应对这些挑战，就必须对国际局势进行清晰的评估。（李）

9

原文： More children, both boys and girls, are achieving greater levels of education and more women are entering the political world than ever before.

原译： 接受更高程度教育的儿童（包括男童和女童）和步入政坛的妇女数量史无前例。（马）

改译： 接受更高程度教育的儿童（包括男童和女童）和步入政坛的妇女数量比以往任何时候都多。（程）

李：前置定语尽量简短。"史无前例"与"前所未有"区别在于：前者偏重在"史"和"例"，用于强调历史上从未有过；而"前所未有"指以前没有，语气较轻，适用范围更广。

建议译法： 有更多的儿童（包括男童和女童）教育程度提高，步入政坛的妇女也比以往任何时候都多。（李）

10

原文： This progress represents concentrated efforts by United Nations Member States to work towards these and other development goals.

原译： 以上进步体现了联合国会员国为实现这些和其他发展目标作出的集中努力。

马：术语都在 www.unterm.org（联合国术语库）中查过。搜索结果统一使用"会员国"，而非"成员国"。

改译1： 这些进步是联合国会员国全力以赴实现这些和其他发展目标的结果。（程）

李:"集中力量"和"全力以赴"还是有所不同。全力以赴,是指用的力量大;集中努力,是指用的力量集中于一处。原文是 concentrated,用集中努力似乎更好。

> **建议译法**:这一进步是联合国会员国为实现这些和其他发展目标而集中努力的结果。(李)

李:"发展目标"是指 2015 年之前的 MDG(千年发展目标)和之后的 SDG(可持续发展目标)。these development goals 是指跟减贫、儿童教育和妇女参政相关的发展目标。

11

> **原文**:Yet after years of decline, the number of conflicts is on the rise and they are lasting longer, fuelled by the spread of terrorism and violent extremism, transnational criminal networks and deep regional divisions.
> **原译**:然而,由于恐怖主义、暴力极端主义、跨国犯罪网络和严重区域分裂的蔓延,本已连年减少的冲突开始增多,持续时间也更长。(马)

李:spread of 只能修饰一个。如果说修饰 networks 还勉强的话(network 的动词搭配应当是 expand),修饰 division 意思上不可能。因此只能修饰一个。但翻译的时候,光说一个"网络"与其他两个短语不平衡,只能再加一个"扩大"。

关于 regional divisions,这是一份资料:

The choice of candidates has opened up deep regional divisions largely based around colonial divisions between Francophone and Anglophone countries in the world's poorest continent. "Whatever may be the African position, whatever may be the offer we may have, if the continent is not united we may never be able to win," said Alpha Oumar Konare, AU Commission chairperson, earlier in opening remarks at the meeting in Abuja. "The strength of the continent is the ability to speak with one voice and its ability to act together."

https://www.globalpolicy.org/security-council/security-council-reform/41206.html?itemid=913

联合国把世界分为几个层级：global、regional、national、sub-national、local，此处的 regional divisions 就是指"区域"层面（即非洲地区）的分裂／矛盾。"区域分裂"的意思不明确，调整为"地区矛盾"更清楚一些。

王：世界银行与联合国共同发布的有关冲突问题的报告可见，与 2014 年相比，2015 年的冲突数量有所增加，虽然没有找到 2016 年和 2017 年的具体数据，但是由此推测，翻译成"连年减少"并不准确。

http://www.un.org/pga/70/wp-content/uploads/sites/10/2016/01/Conflict-and-violence-in-the-21st-century-Current-trends-as-observed-in-empirical-research-and-statistics-Mr.-Alexandre-Marc-Chief-Specialist-Fragility-Conflict-and-Violence-World-Bank-Group.pdf

> **建议译法**：然而，由于恐怖主义和暴力极端主义蔓延、跨国犯罪网络扩大和深刻的地区矛盾，冲突的数量经历数年下降之后又重新上升，而且冲突持续的时间也在加长。（李、王）

12

> **原文**：The threat of famine in several countries, resulting from violence compounded by drought, lurks just around the corner.
>
> **原译**：在一些国家，暴力引发的饥荒威胁因干旱变得更为严峻，迫在眉睫。（马）

李：我原以为"迫在眉睫"用以说明需要紧急采取行动，但看了语料库用法，饥荒也可以迫在眉睫。所以，"迫在眉睫"可以使用，但要加个主语：在一些国家，暴力引发的饥饿威胁因干旱变得更为严峻，饥荒迫在眉睫。因为不是"威胁"迫在眉睫；威胁是现实存在的。另外，用"饥饿"和"饥荒"两个词，避免用词重复。

原文似乎应该添加一个"and"：resulting from violence [and] compounded by drought，不添加 and，compound 就修饰 violence。但检索全文发现：

a) Tragically, famine threatens four States today, caused by drought and conflict.

b) Conflict, drought and violence have carried the threat of famine that has affected 20 million people in Nigeria, Somalia, South Sudan and Yemen.

因此，compound 应该修饰 threat of famine。原译理解正确，可能是知情判断，也可能是凭直觉碰对了。

建议译法：在一些国家，暴力引发的饥饿威胁因干旱变得更为严峻，饥荒随时都会发生。（李）

13

原文：These contradictory trends are exacerbated by international power dynamics that are in flux.

原译：国际力量格局不断变化，令这些矛盾趋于激烈。（马）

王：什么是 international power dynamics？直接在谷歌上搜索 international power dynamics，没有找到权威定义。搜索 dynamics of power，找到政治学文献中的定义，可以由此窥视 dynamics of power 的含义：

"Power can be defined as the degree of control over material, human, intellectual and financial resources exercised by different sections of society. The control of these resources becomes a source of individual and social power. Power is dynamic and relational, rather than absolute — it is exercised in the social, economic and political relations between individuals and groups. It is also unequally distributed – some individuals and groups having greater control over the sources of power and others having little or no control. The extent of power of an individual or group is correlated to how many different kinds of resources they can access and control."

(VeneKlasen, Miller, Budlender, & Clark, 2002)

由此可见，原译把 dynamics 译为"格局"是可取的。power 译为"权力"（不是"权利"）似乎更容易理解。

李：按照原文的信息顺序翻译，与上文衔接更紧密。

> **建议译法**：上述相互矛盾的趋势，因国际权力格局的不断变化而更加严峻。（王、李）

14

> **原文**：As we move towards a multipolar world order composed of multiple and shifting centres of power, there is an added feeling of unpredictability.
>
> **原译**：世界秩序正朝着多极化演变，权力中心不止一个，而且还在不停变换，我们愈发感觉前路难以预知。（马）
>
> **改译**：世界秩序正朝着多极化演变，权力中心不断变化，而且不止一个，我们愈发感觉前路难以预测。（程）

李：两种译法都可以。也许可以再正式一些。

> **建议译法**：随着权力中心的不断变化和多元化，世界秩序走向多极，我们愈发感到世事难料。（李）

15

> **原文**：threatens lives, livelihoods and infrastructure
> **原译**：威胁生活、生计和基础设施（马）

王：life 经常译为"生命"或"生活"。在此以复数形式出现，指的是生命。

> ⑤ [C] existence of an individual human being 人命；（人的）性命： *Doctors worked through the night to save the life of the injured man.* 医生彻夜工作以拯救伤者的生命. * *Three lives were lost* (ie Three people died) *in the accident.* 事故中三人丧生.
>
> （牛津高级英汉双解词典）

再者，从意思搭配上来看，极端天气会"威胁"生命／生存，但"影响"生活。

livelihood 也有不同意思。Oxford English Dictionary 对 livelihood 的定义是：1. Course of life, lifetime; kind or manner of life 2. Means of living, maintenance, sustenance。根据语境判断，此处应为第 2 条释义，即生计，或生活手段。

> **建议译法**：威胁生命、生计和基础设施（王）

16

> **原文**：The planet's population will grow to nearly 10 billion people by 2050, two thirds living in cities that could be left unprepared for such rapid growth unless urban leaders grasp this opportunity to prosper by utilizing concentrated habitats to build more efficient infrastructures.
>
> **原译**：地球人口到 2050 年将增至近 100 亿，其中三分之二将生活在城市。如果城市领导者不抓住机会实现发展，利用密集居住地建设更为高效的基础设施，这些城市将无法承受如此快速的人口增长。（马）

李："密集居住地"意思不太清楚，此处可以译为"集中住区"。

habitat 一般是指动植物的栖息地或生存环境。

habitat

noun [C or U] ● UK 🔊 /ˈhæb.ɪ.tæt/ US 🔊 /ˈhæb.ə.tæt/

⊙ C1 **the natural environment in which an animal or plant usually lives:**
With so many areas of woodland being cut down, a lot of wildlife is losing its natural habitat.

但也用于表示人类住区。联合国有个机构就简称 UN-Habitat（中文简称：人居署；英文全称：The United Nations Human Settlements Programme，中文全称：联合国人类住区规划署）。UN-Habitat is the United Nations programme working towards a better urban future. Its mission is to promote socially and environmentally sustainable human settlements development and the achievement of adequate shelter for all.

建议译法：地球人口到 2050 年将增至近 100 亿，其中三分之二生活在城市。如果城市领导者不抓住机遇谋发展，利用集中住区建设更为高效的基础设施，这些城市将无法承受如此快速的人口增长。（李）

17

原文：People are on the move, to cities and all parts of the world, in search of opportunity and safety.

原译：人们为了寻找机遇、寻求安全，而向城市和世界各地迁移。（马）

李：尽量不破坏原文的信息流，否则重点会改变。

建议译法：人口在不断流动，流向城市，流向世界各地，去寻找机遇和安全的环境。（李）

18

原文：Population displacement and migration on a scale not seen since the Second World War bear witness to enduring challenges grounded in escalating conflicts and systemic inequalities.

原译：自第二次世界大战以来，人口流离失所和移民的规模前所未有，见证了不断升级的冲突和系统性不平等给我们带来的持久的挑战。（马）

李："人口"可以省略，已经隐含在"流离失所"中。

systemic 和 systematic 意思不同。Systemic refers to something that affects an entire system. In this sense it is *complete*.

- For centuries, government has been a tool for systemic oppression.
- Jake has developed a systemic condition that hinders the function of his digestive tract.

Systematic refers to something done according to process or plan.

- The power plant had planned a systematic transition to offline status, but that was before the tsunami.

- The hacker's new script ran a systematic process that was designed to take down the target's servers.

详细解释见：https://writingexplained.org/systemic-vs-systematic-difference 或搜索 difference between systemic and systematic。

这两个意思都可以翻译为"系统性的"，因为汉语的"系统"，有三个意思，前两个可以归入 systemic，第三个即 systematic。

> 现代汉语词典第3版
> **系统**
> （1）在动、植物和人体内许多器官联合组成的结构。这些器官在组织形态上有相似的特征，在机能上完成一种连续性的生理作用。（2）同类事物按一定的关系联合起来，成为一个有组织的整体：组织~｜灌溉~。（3）有条理的，连贯的：~地学习马克思主义理论。

本句翻译为"系统性不平等"没问题，但如果希望更具体，可以翻译为"制度性的"。

> 现代汉语词典第3版
> **制度**
> （1）要求大家共同遵守的办事规程或行动准则：工作~｜财政~。（2）在一定历史条件下形成的政治、经济、文化等方面的体系：社会主义~｜封建宗法~。

"制度"（义项2）性的，一定是影响到全体的。

顺便提及，汉语中的"有序"（如"有序推进"），可以译为 systematically 或 according to plan，不一定要说 in an orderly manner。

> **建议译法**：自第二次世界大战以来，流离失所和移民的规模前所未有，见证了冲突不断升级和制度性不平等带给我们的持久挑战。（李）

19

> **原文**：While some countries have been willing to open their arms to people in need, others have reacted by succumbing to deep national and international tensions and polarization.
>
> **原译**：面对需要帮助的人，一些国家愿意敞开怀抱，而另一些国家却屈从于国内和国际的极度紧张关系和两极分化状况。（马）

李：national and international tensions and polarization 是指国内和国际上由于因移民问题产生的紧张关系和两极分化意见。

王：以下段落摘自 *Adjusting to a World in Motion: Trends in Global Migration and Migration Policy* edited by Edited By Douglas J. Besharov, Mark H. Lopez：

Public attitudes toward migration differ among receiving countries. In 2011, for example, a majority of adults in Spain, the United Kingdom, and the United States told the German Marshall Fund's (GMF) Transatlantic Trends Survey (2011) that "immigration is more of a problem" than "an opportunity" (p.5). In other countries, such as Germany, Italy, and the Netherlands, the GMF survey found that opinion about migration was split: just about as many adults said that "immigration is a problem" as said "immigration is an opportunity" (p. 5). Only among Canadian adults (surveyed through 2010) did the GMF survey find a majority who see immigration as more of an opportunity (German Marshall Fund 2010, 4). These differences are likely attributable to a number of factors, including the receiving country's social values and economic situation, as well as the history and characteristics of migration in that country. Views of migration in sending countries are also mixed. In a 2012 Pew Research Center's Global Attitudes Project Center survey, half of Mexican adults (50 percent) said "people leaving [Mexico] for jobs in other countries" was "a very big problem" for Mexico (Pew Global Attitudes 2012, 15). The same survey, however, found other issues were more likely to be rated much higher as "very big problems" (p.16) for Mexico: cartel-related violence (according to 75 percent of Mexican adults), human rights violations by the military and police (74 percent), crime (73 percent), corrupt political leaders (69 percent), economic problems (68 percent), illegal drugs (68 percent), terrorism (62 percent), and pollution (58 percent).

由此可见各国对待移民的整体态度和一国之内对待移民的态度有很大差距。

建议译法：面对需要帮助的人，一些国家愿意敞开怀抱，而另一些国家则屈从于深刻的国内国际矛盾和两极化意见。（李）

20

原文：Inequality and exclusion underlie many of today's challenges
原译：当今许多挑战都源自不平等和排斥现象

李："现象"过于具体。不平等和排斥实为制度和/或心态。Exclusion: the process or state of excluding or being excluded。但去掉"现象"，节奏上欠缺一些。加上"社会"，凑齐音节。"排斥"隐含了社会性：有不同群体才会有排斥。

建议译法：今天的许多挑战都源自不平等和社会排斥。（李）

21

原文：Globalization has brought immense gains in the fight against poverty worldwide and has improved living conditions nearly everywhere.
原译：全球化为世界消除贫困带来巨大帮助，改善了几乎各地的生活条件。

王：原译"全球化……带来巨大帮助"不太符合中文表达习惯。

改译1：全球化使世界消除贫困工作取得巨大成就，改善了几乎各地的生活条件。（王）
改译2：全球化为世界范围内消除贫困（或"世界范围内的反贫困斗争"）作出巨大贡献，改善了几乎所有地区的生活条件。（程）

李：改译2很好。另外，"各地"尽管可以理解为"所有地方"，但通常用来表示"地方"的复数。要强调"所有"，就直接说"所有地区"。

建议译法： 全球化为世界范围内消除贫困（或"世界范围内的反贫困斗争"）作出巨大贡献，改善了几乎所有地区的生活条件。（程）

22

原文： But it has been cruelly unfair...
原译： 然而，全球化又是残酷而不公的。（马）

李：处理为并列不妥，应当是不公平以至于达到残酷的程度。

建议译法： 然而，全球化带来了残酷的不公。（李）

23

原文： ...as wealth has increased, so too has its asymmetry, leaving millions behind in all parts of the world.
原译： 随着财富的增加，财富分布也愈发失衡，将世界各地数百万人甩在后面。

王：原文 so too has its asymmetry 完整结构为 so too has the asymmetry [of wealth increased]。asymmetry 就是 lack of equality。

> Lack of equality or equivalence between parts or aspects of something; lack of symmetry.
> 'there was an asymmetry between the right and left ears'
> 'the global system is marked by great asymmetry: the most important goods are controlled by groups in a relatively small number of countries'
> [count noun] 'gravitational asymmetries had pulled the sphere out of shape'

https://en.oxforddictionaries.com/definition/asymmetry

所以，译为"不平等""失衡"都可以。不必拘泥于"对称"之类的说法。

李："数百万人"太具体；"千百万人"范围更大。

建议译法：随着财富的增加，财富分配也愈发不平等，在世界所有地方，都有千百万人被甩在后面。（王、李）

24

原文：Both developed and developing countries, North and South, face greater inequality and marginalization now than they did 20 years ago.
原译：无论发达国家还是发展中国家，北方还是南方，不平等和边缘化都甚于二十年前。（马）

王：The **North–South divide** is broadly considered a socio-economic and political divide. Generally, definitions of the Global North include the United States, Canada, Western Europe, and developed parts of Asia, as well as Australia and New Zealand, which are not actually located in the Northern Hemisphere but share similar economic and cultural characteristics as other northern countries. The Global South is made up of Africa, Latin America, and developing Asia including the Middle East. The North is home to all the members of the G8 and to four of the five permanent members of the United Nations Security Council.

The North mostly covers the West and the First World, along with much of the Second World, while the South largely corresponds with the Third World. While the North may be defined as the richer, more developed region and the South as the poorer, less developed region, many more factors differentiate between the two global areas.

https://en.wikipedia.org/wiki/North%E2%80%93South_divide

李：边缘化是一样外在表现，是一种现象，也可以说是"问题"。不增词，语感上感觉不完整。更口语的说法是"不平等和边缘化问题／现象，都比二十年前严重。"

建议译法：无论发达国家还是发展中国家，无论是北方还是南方，不平等和边缘化现象都甚于二十年前。（李）

25

原文：Unless we work together, the coming decades are likely to drive poverty more deeply into fragile low-income countries, pushing them even further onto the sidelines, while even larger numbers of people struggling with poverty live in middle-income countries.

原译：除非我们通力合作，否则在未来几十年里，本就脆弱的低收入国家将在贫困中陷得更深，被推到更为边缘的境地，中等收入国家甚至会有更多贫困人口。（马）

王：decades 没有行为能力，无法"drive"，所以，drive 仅仅是个比喻的说法，译文不必纠结这个词的翻译。drive poverty more deeply into fragile low-income countries 的意思为本就脆弱的国家会更加贫困。

改译：除非我们通力合作，否则在未来几十年里，本就脆弱的低收入国家将更加贫困，进一步陷入边缘化境地，中等收入国家甚至会有更多贫困人口。（王）

建议译法：除非我们通力合作，否则在未来几十年里，本就脆弱的低收入国家将更加贫困，进一步陷入边缘化境地，甚至中等收入国家也会出现更多贫困人口。（李）

李："甚至"的位置微调一下，逻辑更通顺：不仅低收入国家更穷，中等收入国家贫困人口也会增加。

26

原文：Furthermore, this sense of exclusion is not limited to the poorest countries but is vividly on the rise in developed countries as well, fuelling trends of nationalism and a lack of trust in national and multilateral institutions. Our hard-won collective progress towards combating poverty and promoting common security is newly at risk.

原译： 此外，这种被排斥感不仅存在于最贫穷国家，在发达国家也愈渐加深，助长民族主义趋势，使人们失去对国家机构与多边机构的信任。在消除贫困和促进共同安全方面，我们的共同进步来之不易，如今又再次面临风险。（马）

王 & 李： 用及物动词"侵蚀"替换"使……失去"，表达更为直接；collective progress 是集体努力取得的进步。

建议译法： 此外，这种被排斥感不仅限于最贫穷的国家，在发达国家也明显增加，从而助长民族主义趋势，侵蚀人们对国家机构与多边机构的信任。在消除贫困和促进共同安全方面，我们集体取得的进步来之不易，如今却面临新的风险。（王、李）

27

原文： Countries and institutions are struggling to fully deliver
原译： 国家和机构勉力实现承诺

王 & 李： 这句话考验联系上下文的能力。具体 deliver 什么，全文有多处提示，如：

a) …how we can better deliver *on the promise* of the United Nations. (Para.1)

b) Overwhelmed, *a significant number* of States across the world are struggling to effectively address today's major challenges and deliver the *services* needed by their populations. (Para. 9)

这个标题下指出，不少国家在服务人民需求方面出现困难。通篇来看，deliver 是指兑现承诺（提供服务也是兑现承诺）。因为找不到一个不及物动词来翻译 deliver，必须添加一个宾语，用 promise 比用 service 更有包容性。

改译 1： 国家和机构无法充分实现承诺（李）
改译 2： 在充分实现承诺方面力不从心 / 举步维艰（李）

程：这里的问题是 struggling。我的理解是"艰难地、努力地做某件事情"。此处的 struggling 表明，各国和各机构是在努力做，但是困难重重，包括财力、物力、人力等方面都非常不给力。尽管如此，他们也仍在千方百计地努力着。这样，我们是否可以改为："国家和机构正艰难地努力全面实现承诺"呢？有很多时候，我们在工作中遇到困难，进展不顺利，当别人问你，项目进度如何？工作情况怎么样？有的人会说，I am struggling. I am struggling to finish it on time.

> **改译 3**：国家和机构正艰难地努力全面履行承诺。（程）

李：并非所有国家和机构。第 9 段明确说 a significant number of States，所以，可以笼统地说"一些国家"。确实，改译 1 和 2 的表述方式有些消极，秘书长是从正面来谈这个问题：尽管难，还是在努力。综合程老师的意见继续修改。

> **建议译法**：一些国家和机构在通过艰难努力，全面兑现承诺。（李）

28

> **原文**：fragile States
> **建设译法**：脆弱国家（马）

王：A fragile state is a low-income country characterized by weak state capacity and/or weak state legitimacy leaving citizens vulnerable to a range of shocks. The World Bank, for example, deems a country to be 'fragile' if it (a) is eligible for assistance (i.e., a grant) from the International Development Association (IDA) (b) has had a UN peacekeeping mission in the last three years, and (c) has received a 'governance' score of less than 3.2 (as per the Country Performance and Institutional Assessment (CPIA) index of The World Bank).

While many countries are making progress toward achieving the Millennium

Development Goals, a group of 35 to 50 countries (depending on the measure used) are falling behind. It is estimated that out of the world's seven billion people, 26% live in fragile states, and this is where one-third of all people surviving on less than US$1.25 per day live, half of the world's children who die before the age of five, and one-third of maternal deaths occur.

https://en.wikipedia.org/wiki/Fragile_state

29

> 原文：violent extremism
> 建议译法：暴力极端主义（马）

王：Violent extremism refers to the beliefs and actions of people who support or use ideologically motivated violence to achieve radical ideological, religious or political views. Violent extremist views can be exhibited along a range of issues, including politics, religion and gender relations. No society, religious community or worldview is immune to violent extremism. Though "radicalization" is a contested term to some, it has come to be used to define the process through which an individual or a group considers violence as a legitimate and a desirable means of action. Radical thought that does not condone the exercise of violence to further political goals may be seen as normal and acceptable, and be promoted by groups working within the boundaries of the law. It is often used as a code name for Islamic terrorism.

https://en.wikipedia.org/wiki/Violent_extremism

同时，由联合国网站新闻判断，violent extremism 多指伊斯兰国组织、基地组织和博科圣地。资料：

PLAN OF ACTION TO PREVENT VIOLENT EXTREMISM

In recent years, terrorist groups such as ISIL, Al-Qaida and Boko Haram have shaped our image of violent extremism and the debate about how to address this threat. Their message of intolerance – religious, cultural, social – has had drastic consequences for many regions of the world. Holding territory and using social media for real-time communication of their atrocious crimes, they seek to challenge our shared values of peace, justice and human dignity.

https://www.un.org/counterterrorism/ctitf/en/plan-action-prevent-violent-extremism

30

原文：inclusive institutions
原译：包容型机构（马）
建议译法：包容性机构（李）

李：什么是包容性机构？如下：

What do inclusive/exclusive institutions look like?

Inclusive institutions:

- Bestow *equal* rights and entitlements, and enable equal opportunities, voice and access to resources and services.
- Are typically based on principles of universality, non-discrimination, or targeted action. Targeted action is needed where some people and groups are particularly disadvantaged, and therefore require differential treatment to achieve the equivalent outcomes.

Examples of inclusive institutions

- **Universal**: universal age-related state pension; universal access to justice or services.
- **Non-discriminatory**: meritocratic recruitment in the civil service; inheritance laws that protect widows' land rights.
- **Targeted**: affirmative action to increase the proportion of women political representatives; budget rules that prioritise investment in disadvantaged areas.

https://gsdrc.org/topic-guides/inclusive-institutions/concepts-and-debates/what-do-inclusiveexclusive-institutions-look-like/

31

> 原文: We must collectively invest more to help countries build inclusive institutions and resilient communities capable of thriving in a globalized world.
> 原译: 我们必须共同加大投入，帮助各国建设能在全球化世界中蓬勃发展的包容型机构和韧性社区。（马）
> 以下为关于 resilient community 的翻译的讨论:
> **建议译法 1:** "韧性社区"（马）
> **建议译法 2:** "柔韧社区"（李）
> **建议译法 3:** 复原能力强的社区（李）

李：原译"韧性社区"我觉得可以理解，加上引号更好。译为"柔韧社区"也可以。也可以翻译为"复原力强的社区"，这是联合国常用的译文。resilient 不容易翻译，往往需要根据具体情灵活处理。但联合国有个不好的习惯：为求统一而将一个词的翻译固化，导致一些情况下语言不太通顺。但在此处，"复原力强的社区"是可以用的。

resilient community 还可以处理为"抗逆性强的社区"。我多年前在曼谷 UNESCAP 做短期翻译，曾把 resilience 译为"抗逆性"，觉得能够用于多种情形。

> **建议译法 4:** 复原力强的社区（程）

程：resilient 这个词现在经常使用。我们在日常聊天中，可能会说这个人很有韧性、有韧劲，但是好像不太说社区抗逆性强。其实这个词指的是，任何地方，包括城市、社区在遇到灾难后能够迅速地恢复各项功能，包括交通、运输、食物供给、医疗救治等等，使城市和社区迅速恢复正常。比如纽约市就是一个非常 resilient 的城市。"9·11"事件以及前两年发生的一次飓风，都使纽约市遭受重创，但是，他们从市政府到各个机构都在很短的时间里，就让整个城市继续运转起来，让百姓的生活恢复正常。也就是说，纽约这个城市的抗击打能力超强。而前几年在路易斯安娜那里发生了一次水灾，那里到现在仍然是一蹶不振。那个城市就不能说是 resilient。

李:"复原力强"是一个很好的说法。可以改为"复原力强",但不否定其他译法。

王:有译者提出 communities 究竟是应该理解成"社区"还是"社会",以下为李长栓老师给出的意见。

李:这里的 communities 用的是复数,应该和 institutions 一样,属于社会的具体组成单位(社区、村镇、市镇);而"社会"是个整体概念。从其他文本中的使用来看,也是指一个小地方(社区)。所以,我的意见还是翻译为"社区"。当然,communities 既可以指一个地方,也可以指一群有共同之处的人,所以,有时翻译为"社群"。

32

原文:Overwhelmed, a significant number of States across the world are struggling to effectively address today's major challenges and deliver the services needed by their populations.

原译:许多国家在重负之下,艰难地争取有效应对当今的主要挑战,提供本国人民所需的服务。(马)

李:"重负之下"是什么负担,不清楚。overwhelmed 是指挑战太多、服务需求太大,国家感到应接不暇。struggling 这个词是指力不从心、苦苦挣扎。鉴于句首和句尾都可以放置重要信息,改译调整了一下顺序。

建议译法:面对今天的重大挑战和人民的服务需求,世界许多国家在苦苦挣扎,艰难应对。(李)

33

原文:Tensions are exacerbated by a lack of opportunities and by a strong sentiment among many peoples — their youth especially — that they are being excluded by the very institutions meant to serve them.

原译:许多人,尤其是年轻人,不仅缺少机会,而且强烈感受到自己被排斥在本应为他们服务的机构之外,造成紧张局势加剧。(马)

peoples 是指一个民族或族群：

> 5 *plural* **peoples** : a body of persons that are united by a common culture, tradition, or sense of kinship, that typically have common language, institutions, and beliefs, and that often constitute a politically organized group
>
> https://www.merriam-webster.com/dictionary/people

这句暗示一些国家歧视特定族群或群体。a strong sentiment 不容易翻译。Linguee 双语语料库有些启发：

- There is *strong sentiment* today that neither the existence of universal museums nor their multiplication in different sites [...]
- 今天，有观点坚信，现在存在的世界性博物馆或未来在不同地方建立更多这样的博物馆都无法取代一件文物同昨天、今天与明天的社会之间的联系。（ods.un.org）

看来可以把 strong sentiment 具体化。此处的情绪毫无疑问是"强烈不满"。

> **建议译法**：许多族群，尤其是其中的青年人，由于缺乏机会，并强烈不满本应为之服务的机构却排斥他们，造成社会矛盾进一步加剧。（李）

34

> **原文**：Few countries or institutions appear to have a long-term vision to meet peoples' needs or strategies to manage today's interlinked crises, instead finding themselves entangled in reactive responses.

王：代表"国家"或"机构"的 they (themselves)，应该翻译为"他们"还是"它们"？这是个令人纠结的问题。按照通常的理解，不表示"人"，就用"它"，似乎应该翻译为"它们"，联合国的翻译语料中基本也是这么翻译。但纯中文语境下的用例，是另一种情景：

a. 以下段落摘自中华人民共和国常驻联合国代表团网站：

"十年前，各国首脑齐聚布鲁塞尔，通过了《布鲁塞尔行动纲领》，对最不发达国家未来十年的发展做出了庄严的政治承诺，为国际社会帮助最不发达国家摆脱贫困、实现发展制定了时间表和路线图。十年来，最不发达国家为此进行了不懈努力，使经济建设和社会发展不断改善。然而，由于最不发达国家长期以来基础差，能力弱，其内在的脆弱性没有得到根本改变，特别是全球金融危机后，他们面临的挑战有增无减，全面实现《布鲁塞尔行动纲领》目标的前景不容乐观。因此，最不发达国家需要做出新的努力，国际社会需要给予更大的支持。"

b. 以下摘自外交部网站：

"中国政府和中国外交部昨天发表的两个声明、中国政府今天发表的白皮书已经比较完整和系统地阐述了中方在所谓南海仲裁案问题上的立场。我不再重复。我知道很多记者已经参加了上午国新办的发布会，听取了刘振民副部长介绍的情况。在此，我仅就上述这三四个国家仍然执着所谓"仲裁结果符合国际法"这么个表态，谈几点看法：

第一，我们注意到，自从中方提醒"七八个国家代表不了国际社会"后，上述这几个国家在他们的表态中没再以"国际社会"自居。这很好。"

c. 同时，现代汉语语料库检索中，"他们"与国家的模糊匹配为 255 条，"它们"为 138 条。

以上例子说明，至少在把一个国家或机构当成一群人的时候，可以用"他们"来指代。

王：reactive response 意思应理解为"被动应对"，与"主动应对"相对应。

Q: What is the difference between proactive and reactive?

A: QUICK ANSWER
A proactive approach focuses on eliminating problems before they have a chance to appear and a reactive approach is based on responding to events after they have happened. The difference between these two approaches is the perspective each one provides in assessing actions and events.
CONTINUE READING ▼

https://www.reference.com/education/difference-between-proactive-reactive-a7e0b62f5c80ac8c#

以下段落选自一篇联合国新闻中心的报道。报道谈及联合国维和任务在刚果民主共和国"主动应对"的必要性。

He affirmed that the UN's presence in critical areas of danger was "not enough" and that "presence without action, in the face of violence, undermines our credibility." To that point, he called on MONUSCO troops to engage with civilians, "pursue the danger where it lies," and "march for days into the jungle," if necessary, in order to guarantee the protection of civilians.

"Action, not inaction; proactive, not reactive; mobile forces, not static battalions; feet, not wheels," Mr. Kobler stated. "When civilians are at risk, 'Act, don't ask!'"

http://www.un.org/apps/news/story.asp?NewsID=49172#.WZrDhz6GPcs

建议译法: 似乎没有什么国家或机构能够放眼长远,满足人民的需求,或制定战略,管理当今社会各种相互关联的危机;相反,他们陷于被动应对而不能自拔。(李)

第八单元 法律

Exercise 8 An Engagement Letter

翻译情景

本单元选自一份委托书（Engagement Letter），Dragon Systems（声龙公司）委托高盛公司（Goldman Sachs）办理声龙公司的出售事宜。委托书由高盛起草。后来因为升这桩并购案，贝克夫妇将高盛公司告上法庭。这份委托书是其中一份重要证据。

假定你是自由职业译员，对诉讼案件一无所知。现在承接了委托书的翻译任务，将来译文用于编写英汉对照的案例集。请翻译委托书节选，共737词。全文可截取原文任意片段，在网上搜索查看。

训练重点

虽然每次的作业翻译都要调动各项翻译能力，但每篇作业特点不同，需要调动的能力有所不同。本篇文章需要重点调动全局意识、查证能力和逻辑思维能力。全局意识是在译者对作者、知识背景和翻译情景一无所知的情况下，主动了解相关信息，避免方向性错误；查证能力帮助译者调动各种资源，查找相关知识；逻辑思维和查证能力相辅相成，促使译者透彻理解原文，并以简洁、清晰、严谨的方式形成译文。

训练难点

这封委托书不仅体现了法律文件用词的严谨性，也提醒译者在工作中必须锱铢必较。本单元的难点首先在于通过查证，掌握原文背景和事件脉络，理解原文的每个细节；其次是如何以专业、清晰的方式传递信息。

训练方式

本次练习分原文、翻译提示、参考译文、译者注四部分。请先尝试自己翻译原文。做完以后再参看翻译提示，并再次调查、修改、润色，形成第二稿。形成二稿之后，再看参考译文和译者注。翻译能力是在实践过程中不断提升的，希望你充分利用每一单元，一步步取得翻译能力上的飞跃！

原文[1]

Engagement Letter[2][3]

PERSONAL AND CONFIDENTIAL

December 2, 1999

Ellen Chamberlain

Chief Financial Officer

Dragon Systems, Inc.

320 Nevada Street

Newton, MA 02460

Janet M. Baker, Ph.D.

Dragon Systems, Inc.

320 Nevada Street

Newton, MA 02460

Donald L. Waite

Executive Vice President and Chief Administrative Officer

Seagate Technology, Inc.

920 Disc Drive

P.O. Box 66360

Scotts Valley, CA 95067-0360

Ladies and Gentleman[4]:

We are pleased to confirm the arrangements under which Goldman, Sachs & Co. ("Goldman Sachs") is exclusively engaged by Dragon systems, Inc. (the "Company") as financial advisor in connection with[5] the possible sale of all or a portion of the Company.

During the term of our engagement, we will provide you[6] with financial advice and assistance in connection with this potential transaction, which may include performing valuation analyses, searching for a purchaser acceptable to you, coordinating visits of potential purchasers and assisting you in negotiating the financial aspects of the transaction.

In connection with this engagement, the Company shall pay us a quarterly fee of $150,000, payable in cash, commencing on February 1, 2000, which to the extent paid shall be applied against[7] any transaction fee which may become payable pursuant to this letter agreement. If the purchase of 50% or more of the outstanding common stock or the assets (based on the book value thereof) of the Company is accomplished ("a sale of the Company") in one or a series of transactions, including, but not limited to, private purchases of stock, a merger or a sale by the Company of its stock or assets, we will charge a transaction fee based on the eventual buyer ("the Buyer") of the Company as set forth[8] below.

…

If less than 50% of the outstanding common stock or the assets (based on the book value thereof) of the Company is acquired in the manner set forth above, we will charge a transaction fee to be mutually agreed upon by Goldman Sachs and the Company but in no event less than $2 million. Notwithstanding the foregoing, in the event that either Sony Corporation or Psion PLC, or their respective affiliates, invest $40 million or less in the Company through a private issuance of new shares by the Company, no fee shall be payable in connection with such transaction. Except as provided herein, a transaction fee will be paid to us in cash upon consummation of each transaction.

The aggregate consideration for purposes of calculating a transaction fee shall be:

(i) in the case of the sale, exchange or purchase of the Company's equity securities, the total consideration paid for such securities (including amounts paid to holders of options, warrants and convertible securities), plus the principal amount of all indebtedness for borrowed money as set forth on the most recent consolidated balance sheet of the Company prior to the consummation of such sale, exchange or purchase, and

(ii) in the case of a sale or disposition by the Company of assets, the total consideration paid for such assets, plus the net value of any current assets not sold by the Company and the principal amount of all indebtedness for borrowed money expressly assumed by the purchaser.

Amounts paid into escrow and contingent payments in connection with any transaction will be included as part of the aggregate consideration. Fees on amounts paid into escrow will be payable (a) upon the establishment of such escrow or (b) upon the release of such amounts from escrow to the extent the related escrow agreement provides that the escrow agent shall pay such fees to Goldman Sachs at or prior to the payment of such amounts to the Company or its stockholders. For purposes of the foregoing sentence,[9] Goldman Sachs shall not be entitled to fees on amounts released from escrow that are paid to the Buyer. If the consideration in connection with any transaction may be increased by payments related to future events, the portion of our fee relating to such contingent payments will be calculated and paid if and when such contingent payments are made. Aggregate consideration also shall include the aggregate amount of any (i) dividends or other distributions declared by the Company with respect to its stock after the date hereof, other than normal recurring cash dividends in amounts not materially greater than currently paid, and (ii) amounts paid by the Company, to repurchase any securities of the Company outstanding on the date hereof.[10]

翻译提示

1 **全局意识**
请大家针对原文和译文，分别回答 Who is talking to whom? About what? When, where and why? And how? 然后再开始翻译。

2 **全局意识：事件主角与来龙去脉**
翻译之前，需要了解事件的主角和来龙去脉，也就是全局意识当中涉及的 6Ws（who is talking to whom, about about, when, where and why）。可以将事件主题词 "Goldman Sachs and the $580 Million Black Hole" 输入到谷歌当中，搜索词条第一条即是《纽约时报》的相关内容。也可以试着检索其他信息，比如法院"备忘和裁定"（Memorandum and Order）（参考网站：https://www.casemine.com/judgement/us/59146636add7b0493429b237#）。

3 **查证能力 / 逻辑思维**
通过查证，engagement letter 应该有很多翻译版本，译者需要做的不是机械地对照，而是选择有理论依据、素材支撑的版本即可，不必过于拘泥于一种译本。

4 **全局意识：细节处理**
译者在校验时，要注意这里的单复数情况。

5 **用词准确性**
是否而可以翻译为"处理"？高盛的作用是什么？

6 **you 的指代**

这个词如何解释,有争议,需慎重处理。

7 **理解 / 查证能力**

理解这句话的关键,是弄清楚 apply against 的意思,是支付还是不支付?建议查询一下投行的支付方式。

8 **修饰关系**

请研究一下 as set forth 修饰谁。

9 **全局意识:上下文**

for purposes of the foregoing sentence 的意思要结合上句话来理解。

10 **修饰关系**

想要翻译清楚法律原文,准确理解、分析原文句子结构非常重要。在 (i) 和 (ii) 中,请译者辨析第一个 hereof 修饰的是谁?是 stock 还是 declare?同理,第二个 hereof 修饰的是 securities,还是 outstanding?

参考译文[1]:

委托书[2]

私人保密通信[3]
1999 年 12 月 2 日
埃伦 · 张伯伦
首席财务官
声龙系统公司[4]
内华达大街 320 号
马萨诸塞州牛顿市

邮编 MA 02460[5]

珍妮特·M·贝克博士
声龙系统公司
内华达大街 320 号
马萨诸塞州牛顿市
邮编 MA 02460

唐纳德·L·韦特
执行副总裁兼首席行政官
希捷科技公司[6]
迪斯科车道 920 号[7]
邮政信箱 66360 号[8],
加利福尼亚州斯科茨谷
邮编 CA 95067-0360

各位女士/先生[9]：

  我们很高兴确认如下安排：声龙系统公司（简称"贵公司"）独家委托高盛集团（简称"高盛"）作为财务顾问,[10] 就贵公司可能出售全部或部分业务事宜[11] 提供顾问服务。[12]

  受委托期间，我们将就此项潜在交易向你们提供财务建议和协助，其中可能包括估值分析、寻找你们可以接受的买方、协调潜在买家的访问、协助你们谈判交易中的财务事宜。[13]

  为此次委托之目的，自 2000 年 2 月 1 日起，贵公司每季度应以现金形式支付我们 15 万美元。根据本委托协议可能需要支付的任何交易费用，应扣除已按季度支付的费用。[14] 若通过一次或一系列交易——包括但不限于非公开购买贵公司股票、公司合并或贵公司出售股票或资产,[15] 投资者完成收购贵公司 50% 或以上的流通普通股或资产（以账面价值计算）（简称"完成贵公司出售"），我们将根据贵公司的最终买方（简称"买方"），按以下方式收取交易费。[16]

若以上文所述方式收购的贵公司流通普通股或资产（以账面价值计算）少于50%，我们将按照高盛与贵公司共同商定的数额收取交易费，但无论如何，该费用不低于200万美元。[17] 虽有上述规定，[18] 若索尼公司或Psion公共有限公司，[19] 抑或两者各自的关联公司，[20] 以购买贵公司未公开发售新股的方式，向公司投资4000万美元或以下数额，则贵公司无须就此交易支付任何费用。[21] 除本协议另有约定外，交易费用应在完成每笔交易后，以现金方式支付给我们。[22]

为计算每次交易费之目的，总对价[23] 应做如下理解[24]：

(i) 如果是出售、交换或购买贵公司的股本证券，[25] 总对价即为投资者购买此类证券支付的总对价（包括支付给期权、认股权证[26]、可转换证券[27] 持有者的费用），加上完成此类出售、交换或购买之前，贵公司最新合并[28] 资产负债表中所借款项的全部债务本金。[29]

(ii) 如果是贵公司出售或处置[30] 资产，总对价即为投资者购买这些资产支付的总对价，加上贵公司未出售的流动资产净值，以及由购买方[31] 明确承担的所借款项的全部债务本金。[32]

支付到托管账户[33] 的资金及与任何与交易相关的或有[34] 付款均计入总对价。[35] 支付到托管账户的资金，按以下时间点支付费用[36]：(i) 设立托管账户之时；或 (ii) 托管账户释放托管资金之时，条件是相关托管协议规定托管代理人向贵公司或其股东释放托管资金之时或之前，[37] 先行向高盛支付相关费用[38]。为上句话之目的，高盛不应就托管账户释放给买方的资金收取费用[39]。若因与未来事件相关的付款导致任何交易的对价增加，高盛将在或有付款支付完成时，计算并收取与此或有付款有关的费用。[40] 总对价还应包括：(i) 本协议日之后贵公司宣布的[41] 股票红利和其他利益分配，[42] 总额，不包括正常支付的经常性现金红利，[43] 但大大高于当前支付水平的除外；以及 (ii) 贵公司为回购本协议日仍在流通的普通股支付的费用总额。[44]

第八单元·法　律

译者注

1　全局意识：
　　事件主角和来龙去脉

　　这份委托协议后来演变成为一桩诉讼。原告是 Dragon Systems（声龙公司）的两位创始人，被告是高盛公司（Goldman Sachs）。据《纽约时报》报道，L&H 有意购买声龙公司，贝克夫妇急于出售。声龙创始人詹姆斯·贝克(James Baker) 和珍妮特·贝克 (Janet Baker) 委托高盛做财务顾问，以完成这项并购。虽然公司价值数亿美元，但对高盛来说是小菜一碟，因此高盛没有给予应有重视，仅仅安排四个二十多岁的毛头小伙，来协调收购事宜。声龙依赖高盛，而高盛显然没有尽职地调查（高盛说自己本来就没有尽职调查的责任），就匆匆忙忙把声龙卖给涉嫌财务诈骗的 L&H 公司。后者没有足够现金，全部以公司股票支付对价。2 个月后财务骗局曝光，公司随即破产清算，本来价值数亿美元的公司，贝克夫妇仅拿到数百万，经济损失 3 亿美元，还损失了凝聚 18 年心血的语音识别技术（清算中被卖给其他公司）。

　　贝克夫人以"违约"等多项事由，将高盛告上法庭。被告认为，这封委托书是高盛和声龙两家公司签署的，要打官司，只有声龙公司有资格，但声龙已经不复存在；贝克夫人作为股东，不是委托书当事方，所以没有诉讼资格（standing）。贝克夫人认为，她的名字既然出现在委托书的收件人中（贝克先生不是收件人），委托书当中的 you，也包括自己，高盛对其承担直接的合同义务，所以她有诉讼资格。法院认为，在委托书上主体部分签字的，只有声龙代表 CFO 张伯伦，没有贝克夫人，所以，不需要考虑 you 是否包括贝克夫人，就可以判定贝克夫人不是委托书当事人；而且贝克夫人还签订了不起诉协议。

　　案件最终以贝克夫妇败诉告终，贝克夫妇上诉后，上诉法院维持原判。

　　关于事件的来龙去脉，《纽约时报》有详细报道（包括中文译文）。如果无法查看《纽约时报》，请查看其他网站的转载，比如 CNBC。请把下列内容输入谷歌搜索框搜索："Goldman Sachs and the $580 Million Black

249

Hole",搜索结果中的第一条即是《纽约时报》的报道。这里摘录《纽约时报》报道中的几段内容。

贝克夫妇的主张:

THE Bakers' case against Goldman is simple. Their lawyer, Alan K. Cotler of Philadelphia, captured it in a single sentence in a motion for summary judgment (简易程序判决): "The Goldman Four were unsupervised, inexperienced, incompetent and lazy investment bankers who were put on a transaction that in the scheme of things was small potatoes for Goldman."

高盛的抗辩:

Summarizing Goldman's defense is more complicated. Based on the firm's response to the complaint, its motion for summary judgment and testimony of the people it employed, most of that defense falls under one of three rubrics: The Bakers do not have standing to sue. Goldman had no obligation to do a financial analysis of L.& H. And Goldman's bankers actually performed quite well. The firm released a statement that asserted, "Goldman Sachs was retained as a financial adviser by Dragon Systems, *not its shareholders*, and performed its assignment satisfactorily in all respects."

跟委托书相关的一段:

Goldman's lawyer, John D. Donovan of Ropes & Gray in Boston, has argued that *under the terms of the engagement letter*, only Dragon Systems had the right to sue, and Dragon no longer exists. Goldman has even filed a countersuit against Ms. Baker, contending that by suing Goldman she had breached the contract. Even though Ms. Baker lost everything in a deal Goldman orchestrated, the firm says Ms. Baker should now pay its legal fees.

https://www.nytimes.com/2012/07/15/business/goldman-sachs-and-a-sale-gone-horribly-awry.html

还可以检索其他信息。这是马萨诸塞州地区法院"备忘和裁定"(Memorandum and Order) 当中涉及委托书的一段:

Defendants contend that the Bakers have no cause of action for breach of contract because the Bakers were not parties to the Engagement Agreement between Dragon and Goldman, and that Goldman's duties ran exclusively to Dragon. The Bakers respond that Goldman owed them a direct contractual duty independent of the contractual duty it owed to Dragon. The Bakers predicate this argument on the language of the second sentence of the Engagement Agreement, which reads,

> During the term of our engagement, we will provide *you* with financial advice and assistance in connection with this potential transaction, which may include performing valuation analyses, searching for a purchaser acceptable to *you*, coordinating visits of potential purchasers and assisting *you* in negotiating the financial aspects of the transaction.

https://www.casemine.com/judgement/us/59146636add7b0493429b237#

什么是engagement letter? engagement letter，中文一般翻译为"委托书"或者"约定书"。通过如下解释可以得知，委托书一般是专业服务公司（如金融、会计、法律、咨询公司）与客户之前签订的协议，用来界定委托与受托关系、责任目标和范围等事宜：

An engagement letter is a written agreement to perform services in exchange for compensation. Engagement letters are traditionally used by certain professional service firms, particularly in the fields of finance, accounting, law and consulting, to define the specifics of the business relationship. The letter is usually sent by the service firm to an officer of the engaging company, and once the officer has signed it, the letter serves as a contract.

Since an engagement letter serves the same purpose as a traditional contract, it is important to carefully lay out the scope of the engagement, any contingencies that must be addressed, completion deadlines and compensation arrangements. Ensuring that these details are correct at the outset helps to avoid costly misunderstandings later on in the assignment. Since an engagement letter is more informal by its nature, it can be a good way to establish a written agreement when the parties would otherwise be reluctant to enter into a full contract.

http://www.investopedia.com/terms/e/engagement-letter.asp

全局意识：
who is talking to whom

尽管是声龙委托高盛，但这封委托书却是高盛起草的，旨在确认声龙与高盛的聘任关系。委托条件，双方肯定已经私下谈妥。收件人是 1：Ellen Chamberlain，声龙的首席财务官（CFO）；2：Janet Baker，声龙的总裁和共同创办人；3：Donald L. Waite，希捷科技 (Seagate Technology，声龙股东) 的行政副总裁。

2

> **原文：** Engagement Letter
> **原译：** 财务顾问协议（谢）

谢： 最初译为"委托书"。参考资料：

故事到了 1999 年 12 月，对并购事宜完全一头雾水的贝克夫妇，签署了一份由高盛起草的五页委托书。在委托书中，高盛承诺提供"与此项潜在交易相关的财务咨询和协助，可能包括开展估值分析、寻找贵方所能接受的买家、协调安排潜在买家来访，并协助贵方洽商此项交易的财务条款。"

https://cn.nytimes.com/business/20120806/c06goldman/?mcubz=3

后来询问金融圈人士，他们建议翻译成"财务顾问协议"，以便在标题上就点明协议的内容。译者思考后也认为这里应该翻译成"财务顾问协议"。一是这一标题非常清楚，作为一个法律文件来说是需要说明白的。二是译者认为，"协议"一词更符合本文的内容，因为这是双方基于共识签订的法律文书。参考资料：

关于并购业务顾问收费问题，一直是投行圈从业人士的主要收益来源，尤其是并购居间人，经常跟买方或卖方甚至两方签署《并购居间财务顾问服务协议》来锁定未来并购交易完成后的服务费。

http://blog.sina.com.cn/s/blog_621583480102wot3.html

王： 我觉得谢的论证有理有据，值得信服。但看了叶俊文的查证，也觉得聘用书、委托书没有问题。通过查证，发现 engagement letter 并没有统一说法。我觉得只要意思清楚都可以,还是烦请李老师定夺一下。

李:翻译很难有统一的译法,况且这个名称也不是未来案件的争议要点,所以,我觉得"聘书""委托书""委托代理协议""财务顾问协议"都没问题;姑且译为"委托书"。

> **建议译法:** 委托书(李)

3

> **原文:** PERSONAL AND CONFIDENTIAL
> **原译:** 私人机密(谢)
> **建设译文:** 私人保密通信(李)

李:这是说明这封信的性质。根据英文的密级,属于"秘密"。但要说"私人秘密通信",似乎有什么见不得人的秘密。"保密"可能更达意。

关于密级,百度百科这样说:"密级"指国家事务秘密程度的等级,一般分为绝密、机密、秘密三级。自2017年10月1日起,军队中在原三级基础上增加新增"绝密·核心"密级,成为四级密级制,新密级暂时仅用于军事机关。

维基百科 classified information 词条有相应的英文说法,可以参考。这是目录的一部分:

Contents [hide]
1 Government classification
2 Typical classification levels
    2.1 Top Secret (TS)
    2.2 Secret
    2.3 Confidential
    2.4 Restricted
    2.5 Official
    2.6 Unclassified
    2.7 Clearance
    2.8 Compartmented information
3 International
    3.1 NATO classifications
    3.2 International organisations

https://en.wikipedia.org/wiki/Classified_information

4

原文：Dragon Systems, Inc. 的译法，参考了以下平行文本：

2000年5月8日，中国北京——作为拥有世界领先语音识别技术的Dragon Systems（声龙）公司"龙年"活动的一部分，该公司宣布，今天发布的"声龙普通话龙年版"软件是该公司专门为开拓亚洲市场而设计的最先进的语音识别产品。

http://tech.sina.com.cn/news/it/2000-05-11/24847.shtml

5

> **原文**：Newton, MA 02460
> **原译**：马萨诸塞州，牛顿市，02460（谢）

1、美国邮编：（美国一般叫zip code）

美国邮编有两种，一是5位数字-4位数字，比如：15894-4589，

二是5位数字，例如：95874

李：信件左上角的收件人信息，除了姓名和职称外，其实都没有必要翻译。至少联合国出版物上的地址，都是不翻译的。这次翻译任务，假定是编写英汉对照的案例，为了便于读者学习，可以翻译出来。MA 也可以翻译两遍，让大家多学点知识。参考译文以行为单位来翻译；如果是文章中的叙述性文字，可以按照中文习惯从大到小重新排列。

> **建议译法**：马萨诸塞州牛顿市，邮编 MA 02460（李）

6

Seagate Technology, Inc. 的背景资料：

Seagate Technology knows that if you want to survive in the storage market, you'd better have drives. The company is a leading independent maker of storage systems for electronic data. It makes hard disk drives (HDDs), solid state drives (SSDs), and solid state hybrid drives (SSHDs) as well as devices for managing storage. Seagate's drives are used in systems ranging from personal computers and consumer electronics to high-end servers and mainframes. The company sells directly to computer manufacturers and through distributors. The company sells directly to OEM customers including HP Inc. and Dell and to distributors and retailers. Seagate generates around 70% of its sales outside the US. France-based LaCie is a Seagate subsidiary.

http://www.vault.com/company-profiles/computer-hardware/seagate-technology-llc/company-overview

声龙和希捷的关系（来自《纽约时报》报道）：

For years, the Bakers pressed on, convinced that they were on track to create a program that would recognize continuous speech.

To do that, however, they eventually decided that they needed more capital. While Mr. Baker worked on the technology, Ms. Baker brokered a deal with Seagate Technology, the disk drive manufacturer. *Seagate bought 25 percent of Dragon for $20 million.* Then, in 1997, Dragon introduced Dragon NaturallySpeaking, a program that recognized more words than could be found in a standard collegiate dictionary.

Seagate Technology, Inc. 的译法，参考了以下资料：

希捷科技（英语：Seagate Technology）是全球主要的硬盘厂商之一，于1979年在美国加州成立，在开曼群岛注册。希捷的主要产品包括桌面硬盘、企业用硬盘、笔记本电脑硬盘和微型硬盘，它的第一个硬盘产品容量是5MB。在2006年5月，希捷科技收购了另一间硬盘厂商迈拓公司（Maxtor）。产品销量方面，希捷宣称为销量第一的公司，售出十亿个硬盘产品。

https://zh.wikipedia.org/wiki/ 希捷科技

7

翻译 Disc Drive 的参考资料：

王：drive，车道，一般指连接私人住宅和街道 / 公路的那段路。

Blvd, boulevard，城市里的大道，类同 avenue，或由于是来自法语，显得更雍容一些，例如：日落大道 Sunset Boulevard。

Ave, avenue，城市里的大道，有绿化带，较宽，多为商业区，繁华热闹。

St, street，城市里的街道，少或没有绿化带，较窄，多为住宅区。

Fwy, freeway，高速公路，基本等同于 expressway，也可指市区快速路，中国的高速路统称为 expressway（或许 freeway 来自 toll-free way，免费高速，所以中国不适用）。

Rd, road，道路，可用于普通公路（国道、省道、县道），也可指城市内的普通街道。

此外，美国地址还有：

xxx Wy, way，路 / 街

xxx Cir, circle，环路

xxx Ln, lane，弄 / 巷

http://wenren.com/thread-2425-1-1.html

8

> **原文**：P.O. Box 66360
> **原译**：66360 邮箱（谢）

谢芮：根据以下文本：

P.O. BOX 是 Post Office Box 的缩写，也可以写为 Postal Box，意思是"邮政信箱"，目前在世界各地使用都很普遍，是当地邮局专门设置的可上锁的、唯一编号的、可寻址的小铁箱子，可以个人租用也可以企业租用。根据邮箱大小及放置位置不同，租用价格有所不同，邮箱越大价格会越高，而在中心商业区的价格也相对高些。

https://www.liankuaiche.com/question/51678

王：原译"邮箱"可能被理解为 mailbox。

> **改译1**：66360 邮政信箱（王）
> **建议译法**：邮政信箱 66360 号（李）

9

> **原文**：Ladies and Gentleman
> **原译**：女士们、先生们（谢）

叶：原文 Gentleman 用的是单数，因为是给三个人写的，两名女性，一名男性。称呼"先生们"觉得有些别扭，是否可以译"女士们、唐纳德先生"？或"女士们、这位先生"？

王：是否可以处理为"各位女士，各位先生"？

不指名道姓，且"各位"指参与其中的每一位，但不像"们"那样突出复数。具体指代谁，我们可以加注进一步解释，不然我担心会给读者造成困扰。

改译1：各位女士、各位先生（王）

李：毕竟只有一位先生。加上"各位"，还是别扭。用斜线隔开，可能复数概念不太突兀。

建议译法：各位女士 / 先生（李）

10

原文：financial advisor
原译：财务顾问
改译：（维持不变）

李："财务顾问"是高盛业务的一部分：

表2 高盛及附属公司提供的服务以及其他活动（2011年）		
投资银行	财务顾问	并购重组的战略咨询，资产剥离，收购防御策略，风险管理，重组和分拆上市一站式并购融资和跨境重组，管理资本金、资产和负债风险，与并购安排相关的贷款承诺、银行贷款、过桥贷款。
	股票承销	普通股、优先股、可转换和可交换证券。
	债券承销和设计债务融资工具	投资级债券、高收益债券、银行贷款、过桥贷款和新兴市场债券和结构化的证券。

http://www.sac.net.cn/yjcbw/zgzqzz/2012/2012_11/201212/P020121214387219821574.pdf

财务顾问费是利润主要来源

目前并购财务顾问的收费没有一个统一的收费标准，因并购操作复杂程度、并购标的额大小、操作周期长短、谈判双方的谈判实力不同而高低不一，但是总体的区间基本上都落在 150 万到 500 万之间，有少数标的额较大且操作较复杂的并购案，财务顾问金额在 600 万元以上。一般来说，上市公司并购顾问费高于非上市公司并购，涉及国有股权的上市公司并购顾问费高于法人股的上市公司并购，要约收购的并购顾问费高于普通的协议收购。

http://www.goingconcern.cn/article/2914

11

原文：. . . as financial advisor in connection with the possible sale of all or a portion of the Company.
原译：作为财务顾问，负责协助全部或部分公司的潜在出售（谢）

谢：应该是由公司来处理自己的出售，而财务顾问提供的是建议和服务。

改译 1：就全部或部分出售贵公司的可能性问题，提供财务顾问服务。（谢）

李："可能"放在哪里都不顺。省略算了。意思已经隐含在句子中了。

建议译法：……作为财务顾问，就贵公司出售全部或部分业务事宜提供顾问服务。（李）

12

原文：We are pleased to confirm the arrangements under which Goldman, Sachs & Co. ("Goldman Sachs") is exclusively engaged by Dragon systems, Inc. (the "Company") as financial advisor in connection with the possible sale of all or a portion of the Company.

原译：我司很高兴确认如下安排：声龙系统公司（简称"贵司"）聘请高盛集团（简称"高盛"）作为专属财务顾问，负责协助全部或部分公司的潜在出售。（谢）

王：还是建议全篇都改用"公司"，"我司"这种说法总让人联想到国家部委，而且在经济领域，一般还是说"公司"。

改译1：我公司很高兴确认如下安排：声龙系统公司（简称"贵公司"）聘请高盛集团（简称"高盛"）作为专属财务顾问，负责协助全部或部分公司的潜在出售。（王）

李：既然 you 引起了争议，这个 we 我们也严格处理吧。

李：后来出现争议的词语还包括"exclusively engage"（见下），这两个词也翻译为一个整体吧（"独家委托"）。

4. The parties disagree on the meaning of the term "exclusively engage" in the Engagement Agreement. Defendants argue it means Dragon was Goldman's exclusive client. Plaintiff argues that it means Goldman was the exclusive investment banker acting as a financial advisor to Dragon. However, because Ms. Chamberlain, Dragon's CFO, was the only party to sign the body of the contract, and because the contract only contemplated the provision of consideration by Dragon, the textual dispute between the parties is not a determinative issue.

建议译法：我们很高兴确认如下安排：声龙系统公司（简称"贵公司"）独家委托高盛集团（简称"高盛"）作为财务顾问，就贵公司出售全部或部分业务事宜提供顾问服务。（李）

13

> 原文：During the term of our engagement, we will provide you with financial advice and assistance in connection with this potential transaction, which may include performing valuation analyses, searching for a purchaser acceptable to you, coordinating visits of potential purchasers and assisting you in negotiating the financial aspects of the transaction.
>
> 原译：聘用期间，我司将为贵司提供与此潜在交易有关的财务咨询及协助，包括开展估值分析、寻找合适买家、协调潜在买家来访及协助贵司谈判交易的财务事项。（谢）

谢：valuation analyses：

A form of fundamental analysis that looks to compare the valuation of one security to another, to a group of securities or within its own historical context. Valuation analysis is done to evaluate the potential merits of an investment or to objectively assess the value of a business or asset.

Valuation analysis is one of the core duties of a fundamental investor, as valuations (along with cash flows) are typically the most important drivers of asset prices over the long term.

http://www.investopedia.com/terms/v/valuation_analysis.asp

valuation analyses 的翻译参考以下文本：

公司估值是指着眼于公司本身，对公司的内在价值进行评估。公司内在价值决定于公司的资产及其获利能力。

http://wiki.mbalib.com/wiki/ 公司估值

王：you 的指代，可能是 engagement letter 最具有争议性的地方，全文中出现多次。当事人 Janet Baker 以这封 engagement letter 起诉高盛。但是，这封信写得模棱两可，最关键的就是信中 you 指代不清（不确认是公司还是 Janet 本人），因此法院最终判高盛无罪。因此，我想在翻译时，我们也要模糊处理。我暂时把这里改成"您"。

> **改译 1**：协议期间，我公司将为您提供与此潜在交易有关的财务建议及协助，其中可能包括进行估值分析、寻找您可以接受的买方、协调潜在买家来访及协助您谈判交易的财务事项。（王）

王：如果标题 engagement letter 决定翻译为"财务顾问协议"，那 During the term of our engagement 要改为协议期间；如果翻译为"委托书"，此处就是"受委托期间"。

李：我花了一天时间研究这个案件。从这封信的整体来看，这个 you 显然是指公司，挺清楚的，不是高盛故意含糊；法官也作出了这样的认定。之所以出现争议，是因为这笔交易被高盛做砸了，贝克夫妇很恼火，因此就想办法起诉高盛。要起诉，就必须有事由，即你哪些受保护的权利受到侵害。The Bakers assert seven claims: (1) breach of fiduciary duty; (2) violation of the Massachusetts Unfair Trade Practices statute, Mass. Gen. Laws Ch. 93A; (3) breach of contract; (4) breach of contract/third party beneficiary; (5) breach of the implied covenant of good faith and fair dealing ; (6) negligence; (7) negligent misrepresentation.［马萨诸塞州地区法院的备忘和裁定(Memorandum and Order)］，其中的第三项事由是 breach of contract。贝克夫妇如果要指责高盛违约，自己必须是协议当事人。但高盛说，协议是跟声龙公司签的（由 CFO 代表），股东（贝克夫妇）不是协议当事方。贝克夫人说，收件人当中也提了我的名字，里面的 you 也一定包括我个人。但法院不认同贝克夫人的主张。

如果不是出现诉讼，译员其实可以根据上下文，把 you 翻译为"贵公司""贵方"。但因为 you 是个争点，我们就不能那样自由了。翻译为"您"，显然是不对的，因为收件人是三个。既然是写给三个人的，其中的 you 一定是复数"你们"。

另外，这是一起民事诉讼，所以，不可能出现"有罪"的说法。有罪是违反刑法时，法院作出的认定。民法上，有过错的一方，要"承担责任"。

建议译法：受委托期间，我们将就此项潜在交易向你们提供财务建议和协助，其中可能包括估值分析、寻找你们可以接受的买方、协调潜在买家的

访问、协助你们谈判交易中的财务事宜。（李）

14

> **原文**: In connection with this engagement, the Company shall pay us a quarterly fee of $150,000, payable in cash, commencing on February 1, 2000, which to the extent paid shall be applied against any transaction fee which may become payable pursuant to this letter agreement.
>
> **原译**：按照协议规定，自 2000 年 1 月起，贵司每季度现金支付我司 15 万美元，但该金额不包括依本协议应支付的任何交易费用。（谢）

王：理解有误。这句话的意思翻反了，apply against 不是不支付，而是要支付那些可能产生的额外费用。

> **改译**：按照协议规定，自 2000 年 1 月起，贵公司每季度应以现金形式支付我公司 15 万美元，并应支付根据本协议可能产生的任何交易费用。（王）

李：这句话我一开始也看不懂，主要是不知道 apply against 是什么意思。后来我查看了投行的收费方式。通常有固定费用，加上交易成功后按比例收取的费用（成功佣金）；固定费用保底，成功佣金按递增或递减的比例收取。仔细思考了一下，觉得只有一种可能：如果交易成功，这笔固定费用可以从成功佣金中扣除。如果交易不成功，反正也收了这笔费，怎么着都赚钱。

王：用 Linguee 查到一些 apply against 的平行文本。打开一个链接看到如下内容：

2.4 The operating/management costs of the Prize, including all costs related to the award ceremony and public information activities, shall be fully covered by the interest earned from the donation made by the Japan Shipbuilding Industry Foundation. To this end, the Director-General shall determine a mandatory overhead cost amount to be applied and charged against the funds in the Special Account, which is to be established under the Financial Regulations for the Prize.

但相应译文似乎不太准确：

2.4 本奖项的所有运作/管理费，包括颁奖仪式和公众宣传活动的所有费用全部由日本造船工业基金会捐赠所得利息提供。为此，总干事将依照本奖项《财务条例》而设立的特别账户支付法定管理费。

但从这个例子似乎可以看出，be applied against 和 be charged against 意思应该相同，都是"从……中支付"的意思，就是李老师说的"从……中扣除"。

李：我在 Linguee 的英语－西班牙语语对中，看到很多例句，比如：

> Contributions of varying amounts, totalling $0.1 million, were received from Member States to be applied against the 2002 assessment.
>
> Se han recibido contribuciones en cantidades diversas de los Estados Miembros, por un valor total de 0,1 millones de dólares, cuyos importes se deducirán de las respectivas cuotas para 2002.

用谷歌翻译把西班牙语再翻译回英文，是这样的：

Contributions have been received in various amounts from Member States, for a total value of $ 0.1 million, the amounts of which will be deducted from the respective quotas for 2002.

很显然，be applied against 就是从后面的数字中扣除。

> **建议译法**：为此次委托之目的，自 2000 年 2 月 1 日起，贵公司每季度应以现金形式支付我们 15 万美元。根据本委托协议可能需要支付的任何交易费，应扣除已按季度支付的费用。（李）

15

> **原文**：... merger or a sale by the Company of its stock or assets.

谢：merger or a sale by the Company of its stock or assets 原来译为"合并或公司出售股票或资产"，但同学审校指出，merger or a sale by the Company of its stock or assets 正好就是 merger and acquisition。参考资料：

（一）公司合并与公司并购

经济学上常用公司并购（Merger & Acquisition）的概念，公司并购与公司合并既有联系又有区别。公司并购是指一切涉及公司控制权转移与合并的行为，它包括资产收购（营业转让）、股权收购和公司合并等方式，其中所谓"并"（Merger），即公司合并，主要指吸收合并，所谓"购"（Acquisition），即购买股权或资产。

……

（三）公司合并与资产收购

公司合并不同于公司的资产收购，资产收购是一个公司购买另一个公司的部分或全部资产，收购公司与被收购公司在资产收购行为完成之后仍然存续。

……

（四）公司合并与股权收购

公司合并也不同于公司的股权收购，公司的股权收购是指一个公司收买另一个公司的股权，以取得控股权，收购公司和被收购公司在股权收购行为完成之后仍然存续。

http://www.pkulaw.cn/fulltext_form.aspx?Gid=1711276275&Db=refk

所以改为"公司并购"。

李：我们不是公司内部的译员，对金融知识了解有限。在不确信的情况下，还是慎重一些好。

建议译法：公司合并或贵公司出售股票或资产（李）

16

原文：If the purchase of 50% or more of the outstanding common stock or the assets (based on the book value thereof) of the Company is accomplished ("a sale of the Company") in one or a series of transactions, including, but not limited to, private purchases of stock, a merger or a sale by the Company of its stock or assets, we will charge a transaction fee based on the eventual buyer ("the Buyer") of the Company as set forth below.

原译： 若在一笔或一系列交易中售出 50% 或以上的贵司流通普通股或资产（以账面价值计算）（简称"贵司出售"），且交易包括但不限于私人收购股票或并购，我司将根据以下列出的最终买家（简称"买家"）收取交易费用。（谢）

谢：outstanding stock:

http://www.investorwords.com/3536/outstanding_stock.html

common stock:

What is a 'Common Stock'

Common stock is a security that represents ownership in a corporation. Holders of common stock exercise control by electing a board of directors and voting on corporate policy. Common stockholders are on the bottom of the priority ladder for ownership structure; in the event of liquidation, common shareholders have rights to a company's assets only after bondholders, preferred shareholders and other debtholders are paid in full.

http://www.investopedia.com/terms/c/commonstock.asp

outstanding common stock 的翻译参考了以下资料：

http://lawyer.get.com.tw/Dic/DictionaryDetail.aspx?iDT=67877

出。从股票类型看，美国上市公司只有普通股和优先股之分，没有流通股与不流通股之分。而中国上市公司分成国家股、法人股、外资股和社会公众股，只有 1/3 的股份流通，造成同股不同价、不同权、不同利等一系列问题，并几乎成为中国股票市场一切制度性缺陷的根源，制约着中国股市规范化和市场化的进程。

https://books.google.com.hk

花旗集团曾于 7 月底表示，其 203 亿美元优先股和信托优先证券都能转换成普通流通股，美国联邦政府将约 395 亿美元优先股转换成普通股。

http://finance.sina.com.cn/stock/usstock/c/20090903/23176704587.shtml

谢：book value：

Book value of an asset is the value at which the asset is carried on a balance sheet and calculated by taking the cost of an asset minus the accumulated depreciation. Book value is also the net asset value of a company, calculated as total assets minus intangible assets (patents, goodwill) and liabilities. For the initial outlay of an investment, book value may be net or gross of expenses such as trading costs, sales taxes, service charges and so on.

http://www.investopedia.com/terms/b/bookvalue.asp

book value 的翻译参考了以下资料：

账面价值（英语：book value）是公司之会计纪录上所记资产的价值，它通常指资产的取得成本减去累积折旧的余额，并非现金流量，使用不同的折旧方法会有不同的账面价值。

https://zh.wikipedia.org/wiki/ 账面价值

谢：sale 的意思是 stock purchase：

Summary: A stock purchase is conceptually very straightforward; the buyer simply purchases the outstanding stock of your company directly from the stockholders. The name of your company, operations, contracts, etc. all remain in place, just with new owners.

Advantages: As noted above, this is a very simple and straightforward transaction structure. There is no need to form a merger sub and in many cases this will not impact anti-assignment provisions. If there are a small number of stockholders that are operating in unison, this may be a preferred form of transaction.

Disadvantages: Often, a company has a large number of stockholders, some of whom might own small amounts of stock or might be difficult or impossible to contact. In those situations, it doesn't make sense to bring such stockholders into the sale negotiations as it might make such negotiations difficult. Additionally, with a large and diverse stockholder base, it's not assured that all of stockholders will actually agree to sell their shares, and few buyers are looking to acquire less than 100% of your company. Therefore, unless your company is closely held and you are confident that you can get all of the stockholders to agree to the sale, stock purchase may not be feasible.

Asset Purchase

Summary: In an asset purchase, a buyer only buys selected assets from your company, and your company will continue to exist, and potentially continue to operate, following the sale. Relatedly, the buyer may not assume all of the liabilities of your company, which will remain with your company post-closing if not explicitly assumed.

Advantages: From the buyer's perspective, this may be a favorable structure because it allows the buyer to pick and choose only the assets it actually wants to acquire or thinks are valuable, while leaving unwanted assets (and liabilities, both known and unknown) behind, all without having to deal directly with your company's stockholders. There may also be significant tax benefits to the buyer associated with an asset purchase (the buyer will get a "step up in basis" with respect to assets it purchases).

Disadvantages: If a buyer is only looking to buy a single line of business, it can often become time consuming and expensive, as well as impractical, to separate the acquired assets and associated contracts relating to such assets from the rest of your company (as often times, assets and contracts are not confined to a single line of business and many assets, including intellectual property assets, may be shared between business lines). Additionally, as with other structures, an asset purchase might trigger certain provisions in contracts, or might not be permitted at all (for example, government permits are often nontransferable, while certain other transfers such as intellectual property might require government filings). Finally, the concepts of "successor liability" and "fraudulent conveyance" somewhat limits the ability of a buyer to leave behind or otherwise insulate itself from unwanted liabilities in your company.

https://www.cooleygo.com/selling-your-company-merger-vs-stock-sale-vs-asset-sale/

> **改译**：若在一笔或一系列交易中售出 50% 或以上的贵公司流通普通股或资产（以账面价值计算）（简称"贵公司出售"），且交易包括但不限于私人收购股票或并购，我公司将根据下文所述的本公司的最终买方（简称"买方"）收取交易费。（王）

李："且"字删掉。虽然只错一个字，但从属关系（"transactions including"）变成并列关系（"若……售出……且交易包括"），是个大错。including 修饰 transactions，补充说明交易的类型。

Think global。我们的节选到这里省略了几段，不意味着可以不看下面几段中。如果看看这几段：

If the Buyer is Light or Alabama and its affiliates ("Alabama"), we will charge a transaction fee based on the following schedule.

Aggregate Consideration	Fee Payable
Up to $560 million	Minimum Fee shall be $2 million (the "Minimum Fee"), and such Minimum Fee may be increased up to a total of $5 million at the sole discretion of the Company
Over $560 million	Minimum Fee plus 5% of the aggregate consideration in excess of $560 million

If the Buyer is not Light or Alabama, we will charge a transaction fee based on the following schedule.

Aggregate Consideration	Fee Payable
Less than $375 million	$3.25 million
$375 - $650 million	0.87% of aggregate consideration
Over $650 million	$5.63 million plus 3% of the aggregate consideration in excess of $650 million

就会发现，买主不同，收费方式不同。这就是 charge a transaction fee based on the eventual buyer ("the Buyer") of the Company as set forth below 的意思。as set forth below 修饰 charge。

> **建议译法**：若通过一次或一系列交易——包括但不限于非公开购买贵公司股票、公司合并或贵公司出售股票或资产，投资者完成收购贵公司 50% 或以上的流通普通股或资产（以账面价值计算）（简称"完成贵公司出售"），我们将根据贵公司的最终买方（简称"买方"），按以下方式收取交易费。（李）

17

> **原文**：If less than 50% of the outstanding common stock or the assets (based on the book value thereof) of the Company is acquired in the manner set forth above, we will charge a transaction fee to be mutually agreed upon by Goldman Sachs and the Company but in no event less than $2 million.
>
> **原译**：若以上文提到的方式，50% 以下的贵司流通普通股或资产（以账面价值计算）被收购，我司将收取经高盛与公司共同商定的交易费用。但在任何情况下，费用不得低于 200 万美元。（谢）
>
> **改译**：若以上述方式收购少于 50% 的贵公司流通普通股或资产（以账面价值计算），我们将收取经高盛与贵公司共同商定的交易费用。但在任何情况下，费用都不得低于 200 万美元。（王）
>
> **建议译法**：若以上文所述方式收购的贵公司流通普通股或资产（以账面价值计算）少于 50%，我们将按照高盛与贵公司共同商定的数额收取交易费，但无论如何该费用不低于 200 万美元。（李）

李：原译和改译的前半部分都不太通顺。

18

notwithstanding the foregoing:

"Notwithstanding the foregoing" means in spite of what was just said or written. The word "notwithstanding" means in spite of or despite. The word "foregoing" means what has come earlier.

https://www.reference.com/government-politics/notwithstanding-foregoing-mean-6dde9133158d719a#

notwithstanding the foregoing 的翻译参考了以下资料：

承运人对于在接受货物加以监管之前和交付货物之后因任何原因产生的货物损失或损坏不应承担任何责任。虽有上述规定，如任何适用强制性法律作出相反规定，即使损失或损坏不是在海上发生，在此附加性强制责任期内，承运人仍可在此强制性法律所规定的范围内行使条款 5.1 中引用的海牙规则中之每一权利、抗辩、限制和特权。

http://terms.maerskline.com/carriage_china

19

李琦：这里的 Psion PLC 应该是"公共有限公司"而非"私人有限公司"。查证结果如下：

Psion was a designer and manufacturer of mobile handheld computers for commercial and industrial applications. The company was headquartered in London, England with major operations in Mississauga, Ontario, Canada and additional company offices in Europe, the United States, Asia, Latin America, and the Middle East. It was a public company listed on the London Stock Exchange (LSE: PON) and was once a constituent of the FTSE 100 Index.

20

谢：affiliate 与 subsidiary 不同。

All three of these terms – affiliate［关联公司］, associate［关联公司］, and subsidiary – refer to the degree of ownership that a parent company holds in another company. In most cases, the terms affiliate and associate are used synonymously to describe a company whose parent only possesses a minority stake in the ownership of the company.

A subsidiary［子公司］, on the other hand, is a company whose parent is a majority shareholder. Consequently, in a wholly owned subsidiary, the parent company owns 100% of the subsidiary. For example, the Walt Disney Corp. (DIS) owns an equally held joint venture with Hearst Corporation called A&E Television Networks, an 80% stake in ESPN and a 100% interest in the Disney Channel. In this case, A&E Television Networks, which is independently run is an affiliate company, ESPN is a subsidiary, and the Disney Channel is a wholly owned subsidiary company.

http://www.investopedia.com/ask/answers/06/subsidiaries.asp

subsidiary 是受到母公司绝对控制（50% 以上的股权）的，但 affiliate 通常也受到母公司的控制（这与 affiliate 本身的词义一致），但母公司的股份一般低于 50%。

子公司

子公司是指一定数额的股份被另一公司控制或依照协议被另一公司实际控制、支配的公司。子公司在经济上受母公司的支配与控制，但在法律上，子公司是独立的法人。

https://baike.baidu.com/item/ 子公司

附属公司

附属公司，是指被另一个企业（称为母公司）控制的企业，一般是为签约方所拥有控制，或是与签约方有关联的公司。在服务合同中，与签约方同为另一家公司所拥有或控制的其他公司，也可以被列为附属公司里。

https://baike.baidu.com/item/ 附属公司

维基百科子公司的词条里认为子公司又称为附属公司，是逻辑上的包含关系。

王：根据你们的查证，我觉得"关联公司"更好些，强调关联性，而非所属性。

21

原文：Notwithstanding the foregoing, in the event that either Sony Corporation or Psion PLC, or their respective affiliates, invest $40 million or less in the Company through a private issuance of new shares by the Company, no fee shall be payable in connection with such transaction.

原译： 虽有上述规定，但若索尼公司或 Psion PLC 公司，抑或两者各自的附属公司，购买贵司非公开发行的新股，且支付对价为 4000 万美元或以下，则该交易不收取费用。（谢）

改译： 虽有上述规定，若索尼公司或 Psion PLC 公司，抑或两者各自的关联公司，通过私下发行公司新股份，向公司投资 4000 万美元或以下数额，则贵公司无须就此类交易支付任何费用。（王）

建议译法： 虽有上述规定，若索尼公司或 Psion 公共有限公司，抑或两者各自的关联公司，以购买贵公司非公开发售新股的方式，向公司投资 4000 万美元或以下数额，则贵公司无须就此交易支付任何费用。（李）

李：改译 1"……关联公司，通过私下发行公司新股"有歧义。是"贵公司"发行股票，不是投资公司。还是要增加"购买"。

22

原文： Except as provided herein, a transaction fee will be paid to us in cash upon consummation of each transaction.

原译： 除另有规定外，每笔交易完成后，交易费用应以现金支付我司。（谢）

改译： 除另有规定外，每笔交易完成后，交易费用应以现金方式支付给我们。（王）

建议译法： 除本协议另有规定外，交易费用应在完成每笔交易后，以现金方式支付给我们。（李）

李：herein=in this letter；建议译法的后两小句共用一个主语。

23

consideration:

    Money or other payment provided in exchange for an act or service that helps a business. Consideration may be cash in which case, it is more like a sale or payment-in-kind. For example, a person may receive a certain amount of equity in a business in exchange for giving or allowing the business to use the person's intellectual property.

http://financial-dictionary.thefreedictionary.com/consideration

Definition

Something of value, such as money or personal services, given by one party to another in exchange for an act or promise.

http://www.investorwords.com/1040/consideration.html

consideration 的翻译参考资料：

收购对价

以股票为收购对价是指收购要约人增加发行本公司的股票，以新发行的股票或以其持有的其他法人团体的股票替换目标公司的股票而实现控股目的的一种对价方式。

http://wiki.mbalib.com/wiki/ 收购对价

对于卖方而言，需要确保的主要是买方有足够的资产来支付，所以尽职调查更会关注在买方的资产方面。会关注买方的财报、现金流、债务文件，如果买方选择用自己股票来作为并购对价(consideration)，还要研究买方的股票是否是有效发行(validly issued)，公司章程是否允许增发股票等等。

https://www.zhihu.com/question/24328767

24

原文：The aggregate consideration for purposes of calculating a transaction fee shall be: . . .

原译：计算交易费用时，总对价应为：……（谢）

改译1：计算交易费用的总对价应为：……（王）

改译2：为计算交易费之目的，对总对价做如下定义：……（李）

建议译法：为计算每次交易费之目的，总对价应做如下理解……（李）

25

equity securities:

 An instrument that signifies an ownership position (called equity) in a corporation, and represents a claim on its proportional share in the corporation's assets and profits. Ownership in the company is determined by the number of shares a person owns divided by the total number of shares outstanding. For example, if a company has 1000 shares of stock outstanding and a person owns 50 of them, then he/she owns 5% of the company. Most stock also provides voting rights, which give shareholders a proportional vote in certain corporate decisions.

      http://www.investorwords.com/1737/equity_security.html#ix-
                  zz4qORVQV3o

谢：从我的查证上看，"股本证券"是更为常见的说法：

The subject of trade in an alternative system may be shares, the rights to shares (PDA), rights, depositary receipts and other **equity securities**.　➔ paiz.gov.pl	在新版市场交易的客体可以是 股票、认股权证（PDA）、权利、存券收据以及股权证券。　➔ paiz.gov.pl
The real estate investment trust and listed **equity securities** are denominated in HK dollars.　➔ wingtaiproperties.com	房地產投資信託基金及上市股本證券 以 港元 計值。　➔ wingtaiproperties.com
[...] conflicts of interest that may arise when securities analysts recommend **equity securities** in research reports and public appearances.　➔ legco.gov.hk	證券交易委員會有責任制訂規則，以處理有關 證券分析員在研究報告或公開場合推介股 本證券 時 或會出 現的利益衝突。　➔ legco.gov.hk
The Group did not have investment in any debt or **equity securities**.　➔ asiasat.com	本集團沒有投資於任何債務及股本證 券。　➔ asiasat.com

李：注意，双语语料库提供的译法仅供参考，还需要核实。百度百科："股本证券即一般所指的股票，大致可分为普通股及优先股"。

26

warrants:

 In finance, a warrant is a security that entitles the holder to buy the underlying stock of the issuing company at a fixed price called exercise price until the expiry date.

 Warrants and options are similar in that the two contractual financial instruments allow the holder special rights to buy securities. Both are discretionary and have expiration dates. The word warrant simply means to "endow with the right", which is only slightly different from the meaning of option.

https://en.wikipedia.org/wiki/Warrant_(finance)

warrants 的翻译参考：

认股权证

认股权证，又称"认股证"或"权证"，其英文名称warrants，故在香港又俗译"窝轮"。认股权证是授予持有人一项权利，在到期日前（也可能有其它附加条款）以行权价购买公司发行的新股（或者是库藏的股票）。

按照权利内容，权证分为认购权证和认沽权证。如果在权证合同中规定持有人能以某一个价格买入标的资产，那么这种权证就叫认购权证。如果在权证合同中规定持有人能以某一个价格卖出标的资产，那么这种权证就叫认沽权证。

https://baike.baidu.com/item/ 认股权证

27

convertible securities:

What is a 'Convertible Security'

A convertible security is an investment that can be changed into another form. The most common convertible securities are convertible bonds or convertible preferred stock, which can be changed into equity or common stock. A convertible security pays a periodic fixed amount as a coupon payment (in the case of convertible bonds) or a preferred dividend (in the case of convertible preferred shares), and it specifies the price at which it can be converted into common stock.

http://www.investopedia.com/terms/c/convertible-security.asp

convertible securities 的翻译参考：

可转换证券（Convertible Security）是指持有者可以在一定时期内按一定比例或价格将其转换成一定数量的另一种证券。例如有些债券可换成发行公司的普通股票，但有时则只能转换成发行公司的优先股或其他公司的股票。在可转换证券中，用得最多的是可转换债券。可转换证券在公开发行的证券中占有重要地位。

https://baike.baidu.com/item/ 可转换证券

28

consolidated balance sheet:

A consolidated balance sheet is a compilation of a company's balance sheet information and all its subsidiaries. Generally Accepted Accounting Principles (GAAP) requires companies with multiple business divisions, special purpose entities, or partially owned subsidiary businesses to be included in the parent company's balance sheet information. This consolidated statement allows banks, lenders or private investors to have a clear picture of the company's financial health. The format also presents a snapshot of the company's current asset and liability balances.

The balance sheet includes all the assets, liabilities, and retained earnings or owner's equity of the company. This information usually represents the wealth created by the company, rather than its net income for the current accounting period. Banks and investors use this information to determine the value of the company's assets and how much debt the company has incurred to purchase these assets or run its daily operations. While the parent company's consolidated balance sheet is most important to external users of financial information, they may also be interested in the individual subsidiary's balance sheet.

http://www.wisegeek.com/what-is-a-consolidated-balance-sheet.htm

consolidated balance sheet 的翻译参考资料：

合并资产负债表

反映以母公司为核心的企业集团在某一特定日期财务状况的报表。它是在母公司和需纳入合并范围的子公司的个别资产负债表的基础上，再抵销个别资产负债表所包括的企业集团内部子公司之间的影响企业集团资金总额计量的往来事项编制的。

由企业集团中的母公司于会计年度终了编制，主要服务于母公司的股东和债权人。编制合并资产负债表时，必须将母、子公司的内部往来项目予以抵消，只有非内部交易项目才予以合并。在复杂权益法下，合并后合并资产负债表的股东权益和留存利润数分别等于母公司资产负债表中的股东权益数和留存利润数。

https://baike.baidu.com/item/ 合并资产负债表

29

> 原　文：(i) in the case of the sale, exchange or purchase of the Company's equity securities, the total consideration paid for such securities (including amounts paid to holders of options, warrants and convertible securities), plus the principal amount of all indebtedness for borrowed money as set forth on the most recent consolidated balance sheet of the Company prior to the consummation of such sale, exchange or purchase ...
> 原译：(1)在公司权益性证券的出售、交换或购买中，证券的总对价（包括对期权、认股权证、可转换证券持有者支付的费用）加上出售、交换或购买之前，公司最新合并资产负债表中的债务本金。（谢）

谢：principal amount:

　　Principal is a term that has several financial meanings. The most commonly used refer to the original sum of money borrowed in a loan, or put into an investment. Similar to the former, it can also refer to the face value of a bond.

　　Principal can also refer to an individual party or parties, the owner of a private company, or the chief participant in a transaction.

http://www.investopedia.com/terms/p/principal.asp

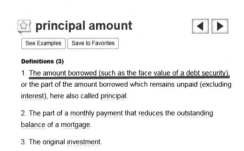

http://www.investorwords.com/3841/principal_amount.html

谢：principal amount：本金（principal）即贷款、存款或投资在计算利息之前的原始金额。

https://baike.baidu.com/item/ 本金

277

> **改译**：（1）就出售、交换或购买本公司股本证券而言，此类证券的总对价（包括支付给期权、认股权证、可转换证券持有者的费用）加上完成出售、交换或购买之前，公司最新合并资产负债表中的债务本金。（王）
>
> **建议译法**：(i) 如果是出售、交换或购买贵公司的股本证券，总对价即为投资者购买此类证券支付的总对价（包括支付给期权、认股权证、可转换证券 持有者的费用），加上完成此类出售、交换或购买之前，贵公司最新合并资产负债表中所借款项的全部债务本金。（李）

李：原文的结构是一句话：The consideration shall be: (i) the total consideration plus…; (ii) the total consideration plus… 但这句话太长，所以，主语部分单独成句（"为计算每次交易费之目的，总对价应做如下理解"），其余两款也分别成句，叙述起来比较从容。

30

disposition:

Disposition refers to the act of getting rid of an asset or security through a direct sale or some other transfer method. Insider trades often report a disposition of a certain number of shares to board members and executives, which simply means that they have sold the assets in question.

"Disposition" is the technical term for selling shares of stock in a publicly traded company in all cases. When an investor sells a piece of equity, he is giving up ownership of those shares, transferring ownership to another investor or organization. Any time a person buys stock on a public exchange, an act of disposition occurs by the selling party.

"Disposition" can also be used to encompass the sale of shares or equity to collateralize a loan with a lending institution. If an investor has a margin account, for example, and a broker sells shares within that margin account, it's considered a disposition of equity.

http://www.investopedia.com/terms/d/disposition.asp

31

谢：我觉得 purchaser 和 buyer 都是没有区别的，只是换了一个说法而已，译文不必区别对待。

32

原文：(ii) in the case of a sale or disposition by the Company of assets, the total consideration paid for such assets, plus the net value of any current assets not sold by the Company and the principal amount of all indebtedness for borrowed money expressly assumed by the purchaser.

原译：(ii) 在公司资产出售或处理中，资产的总对价加上公司未出售的流动资产净值以及由买家明确承担的债务本金。（谢）

改译：(2) 在公司出售或处置资产的情况下，为这些资产支付的总对价，加上贵公司未出售的流动资产净值以及由买方明确承担的债务本金。（王）

李：principal amount of all indebtedness for borrowed money 虽然很啰唆，但我们不是专业人士，不敢省略"债务本金"。

建议译法：(ii) 如果是贵公司出售或处置资产，总对价即为投资者购买这些资产支付的总对价，加上贵公司未出售的流动资产净值，以及由购买方明确承担的所借款项的全部债务本金。（李）

33

escrow:

Escrow is a legal concept in which a financial instrument or an asset is held by a third party on behalf of two other parties that are in the process of completing a transaction. The funds or assets are held by the escrow agent until it receives the appropriate instructions or until predetermined contractual obligations have been fulfilled. Money, securities, funds, and other assets can all be held in escrow.

When parties are in the process of completing a transaction, there may come a time when it is only interesting to move forward for one party if it knows with absolute certainty that the other party will be able to fulfill its obligations. This is where the use of escrow comes into play.

http://www.investopedia.com/terms/e/escrow.asp

叶俊文：escrow 建议译者"第三方托管（escrow）"。中国工商银行网站上直接用 escrow，是因为其产品概况的第一句就介绍了什么叫作 escrow 托管。但原文没有解释何为 escrow，因此我觉得不妨把"第三方"这个重要特征译出，括号加注英文。

李：不用添加"第三方"。我们翻译的东西假定是专业人士看的，不是面向老百姓。法律翻译能不添加，就不添加。

34
contingent:

http://www.businessdictionary.com/definition/contingent-payment.html

谢：contingent 就是比 possible 的可能性还要低的意思，中文翻成"或有"。

contingent 作为形容词时，还有一个常用的固定搭配：contingent expenses，中文常翻译为："或有费用"（即该费用有可能发生，也可能不发生。possible but not certain to occur。）。如：They had to plan for contingent expenses.（他们不得不规划或有费用）。

http://www.learnenglishwithwill.com/contingent-upon-on-meaning-definition-usage-example/

35

> 原文：Amounts paid into escrow and contingent payments in connection with any transaction will be included as part of the aggregate consideration.
>
> 原译：第三方托管业务（ESCROW）款项及任何交易的或有费用都将计入总对价。（谢）
>
> 改译：第三方托管费用及任何与交易相关的或有费用都将计入总对价。（王）

李：第三方托管费用是给第三方的费用。这里是指声龙暂时交给第三方托管的钱。这些钱也算作对价，要跟高盛分成。原文既然有 paid into，说明 escrow 是个基金。

escrow noun

es·crow | \ ˈe-ˌskrō 🔊, e-ˈskrō\

Definition of *escrow* (Entry 1 of 2)

1 : a deed, a bond, money, or a piece of property held in trust by a third party to be turned over to the grantee only upon fulfillment of a condition

2 : a fund or deposit designed to serve as an escrow

in escrow

: in trust as an escrow
// had $1000 *in escrow* to pay taxes

> 建议译法：支付到托管账户的资金及与任何与交易相关的或有付款均计入总对价。（李）

36

李：Fees on amounts paid into escrow 接上一句，讲的是高盛何时针对托管资金的收取费用。支付给托管方的费用，高盛不感兴趣。

37

李：escrow agent 指的是接受托管的第三方机构：

An escrow agent is a person or entity that holds property in trust for third parties while a transaction is finalized or a disagreement is resolved. The role of escrow agent is often played by an attorney (or notary in civil law jurisdictions). The escrow agent has a fiduciary responsibility to both parties to the escrow agreement.

http://www.investopedia.com/terms/e/escrow_agent.asp

38

> 原文：... (b) upon the release of such amounts from escrow to the extent the related escrow agreement provides that the escrow agent shall pay such fees to Goldman Sachs at or prior to the payment of such amounts to the Company or its stockholders.
>
> 原译：(2) 相关 ESCROW 托管协议规定在向贵司或其股东支付总款项之时或之前，托管代理应向高盛支付交易费用，则托管人应在 ESCROW 托管业务费用发放之时进行支付。(谢)
>
> 改译：(2) 在向贵公司或其股东支付总款项之时或之前，按照托管协议规定，托管代理人向高盛支付此类费用时。(王)
>
> 建议译法：(ii) 托管账户释放上述资金之时，条件是相关托管协议规定托管代理人向贵公司或其股东释放上述资金之时或之前，向高盛支付相关费。(李)

李：这还是很长的一句话，结构是：Fess will be payable upon ... and upon... 还是先把总括部分独立出来（"支付到托管账户的资金，按以下时间点支付费用"），再分别翻译两个时间点。主要还是理解。之所以说"释放"，是因为第三方暂时看管一下这些钱，满足一定条件后，释放给原来的主人。

39

原文: For purposes of the foregoing sentence, Goldman Sachs shall not be entitled to fees on amounts released from escrow that are paid to the Buyer.

原译: 就上述情况而言,高盛不得从为买家提供的 ESCROW 托管业务中收取费用。(谢)

建议译法1: 如上文所述,高盛无权收取支付给买方的托管费用。(王)

建议译法2: 为上句话之目的,高盛不应就托管账户释放给买方的资金收取费用。(李)

李: for purposes of the foregoing sentence,还是要结合上句话来理解。上句话说,释放资金时给高盛钱。但第三方托管账户里,不仅放着声龙的钱,还可能放着买家的钱。释放买家的钱款时,不用给高盛钱。for purposes of the foregoing sentence 是用来为上句话设定限制的。

40

原文: If the consideration in connection with any transaction may be increased by payments related to future events, the portion of our fee relating to such contingent payments will be calculated and paid if and when such contingent payments are made.

原译: 若任何交易的对价会因未来活动有关的费用而增长,且当或有费用产生之时,高盛将计算并收取该款项的费用。(谢)

改译: 若任何交易的对价可能因与未来事件有关的费用而增长,且当产生或有费用时,高盛将计算并收取与这种或有费用有关的部分费用。(王)

建议译法: 若因与未来事件相关的付款导致任何交易的对价增加,高盛将在或有付款支付完成时,计算并收取与此或有付款有关的费用。(李)

李：意思是，将来发生了什么事，别人给了声龙一笔钱，这笔钱，也要按一定比例给高盛。

41

王：dividends or other distributions *declared* by the Company，其中的 declare 应该不是"发行"，而是"宣布"或者"宣派"。

Definition of declared dividends

A portion of a company's profits that have been decided to be paid out as dividends to the shareholders by the board of directors. The declaration thereby creates a liability for the associated payments.

http://www.investorwords.com/15332/declared_dividend.html#ixzz5GDDabEEQ

42

谢：根据审校同学调查，distribution 的范围比"实物股利"更广。

国外对股利的概念通常比较明确。在大陆法系国家，股利作为对公司利益的分配，"主要是指公司以股息或红利形式向股东所作的支付与负债"。美国对股东的资产受益有两种不同的称呼，一为 dividend，指公司从现在或过去之盈余中向股东所支付的款项；另一为 distribution，泛指公司向股东做出的任何给付，通常除 dividend 外，还包括公司以回购股份或股票的形式对股东所做的支付与负债（即 distribution 包括 dividend）。

在我国，无论是股利、股息还是红利，都来源于公司之盈余，而公司回购股份或股票在我国作为一项单独的制度，与股利分配并不相同，因此，我国的"股利"应该与大陆法系国家的公司利益分配和美国的 dividend 相当。确切地说，股利在我国就是指依法定条件和程序，主要是《公司法》第 177 条，从公司的盈余中向股东做出的分配。

http://blog.sina.com.cn/s/blog_4839d9b30102vjhx.html

李：distribution 可以译为"利益分配"。

43 专业知识

What is a 'Special Dividend'

A special dividend is a non-recurring distribution of company assets, usually in the form of cash, to shareholders. A special dividend is larger compared to <u>normal dividends</u> paid out by the company.

A cash dividend:

A cash dividend is money paid to stockholders, normally out of the corporation's current earnings or accumulated profits. All dividends must be declared by the board of directors, and they are taxable as income to the recipients.

http://www.investopedia.com/terms/c/cashdividend.asp

44

原文： (i) dividends or other distributions declared by the Company with respect to its stock after the date hereof, other than normal recurring cash dividends in amounts not materially greater than currently paid, and (ii) amounts paid by the Company, to repurchase any securities of the Company outstanding on the date hereof.

原译： 总对价还应包括：(i) 本协议日之后贵公司宣布的 股票红利和其他利益分配总额，不包括正常支付的经常性现金红利，但大大高于当前支付水平的除外；以及 (ii) 贵司即日回购自己发行的流通证券所支付的费用。（谢）

改译： 总对价还应包括：(i) 本协议日之后贵公司宣布的 股票红利和其他利益分配总额，不包括正常支付的经常性现金红利，但大大高于当前支付水平的除外；以及贵公司为回购当日尚未发行的本公司证券所支付的费用。（王）

李：从语法来讲，after the date hereof 应该修饰最近的 stock，但意思上，"协议日之后的股票"说不通，declare...after a date 才说得通；第二句 on the date hereof 修饰 out-standing，不是修饰 securities。两者的共同之处，是均

修饰动词（declare 和 stand out）。我是凭借一点点专业知识判断的。

> **建议译法**：总对价还应包括：(i) 本协议日之后贵公司宣布的 股票红利和其他利益分配总额，不包括正常支付的经常性现金红利，但大大高于当前支付水平的除外；以及(ii) 贵公司为回购本协议日仍在流通的普通股所支付的费用。（李）

第九单元　科学技术

Exercise 9　The Seven Deadly Sins of AI Predictions

翻译情景

以下段落摘自 MIT Technology Review（www.technologyreview.com）上发表的 The Seven Deadly Sins of AI Predictions。可截取节选任意片段检索全文。作者 Rodney Brooks 是麻省理工学院计算机科学与人工智能实验室 Rethink Robotics 和 iRobot 的创始人，具有深厚的专业背景知识和学术修养。*MIT Technology Review* 过去专业性较强，现在逐渐转变为面向大众的读物，不过目标读者仍是业内人士，或对前沿科技感兴趣的科技爱好者。请翻译本单元选段，共 543 词。假设译文读者为同类人群。

训练重点

本篇文章应重点调动全局意识和逻辑思维能力。全局意识贯穿翻译始终，要求译者时刻从宏观层面思考具体问题的解决方法。译者的视野要远超语篇，把语篇当作整个世界的有机组成部分来理解和重构，包括查清原文出处、作者情况、写作背景、逻辑结构、中心思想、语言风格、读者群体等；同时还要考虑译文读者和译文使用情景。其次，在翻译过程中，如果原文逻辑不甚严密，译者应充分利用逻辑思维，让译文逻辑更为紧凑、严密。

训练难点

本篇的难点之一是如何抓住原文和展现原文逻辑，二是以读者可以理解和接受的语言表达原文内容，同时尽量不失原作风格。

训练方式

本次练习分原文、翻译提示、参考译文、译者注四部分。请先尝试自己翻译原文。做完以后再参看翻译提示，进一步调查研究，修改、润色，形成第二稿。形成二稿之后，再看参考译文和译者注。翻译能力是在实践过程中不断提升的，希望你可以充分利用每一章教材，一步步取得翻译能力上的提升！

原文[1]

The Seven Deadly Sins of AI Predictions

Exponentials
Many people are suffering from a severe case of "exponentialism[2]."
Everyone has some idea about Moore's Law, which suggests that computers get better and better on a clockwork-like schedule. What Gordon Moore actually said was that the number of components that could fit on a microchip would double every year. That held true for 50 years, although[3] the time constant for doubling gradually lengthened from one year to over two years, and the pattern is coming to an end.

Doubling the components on a chip has made computers continually double in speed. And it has led to memory chips that quadruple in capacity every two years. It has also led to digital cameras that have better and better resolution, and LCD screens with exponentially more pixels.

The reason Moore's Law worked is that it applied to a digital abstraction of a true-or-false question[4]. In any given circuit, is there an electrical charge or voltage there or not? The answer remains clear as chip components get smaller and smaller—until a physical limit intervenes, and we get down to components with so few electrons that quantum effects start to dominate. That is where we are now with our silicon-based chip technology[5].

When people are suffering from exponentialism, they may think that the exponentials they use to justify an argument are going to continue apace. But Moore's Law and other seemingly exponential laws can fail because they were not truly exponential in the first place.

Back in the first part of this century, when I was running MIT's Computer Science and Artificial Intelligence Laboratory (CSAIL) and needed to help raise money for over 90 different research groups, I tried to use the memory increase on iPods to show sponsors how things were continuing to change very rapidly. Here are the data on how much music storage one got in an iPod for $400 or less:

year	gigabytes[6]
2002	10
2003	20
2004	40
2006	80
2007	160

Then I would extrapolate a few years out and ask what we would do with all that memory in our pockets.[7]

Extrapolating through to today [8]we would expect a $400 iPod to have 160,000 gigabytes of memory. But the top iPhone of today (which costs much more than $400) has only 256 gigabytes of memory, less than double the capacity of the 2007 iPod. This particular exponential collapsed very suddenly once the amount of memory got to the point where it was big enough to hold any reasonable person's music library and apps, photos, and videos. Exponentials can collapse when a physical limit is hit, or when there is no more economic rationale to continue them.

Similarly, we have seen a sudden increase in performance of AI systems thanks to the success of deep learning. Many people seem to think that means we will continue to see AI performance increase by equal multiples on a regular basis. But the deep-learning success was 30 years in the making, and it was an isolated event.

That does not mean there will not be more isolated events, where work from the backwaters of AI research suddenly fuels a rapid-step increase in the performance of many AI applications. But there is no "law" that says how often they will happen.

翻译提示

1. **全局意识**

   请大家针对原文和译文，分别回答 Who is talking to whom? About what? When, where and why? And how? 然后再开始翻译。尤其要关注作者的背景、立场和原文风格。

2. **标点符号**

   这里有同学提出原文标点错误，认为句号应该放在引号之外。在审校二稿时，同学们可以仔细查查，原文标点是否有误。

3. **逻辑思维**

   李：请查英英词典看 although 的意思。结合作者对指数式增长的态度，判断这句话主句是重点,还是从句是重点;重点置于句首,还是句末?

4 全局意识/专业知识/逻辑思维
想要准确理解这句话,恐怕要弄清楚 digital abstraction of a true-or-false question 是什么意思。恐怕要查查 digital abstraction 是什么意思,抽象的过程有没有什么样的标准(benchmark)。记住,翻译的一切前提的理解,没有理解,语言表达就无从谈起。

5 全局意识/专业知识/逻辑思维
为什么作者要谈到量子效应?可以查查量子效应和隧穿效应的关系,在脑海中勾勒出形象的图画帮助理解。译者也可以查查 silicon-based technology 面临的问题,构架出 quantum effects 和 silicon-based technology 之间的关系。

6 全局意识:读者意识
gigabytes 是用专业的表达,还是用我们通常比较熟悉的用法?

7 全局意识/语言能力:时态理解
Then I would [思考:这是在回顾当时拉赞助的情形,还是表示 I would like to?] extrapolate a few years out and ask [问谁?是问赞助商,还是今天的读者?] what we would do with all that memory in our pockets.

8 全局意识/逻辑思维
extrapolating through to today 是表示回到今天,还是继续在回顾过去?

参考译文[1]

AI 预测的七宗罪

指数式增长[2]

许多人都严重迷信"指数式增长论"。[3]

大家都或多或少听说过摩尔定律。该定律认为，计算机性能会以时钟般的固定周期不断改进。[4]但戈登·摩尔（Gordon Moore）实际上说的是，芯片上可容纳的元件数量会逐年翻番。[5]这一规律一直持续了50年。但到了后来，翻番的时间逐渐从一年延长至两年，现在这一规律行将失效。[6]

单个芯片容纳电子元件数量不断翻番的结果是，计算机速度持续翻番，内存卡容量两年翻两番，数码相机分辨率不断提高，LCD液晶屏像素呈指数式增长。[7]

摩尔定律之所以曾经有效，在于它适用于能够以抽象的数字表达"是/否"的情形——即在任何给定电路中是否存在电荷或电压。在达到某种物理极限前，答案是清楚无误的。但当芯片上的元件越来越小，致使电子过少时，量子效应便趋于主导。硅芯片技术目前就发展到了这种状态。[8]

指数论者可能会认为，支撑自己观点的指数式增长会快速继续下去。然而，摩尔定律和其他指数类定律都可能会失效，因为它们根本就不是真正的指数定律。[9]

本世纪初，我担任麻省理工学院的计算机科学和人工智能实验室（CSAIL）的主管，需要为90多个研究小组筹集资金。为了向赞助商证明科技发展瞬息万变，我给他们展示了iPod内存增长的例子。以下是400美元以下的iPod音乐存储空间[10]：

年份	内存（GB）
2002	10
2003	20
2004	40
2006	80
2007	160

然后，我推算几年后的情况，并问大家，口袋里装这么大的内存做什么？[11]

按此增长速度，现在400美元的iPod得有16万G内存了。但如今最好的iPhone（售价远超400美元）也只有256G，不到2007年iPod的两倍。一旦内存足够大，满足了任何人对音乐库、应用程序、照片和视频存储的合理需求，这个指数增长神话便瞬间破灭。因此，当达到一定物理极限，或继续下去没有经济上的理由时,指数函式是增长就会崩溃。[12]

同理,由于深度学习大获成功,人工智能系统的性能也迅速提高。如此一来,许多人似乎认为,人工智能的性能也会像过去一样。然而,深度学习的成功是过去30年来累积研究的结果,而且是一个孤立事件。[13]

当然了,孤立事件可能还会有。比方说,人工智能研究的冷门领域突然取得突破,带动人工智能应用程序的性能快速提高。然而,这样的事多久会出现一次,并无任何"定律"作出预测。[13]

译者注

1　全局意识: 作者背景

王: 本文作者为 Rodney Brooks,原文文末有对作者的简单介绍:

Rodney Brooks is a former director of the Computer Science and Artificial Intelligence Laboratory at MIT and a founder of Rethink Robotics and iRobot. This essay is adapted with permission from a post that originally appeared at rodneybrooks.com.

https://www.technologyreview.com/s/609048/the-seven-deadly-sins-of-ai-predictions/

在维基百科上也可以查到作者的资料:

Rodney Allen Brooks (born 30 December 1954) is an Australian **roboticist**, Fellow of the Australian Academy of Science, author, and robotics entrepreneur, most known for popularizing the actionist approach to robotics. He was a Panasonic Professor of Robotics at the Massachusetts Institute of Technology and former director of the MIT Computer Science and Artificial Intelligence Laboratory. He is a founder and former Chief Technical Officer of iRobot and co-Founder, Chairman and Chief Technical Officer of Rethink Robotics (formerly Heartland Robotics). Outside the scientific community Brooks is also known for his appearance in a film featuring him and his work, *Fast, Cheap & Out of Control.*

https://en.wikipedia.org/wiki/Rodney_Brooks

可见本文作者是机器人领域的专家，曾是麻省理工学院的教授，也是作家和企业家，所以本文内容具有权威性。

全局意识：作者立场

王：通读全文，作者主要讲述人们在预测人工智能未来时的七个倾向，作者对这些倾向持批判态度。文章开头就十分清晰地表明了作者的立场：

We are surrounded by **hysteria** about the future of artificial intelligence and robotics—**hysteria** about how powerful they will become, how quickly, and what they will do to jobs.

I recently saw a story in MarketWatch that said robots will take half of today's jobs in 10 to 20 years. It **even** had a graphic to prove the numbers.

The claims are **ludicrous**. (**I try to maintain professional language, but sometimes** …) For instance, the story appears to say that we will go from one million grounds and maintenance workers in the U.S. to only 50,000 in 10 to 20 years, because robots will take over those jobs. **How many robots are currently operational in those jobs?** *Zero.* **How many realistic demonstrations have there been of robots working in this arena?** *Zero.* Similar stories apply to all the other categories where it is suggested that we will see the end of more than 90 percent of jobs that currently require physical presence at some particular site.

https://www.technologyreview.com/s/609048/the-seven-deadly-
sins-of-ai-predictions/

加粗的词语和句子都体现出作者对于一些不切实际的预测的态度，语气相当激烈。翻译时的理解和表达，不能偏离这个基本态度，不能以肯定的口气，描述作者反对的事物。

全局意识：原文风格

王：此处补充梁嘉琳同学对原文杂志风格和作者语言风格的分析：

本文出自 *MIT Technology Review* 的 **Intelligent Machines** 栏目，发表于 2017 年 10 月 6 日。

MIT Technology Review is a magazine published, but not owned by the Massachusetts Institute of Technology. It was founded in 1899 as *The Technology Review*, and was re-launched without "The" in its name on April 23, 1998 under then publisher R. Bruce Journey. In September 2005, it underwent another transition under its then editor-in-chief and publisher, Jason Pontin, to a form resembling the historical magazine.

https://en.wikipedia.org/wiki/MIT_Technology_Review

MIT Technology Review 网页对杂志作了如下介绍：

What We Do

Every day, we provide an **intelligent, lucid, and authoritative** filter for the overwhelming flood of **information about technology**. We do this with serious journalism, written in **clear, simple language**, by a knowledgeable editorial staff, governed by a policy of accuracy and independence. We do this in features, news analysis, business reports, photo essays, reviews, and interactive digital experiences that invite our readers to **probe deeper, examine data, and get to know experts and their opinions to see, explore, and understand new technologies and their impact**. We do this with beautifully designed platforms and publications online, in print, on mobile, and in person at live events around the world.

Who We Are

We're an innovative, digitally oriented global media company whose reach is rapidly expanding. Our **mission** is to **equip our audiences with the intelligence to understand and contribute to a world shaped by technology**. Founded at the Massachusetts Institute of Technology in 1899, *MIT Technology Review* derives its authority from the world's foremost technology institution and from our editors' deep technical knowledge, capacity to see technologies in their broadest context, and unequaled access to leading innovators and researchers. **Accuracy and independence** are our highest priorities: our coverage is independent of any influence, including our ownership by MIT.

Who We Serve

Our audience is anyone, anywhere, who believes that technology can solve hard problems, grow prosperity, and expand human possibilities. It is a global community of business and thought leaders, innovators and early adopters, entrepreneurs and investors, as well as all of MIT's alumni.

https://www.technologyreview.com/about/

根据杂志对自己的介绍，可以知道杂志提供科技专家对相关问题和事件的评论分析，**内容清晰**并且具有**权威性**，注重内容的**准确性和独立性**。杂志**语言风格清晰、易于理解**。杂志旨在让读者深入了解科技问题、与读者分享专家的观点，激发读者对相关问题的思考和探索。杂志创刊于麻省理工学院，因此作者为领域专家，有权威性，但杂志本身不是专业科学杂志，而是面向大众、面向一切对科技感兴趣的人。所以在翻译文章时，语言应该清晰易懂，不应该过于晦涩。

祁欣同学的查证为杂志的风格变化提供了依据：

- 这本杂志原名为The Technology Review，之后更换过一次名字，以下是对这本杂志的介绍：
- The historical magazine had been published by the MIT Alumni Association, was more closely aligned with the interests of MIT alumni, **and had a more intellectual tone and much smaller public circulation. The new version focused on new technology and how it is commercialized; was mass-marketed to the public**; and was targeted at senior executives, researchers, financiers, and policymakers, as well as MIT alumni.

https://en.wikipedia.org/wiki/MIT_Technology_Review

- 人们将它评价为a clearing house of information and thought，从杂志定位可以看出它学术性和科技性较强，受众主要为接受过高等教育、有相关背景的群体。**不过杂志改版之后更加面向大众，不会太过艰深复杂。**

张旭同学在课上对作者的背景和原文风格作了进一步补充：作者有很强的逻辑思维，又有深厚的学术背景，但是作者的逻辑思维不应该体现在语言的晦涩上，而是严密的逻辑上。

2

> 原文: exponentials
> 原译: 指数(谢)
> 建议译法: 指数式增长(王)

王 & 李: exponential 一般做形容词用,但文中标题显然是名词。在 free dictionary 上找到它的名词用法,应解释为"指数":

Noun 1. **exponential** - a function in which an independent variable appears as an exponent
≡ **exponential function**
↔ function, mapping, mathematical function, single-valued function, map - (mathematics) a mathematical relation such that each element of a given set (the domain of the function) is associated with an element of another set (the range of the function)
Adj. 1. **exponential** - of or involving exponents; "exponential growth"

"CITE" Based on WordNet 3.0, Farlex clipart collection. © 2003-2012 Princeton University, Farlex Inc.

Collins 的解释是"极快的":

exponential
(ɪkspənenʃəl)

adjective [usually ADJECTIVE noun]
Exponential means growing or increasing very rapidly.
[formal]
The policy tried to check the exponential growth of public expenditure.
exponentially adverb [ADVERB after verb]
The quantity of chemical pollutants has increased exponentially.

COBUILD Advanced English Dictionary. Copyright © HarperCollins Publishers

联系上下文可知,exponentials 是人们预测 AI 发展的七大倾向之一,意为翻番式的增长。因此,与其翻译成"指数",不如译为"指数式增长",更能概括下面几段话的意思。译者不能"鼠目寸光";要放眼世界,才能认识自我。

3

> 原文: Many people are suffering from a severe case of "exponentialism".
> 原译: 许多人正在遭受"指数论"的荼毒。(谢)

王：按照原文的形式翻译，没有问题。但是，感觉意思不明确，中国读者不清楚是什么意思。这里是说一种谬误的观点，也就是人们容易过度相信所谓的"指数论"，但其实不然。

标点符号

王：李老师提醒，原文标点并没有错误，只是各国标点规则不同。

李：原文没错。是因为英美用法不同。

Quotation marks:

This is one of the most common mistakes made by writers in Australian English.

American English uses double quotation marks, and only uses single quotations marks when quoting inside a quotation; for example:

According to Lines (2010), "these soldiers served as models of the 'New Woman.'"

In Australian English, single quotation marks are used, with double quotation marks only used to quote within quotations:

According to Lines (2010), 'these soldiers served as models of the "New Woman"'.

Punctuating quotations:

You will also notice in the example quotations above that the punctuation at the ends of the sentences are different.

In American English, the punctuation mark (i.e., the full stop or comma) always comes before the closing quotation mark. Conversely, in Australian English, the punctuation mark will usually come *after* the closing quotation mark, unless the quotation is also a complete sentence. Compare the following two examples. (Both use Australian English).

The salsola is a salt marsh plant. 'It stores the salt in its leaves, so is a naturally seasoned plant.'

The salsola is a salt marsh plant. As salt is stored in its leaves, it is 'naturally seasoned'.

Note that in the first example, the quotation and the complete sentence (from capital letter to full stop) are one and the same. Therefore, in Australian English, the punctuation mark is placed inside the quotation marks. In all other instances, the punctuation mark is placed outside the quotation marks.

By keeping just these few differences in mind while writing, you will dramatically reduce the number of stylistic errors in your text caused by confusion between the conventions of American and Australian English.

However, we additionally recommend having your document edited by a professional editing service such as Elite Editing. A comprehensive edit to remove stylistic errors and ensure consistency in language use is just part of the service we provide.

改译1：许多人都过度迷信"指数论"。（王）

李：suffer from a severe case of 既可以形象地翻译出来，也可以只翻译意思。

改译2：许多人都患有"指数式增长论"的毛病。（李）
建议译法：许多人都严重迷信"指数式增长论"（李）

4

原文：Everyone has some idea about Moore's Law, which suggests that computers get better and better on a clockwork-like schedule.

谢：Moore's Law 中文译名为"摩尔定律"。

摩尔定律（英语：Moore's law）是由英特尔（Intel）创始人之一戈登·摩尔

提出来的。其内容为：集成电路上可容纳的电晶体（晶体管）数目，约每隔两年便会增加一倍；经常被引用的"18 个月"，是由英特尔首席执行官大卫·豪斯（David House）所说：预计 18 个月会将芯片的性能提高一倍（即更多的晶体管使其更快）。

https://zh.wikipedia.org/wiki/摩尔定律

> **原译**：每个人多少知道些摩尔定律。该定律认为，计算机的性能以发条般精准的时间表不断完善。（谢）

王 & 李：把 everyone 直接翻译成"每个人"，读起来总是觉得有些绝对，强调没有例外。改为"大家"，语气缓和一些。

王：like clockwork 的意思就是指非常有规律、可预测。

like clockwork

Predictably and dependably. *Everything is going like clockwork, so we should be ready to start construction by the end of the month. The conference went like clockwork from beginning to end.*

Also, regular as clockwork. With extreme regularity, as in *Ruth arrives every Wednesday morning just like clockwork*, or *You can count on his schedule, which is regular as clockwork*, or *Their assembly line runs like clockwork*. This idiom alludes to the mechanical and therefore very regular action of a clock. [Second half of 1600s]

https://idioms.thefreedictionary.com/like+clockwork

> **改译**：大家都或多或少听说过摩尔定律。该定律认为，计算机性能会有规律地逐步完善。（王）

李："有规律"过于平淡；作者的语气比较强烈，语言也更加生动。

> **建议译法**：大家都或多或少听说过摩尔定律。该定律认为，计算机性能会以时钟般的固定周期不断改进。（李）

5 全局意识：think global

> **原文**：What Gordon Moore actually said was that the number of components that could fit on a microchip would double every year.
>
> **原译**：高登·摩尔（Gordon Moore）的原话是，芯片可容纳的元件数量每年都会翻一番。（谢）
>
> **建议译法**：但戈登·摩尔（Gordon Moore）实际上说的是，芯片上可容纳的元件数量会逐年翻番。（王）

王：这句话看似孤立，但和上文有密切联系。作者的逻辑是：大家都认为摩尔那样说，但实际上他是这么说的。中间有个转折，译文需要体现出来。

6

> **原文**：That held true for 50 years, although the time constant for doubling gradually lengthened from one year to over two years, and the pattern is coming to an end.
>
> **原译**：尽管这一时间由一年逐渐延长至两年，规律也逐渐消失，但 50 年来，这一说法的确是正确的。（谢）
>
> **改译**：尽管翻倍的时间常数从一年逐渐延长至两年，规律也逐渐消失，但在过去 50 间它是成立的。（王）
>
> **建议译法**：这一规律一直持续了 50 年。但到了后来，翻番的时间逐渐从一年延长至两年，现在这一规律行将失效。（李）

李：although 才是重点。建议译法这样修改才是旗帜鲜明地否定摩尔定律。作者整体逻辑是批判摩尔定律。所以说，尽管这个定律管用了 50 年，但越往后，越不管用（一年变两年），到现在，几乎失效了。原因是根本不存在这样的定律。如果把管用了 50 年后置，就是肯定摩尔定律：尽管这几年有点不太符合，但过去 50 年运作挺好。这不符合作者对摩尔定律的整体评价。

7

原文：Doubling the components on a chip has made computers continually double in speed. And it has led to memory chips that quadruple in capacity every two years. It has also led to digital cameras that have better and better resolution, and LCD screens with exponentially more pixels.

原译：芯片元件翻番，计算机速度每年也持续翻倍。内存卡的容量每两年翻两番。数码相机清晰度逐渐攀升，LCD 液晶屏像素呈指数增长。（谢）

改译：芯片元件翻番，计算机速度就会持续翻倍。此外，内存卡容量也会每两年翻两番，数码相机分辨率会更高，LCD 液晶屏像素也会呈指数式增长。（王）

王：这里还是应该注意语篇衔接问题。句首 doubling the components on a chip 是这句话的主语，后面两句的主语 it 都指向这个主语。也就是说，芯片元件翻番，会带来计算机速度、内存卡容量、数码相机分辨率、LCD 液晶屏像素等的逐步变化。原译和改译用句号，割裂了这种联系。不如一气呵成。

李："会"是未然；此处讲的是"已然"。

建议译法：单个芯片容纳电子元件数量不断翻番的结果是，计算机速度持续翻番，内存卡容量两年翻两番，数码相机分辨率不断提高，LCD 液晶屏像素呈指数式增长。（李、王）

8

原文：The reason Moore's Law worked is that it applied to a digital abstraction of a true-or-false question. In any given circuit, is there an electrical charge or voltage there or not? The answer remains clear as chip components get smaller and smaller—until a physical limit intervenes, and we get down to components with so few electrons that quantum effects start to dominate. That is where we are now with our silicon-based chip technology.

> **原译**：摩尔定律有效的原因，是因为其适用于真假问题的数字抽象。一个任意给定电路是否存在电流或电压？即使芯片元件越来越小，该问题的答案仍不言而喻。然而，当达到物理极限，元件电子太少，量子效应开始主导，情况就会不同。这就是硅芯片技术的现状。（谢）
>
> **改译**：摩尔定律之所以有用，是因为它把复杂问题简单化，就像数字电路一样，只存在有或无的问题。这就好比在问，在任何给定电路中，是有还是没有电流或电压？答案是显而易见的。但当芯片元件越来越小，达到物理极限，致使元件电子太少时，量子效应便趋于主导，这时情况会大为不同。这就是硅芯片技术的现状。（王）

全局意识 / 专业知识

李：我虽然不懂编程，但我知道计算机只用 0 和 1。"计算机就是用晶体管的导通和不导通这两种状态来分别代表 0 和 1 的"（https://blog.csdn.net/saintyyu/article/details/64944878）所谓的 digital abstraction of a true-or-false question，意思就是把"通 / 不通"这样的是否问题，抽象表达为数字（0/1）。

In any given circuit... 这句话，不过是举了一个 true-or-false 的例子，翻译时要确保与上句话之间建立联系。

所谓 physical limits 就是指，原件越来越小，小得不能再小了。

The answer remains... 这句话，实际上存在逻辑瑕疵，改通顺是这样：

The answer remains clear until a physical limit intervenes—as chip components get smaller and smaller, we get down to components with so few electrons that quantum effects start to dominate.

这句话当中我还没有弄懂的地方是：什么是"量子效应"？"量子效应趋于主导"意味着什么？我的推断是：发生量子效应时，有电无电就很难判断了，因为电子太少了。我不知道这个理解是否正确。等下看同学的查证。

逻辑思维

王：true-or-false question，同学们的译法主要有以下几种：是非题、判断题、真假题、电路正负、0 或 1。我认为，无论翻译成什么，都要和后一句 In any given circuit, is there an electrical charge or voltage there or not 衔接起来。

联系这句话，其实这个 true-or-false question 就是指有无电流的问题。

王：什么是 digital abstraction？经调查，发现 digital abstraction 是数字电路（digital circuit）中的一个概念，指以简单的二元对立（0 或 1，是或否，开或关）形式，来表示电压的有无，相当于把复杂问题抽象化、简单化：

The term a digital circuit refers to a device that works in a binary world. In the binary world, the only values are zeros and ones. Hence, the inputs of a digital circuit are zeros and ones, and the outputs of a digital circuit are zeros and ones. Digital circuits are usually implemented by electronic devices and operate in the real world. In the real world, there are no zeros and ones; instead, what matters is the voltages of inputs and outputs. Since voltages refer to energy, they are continuous. So we have a gap between the continuous real world and the two-valued binary world. One should not regard this gap as an absurd. Digital circuits are only an abstraction of electronic devices. In this chapter we explain this abstraction, called the digital abstraction. In the digital abstraction one interprets voltage values as binary values.

http://www.eng.tau.ac.il/~guy/Computer_Structure03/lecture_notes/chapter1.pdf

通常译为"数字抽象"。但李老师用"以抽象数字表达"，意思更加清楚易懂。

王：张旭同学对 digital abstraction 的查证很透彻：

- 更加惊人的是，这篇文章也是 Rodney Brooks 写的，因此这个说法应该是他常用的。这篇文章更加详细地解释了数字抽象的具体含义。也就是说，摩尔定律对"电路里是否有电荷和电压"进行数字抽象，多少以上是 yes，多少以下是 no。然后根据这个标准判断是否能够继续增加晶管体的数量，升级芯片。

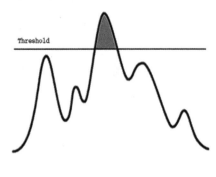

王：吴秀倩同学查证结果很形象，说明晶体管太小就会漏电：

- 前半句 "The answer remains clear as chip components get smaller and smaller" 说的应该是<u>虽然元件不断变小，但是人们还是能清楚地知道晶体管究竟处于"开"与"关"中的哪个状态</u>。

- 后半句 "until a physical limit intervenes," 指的是，元件的体积突破了一个界限，使得人们无法清楚判断晶体管的开关。下面材料解释了背后的原因：

- 这些开关都是由硅制备的，硅是一种半导体，电学性能是介于导体（电流很容易通过）和绝缘体（电流不能通过）之间，半导体的电学性能也是可以调节的，既可以通过称之为"掺杂"的工艺：材料中的原子被其它元素取代，例如砷或者硼，也可以通过施加电场进行调节。

- 在硅基的半导体中，沟道是由被掺杂一种材料构成，而源极和漏极是由被掺杂了另外一种材料构成。"掺杂"改变了载流子在半导体内流动所需要的能量，所以两种不同掺杂后的材料靠近时，电流是不能通过的（此处讲的应该是PN结的"整流效应"，译者注）。但是，<u>当器件在"开"的状态时，栅极电场诱导出一层很薄的通道，联通了整个电路，使得电流可以通过</u>。

- 在很长的一段时间内，由于晶体管变得越来越小，基于以上的设计的芯片运行得越来越好。<u>但小到一定尺度后，器件开始崩溃了。在现在的晶体管内，源极和漏极已经靠得非常近了，只有20纳米左右。这使得即使在"关"的状态下，沟道也很容易发生"漏电流"，从而浪费了电量，而且还产生了不必要的热量。</u>

王：综上，李老师的问题可以这样解答。数字抽象是为了判断有电流还是无电流的问题。因为晶体管的运作不需要知道具体的电流数字，只需要知道有还是没有电流就可以了。只是，我们需要人为设置一个有无电流的标准，即多少电流以下算有，多少以下算无。当芯片元件越来越小，就会出现量子效应。我们可以把量子效应想象成守门员守球，当球太小的时候，守门员防不住，那么球就进门了，也就相当于量子趋于主导，产生了遂穿效应。如果出现这种情况，那么数字抽象就没有用了，因为无法准确测算出究竟有多少电流流过。这个问题和 silicon-based technology 问题很相似，根据查证，silicon-based technology 的发展面临两个主要问题。一个是过热的问题，一个是漏电。过热问题就会让晶体管融化掉，那何来测量电流一说呢？如果漏电的话，那么测量数据就不准确了，也无法给出电流量大小的准确答案。

- That is where we are now with our 【silicon-based chip technology.】

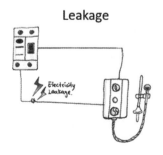

建议译法：摩尔定律之所以曾经有效，在于它适用于能够以抽象的数字表达"是/否"的情形——即在任何给定电路中是否存在电荷或电压。在达到某种物理极限前，答案是清楚无误的。但当芯片上的元件越来越小，致使电子过少时，量子效应便趋于主导。硅芯片技术目前就发展到了这种状态。（李）

9

原文：When people are suffering from exponentialism, they may think that the exponentials they use to justify an argument are going to continue apace. But Moore's Law and other seemingly exponential laws can fail because they were not truly exponential in the first place.

原译：当人们深受指数论荼毒，他们会认为用来证明一个观点正确的指数还会继续有效。然而，摩尔定律和其他徒有其表的指数定律则会失效，因为这些定律本身没有真正的指数性。（谢）

改译1：对"指数论"深信不疑的人可能会认为，支持自己观点的指数将继续快速增长。然而，摩尔定律和其他类似的指数定律都可能会失效，因为它们根本不是真正的指数（王）

改译2：指数论者可能会认为，支撑自己观点的指数式增长会快速继续下去。然而，摩尔定律和其他指数类定律都可能会失效，因为它们根本就不是真正的指数定律。（李）

李：people are suffering from exponentialism 可以简化为"指数论者"，或者说"相信指数论的人"。

"指数"不会加速增长。所谓指数式增长，就是1变2，2变4，4变16，或者说从2的0次方变成1次方、2次方、3次方、4次方。本文中作者列举的存储能力增长就是这种增长。指数式增长也叫几何增长。

geometric growth

A pattern of growth that increases at a geometric rate over a specified time period, such as 2, 4, 8, 16 (in which each value is double the previous one). Contrast arithmetic growth, exponential growth.

www.oxfordreference.com

所以，其中的"指数"（0-1-2-3-4）增加是恒定的，不是加速的，但增长本身是加速的。因此不能说"指数将快速增长"，但可以说"增长将加速"。

> **建议译法**：指数论者可能会认为，支撑自己观点的指数式增长会快速继续下去。然而，摩尔定律和其他指数类定律都可能会失效，因为它们根本就不是真正的指数定律。（李）

10

> **原文**：Back in the first part of this century, when I was running MIT's Computer Science and Artificial Intelligence Laboratory (CSAIL) and needed to help raise money for over 90 different research groups, I tried to use the memory increase on iPods to show sponsors how things were continuing to change very rapidly. Here are the data on how much music storage one got in an iPod for $400 or less:
>
> **原译**：本世纪初，我管理着麻省理工学院的计算机科学及人工智能实验室（CSAIL），需要为90多个不同的科研组筹措资金。我试着用iPod存储空间在不断提高这一事实，向赞助商展示一切都在快速变化。以下数据描述了400美元以下的iPod音乐存储容量：（谢）
>
> **改译**：本世纪初，我还在管理麻省理工学院的计算机科学和人工智能实验室（CSAIL），那时我需要为90多个研究小组筹集资金。为了向赞助商证明科技发展日新月异，我给他们展示了iPod内存变大的例子。以下是价值400美元或更低的iPod内存量：（王）

全局意识

李："空间提高"搭配不当；grow very quickly 不仅是快速变化，而且是变得更快；原文 the first part of this century 没有表达清楚，其实就是指 the first decade of this century。我查看了一下，本文写于 2017 年，下面提供的一组数据到 2007 年，他当时一定还在 MIT。所以，他所说的 first part，一定是指本世纪前十年，而不是前 50 年。译为"本世纪初"是站得住脚的。

> **建议译法**：本世纪初，我担任麻省理工学院的计算机科学和人工智能实验室（CSAIL）的主管，需要为 90 多个研究小组筹集资金。为了向赞助商证明科技发展瞬息万变，我给他们展示了 iPod 内存增长的例子。以下是 400 美元以下的 iPod 音乐存储空间：（李）

11

> **原文**：Then I would extrapolate a few years out and ask what we would do with all that memory in our pockets.
>
> **原译**：接下来，我将往后推算几年，探讨如何利用口袋里的存储空间。（谢）
>
> **改译**：然后，我推断出几年后的情况，并问大家，这么大的内存能拿来做什么？（王）

学生的疑问：I would 是否可以理解为 I would like to do something？如果这样理解，那么这里这个 we 是否就不是指当时的潜在赞助商，而是指我们读者呢？也就是说，作者这个时候是对读者说：我要跟大家解释一下，照这样推断，几年以后的内存会有多大？

以下是李老师的分析：

> Back in the first part of this century, when I was running MIT's Computer Science and Artificial Intelligence Laboratory (CSAIL) and needed to help raise money for over 90 different research groups, I tried to use the memory increase on iPods to show sponsors how things were continuing to change very rapidly. Here are the data on how much music storage one got in an iPod for $400 or less: [现在到了 2017 年，但他没有提供更新的数据，说明是在描述当时的情况。以下数据，显然是他写这篇文章的时候，找到了当时用来说服赞助人的数据。]

第九单元 · 科学技术

year	gigabytes
2002	10
2003	20
2004	40
2006	80
2007	160

Then I *would* extrapolate *a few years out* and *ask* what we would do with all that memory in our pockets. [（1）这一段和上一段意思最紧密，都是在描述过去，would 也是在描述当时常做的事情。如果不是中间隔了一张表，这两段就是同一段；再说了，就这一句话，也不太可能单独成段。（2）这里说再往后推算几年（a few years out），大不了就三四年，也就到了 2011 年。那时候理论上就是 160*2*2*2=2560G，装在口袋书已经没用了。（3）这一段如果理解为面向本文读者说话，逻辑上和下一段有冲突：现在已经是 2017 年，为什么只是往后推算几年？为什么不直接推算到今天？前一段往后推算几年，下一段再推算到今天，都是为了说明同样道理，那不是重复吗？所以只能理解为，两段面向不同对象，推算不同年数］

Extrapolating through to today [此处的 today，相对于 back in the first part of this century。如果把前面两段视为一整段，则上面一段谈过去，这一段回到现在，所以，从逻辑上看，上一段的 we 是指作者和赞助商。本段的 we 是指作者和今天的读者]，we *would* [这个是虚拟语气] expect a $400 iPod to have 160,000 gigabytes of memory. ...

would 也没有 would like to 的意思。此处的 would 表示频率：

would *modal verb* (FREQUENCY)

● B2 ALSO 'd used to talk about things in the past that happened often or always:
He would always turn and wave at the end of the street.

● ALSO 'd DISAPPROVING used to suggest that what happens is expected because it is typical, especially of a person's behaviour:
"Madeleine called to say she's too busy to come." "She would - she always has an excuse."

309

李：关于这句话的更多分析，简单来说，是在回顾当时拉赞助的情形。赞助商怎么回答作者的提问，这里没有交代。想必赞助商会回答：没啥用。这时作者就会说：没错。别往内存投钱了。投到我这里吧。我这里是新科技。

建议译法：然后，我推算几年后的情况，并问大家，口袋里装这么大的内存做什么？（李）

12

原文：Extrapolating through to today, we would expect a $400 iPod to have 160,000 gigabytes of memory. But the top iPhone of today (which costs much more than $400) has only 256 gigabytes of memory, less than double the capacity of the 2007 iPod. This particular exponential collapsed very suddenly once the amount of memory got to the point where it was big enough to hold any reasonable person's music library and apps, photos, and videos. Exponentials can collapse when a physical limit is hit, or when there is no more economic rationale to continue them.

原译：按照推算，现在400美元的iPod存储空间应达160000千兆。但现在最好的iPhone（售价远超400美元）仅有256千兆的存储空间，比2007年的两倍还要少。一旦存储空间足够大到可以容纳任何普通人的乐库、应用、照片和视频，这一指数就会骤降。当达到物理极限，或没有经济原理能够维持指数时，指数就会崩溃。（谢）

改译：要这样推断，现在400美元的iPod得有16万G内存了。但如今最好的iPhone（售价超过400美元）也只有256GB的内存，还不到2007年iPod内存的两倍。一旦内存足够大，满足任何人对音乐库、应用程序、照片和视频的合理存储需求，这个特定的指数式增长就会骤然失效。因此，当变化达到物理极限，或没有经济效益时，指数论便不再成立。（王）

李：extrapolating through to today 表示又回到了今天，不再是回顾过去。

李：译者对语言要有敏感性，时刻注意表达的逻辑性。"足够大到可以"是句式杂糅。或者改为"足够大，可以"，或者改为"大到足以"。"指数骤降"也无意义。"指数"就是几次方。几次方骤降又是什么？这句话无非是说，所谓的指数式增长，便不攻自破了。可以灵活选择生动的语言。

建议译法：要这样推断，现在 400 美元的 iPod 得有 16 万 G 内存了。但如今最好的 iPhone（售价远超 400 美元）也只有 256G，不到 2007 年 iPod 的两倍。一旦内存足够大，满足任何人对音乐库、应用程序、照片和视频存储的合理需求，这个指数增长神话便瞬间破灭。因此，当达到一定物理极限，或继续下去没有经济上的理由时，指数式增长就会崩溃。（李）

13

原文：Similarly, we have seen a sudden increase in performance of AI systems thanks to the success of deep learning. Many people seem to think that means we will continue to see AI performance increase by equal multiples on a regular basis. But the deep-learning success was 30 years in the making, and it was an isolated event.

原译：同理，由于深度学习的成功，人工智能系统性能迅速提升。许多人认为，这意味着人工智能系统的性能将会定期以同一倍数增长。但是，深度学习的成功花了 30 年，而且还是独立事件。（谢）

改译 1：同样，由于深度学习大获成功，人工智能系统的性能也迅速提高。如此一来，许多人似乎认为，人工智能的性能也会定期以同等倍数增长。然而，深度学习的成功是过去 30 年来努力的结果，而且它是一个孤立事件。（王）

李："同一倍数""同等倍数"都不是常见的表达方式。基本意思是像过去一样，定期成倍提升。in the making 意思是不间断努力。剑桥词典的解释：

> **in the making**

⭐ if something is a particular length of time in the making, it takes that long to do or achieve it:

The current crisis has been in the making for several years, and it has taken far too long for regulators to act.

isolated events,"孤立事件",可能不会发生第二次:

⭐ happening alone, separately, or only once:

isolated case/incident/instance This is not an isolated case of fraud but one of the biggest corruption scandals in history.

dictionary.cambridge.org

> **建议译法**：同理，由于深度学习大获成功，人工智能系统的性能也迅速提高。如此一来，许多人似乎认为，人工智能的性能也会像过去一样，定期成倍提升。然而，深度学习的成功是过去 30 年来累积研究的结果，而且是一个孤立事件。（李）

14

> **原文**：That does not mean there will not be more isolated events, where work from the backwaters of AI research suddenly fuels a rapid-step increase in the performance of many AI applications. But there is no "law" that says how often they will happen.
>
> **原译**：这并不意味着不会再出现独立事件，人工智能科研的回水区仍有可能突然促进许多人工智能应用的快速发展。但事件何时出现，却无定律可循。（谢）

王："回水区"意思不清楚，需要查 backwaters 在文中是什么意思。由下图第二条推测，backwater 指发展滞后或停滞不前的状态。结合文意，backwater 应该指 AI 领域停滞不前的课题。

backwater

noun [C] • UK /ˈbæk.wɔː.tər/ US /ˈbæk.wɑː.tɚ/

⭐ **a part of a river where the water does not flow:**
We tied the boat up in a quiet backwater overnight.

⭐ DISAPPROVING **a place that does not change because it is not influenced by new ideas or events that happen in other places:**
He grew up in a rural backwater.

dictionary.cambridge.org

改译 1：当然了，孤立事件可能还会有。一旦人工智能研究中的攻坚问题取得进展，便能马上带动人工智能应用性能的快速发展。然而，这样的事多久会出现，并无规律可循。（王）

改译 2：当然了，孤立事件可能还会有。比方说，某个本来默默无闻的人工智能领域突然取得突破，带动人工智能应用程序的性能快速提高。然而，这样的事多久会出现一次，并无任何"定律"作出预测。（李）

建议译法：当然了，孤立事件可能还会有。比方说，人工智能研究的冷门领域突然取得突破，带动人工智能应用程序的性能快速提高。然而，这样的事多久会出现一次，并无任何"定律"作出预测。（李）

李："冷门"应该能够表达 backwater 的意思。

> Some scientists change their direction to be at the cutting edge of science, whereas others continue in the former areas of research. Those that do not pursue the major advances are often said to be engaging in backwater research. These scientists can still make breakthroughs independent of the current fad. While the avant-garde scientists are at the frontier of new knowledge and theory, the backwater scientists doing applied research are the primary source of technological invention. Their discoveries may not give rise directly to new theories, but they do give rise to new holistic understanding within an existing paradigm. Both kinds of research are essential and form a vital continuum.

第十单元　建筑设计

Exercise 10 Architecture

翻译情景

本单元选自澳大利亚塔斯马尼亚州 MONA（Museum of Old and New Art）博物馆网站对该馆的介绍，内容为该博物馆资深撰稿人兼"研究策展人"（Research Curator）Elizabeth Pearce 与博物馆建筑师 James Pearce 之间的对话。

博物馆的建筑设计公司为 Fender Katsalidis。设计团队包括首席建筑师 Nonda Katsalidis（与博物馆创始人 David Walsh 密切合作），建筑设计总监 James Pearce，以及场地项目经理 Steve Devereaux 等。

假定博物馆网站制作中文网页，请你把这篇对话翻译为中文。可通过网站（mona.net.au/museum/architecture）或截取节选任意片段检索全文；或通过谷歌查找视频或图片；真实的翻译情景中还可能需要到现场参观或请博物馆提供视频、图片或解释。在表达方面，注意对话双方是夫妻关系，在照顾专业性的同时，尽量让对话朴实自然，不要过于正式或浮夸。

训练重点

本单元主要训练译者的全局意识、查证能力和语言能力。全局意识就是对语篇内容和语篇外情景的感知和运用。译者需要清楚选段的语言风格、对话人背景、目标读者等；同时，建议博物馆建筑设计的空间感和视觉效应，单单借助对话本身的文字材料是无法充分理解的；译者还需要借助其他图片、音视频等外部资料，才能更清楚原文文字描述的深刻含义。

训练难点

本篇的难点之一在于宏观把握原文的语言风格，用自然、得体的语言产出译文；第二个难点是如何通过查证，准确理解原文中具有空间感的建筑设计。

训练方式

本次练习分原文、翻译提示、参考译文、译者注四部分。请先尝试自己翻译原文。做完以后再参看翻译提示，并继续调查研究，修改、润色译文，形成第二稿。形成二稿之后，再看参考译文和译者注。最后几个单元，希望你充分利用所学知识，综合运用各项能力，更上一层楼！

原文 [1]

Architecture

...

Also, there're no extraneous finishes. The building is comprised of just what you see. When you get inside, there are no plasterboard linings and stuff like that, just the raw structure.

JP: It gives the building a robustness. It can take a lot of wear and tear, and still look good, not get scuffed or dirty². It also provides a natural character. In most museums you have some sort of expression on the outside, but this is not carried through, so the white box³ in the interior bears no relation to its structure. We didn't want to create a neutral space for the art⁴, but an active, living one—a space the art responds to.

...

JP: There had been a colonnade[5] on the existing building, that Grounds had originally designed for it. It had been demolished by the time we got there. There was some argument about the fact that we should not reinstate it, but create a new kind of entry piece on the same spot—some sort of statement or marker. The idea behind the mirror entry is about the event horizon[6] surrounding black holes, the point of no return when you can't escape the pull of gravity.

...

EP: Down in the bottom level of the gallery, that sandstone wall—it sets this mood of damp apprehension I think.

JP: The sandstone reflects sound in a particular way. And a massive rock like that has a certain sense of gravity and presence. A lot of that is to do with the lighting as well. But what's great about the natural material is it has a variety and life, and you can see all the strata and realise what you're looking at is hundreds of millions of years old.

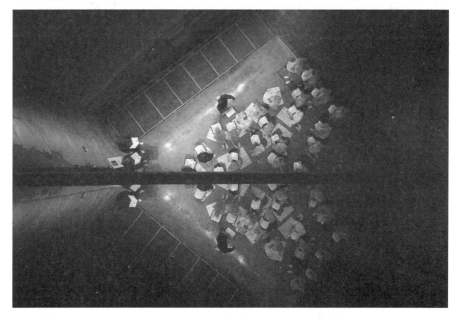

...

To start off with, we had a space frame truss. He never liked that. He said,

'It should just be a big, steel beam.' So that's what we ended up with. However, I did convince him to—well, whether I convinced him, or whether he just didn't notice, or saw it and liked it, I don't know. But we did shape the beam so that it was deeper in the middle[7] and thinner at the ends, otherwise it doesn't give you a sense that it's holding something up. This gave it a bit of a dynamic. So we got that one through.

…

But up on top of the museum, on the plaza, we wanted people to be able to see through, so we solved that problem with the rusted steel blades[8], shaped to continue the line of the wall. So that was a pretty neat solution.

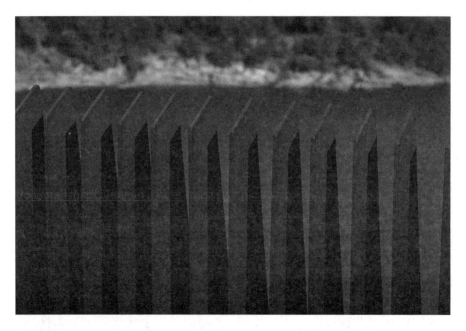

But we started with a whole lot of other ideas to solve the balustrade problem. Inside the museum, Nonda had this idea of steel rods connecting a steel handrail at the top but the bottom was on a zigzag so the rods sort of wove in and out around the void[9]. David hated it.

EP: Because, again, it was too fussy?

JP: Probably. So we ended up with just the cantilever glass balustrades, which you won't even have noticed. We avoided the traditional patch-fitting type thing on the balustrade, with the stainless steel dots that you typically see holding up the glass. We invented our own little thing that clips over the glass at the top and then curved out to support it.

...

JP: It wasn't a huge falling out really, but there was definitely a discussion. It came about because of the mirror entry. The idea was that the reflections give you this whole distorted space effect. Nonda came up with the line that it would be good if it reflected the colour green—something like the colour of a tennis court. And David said, 'I know what's the colour of a tennis court…'

...

EP: What's your favourite thing?

JP: Hmm. The precast concrete wall that wraps around the main gallery space has a grid pattern on it, the same pattern that's in the ceiling. The important thing for us was that it not look like a whole lot of concrete panels—particularly at the corners. That's very hard to do, and it's important, because it's at the corners that the impression of a three-dimensional object is created. We detailed a panel so it would wrap around the corner, creating a seamless, three-dimensional texture. The grid gets cut off halfway through, at the top and the bottom, so it gives a sense that it just continues.

翻译提示

1 **全局意识**

请大家针对原文和译文，分别回答 Who is talking to whom? About what? When, where and why? And how? 然后再开始翻译。

2 **表述准确性**

注意分析 get scuffed or dirty 讲的是可能性，还是已经发生的情况。这两种理解翻译出来的译文意思上会有很大差别。

3 **语言能力 / 文化沟通**

通过简单的查证可知，white box 是西方引入的一个概念，译者需要衡量是直译还是意译，两种策略会产生什么样的效果，是否可以将两种策略结合。

4 **语言能力**

注意这里 art 前面用了定冠词，检查时要区分 art 是指艺术，还是指艺术品。

5 **词义**

注意看一下 colonnade 是指一根柱子，还是一排廊柱？可借助谷歌图片帮助理解。

6 **专有名词**

event horizon 是一个普通人可能不太熟悉的概念，在修改时，译者需要考虑原文的风格和受众，取舍一下是按照专有名词翻译，还是以通俗易懂的方式表达。

7 **查证能力**

原文对这个 deeper in the middle 的文字描述不够清楚，也不够形象。因此，建议译者查找相关视频或者图片来帮助理解。

8 **查证能力**

要查查 rusted steel blades 的图片。百闻不如一见，有了形象的图片，译者就可以解释它是怎么延续墙面线条的了。

9 **查证能力**

需要重点查证 void 是具体的建筑实物，还是一种建筑构造。

参考译文

建筑设计[1]

……

此外,博物馆也没有多余的饰面。[2]使用的建筑材料,一目了然。[3]馆内看不到石膏衬板之类的饰材,只有原始结构。[4]

JP:这让房屋看起来很结实,无论怎么使用,都不会磨损或弄脏。什么时候都完好如初。[5]另一个好处是天然无华。[6]大多数博物馆,外部看起来挺有特色,但这种特色没有贯穿始终。里面的"白盒子"中性展厅[7]跟外部结构毫无关联。[8]我们不想为展品打造中性空间,而是活跃、有生命力的空间,让展品与空间产生互动。[9]

……

JP:原来的建筑物本来有一排柱廊,格朗兹(Grounds)设计的。我们来的时候已经拆了。[10]当时提出来不去重建柱廊,而是在原地打造新的入口,当作某种宣示或标志,为此我们还有些争论。[11]镜面入口的设计灵感,源自黑洞周围的"事件视界",也就是无法逃脱重力牵引的"不归点"。[12]

……

EP:我想,美术馆最底层的砂岩墙,营造出阴郁不安的气氛。[13]

JP:砂岩反射声音的方式很独特。这么大的石块,给人带来某种厚重感和存在感。这种感觉与灯光也有很大关系。[14]但是,这种天然材料的好处,在于它的多样性和生命力,你可以看到所有的岩层,感慨眼前的一切已经有数亿年历史。[15]

……

起初,我们想采用太空桁架,但他不喜欢。[16]他说:"一根大钢梁就行了。"[17]所以最后改成了钢梁。不过,我确实说服了他——呃,不知道是我说服了他,还是他没注意到,还是他看到后喜欢——但我们的确改造了钢梁,让它中间粗、两头细,这样才有支撑的感觉。也有些动感。[18]钢梁就这么确定了。[19]

第十单元 · 建筑设计

……

但是博物馆顶上,也就是广场上,为了不遮挡视线,我们用了锈钢板片,延续墙体轮廓,让问题迎刃而解。[20]

可是,为了解决围挡的问题,我们一开始想了很多别的办法。[21] 在博物馆内部,农达(Nonda)想用钢护栏,顶部与钢制扶手相连,底部以"之"字形安置,好似在虚空里左右穿行。[22] 但是大卫(David)不喜欢这一设计。

EP:又是因为太过花哨[23]吗?

JP:可能吧。所以最后我们采用了外悬式玻璃围挡,估计你都没注意到。[24] 围挡上没有用传统的玻璃夹,就是大家经常在玻璃门上看到的不锈钢圆点,用来夹持玻璃。我们设计了个小东西,先从顶部夹住玻璃,再向外弯曲固定玻璃。[25]

……

JP:算不上激烈争执,不过的确有所讨论,起因是入口处的镜面墙。当时的想法是,通过镜面反射,产生空间扭曲的整体效果。[26] 农达当时说,最好能反射绿色,就像网球场的颜色。然后大卫说:"你不说,我也知道网球场是什么颜色……"[27]

……

EP:你最喜欢什么?

JP:嗯……主展厅外的混凝土预制板墙。上面有网格状图案,与天花板的图案相同。[28] 我们认为,关键是不能让墙,尤其是墙角,看起来有太多预制板。[29] 这很难办到,但很重要,因为物体的立体感恰恰是在拐角形成的。[30] 我们精心打造了一块转角预制板,包住墙角,创造出无缝衔接的三维效果。[31] 顶部以及底部的网格从中间切断,让人感觉网格会延续下去。[32]

译者注

1 语篇意识

王 & 李:这篇文章以对话形式展开,因此对话要尽量符合口语化表达,不必过于文学化,也不必像文献翻译一样亦步亦趋。interviewer 是 Elizabeth Pearce(妻子),interviewee 是 James Pearce(丈夫),读者可能是对建筑感兴趣的任何人。

另外,要注意语域前后一致,不要一会儿阳春白雪,一会儿下里巴人。

一些背景资料:

博物馆创始人 David Walsh 和博物馆简介:http://news.artintern.net/html.php?id=56237

博物馆俯瞰图:

http://www.huochai.mobi/p/d/1211198/?share_tid=88973b31d3e6&fmid=0

2

> 原文:Also, there're no extraneous finishes.
> 原译:而且博物馆也没有多余的饰面。(莎)

莎:finishes:饰面

Noun 1. **finish** - a decorative texture or appearance of a surface (or the substance that gives it that appearance); "the boat had a metallic finish"; "he applied a coat of a clear finish"; "when the finish is too thin it is difficult to apply evenly"

≡ finishing, coating

↔ **decorativeness** - an appearance that serves to decorate and make something more attractive

↔ **glaze** - a coating for ceramics, metal, etc.

↔ **shoeshine** - a shiny finish put on shoes with polish and buffing; "his trousers had a sharp crease and you could see your reflection in his shoeshine"

第十单元·建筑设计

http://www.thefreedictionary.com/finish

> Design Resources ▲　　Find Us ▼　　　　　　📍 FIND A DEALER
>
> **IMAGES**　　　　　　　**DOCUMENTS**　　　　　　**SURFACE MATERIALS**
>
> Browse, save, and download beautiful images for use in presentations or inspiration boards.　　Browse, save, and download spec guides, certificates, brochures, reports, white papers, case studies, and articles.　　Learn about the wide range of [finishes,] fabrics, and surfaces available on Steelcase products.

https://www.steelcase.com/resources/surface-materials/

> 联系我们 ▼
>
> **图片**　　　　　**文件**　　　　　**饰面材料**
>
> 浏览、保存和下载这些美丽的图片便于在展示板和激励板上使用。　　浏览、保存和下载特别指导、证书、册子、报告、白皮书、案例研究和文章。　　欲了解更多关于产品[饰面]、材质，和表面材料，请点击Steelcase产品一栏。

https://www.steelcase.com/asia-zh/resources/surface-materials/

建议译法：此外，博物馆也没有多余的饰面。（王）

3

原文：The building is comprised of just what you see.
原译：博物馆全是由眼前所见的材料建成的。（莎）
改译 1：你所看到的，就是这幢建筑的构成。（王）
改译 2：建筑是怎么构成的，正如你所见。（陈）

李：意思不明确。

建议译法：使用的建筑材料，一目了然。（李）

325

4

> 原文：When you get inside, there are no plasterboard linings and stuff like that, just the raw structure.
> 原译：馆内的墙也没有石膏衬板之类的东西，只是些原始结构而已。（莎）

莎：谷歌图片搜索 plasterboard lining：

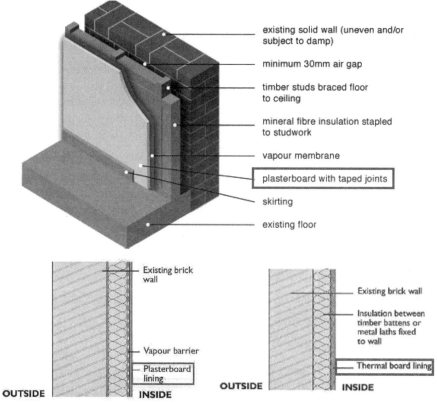

《金属建筑系统：设计与规范》，纽曼

谷歌图书搜索 石膏板 内衬：

表 8.2 所选择组合墙体的 U_0 值

组合墙体	插图	U_0
带 3 英寸玻璃纤维保温棉的金属墙体	图 7.1 和图 7.5	0.13
带 4 英寸玻璃纤维保温棉的金属墙体	图 7.1 和图 7.5	0.12
隐藏式螺钉板，3 英寸玻璃纤维保温棉，金属内衬板和 1/2 英寸石膏板	图 7.2	0.112
隐藏式螺钉板，2 英寸硬制保温板，木质内衬板和 1/2 英寸石膏板	图 7.2（近似）	0.047

根据以上资料可知，plasterboard lining 指的应该是装修的时候涂在最外面的那一层石膏，里面通常有一层绝缘层，然后是木板、石棉等等。

> 改译1：馆内没有石膏衬板之类的东西，只有原始结构。（王）
> 改译2：馆内看不到石膏板之类的东西，只有原始结构。（陈）

王 & 李：根据注释，石膏板是一种装饰材料，所以建议把"东西"改为"饰材"，这样与"只有原始结构"形成对比。

> 建议译法：馆内看不到石膏衬板之类的饰材，只有原始结构。（王）

5

> 原文：It gives the building a robustness. It can take a lot of wear and tear, and still look good, not get scuffed or dirty.
> 原译：建筑因此结实牢靠，即使经历风吹雨打，也依旧美观，耐磨耐脏。（莎）

莎：Robustness:

robustness

NOUN

[mass noun]

1 The quality or condition of being strong and in good condition.
   '*the overall robustness of national and international financial systems*'

   (+ More example sentences)

   1.1 The ability to withstand or overcome adverse conditions or rigorous testing.
   '*we can examine the robustness of our results*'

https://en.oxforddictionaries.com/definition/robustness

> **改译 1**：这赋予建筑一种持久力，使之经久耐磨，美观依旧，没有破损，不会变脏。（王）

表述准确性

王：get scuffed or dirty 讲的是可能性，不是已经发生的；不要表述成"经历了……之后还如何如何"。

陈："使之经久耐磨，美观依旧"似乎跟原文的意思有些细微的差别，"经久耐磨"约等于"美观依旧"。

> **改译 2**：建筑因此有了一种持久力，历经磨损也美观依旧，没有破损，不会变脏。（陈）

李：对话采用口译的方法。不拘泥于字面。

> **建议译法**：这让房屋看起来很结实，无论怎么使用，都不会磨损或弄脏。什么时候都完好如初。（李）

6

> **原文**：It also provides a natural character.
> **改译 1**：也造就了一种天然气质。（陈）

王：汉语很少以"也"字开头单独成句，建议前面加一个"这"。

> **改译 2**：这也造就了一种天然气质。（王）

李：没问题。还可以再改。

> **建议译法**：另一个好处是天然无华。（李）

7

> 原文：white box
> 原译："白盒子"（莎）

莎：这是一个西方引入的概念，因此加引号直接保留。"白盒子"指的是美术馆中用于展览的中立建筑空间。也就是下文所说的 neutral space。

李：查谷歌图片，所谓"白盒子"，就是白色展厅。白色代表中性。White box 见 Museum of Modern Art: Imagining the Future of the Museum of Modern Art, New York：

> **GLENN D. LOWRY**: Terry, I wonder if you would consider elaborating upon a couple of points that you touched upon in your lecture and that also grow out of Mary Lea's and John's comments. The first has to do with the notion of the white box, or its opposite, the black box; that is, what has come to be seen, certainly in some circles, as the need in galleries for—and here I use quotation marks—"neutral spaces," and its implications in terms of the actual experience of looking at art. And as a kind of corollary to that, could you discuss the notion of intimacy and what structures intimacy—that is, what are the experiential components that intimacy demands. I think it is one of the issues that is of great importance for this Museum, as we have come to be appreciated as an institution that has created and sustained an intimate relationship between those who look at art, and the objects themselves.
>
> **TERENCE RILEY**: Actually, discussions have been going on for decades now about the idea of a "white box," a purportedly completely neutral space. They have to be inflected, because, on the one hand, there is an ideological aspect to the white box, which, indeed, as the environment gets less and less formal—as it gets to the point where it has no characteristics whatsoever—the formal characteristics of the work of

谷歌图书搜索 white box art architecture space：

过去几十年来，东方对现代化及其象征的接受、吸收，已反映在当代艺术展场的快速发展上，大部份展场受到西方思维「白盒子」（white box）的高度影响。因此，艺术作品都在抽象的建筑物中展出，这些建筑无形中孤立了这些作品，或是像某些人所说的，让作品得以在专业场域中展出。

《中产阶级拘谨的魅力——当代华人观点》一展，由曾文泉和 Arthub 负责人乐大豆（Davide Quadrio）共同策划，并由李晏祯担任助理策展人。

此展旨在将中国当代艺术移转到不同背景，让它分享一个"亲密"世界、一种私人空间，远离所谓的"白盒子"（white box）经验。

http://www.magician-space.com/cnnews_details.aspx?id=30

根据以上资料可知，white box 应该是指一个完全中性的、客观的建筑空间。简单译为"白盒子"，外行可能看不懂。归化为"中性展厅"，又丧失了介绍外来概念的机会。想来想去，觉得可以把两者结合起来，译为"'白盒子'中性展厅"。

8

原文：In most museums you have some sort of expression on the outside, but this is not carried through, so the white box in the interior bears no relation to its structure.

原译：大部分博物馆的外部多少有些设计表现，却没有一以贯之，导致馆内的"白盒子"与整个建筑毫无联系。（莎）

改译1：在大多数博物馆外部，你都会看到某种结构表现，但我们并没有沿袭这一做法，这样内部的"白盒子"就不会受结构所缚。（王）

改译2：大多数博物馆，你置身馆外，会看到某种结构表现，但这种表现并未贯彻到馆内，导致馆内的"白盒子"和建筑结构毫无关联。（陈）

李：意思理解为，大多数博物馆，虽然外部看起来挺有特色，但这种特色没有贯彻始终，里面的中性展厅千篇一律，跟外部结构/特色毫无关联。言外之意是，Mona 博物馆内外风格如一，都是建材本色，结构表现上有别于其他博物馆。

本句话有个语法问题，可能干扰理解：its structure 当中的 its 按照语法，应该指代 white box。但这说不通（"白盒子内部与盒子的结构无关"），按照前后逻辑，its 应当理解为 the museum's。实际上，这句话隐含 museum：the white box in the interior [of the museum] bears no relation to its structure. 这可能是口语不严谨造成的。好在大家看起来没有受到影响。

改译 3：大多数博物馆，外部看起来挺有特色，但这种特色没有贯彻始终。标准的白色展厅和外部结构毫无关联。（李）

建议译法：大多数博物馆，外部看起来挺有特色，但这种特色没有贯彻始终。里面的"白盒子"中性展厅跟外部结构毫无关联。（李）

9

原文：We didn't want to create a neutral space for the art, but an active, living one—a space the art responds to.

原译：我们不是想要为展品打造一个中立的空间，而是想要打造一片活跃的、有生命力的空间，与展品相呼应。（莎）

莎：这里 the art 用了定冠词，因此不是指"艺术"这个抽象概念，而是指具体的艺术品。art:

2 [uncountable] examples of objects such as paintings, drawings or sculptures
- *an art gallery/exhibition*
- *a collection of art and antiques*

http://www.oxfordlearnersdictionaries.com/definition/english/art_1?q=art

改译 1：我们想为展品打造的，并不是一个中立空间，而是一种活跃的、有生命力的空间，一种与展品相呼应的空间。（王）

陈：原文 space 前的不定冠词似乎并不需要翻译。

改译 2：我们不想为展品打造中立的空间，我们想打造活跃的、有生命力的空间，让展品能与空间相呼应。（陈）

王：两个"我们"作主语稍微有些重复，节奏有点欠缺，这里我比较倾向维持原译。前半句省译不定冠词，是考虑可以让汉语节奏好一些。从后半句看来，是否省略都可以。

改译3:我们想为展品打造的,并非中立的空间,而是活跃、有生命力的空间,是展品与空间相呼应的空间。(王)
建议译法:我们不想为展品打造中性空间,而是有活力、有生命力的空间,让展品与空间产生互动。(李)

10

原文:There had been a colonnade on the existing building, that Grounds had originally designed for it. It had been demolished by the time we got there.
原译:博物馆里本来有一条柱廊,是格荣兹(Grounds)设计的。但是我们来的时候已经被拆除了。(莎)

王:colonnade 是柱廊,不是一根柱子,要注意表述的准确性。

colonnade noun [C] a row of columns separated from each other by an equal distance.

王:原文是 on the existing building,查找到 MONA (MONA Build) 博物馆正前方的图片,图1就是原来的建筑物,Grounds 设计的。

http://www.matthewharding.com.au/work/mona-front-entrance-wall

后来改造成图 2 这个样子：

https://www.discovertasmania.com.au/attraction/museumofoldandnewartmona

王：Grounds 指的是建筑设计师 Roy Grounds。

  Our three-storey, two-bedroom penthouse-equivalent is named after <u>Sir Roy Grounds (1905–81)—the architect</u> behind Mona's Courtyard House (where you enter the museum), and Round House (through the tunnel and into the library).

https://mona.net.au/stay/mona-pavilions/roy

李：Grounds 设计的建筑物，后来成为 MONA 博物馆的入口和图书馆。

  In 2011, with the opening of The Museum of Old and New Art (MONA) in Hobart, Tasmania, two houses designed and built there by Grounds in 1957–9 for Claudio Alcorso on the Moorilla Estate—the Courtyard House and the Round House—became respectively the entrance and the library of Australia's largest private museum.

https://en.wikipedia.org/wiki/Roy_Grounds

莎：这里没有译出 originally，因为上句的"本来"已经可以体现这一点。若译出来，则是"是 Grounds 最初的设计"，这样听起来让人觉得之后有谁又修改过的感觉，容易造成歧义。因此省略。

陈：是否可以更口语一些？

> **改译 1**：这栋楼本来有一排柱廊，最初由格荣兹（Grounds）设计完成。我们来的时候已经拆除了。（陈）

陈：designed for it 当中的 it，指前面说的 building。原本的柱廊以及后来的镜面墙入口所在对比：

李：译为"博物馆""这栋楼"有廊柱都不对。这句是指原来就存在的老建筑现在成了入口。另外，如果人名词典查不到，就按照译音表翻译。网上可找到。

改译 2：原来的建筑物本来有一排柱廊，由格朗兹（Grounds）设计。我们来的时候已经拆除了。（李）

建议译法：原来的建筑物本来有一排柱廊，格朗兹（Grounds）设计的。我们来的时候已经拆了。（陈）

11

原文：There was some argument about the fact that we should not reinstate it, but create a new kind of entry piece on the same spot—some sort of statement or marker.

原译：对此大家曾有些争议，有人认为不应该恢复原样，应该在原地建造新入口——具有声明或者标志意义之类。（莎）

改译 1：一些人认为，我们不应该恢复重建，而应在原地打造新入口，象征一种声明或地标。（王）

改译 2：一些人认为，不该恢复重建，应在原地打造新入口，当作某种声明或地标。（陈）

李：entry piece 应该是指进来首先映入眼帘的东西。下一句所说的 mirror entry (mirrored wall)，就是 entry piece。下图就是 mirror entry。

Mirrored wall on courtyard house, Photo credit: Matt Newton, Images Courtesy of MONA Museum of Old and New Art, Hobart, Tasmania, Australia

李：不是外人和他争论，是当初设计博物馆时，几个人内部的争论。本文多处提到争论，都发生在设计团队。"象征声明"搭配不当。

李：statement 翻译为"声明"意思不清。此处应理解为 marker 的同义词，不一定翻译出来。也许讲话人觉得用词不当，又换成 marker。

王：翻译成"声明"，主要是不符合使用语境。不少同学处理成了"宣示"或者"宣言"，是可取的。这种建筑的表现形式，就像是一种宣言或宣示。这些选词，把建筑拟人化了。

> 改译3：当时提出来不去重建柱廊，而是在原地打造新的迎宾装置，当作某种宣示或标志，为此还有些争论。（李）

王：我个人认为，既然可以表达得更为口语化，不如把 entry piece 直接处理为"入口"。"迎宾"这个词和"装置"不太搭配，而且语域一下子变高了。"为此还有些争论"建议改为"为此我们还有些争论"，这样 some argument 的指代关系就更明确了，是这几个人之间的争论。

> 建议译法：当时提出来不去重建柱廊，而是在原地打造新的入口，当作某种宣示或标志，为此我们还有些争论。（王）

12

> 原文：The idea behind the mirror entry is about the event horizon surrounding black holes, the point of no return when you can't escape the pull of gravity.
> 原译：镜面墙入口的设计灵感来自黑洞周围的"事件视界"，即无法逃脱重力牵引的"不归点"。（莎）

王 & 莎：这两个短语是外来词汇，因此加引号。

事件视界（英语：event horizon），是一种时空的曲隔界线。视界中任何的事件皆无法对视界外的观察者产生影响。在黑洞周围的便是事件视界。在非常巨大的重力影响下，黑洞附近的逃逸速度大于光速，使得任何光线皆不可能从事件视界内部逃脱。根据广义相对论，在远离视界的外部观察者眼中，任何从视界外部接近视界的物件，将须要用无限长的时间到达视界面，其影像会经历无止境逐渐增强的红移；但该物件本身却不会感到任何异常，并会在有限时间之内穿过视界。

https://zh.wikipedia.org/wiki/ 事件视界

In general relativity, an event horizon is a boundary in space time beyond which events cannot affect an outside observer. In layman's terms, it is defined as the shell of "points of no return", i.e., the points at which the gravitational pull becomes so great as to make escape impossible, even for light. An event horizon is most commonly associated with black holes. Light emitted from inside the event horizon can never reach the outside observer.

https://en.wikipedia.org/wiki/Event_horizon

根据上述解释，在广义相对论中，事件视界是时空的界限，超过这个界限事件不会影响外界的观察者。从翻译的角度讲，翻译成"事件视界"需要加上引号，因为它是一个普通人不熟悉的专有名词。当然，这篇文章比较口语化，如果简单处理成非专有名词，意思相同，也是可以接受的。

> **改译1**：镜面入口的设计灵感，源自黑洞周围的"事件视界"，即无法逃脱重力牵引的"不归点"。（王）
>
> **建议译法**：镜面入口的设计灵感，源自黑洞周围的"事件视界"，也就是无法逃脱重力牵引的"不归点"。（陈）

13

> **原文**：Down in the bottom level of the gallery, that sandstone wall—it sets this mood of damp apprehension I think.
>
> **原译**：我觉得，美术馆最底层那几面砂岩墙，制造了一种阴郁的感觉。（莎）

陈：感觉"阴郁"挺好的，"阴"刚好能把"damp"的意味体现出来（地底的潮湿，巨石的压迫）。

改译 1：我想，美术馆最底层的砂岩墙，营造出阴郁与不安的气氛。（陈）

建议译法：我想，美术馆最底层的砂岩墙，营造出阴郁不安的气氛。（李）

14

原文：And a massive rock like that has a certain sense of gravity and presence. A lot of that is to do with the lighting as well.

原译：像这样巨大的岩壁有让人感到些许沉重和压迫，这很大程度上也与灯光有关。（莎）

改译 1：这样的巨石，有一种重力感和存在感，这与灯光也有很大关系。（王）

改译 2：石头如此巨大，透着厚重感和存在感。这种感觉与灯光也有很大关系。（陈）

建议译法：这么大的石块，给人带来某种厚重感和存在感。这种感觉与灯光也有很大关系。（李）

15

原文：But what's great about the natural material is it has a variety and life, and you can see all the strata and realise what you're looking at is hundreds of millions of years old.

原译：但是砂岩的妙处在于形态多样且富有生命力，看着一片片岩层，就会意识到你所凝视的是数亿年的历史。（莎）

改译 1：但是，自然材料的绝妙之处，在于它的多样性和生命力，你能看到所有地层，也能感受到，眼前的一切已有数亿年历史。（王）

李：the natural material 是特指。

王：继续查证，这里特指 sandstone，顺藤摸瓜，找到以下文章，进一步印证了猜测。这篇文章的题目为 *The sandstone really works – MONA, Museum of*

Old and New Art, Hobart, Tasmania – 30 Dec 2014

这种 natural material 就是 sandstone，是最原始的素材，不经过切割加工。

https://daynaa2000.wordpress.com/2015/01/06/tassie-summer-holiday-2014-15/the-sandstone-really-works-mona-museum-of-old-and-new-art-hobart-tasmania-30-dec-2014/

改译 2：但是，天然材料的绝妙之处，在于它的多样性和生命力，你看得到所有地层，感受到，眼前的一切已有数亿年历史。（陈）
建议译法：但是，这种天然材料的好处，在于它的多样性和生命力，你可以看到所有的岩层，感慨眼前的一切已经有数亿年历史。（李）

16

原文：To start off with, we had a space frame truss.
原译：最开始我们设计了一个球节桁架，他很不喜欢。（莎）
改译 1：起初，我们设计的是一个球节桁架，但他不喜欢。（王）
改译 2：起初，我们设计的是球节桁架，但他不喜欢。（陈）

李：什么是 a space frame truss？

In architecture and structural engineering, a **space frame** or **space structure** is a rigid, lightweight, truss-like structure constructed from interlocking struts in a geometric pattern. Space frames can be used to span large areas with few interior supports. Like the truss, a space frame is strong because of the inherent rigidity of the triangle; flexing loads (bending moments) are transmitted as tension and compression loads along the length of each strut. Steel space frames provide great freedom of expression and composition as well as the possibility to evenly distribute loads along each rod and external constraints. With these features, steel space frames can be used to achieve also complex geometries with a structural weight lower than any other solution. The inner highly hyper-static system provides an increased resistance to damages caused by fire, explosions, shocks and earthquakes. Space frames are modular and made of highly industrialized elements designed with a remarkable dimensional accuracy and precise surface finish.

Space frame truss 的图片：

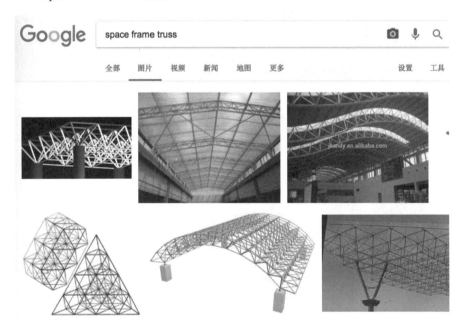

桁架的英文 truss 源自约 1200 年时的古法文 trousse，意思是"许多连结在一起东西的集合"。truss 一词还常常用来描述由许多元件组合的物体，例如曲木框架及屋顶的橡架，不过也常用来表达以下工程上的定义："桁架是由许多个别结构件组成的单一平面框架，结构件的末端互相连接，形成许多三角形，可以延伸很长的距离。"

https://zh.wikipedia.org/wiki/桁架（工程）

建议译法：起初，我们想采用太空桁架，但他不喜欢。（李）

17

原文：He said, 'It should just be a big, steel beam.'

原译：他说："应该放一个大型钢梁"。（莎）

改译：他说："应该就放根大钢梁"。（陈）

建议译法：他说："一根大钢梁就行了"。（李）

18

原文：But we did shape the beam so that it was deeper in the middle and thinner at the ends, otherwise it doesn't give you a sense that it's holding something up. This gave it a bit of a dynamic.

原译：总之我们的确对钢梁进行了改造，让它中间深两边薄，否则没有支撑的感觉。钢梁因此有了些动感。（莎）

改译：但我们的确对钢梁进行了改造，让它中间深两边薄，否则没有支撑感。这让钢梁有了些动感。（王）

此处补充郑瀚文同学的查证。

郑瀚文：原文对此处钢梁形状的描述不够清楚，工程设计方Fellicetti的网站上提供的视频可以看出，桥底部钢梁的下部呈曲线状：

http://www.felicetti.com.au/featured-projects/mona-museum-hobart-2/#more-2714

视频后面也给出了钢梁吊装时的样子：

http://www.felicetti.com.au/featured-projects/mona-museum-hobart-2/#more-2714

可见钢梁是中间粗、两头细。

李：在实际翻译中，恐怕需要与博物馆沟通。但我们权且翻译为"中间粗，两头细"。或者"中间厚，两头薄"。这样翻译虽然不一定正确，但符合逻辑；"深"和"细"不形成对比，即使正确，也会被读者当成错误。

建议译法：但我们的确改造了钢梁，让它中间粗、两头细，这样才有支撑的感觉。也有些动感。（李）

19

原文：So we got that one through.
原译：于是我们就通过了这一设计。（莎）
改译：于是，设计就这么通过了。（陈）
建议译法：钢梁就这么确定了。（李）

李：意思是我们对钢梁的改动，"他"没反对。注意口语化。

20

> **原文**：But up on top of the museum, on the plaza, we wanted people to be able to see through, so we solved that problem with the rusted steel blades, shaped to continue the line of the wall. (So that was a pretty neat solution.)
> **原译**：但是在博物馆顶上，也就是在广场上，我们希望视线不受阻挡，为此，我们设计了锈钢片，其形状延续了墙面的线条。（莎）
> **改译 1**：但是在博物馆顶上，也就是在广场上，为了不挡住公众视线，我们使用了锈钢片，让形状延续墙面线条。（王）
> **改译 2**：但是博物馆顶上，也就是广场上，为了不遮挡视线，我们用了锈钢片，延墙面伸出来的线条排列。（陈）

李：rusted steel blades 是什么？这是查到的图片：

http://wehouse-media.com/ 颠覆性的成人迪士尼乐园 -mona 古今艺术博物馆 /

锈钢板，是指生了锈的钢板。根据生锈的阶段不同，呈现不同的颜色和表面状态。生锈的初期会呈黄色，然后随着生锈进程的推移，逐渐显现金黄色，橙黄色，橙色，橙红，红褐色最后在红褐，或者褐色稳定下来。

https://baike.baidu.com/item/ 锈钢板 /3755445

通过图片，我们也知道了 shaped to continue the line of the wall 是什么意思。文字是苍白的。百闻不如一见。

> 改译3：但是博物馆顶上，也就是广场上，为了不遮挡视线，我们用了锈钢片，延续墙面线条，让问题迎刃而解。（王）

王：按照原文的意思，就是延续墙面线条。但是究竟是怎么延续，是延续哪里的墙面线条，我想很多同学并不清楚。从下图可以看出来，圆圈左边是墙面，右边一点是 steel blades。可以看出，这一圈并不是都是 steel blades，有一些是墙体。设计师的意思就是，在阻碍人视线的地方，用锈钢片，但是它看起来还是墙面的一部分。这样我们翻译就清楚了。

> 改译4：但是博物馆顶上，也就是广场上，为了不遮挡视线，我们用了锈钢板片，延续墙体轮廓，让问题解决得干净利落。（李）
> 建议译法：但是博物馆顶上，也就是广场上，为了不遮挡视线，我们用了锈钢板片，延续墙体轮廓，让问题迎刃而解。（李）

21

> 原文：But we started with a whole lot of other ideas to solve the balustrade problem.

原译：不过一开始我们想了很多办法来解决栏杆的问题。（莎）
改译：为了解决栏杆的问题，我们一开始也想了很多其他办法。（王）

李：虽然字典上用的是"栏杆"，但其实balustrade既包括栏杆，也包括"围栏"：

> **balustrade**
> (bæləstreɪd, US -streɪd)
>
> Word forms: plural **balustrades**
>
> countable noun
>
> A **balustrade** is a railing or wall on a balcony or staircase.
>
> COBUILD Advanced English Dictionary. Copyright © HarperCollins Publishers
>
> https://www.collinsdictionary.com/dictionary/english/balustrade

实际上最后也没有采用"杆"，而使用的"栏"。

建议译法：可是，为了解决围挡的问题，我们一开始想了很多别的办法。（李）

22

原文：Inside the museum, Nonda had this idea of steel rods connecting a steel handrail at the top but the bottom was on a zigzag so the rods sort of wove in and out around the void.

原译：针对馆内栏杆，农达（Nonda）的想法是使用多根钢棍，顶部用一根钢制扶手连成一线，底部设计成"之"字形，这样钢棍穿插交错，中间留有空隙。（莎）

改译1：在博物馆内，农达（Nonda）想用钢棍与顶部钢制扶手相连，而底部设计成"之"字形，这样钢棍就相当于穿插交错于不同空间。（王）

改译2：馆内的栏杆，农达（Nonda）想用钢棍与顶部钢制扶手相连，而底部设计成"之"字形，钢棍就相当于穿插交错，形成某种空间。（陈）

改译3：在博物馆内部，农达（Nonda）想用不锈钢栏杆与顶部钢制扶手相连，底部以"之"字形安置，好像在虚拟障碍中左右穿行。（李）

李：wove: move along by twisting and turning to avoid obstructions, etc 迂回行进（以避开障碍等）：weave (one's way) through a crowd 在人群中迂回前行 * The road weaves through the range of hills. 这条路在群山中绕来绕去．* weave in and out through the traffic 在来往车辆中穿插而行。

王：我又查了一下，发现这个 void 不能当成短语理解，而是 Mona 博物馆里沙墙和博物馆墙面之间的空隙，详见：

THE VOID

Thirteen-metres underground, the Void is a spiffy place to impress your mates. It's home to a Triassic sandstone wall from the museum's excavation, artwork and a full bar. Our huge feast tables seat up to 160 guests or invite 450 of your nearest and dearest for a cocktail party.

Capacity may vary based on which artworks are installed at the time. It's usually Julius Popp's bit.fall, a waterfall of words, which happens to be the most loved Mona artwork of all time.

https://www.aime.com.au/__novadocuments/431514?v=636520104988900000

李：从上面的解释来看，void 不是空隙，而是一个巨大的地下空间。里面可以看到三叠纪的砂石墙、有展品、酒吧、宴席。

王：根据陈阳老师上课的讲解，小写 void 还是应该理解成"虚空"，好像栏杆在虚空中交错。以下为郑瀚文同学画的图，非常形象，课上也介绍了。

郑瀚文：文字太难描述，所以画了一幅图，帮助想象。

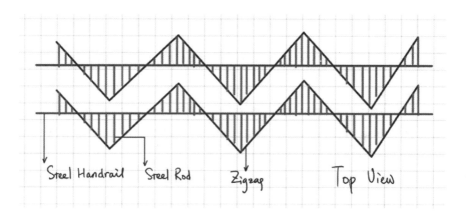

道路向外的突出部分，栏杆也会向外突出，形成锐角，从前后看就像是栏杆摆到了外面。

> **改译 4**：在博物馆内部，农达（Nonda）想用不锈钢栏杆，顶部与钢制扶手相连，底部以"之"字形安置，好似在虚空里左右穿行。（陈）

李：我也是这么想的，但画工不好，没画出来。但仔细想想，这样设计会有现实问题：道路两侧的锐角会绊脚，同时手也够不到相应的栏杆。无论如何，可以按这个想象来翻译。反正没有最终实现，谁也不知道他们脑子里到底怎么想的。把"不锈钢栏杆"改为"钢护栏"吧。不想增加原文没有明说的意思。

> **建议译法**：在博物馆内部，农达（Nonda）想用钢护栏，顶部与钢制扶手相连，底部以"之"字形安置，好似在虚空里左右穿行。（李）

23

李：fussy 的含义：

fuss·y (fŭs′ē)
adj. **fuss·i·er, fuss·i·est**
1. Easily upset; given to bouts of ill temper: *a fussy baby.*
2. Paying great or excessive attention to personal tastes and appearance; fastidious: *He was always fussy about clothes.*
3. Calling for or requiring great attention to sometimes trivial details: *a fussy actuarial problem.*
4. Full of superfluous details: *"It can indeed be fussy, filling with ornament what should be empty space"* (H.D.F. Kitto).

http://www.thefreedictionary.com/fussy

上文节选：

David was always very much against the architects becoming artists. Any time we tried to do something **fancy**, he was like, 'If I wanted art, I'd get an artist to do it.' But we somehow managed to get this stair through. We could explain it to him in a very pragmatic way.

可以看出 David 不想要 fancy 的东西，他希望东西简单实用。所以这里的 fussy 可以理解成 fancy 的近义词。

24

原文：So we ended up with just the cantilever glass balustrades, which you won't even have noticed.

原译：所以最后我们就用了悬臂玻璃扶手，你甚至都不会注意到它。（莎）

改译 1：所以最后我们就用了悬臂玻璃扶手，你甚至都不会注意到它。（王）

改译 2：所以最后我们就用了悬臂玻璃扶手，估计你都没注意到。（陈）

建议译法：所以最后我们采用了外悬式玻璃围挡，估计你都没注意到。（李）

第十单元·建筑设计

http://wehouse-media.com/ 颠覆性的成人迪士尼乐园 -mona 古今艺术博物馆/

注意：玻璃不是扶手，是"围挡"。那根钢条是扶手。

25

> **原文**：We avoided the traditional patch-fitting type thing on the balustrade, with the stainless steel dots that you typically see holding up the glass. We invented our own little thing that clips over the glass at the top and then curved out to support it.
>
> **原文**：我们没有使用传统的玻璃门夹式扶手并配合常见的不锈钢扣来支撑玻璃，而是发明了一个小装置，上方夹住玻璃顶部，下方弯曲以支撑玻璃。（莎）
>
> **改译1**：我们没有使用传统的玻璃门夹式扶手，也就是那种通常用不锈钢扣支撑玻璃的扶手，而是发明了一个小装置，让它从顶部夹住玻璃，再从下方弯曲回来支撑玻璃。（王）

改译2：扶手上没有用传统的玻璃门夹，就是那种通常用来支撑玻璃的不锈钢门夹。我们转而发明了个小装置，先从顶部夹住玻璃，再从下方折回来支撑玻璃。（陈）

改译3：扶手上没有用传统的玻璃门夹，就是那种通常用来支撑玻璃的不锈钢门夹。我们设计了个小东西，先从顶部夹住玻璃，再从下方折回来支撑玻璃。（王）

李：就像口译那样，增加一点也无妨。

patch-fitting type thing 是指"玻璃夹"（此处不是用来夹"门"，只是夹玻璃）：

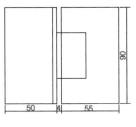

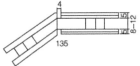

stainless steel dots：

https://www.pinterest.com/pin/415246028124235539/

建议译法：围挡上没有用传统的玻璃夹，就是大家经常在玻璃门上看到的不锈钢圆点，用来夹持玻璃。我们设计了个小东西，先从顶部夹持玻璃，再向外弯曲固定玻璃。（李）

26

原文：The idea was that the reflections give you this whole distorted space effect.

原译：当时的想法是镜面墙的反射有扭曲空间的效果。（莎）

改译：当时的想法是，镜面反射有整体空间扭曲的效果。（陈）

李：whole 修饰 effect。

建议译法：当时的想法是，通过镜面反射，产生空间扭曲的整体效果。（李）

27

原文：Nonda came up with the line that it would be good if it reflected the colour green—something like the colour of a tennis court. And David said, 'I know what's the colour of a tennis court…'

原译：农达当时说反射绿色比较好，类似网球场的颜色。然后大卫说："不用你告诉我网球场是什么颜色……"（莎）

改译1：农达当时说反射线条用绿色比较好，类似网球场的颜色。然后大卫说："不用你告诉我网球场是什么颜色……"（王）

陈：line 在这里就是"话"的意思。

> **8** [N-COUNT 可数名词] 旨在取得某种效果的话语；A particular type of line in a conversation is a remark that is intended to have a particular effect. [with supp]
>
> 'In time perhaps you'll marry again'. 'That's a great line, coming from you!'.
> "有一天也许你会再结婚的。" "这句话真中听啊，难得你能这么说！"
> //…chat-up lines like 'You've got beautiful eyes'.
> 诸如"你的眼睛很漂亮"之类的搭讪语
>
> （柯林斯词典）

> 改译 2：农达当时说了句，最好能反射绿色，类似网球场的绿色。然后大卫说："用不着你告诉我网球场是什么颜色……"（陈）
> 建议译法：农达当时说，最好能反射绿色，就像网球场的颜色。然后大卫说："你不说，我也知道网球场是什么颜色……"（李）

李：短句显得口语化。

28

> 原文：Hmm. The precast concrete wall that wraps around the main gallery space has a grid pattern on it, the same pattern that's in the ceiling.
> 原译：嗯……我最喜欢包裹主建筑的预制混凝土墙，墙是网格图案的，和天花板一样。
> 改译 1：嗯……我最喜欢包裹主建筑的预制混凝土墙，墙上有网格图案，和天花板上的图案一样。（王）
> 改译 2：嗯……我最喜欢包裹主建筑的预制混凝土墙，墙上的网格图案和天花板的网格图案一样。（陈）
> 建议译法：嗯……主展厅外的混凝土预制板墙。上面有网格状图案，与天花板的图案相同。（李）

29

> 原文：The important thing for us was that it not look like a whole lot of concrete panels—particularly at the corners.
> 原译：我们认为，关键是不能让墙看起来像一堆混凝土板，特别是转角处。（莎）
> 改译：我们认为，关键是不能让墙，尤其是墙的转角，看起来像一堆混凝土板。（陈）

李：预制板不可能是"堆放"的。

建议译法：我们认为，关键是不能让墙，尤其是墙角，看起来有太多预制板。（李）

30

原文：That's very hard to do, and it's important, because it's at the corners that the impression of a three-dimensional object is created.

原译：这一点很难做到，但又很重要，因为物体的立体感正是在拐角处形成的。（莎）

改译1：这实在难办，但又很重要，因为物体的立体感恰恰是在拐角处形成的。（陈）

改译2：这很难办到，但很重要，因为物体的立体感恰恰是在拐角处形成的。（李）

建议译法：这很难办到，但很重要，因为物体的立体感恰恰是在拐角形成的。（陈）

31

原文：We detailed a panel so it would wrap around the corner, creating a seamless, three-dimensional texture.

原译：我们精心打造了一块混凝土板，它可以裹住转角，形成一种连续的立体结构。（莎）

莎：这里的 texture 指的是物体的结构。

> **2** [N-VAR 可变名词] (尤指食品、土壤的)结构，构造；The **texture** of something, especially food or soil, is its structure, for example whether it is light with lots of holes, or very heavy and solid.
> This cheese has an open, crumbly texture with a strong flavour...
> 这种奶酪多孔松脆，风味浓郁。
> Earthworms consume large amounts of soil, and produce a rich humus, perfect in texture.
> 蚯蚓吃下大量土壤，排出肥力丰富、物理结构理想的腐殖质。

（柯林斯词典）

改译 1：我们精心打造了一块混凝土板，让它围住转角，营造一种连续的立体结构。（王）

改译 2：我们精心打造了混凝土板用来包住转角，营造连续的立体结构。（陈）

建议译法：我们精心打造了一块转角预制板，包住墙角，创造出无缝衔接的三维效果。（李）

李：从原文最后一张图片可知，拐角处是一块完整的预制板，所以是无缝衔接。如果是两面墙的预制板在此接合，必定在墙角的棱上，留下接缝。

32

原文：The grid gets cut off halfway through, at the top and the bottom, so it gives a sense that it just continues.

原译：在顶部和底部，网格截去一半，这样可以产生一种延续感。（莎）

改译 1：网格从中间被切断，分成顶部和底部，让人感觉它还会延续下去。（王）

改译 2：顶部以及底部的网格从中间切断，让人感觉网格会延续下去。（陈）

建议译法：顶部以及底部的网格从中间切断，让人感觉网格会延续下去。（李）

原文图片上看不到底部的网格，可以想象。

第十一单元　舞蹈艺术

Exercise 11　Gaga

翻译情景

本单元选自 UCLA（加州大学洛杉矶分校）表演艺术中心的网站，介绍了现代舞蹈家 Ohad Naharin 创造的 Gaga 舞蹈理念。该理念与现代舞蹈家鲁道夫·拉班（Rudolf von Laban）创造的拉班舞谱有异曲同工之妙。Gaga 与拉班舞谱一样，不是一种舞蹈，而是一种理念，强调舞者对身体的倾听和与意识的交流。假定网站请你翻译这篇文章，将来在网站发布。节选内容共 458 词。

训练重点

本单元侧重全局意识、文化沟通、查证能力和语言能力。全局意识就是我们不断提及的 6Ws；文化涉及的领域广泛，包括舞蹈艺术。Gaga 舞蹈理念涉及西方舞蹈文化，又与舞蹈家的个人语言风格息息相关，译者应思考如何以简单易懂的语言表达专业舞蹈内容，以达到文化沟通目的。同时，为了深刻理解舞蹈动作特征,译者需要进行全方位的查证。除了文字信息之外,通过图片、音视频甚至现场演示获得的身姿、空间等信息都可以帮助译者理解原文内容。叶子南(2001)先生说过,当译者已经对原文语法结构了然于心时,如果脑海中能够进一步形成图像,就算是真正理解了原文。因此,译者在查证时,不要仅仅限于文字材料,还要多思考如何借助图片、音视频等多模态信息帮助理解。

训练难点

本单元的训练难点:一是平衡原文内容专业性与译文读者理解能力之间的关系;二是充分利用各种材料、调动多重感官帮助理解原文内容。

训练方式

本单元练习分原文、翻译提示、参考译文、译者注四部分。请先尝试自己翻译原文,完成以后再参看翻译提示,再次调查研究,修改润色译文,形成第二稿。形成二稿之后,再看参考译文和译者注。翻译就像带着镣铐的舞者,只有在两种语言之间不断探索,才能展现出极致美感!

原文[1]

Gaga

Gaga[2] is the movement language developed by Ohad Naharin throughout his work as a choreographer and Artistic Director of Batsheva Dance Company[3]. Gaga has two tracks[4]: Gaga/dancers, which is the daily training of Batsheva Dance Company members, now taught also for other dancers in Israel and abroad; and Gaga/people, open to the public and available for anyone at any age, without the necessity of previous experience. Gaga is an experience of freedom and pleasure. The work improves instinctive movement and connects conscious and unconscious movement, and it allows for an experience of freedom and pleasure in a simple way, in a pleasant space, in comfortable clothes, accompanied by music, each person with himself and others[5].

"Gaga challenges multi-layer tasks[6].

"We are aware of the connection between effort[7] and pleasure, we are aware of the distance between our body parts, we are aware of the friction between flesh and bones, we sense the weight of our body parts, yet, our form is not shaped by gravity. ... we are aware of where we hold unnecessary tension, we let go only to bring life and efficient movement to where we let go…We are turning on the volume of listening to our body, we appreciate small gestures, we are measuring and playing with the texture of our flesh and skin, we might be silly, we can laugh at ourselves[8]. We connect to the sense of "plenty of time[9]", especially when we move fast. We learn to love our sweat, we discover our passion to move and connect it to effort. We discover both the animal we are and the power of our imagination. We are "body builders with soft spine". We learn to appreciate understatement and exaggeration. We become more delicate and we recognize the importance of the flow of energy and information through our body in all directions. We learn to apply our force in an efficient way and we learn to use "other" forces.

"We discover the advantage of soft flesh and sensitive hands, we learn to connect to groove even when there is no music. We are aware of people in the room and we realize that we are not in the center of it all. We become more aware of our form since we never look at ourselves in a mirror; there are no mirrors. We connect to the sense of the endlessness of possibilities.

"Yielding is constant while we are ready to snap...

"We explore multi-dimensional movement, we enjoy the burning sensation in our muscles, we are aware of our explosive power and sometimes we use it. We change our movement habits by finding new ones, we can be calm and alert at once. We become available …"

— Ohad Naharin

翻译提示

1. **全局意识**
   请大家针对原文和译文，分别回答 Who is talking to whom? About what? When, where and why? And how? 然后再开始翻译。

2. **全局意识**
   请先上网查找与 Gaga 舞蹈理念相关的中英文资料，并了解舞蹈家 Ohad Naharin 本人的成长经历与语言特点。

3. **语言能力：修饰关系**
   请准确理解 of Batsheva Dance Company 的修饰关系，仔细分析一下它是只修饰 director，还是同时修饰 choreographer？

4. **语言能力：词义**
   请用英英词典查 track 的含义，特别注意结合文内语境理解词义。

5. **全局意识／语言能力**
   译文的风格需要译者根据原文的内容和舞蹈创始人 Ohad 的语言风格做出判断。Gaga 舞蹈理念讲究对身体的倾听，语言比较平实，不建议过于华丽。

6. **查证能力：调动多模态**
   对于 multi-layer tasks 的理解，除了文字模态之外，译者还需要调动图片、视频、甚至亲自尝试跳跳 Gaga 才能感受出来这其中的含义。翻译并不是孤立的语言文字工作，是交际性、社会性的活动。

7. **查证能力**
   effort 的理解需要查一查，译者可以在以下三种译法中选择，是"动力""用力"还是"劲力"比较好？

8 **全局意识 / 语言能力**
要注意语言表达的通顺，同时也不要忘记 Gaga 的舞蹈理念和 Ohad 本人风格都不喜华丽。

9 **全局意识 / 查证能力**
plenty of time 要结合语境来理解。

参考译文

嘎嘎[1]是欧哈德（又译"欧汉"）·纳哈林[2]在其整个编舞生涯及担任巴切瓦舞团艺术总监期间，所创造的动作语言。[3]嘎嘎课程[4]分两种：一种是"舞者嘎嘎"，另一种是"大众嘎嘎"。前者用于以色列巴切瓦舞团专业舞者的日常训练（如今也用于教授国内外其他舞者），[5]后者人人可练，不论年纪，也无需基础。[6]练嘎嘎是自由与愉悦的体验，能升华本能动作，融合有意与无意的肢体运动。在怡人的空间里，舞者穿着舒适的衣服，伴随音乐，以简单的方式享受自由与快乐——自我陶醉，并与他人同乐。[7]

"嘎嘎挑战层层叠加的任务。[8]

"我们能体会劲力[9]与愉悦的关系，感受到身体器官间的距离，觉察肉骨之间的摩擦，感知器官的重量，但我们的型态并非由重力摆布……[10]我们知道身体什么部位绷得太紧，放松是为了让这个地方恢复活力，运动起来更加敏捷……[11]我们调大音量聆听自己的身体，体会肢体的小动作，度量和把玩皮肉的纹理；我们或许像傻瓜，但我们能自嘲。[12]我们想象着"时间还充裕"，尤其在快速移动时。我们学会喜爱自己的汗水，发现舞动的激情，并把激情融于劲力。我们发掘自己的野性与想象力。[13]我们是"脊柱柔软的健美家"。[14]我们学会欣赏低调与夸张。我们变得更加细腻，也明白能量和信息在体内四处流动的意义。[15]我们学会如何省力，也学会如何借力。[16]

"我们发现拥有柔软的躯体和敏感的双手带来的裨益；我们学会捕捉身体的节律，即使没有音乐伴奏。[17][18] 我们知道屋里还有其他人，也明知自己不是人群的中心。[19] 我们对自己的型态感觉更加敏锐，因为我们从来不照镜子；这里没有镜子。我们畅想无尽的可能。[20]

"随顺是常态，但我们能随时爆发（力量）……[21]

"我们探索多维动作，享受肌肉灼热的感觉；我们能感受体内的爆发力，有时还会小试一下。[22] 我们探索新的移动方式，改变移动习惯，我们能从容又警觉。[23] 我们的身体听任使唤……"[24]

——欧汉·纳哈林

译者注

1 全局意识：Gaga 舞蹈理念

周蕴仪：Gaga 不是一种舞蹈，不能称作嘎嘎舞。Gaga 是一种态度，也是一种练舞技巧，更是一个工具箱（toolbox），帮助人将自己的感觉、律动、想象力等，升华为（舞蹈）形态和动作。

关于嘎嘎的介绍：

Gaga is a movement language and pedagogy developed by Ohad Naharin during his time directing and teaching the Batsheva Dance Company, that has defined the company's training and continues to characterize Israeli contemporary dance. A practice that resists codification and emphasizes the practitioner's somatic experience, Gaga is importantly labeled **a movement language rather than a movement "technique"**. Many have noted that Gaga classes consist of a teacher leading dancers through an **improvisational** practice that is based around of a series of images described by the teacher. Naharin explains that such a practice is meant to provide a framework or a "safety net" for the dancers to use to "move beyond familiar limits". The descriptions that are used to guide the dancers through the **improvisation** are intended to help the dancer initiate and express movement in unique ways from parts of the body that tend to be ignored in other dance techniques. One example is the image of "Luna", which refers to the fleshy, semi-circular (like the moon, hence "luna") regions between fingers and toes. **As part of the ideological insistence on moving through sensing and imagining, mirrors are discouraged in a Gaga rehearsal space.**

Gaga pedagogy has two **tracks**, Gaga/Dancers and Gaga/People. Gaga/Dancers is geared towards **extensively trained dancers** and is the daily training of the dancers of Batsheva Dance Company dancers. Gaga/People was created to be accessible **to the general public** and requires no formal dance training to participate in. Gaga was created in Israel, but is now taught around the world.

https://en.wikipedia.org/wiki/Gaga_(dance_vocabulary)

2

于：Ohad Naharin 这个名字国内没有统一译法，我采用的是豆瓣上面的译法。之所以这么选择，是因为豆瓣是知名的文艺爱好者聚集地，对文艺作品资源整合较好。译文读者用"欧汉·纳哈林"进行搜索，可以在豆瓣上发现他更多的作品。所以，为方便读者，作此选择。

十舞 DecaDance

8.9 (51人评价)

类型：舞剧
导演：Ohad Naharin 欧汉·纳哈林
编舞：Ohad Naharin 欧汉·纳哈林
演出团体：Batsheva Dance Company 巴切瓦舞蹈团

https://www.douban.com/location/drama/26869047/

李：Ohad 翻译为"欧汉"，其实是错误的。因为 Ohad 里面没有字母 N，无论如何读不出"汉"。许多翻译爱好者不具备任何翻译知识，人名地名信口开河，贻害无穷。我去查了新华社的人名词典（可在网上搜索 新华社人名词典 下载），里面没有收录。于是上网搜索 Ohad Naharin pronunciation，找到一个网站（https://zh.forvo.com/），可以查找人名地名读音。那里居然有以色列人用希伯来语的发音！按照名从主人的原则，应该翻译为"欧哈德·纳哈林"。可是，为了照顾网友乱起的名字，不妨给出正确译名，括注惯用译名。

3

> 原文：Gaga is the movement language developed by Ohad Naharin throughout his work as a choreographer and Artistic Director of Batsheva Dance Company.
>
> 原译：嘎嘎舞是欧汉·纳哈林在任舞蹈编导和巴切瓦舞蹈团艺术总监时发展出来的动作语言。（于）

王：在舞蹈界，一般说"编舞"就可以了，但大部分情况下是作名词使用。大部分的剧目中，choreographer 还是常译为"编导"而不是"编舞"。

王：根据 Cambridge dictionary，develop 应该作以下理解：

B1 [T] to invent something or bring something into existence:

We have to develop a new policy/strategy to deal with the problem.

The company is spending $650 million on developing new products/technology.

"发展"和"创作"在中文意思上是有区别的。"发展"是在已有事物基础上继续延续、创新，指事物由小到大；"创作"是创造以前没有的事物，指事物从无到有。根据查证，Gaga movement 就是由欧汉·纳哈林开创的。

> 改译1：嘎嘎舞是欧汉·纳哈林在做编舞和巴切瓦舞团艺术总监时创作的动作语言。（王）
>
> 改译2：嘎嘎舞是欧汉·纳哈林在做编舞和巴切瓦舞团艺术总监时创造的动作语言。（李）

周：另外，这句话的结构是有歧义的，即 of Batsheva Dance Company 可能只修饰 director，也可能同时修饰 choreographer。正确的意思是只修饰 director（原译和改译都对，有同学理解错误）。在此补充一些背景资料，Ohad 在纽约时（到 Batsheva 之前）就编舞，是自由编舞，跟他在 Alvin Ailey 首席舞团当舞者的老婆 Mari Kajiwara 合作多年。我上 Gaga 课时问过 Ohad Naharin 本人，他从开始编舞的时候，就已经在用 Gaga 语言，但其练习方式不断演变，理念也不断改变。或许 Gaga 这个词较晚诞生，但 Gaga 理念是一早就有的。

周：找佐证比直接修改的时间长。见下：

CONVERSATIONS | MAY 26, 2012

Ohad Naharin in conversation with Zachary Whittenburg

May 31 through June 3, Hubbard Street Dance Chicago performs its Summer 2012 Series at the Harris Theater for Music and Dance, near Chicago's famous silver "bean" by sculptor Anish Kapoor. Alongside Malditos *by resident choreographer Alejandro Cerrudo, the company unveils its first production of* Quintett *by William Forsythe and revives* THREE TO MAX, *last Spring's world premiere "collage" by Ohad Naharin, director of Batsheva Dance Company. Ohad discusses his approach to dance in a wide-ranging interview with Zachary exclusive to Critical Correspondence.*

Interview Date: February 13, 2011 (By phone between Naharin in Tel Aviv, Israel and Zachary in Chicago, IL.)

Zachary: Glenn Edgerton, artistic director at Hubbard Street Dance Chicago, recalls you asking to teach class when you visited Nederlands Dans Theater, when he was there in the early '90s. Do you remember this and, if so, anything about those classes? Would you consider them the beginning of what became Gaga technique?

Ohad: Hm. [*Pauses*] I need to concentrate. There's a lot of stuff I deleted from my brain. [*Laughs*] I believe that one of the reasons I developed the Gaga movement language is because I needed to have keys to give dancers to work with. And a very important part of the development of it was working with other dancers. I don't recall exactly those classes because that was, really, more than 20 years ago. I do go back even before, if I think of beginnings or the source of the movement language—it is going way back. It's going as way back as I remember myself and it's definitely going back to when I first started teaching, and that was even before those days. It was already happening in New York [but] the movement language evolved a lot since then. It's not that it's so much rooted in what it was, but [that] it needed the process. I think the classes then were more, in terms of their form, more conventional and much more limited in terms of understanding. What today is very fundamental to Gaga is the ability to articulate the scope of sensations and the small details, the small gestures, the attention to details. I think in many ways I was moving in similar ways back then. I think I was dancing for the same reasons, yet [I had] a very different toolbox for the dancers than what [I use] today.

https://movementresearch.org/publications/critical-correspondence/ohad-naharin-in-conversation-with-zachary-whittenburg

周：还有，任何舞团，artistic director 都是最重要的职位。choreographer 可以随时变。多数舞团甚至没有 resident/house/company choreographer。即使有，也会经常会请外面不同的 choreographer 给舞团编舞，但 artistic director 是固定的职位。Ohad 六十几岁，去年刚卸任 artistic director 职位，只留任 house choreographer 一职（因为比较次要）。很多文章，基本都只提他是 artistic director，所以 choreographer 摆在 artistic director 之前，不是说这个职位更重要，而是他做这件事时间更长。下面的资料更说明 of Batsheva 不修饰 choreographer：

Ohad Naharin is *a choreographer, the Artistic Director of Batsheva Dance Company, and creator of the Gaga movement language.*

Naharin was born in 1952 in Mizra, Israel. His mother is a choreographer, dance teacher, and Feldenkrais instructor, and his father was an actor and psychologist. He joined Batsheva Dance Company in 1974 despite having little formal training. During his first year, guest choreographer Martha Graham invited him to join her own company in New York. Between 1975 and 1976,

Naharin studied at the School of American Ballet, The Juilliard School, and with Maggie Black and David Howard. He then joined Maurice Béjart's Ballet du XXe Siecle in Brussels for one season.

Naharin returned to New York in 1979 and made his choreographic debut at the Kazuko Hirabayshi studio the following year. From 1980 until 1990, Naharin presented works in New York and abroad, including pieces for Batsheva Dance Company, the Kibbutz Contemporary Dance Company, and Nederlands Dans Theater. At the same time, he worked with his first wife, Mari Kajiwara, and a group of dancers in New York. Naharin and Kajiwara continued to work together until she died from cancer in 2001.

In 1990, Naharin was appointed Artistic Director of Batsheva Dance Company, and in the same year, he established the company's junior division, Batsheva – the Young Ensemble. He has since created over thirty works for both companies.

https://batsheva.co.il/en/about?open=ohas_naharin

> **建议译法**：嘎嘎是欧汉·纳哈林在其整个编舞生涯及担任巴切瓦舞团艺术总监期间，所创造的动作语言。（周）

4 语言能力：词义

李：下文第二段对 two tracks 的介绍，可以启发对 track 一词的翻译。geared towards, the daily training, requires no formal dance training 以及 taught around the world 等，都在提示我们，这里讲的是"课程"性质的概念。而查到的相关中文文献里，也确实用到了"课程"一词：

- 中国舞者眼中的嘎嘎

2011 年，中国现代舞者谢欣前往纽约留学，也是在那里，她认识了嘎嘎。她介绍，嘎嘎课程分为两种，一种是针对专业舞者训练的"嘎嘎舞者"（Gaga dancer），另一种则是面向普通人的"嘎嘎爱好者"（dancer people）。

http://news.163.com/16/1019/11/C3O39C5I000187VE.html

通过查阅字典，译者还发现，track 一词本身确实也有"班组"的含义：

⑩ Countable American School [按学生能力编成的] 班组
- the top/middle/bottom track
  尖子班/中等班/差班
- to place students in tracks
  把学生分班

王：同意上述分析。再提供一些资料：

Gaga classes are predicated on a deep listening to the body and to physical sensations. The instructions are deployed to increase awareness of and further amplify sensation, and rather than turning from one prompt to another, information is layered, building into a multisensory, physically challenging experience. While many instructions are imbued with rich imagery, the research of Gaga is fundamentally physical, insisting on a specific process of embodiment. Inside this shared research, the improvisational nature of the exploration enables each participant's deeply personal connection with the language.

Gaga provides a framework for discovering and strengthening the body and adding flexibility, stamina, agility, and skills including coordination and efficiency while stimulating the senses and imagination. The classes offer a workout that investigates form, speed, and effort while traversing additional spectrums such as those between soft and thick textures, delicacy and explosive power, and understatement and exaggeration. Participants awaken numb areas, increase their awareness of habits, and improve their efficiency of movement inside multilayered tasks, and they are encouraged to connect to pleasure inside moments of effort. The language of Gaga is in a continual process of evolution, and <u>the classes vary and develop accordingly</u>.

<u>Gaga has two tracks</u>:
- Gaga/dancers, which is the daily training of Batsheva Dance Company, now taught also for other dancers in Israel and abroad
- Gaga/people, open to the public and available for anyone at any age, without the necessity of previous dance experience

http://gagapeople.com/english/about-gaga/

这是在网上找到的资料，与我们的作业内容基本一致。通过划线部分，可知 tracks 就是指代上文的 classes。

5

> **原文**：Gaga has two tracks: Gaga/dancers, which is the daily training of Batsheva Dance Company members, now taught also for other dancers in Israel and abroad; ...
>
> **原译**：嘎嘎舞课程分为两种：一是嘎嘎/舞者，这是巴切瓦舞蹈团成员每日接受的训练，如今在以色列国内国外的其他舞者中也有授课；……（于）
>
> **改译1**：嘎嘎舞课程分为两种：一种是舞者的嘎嘎，即巴切瓦舞蹈团成员的日常训练，如今广授于以色列国内外舞者；……（王）
>
> **改译2**：嘎嘎舞课程 分为两种：一种是舞者的嘎嘎，即巴切瓦舞团成员的日常训练（如今以色列国内外其他舞者也在学习）；……（李）
>
> **改译3**：嘎嘎课程分两种：一种是"舞者嘎嘎"，是巴切瓦舞团成员的日常训练方式，如今也教以色列国内外其他舞者；……（周）
>
> **改译4**：嘎嘎课程分两种：一种是"舞者嘎嘎"，是巴切瓦舞团成员的日常训练方式，如今也教授给以色列国内外的其他舞者。……（周）

李：建议打破原文结构，改为"一种是，另一种是"。前者，后者，这样对比更强烈一些。这不是什么重要的政治法律文件，依着灵活性更大。

> **建议译法**：嘎嘎课程 分两种：一种是"舞者嘎嘎"，另一种是"大众嘎嘎"。前者用于以色列巴切瓦舞团专业舞者的日常训练（如今也用于教授国内外其他舞者），后者人人可练，不论年纪，也无需基础。

李：加括号，也是为了为了便于与后文形成对比。

6

> **原文**：…and Gaga/people, open to the public and available for anyone at any age, without the necessity of previous experience.
> **原译**：二是嘎嘎/爱好者，该课程则面向大众，任何年龄段的任何人都能学习，无需具备一定的基础。（于）
> **改译**：另一种是大众的嘎嘎，面向大众，老少皆宜，无需舞蹈基础。（王）
> **建议译法**：另一种是"大众嘎嘎"，人人可练，不论年纪，也无需基础。（周）

7

> **原文**：The work improves instinctive movement and connects conscious and unconscious movement, and it allows for an experience of freedom and pleasure in a simple way, in a pleasant space, in comfortable clothes, accompanied by music, each person with himself and others.
> **原译**：它改善本能动作，并连接有意识与无意识的动作。嘎嘎舞让每个人可以在舒适的空间里、身着舒服的衣物、伴随着音乐、独自一人或与他人一起简单轻松地体验自由与愉悦。（于）

于：前后两个 movement，中文中如果重复用词还重复句式的话（即"改善……动作，连接……动作"这样的译文），会比较拗口而且显得词穷，所以这边对句子进行了一些新的安排，可能带来的问题就是句子略长。

> **改译1**：它改善本能动作，连接有意识与无意识动作，让人简单地体会自由与快乐：在怡人的空间，身着舒适外衣，伴着音乐，与他人共舞。（王）

周：原文没说得那么确切，不宜过度解读。本能动作，指我们身体内不被驯服或者不可预测的部分，是最原始的自己。Through Gaga, one works to break down physical barriers in order to reach a greater comprehension and control of instinctive movements.

https://nac-cna.ca/en/event/15769

Gaga elevates instinctive motion and links conscious and subconscious movement."

https://www.japantimes.co.jp/culture/2010/04/09/events/events-outside-tokyo/go-gaga-over-israeli-troupe-batsheva/#.WriIZ-huZPY

each person with himself and others 是一种 Gaga 的锻炼方式。老师要我们聆听自己，也要观察辨认（connection），用身体语言对话。

傅天伊：这里最后的部分能否调换一下语序，译为"让每一个人都能在怡人的空间里，穿着舒适的衣服，伴随音乐，与自己或与他人共同享受简单的自由与快乐"？还是需要考虑 each person with himself and others 在原文中的位置呢？

> 改译 2：练嘎嘎是自由与愉悦的体验，能升华本能动作，使有意识与无意识的肢体活动对话交融，让每一个人都能在怡人的空间里，穿着舒适的衣服，伴随音乐，与自己或与他人共同享受简单的自由与快乐。（傅天伊）

周：我翻译时，会尽可能保留原文的节奏，尤其艺术类的文章。你们如果多翻译艺术类文章，就会发现这种结构比比皆是。如果都翻成你们所谓的"符合中文表达方式"，每篇文章都千篇一律了。后面这部分是作者可以抽出来处理的，英文绝对可以写成：

The work improves instinctive movement and connects conscious and unconscious movement. This allows each person to experience the sense of freedom and pleasure with himself and with others in a simple way, in a pleasant space, in comfortable clothes, accompanied by music.

作者没有这么做，就是因为作者要强调自己与自己，以及自己与其他舞者之间的关系。练 Gaga 时，需要看着其他舞者，大家一边跳，一边用眼睛和身体交流，所以 Gaga 舞者自己跟其他舞者在空间中的"对话"极为重要。你们要把后置强调的自己的体验以及自己跟他人的共同体验翻得像白开水，塞在句子中间，说是符合中文表达方式，实际是摒弃 Gaga 的核心思想。况且，这整句英语是比较 poetic 的风格，改译 2 的译文结构丢掉了其中趣致。文字可以改进，但必须符合 Gaga 风格。

> **改译 3**：练嘎嘎是一种自由与愉悦的体验，能升华本能动作，使有意识与无意识的肢体活动对话交融，在怡人的空间里，穿着舒适的衣服，伴随音乐，享受简单的自由与快乐——每一个人，跟自己、跟他人享受。（周）

李：为了去掉最后一个"享受"，试修改如下：

> **建议译法**：练嘎嘎是自由与愉悦的体验，能升华本能动作，融合有意与无意的肢体运动。在怡人的空间里，舞者穿着舒适的衣服，伴随音乐，以简单的方式享受自由与快乐——自我陶醉，并与他人同乐。（李）

李：本来改成"或自我陶醉，或与他人同乐"，但看了周老师的讲解，知道这两件事是同时发生的，原文用了 and。

8　全局意识

Gaga 舞蹈知识

如何理解 multi-layer tasks?

周：上 Gaga 课时，老师会不断给任务，层层叠加，一会儿说 move through honey，然后说 pull the bones out of the flesh，过一会儿又说 smile。这些都是 effort。

　　Never stop: The class is one session, no pauses or exercises, but a continuity of instructions one on top of the other. Each instruction does not cancel the previous one but is added to it, layer upon layer. Therefore, it is important not to stop in the middle of the session. If you get tired or want to work at another pace, you can always lower the volume, work 30% or 20%, float, or rest, but without losing sensations that were already awakened. Do not return to the state your body was in before we started.

http://www.naim.org.il/en/gaga/

In Gaga you analyse how you move in relation to the different movement tasks and suggestions that are given.

…

If you for example notice that your movements are usually symmetric, you will be encouraged to try and explore something else, for example an asymmetric position. When you are aware of your habits and default movement patterns, it opens up the possibility of expanding your range of movements. In this way, you will learn to move with more richness. Eventually, if you do pay attention to this, you will be able to incorporate more layers into your movements. In this way, you will have more nuance and complexity in your movement patterns.

…

In a Gaga class you will often hear the phrase *finding pleasure in movement* mentioned. You will also hear words that are associated with it, like: *smile to each other* and *be silly*. This is all connected to a positive way of thinking. Ohad Naharin explains it like this: "Being attentive to pleasure keeps one aware of taking care of oneself. The pleasure connects the flow of energy and information to your body, it heals you by giving you joy instead of punishment in movement". So the key element here is to feel joy and to connect to pleasure while doing all of the multiple tasks in Gaga.

https://brage.bibsys.no/xmlui/bitstream/handle/11250/2491198/hogstad_masteroppgave_digitalversjon.pdf?sequence=1&isAllowed=y

周：修改是一回事，最花时间的地方是要上网找佐证来证明我的修改。

The notion of finding pleasure while doing something physically challenging is spelled out in phrases such as don't be shy of the effort and enjoy the burring sensation. If you can manage the physical effort by connecting it to the physiological aspect of finding pleasure and enjoying yourself, you can endure more in a class.

> https://brage.bibsys.no/xmlui/bitstream/handle/11250/2491198/hogstad_masteroppgave_digitalversjon.pdf?sequence=1&isAllowed=y

建议译法：嘎嘎挑战层层叠加的任务。（周）

李：周老师有亲身体验，所以理解表达都不费太大力气。费力的是找证据，说明自己的本能正确。这正是专业知识的作用。我们之所以查不胜查，查了还不知道对错，就是因为缺乏某个领域的常识。专业知识从哪里来？一是译者自带的专业背景，二是调查研究。调查研究多了，自然积累了知识。这次翻译嘎嘎查清了100个问题，下次可能只需要查50个。

9

原文：We are aware of the connection between effort and pleasure
原译：我们清楚努力和快乐的关系（于）
改译1：我们知道用力和快乐之间的关系（李）
改译2：我们体会动力与愉悦的关系（周）

周：Effort is a word introduced by Rudolph Laban. According to him, it is a mental impulse from which movement originates. There are four motion factors that constitute it: SPACE (direct or indirect), WEIGHT (strong or light), TIME (sudden or sustained) and FLOW (bound and free). The dynamic of movement is the result of the combination of these factors and its effort qualities.

> https://www.contemporary-dance.org/dance-terms.html

(Gaga methods conceives «effort» to be «different from pain», Summer Intensive 2016), or as a phenomenon of "electrification": the famous Sade's Histoire de Juliette describes how an electric fire flows in the body and sensualises it, promising the lover of pleasure that a «devouring and delicious fire will slip into your nerves, it will light up this electric fluid in which the life principle lives».

> https://danzaericerca.unibo.it/article/download/6605/6434

with the ideal image of the plié. It comes to a contradictory physical effort when there are two opposing directions of movement that cause both holding of energy and bodily pressure. Instead of coordinating direction with physical energy, the dancers are led by two contradictory directions that cause mental effort, which is, in turn, physically applied. In such cases, sensory stimuli are not taken into account as an informative source and therefore the movement cannot be comprehended. As a result, the work of dancing becomes a work of trying to shape and train the body. While working in this pattern, the body is understood as an object of the mind. It becomes a material, *Körper* rather than *Leib*—the dancer has to shape it rather than live it.

Treating the body as merely subject matter gives rise to unreflective effort in doing. It is the exertion needed to overcome the gap between

— Einav Katan-Schmid, *Embodied Philosophy in Dance: Gaga and Ohad Naharin's Movement Research*

其中有 physical effort 和 mental effort，所以"用力"不合适。

Moving though honey and pulling the bones out of the flesh are images that work in the opposite way of the one described in part 2. Here one really uses a lot of bound force and one moves directly and 'push the space'. Pulling the bones out of the flesh has a more inward-looking feeling since it is using the anatomy of the body to describe something (not anatomically correct, but still connected to this.) Moving though honey makes you think of honey and what qualities honey has: sticky, and not easy to move through. Working with these two images makes you use a lot of effort, when you do this you also move in a spatially direct way. Working with these images you do not make sudden changes in speed, the time consumption is sustained.

…

Shake and *quake* are images that are used a lot in Gaga classes. *Shake* is movement quality that has a stir in it, this movement can start in one body part, but it affects the whole body. In Gaga *shake* is described as something that you do on purpose, while *quake* is something that happens to you, like an earthquake. *Spatial focus in *shake* is direct. In q*uake* it is indirect.

https://brage.bibsys.no/xmlui/bitstream/handle/11250/2491198/hogstad_

masteroppgave_digitalversjon.pdf?sequence=1&isAllowed=y

王：我对"动力"的译法还是存疑。根据周老师的查证，effort 是一种 mental impulse，源于 physical effort。这是因为，身体需要控制，所以就要求舞者有 mental effort，强调舞者的意志力和控制力。下图的动作需要极大的控制力和意念，没有控制就没有美。

我查了一下"动力"的中文意思。"动力"即一切力量的来源，主要分为机械类和管理类。当然，舞蹈里面确实也有"动力"这种说法，但是更多在说"主力腿"和"动力腿"，而在做舞蹈动作时，更多的控制（effort）是放在了主力腿上（左图演员的左腿）。这是要求舞蹈演员在做动作时（physical effort）有控制力和意念（mental effort）。因此，我建议此处还是用"用力"比较好。

周："用力"不好。effort 包括身体的力量和心中的意志力。练一次 Gaga 大约 75 分钟（Ohad 的舞团极少上芭蕾的把杆课），75 分钟之内身体的活动不得停止。那种 effort 不限于一般用力。

王：关于 effort 的译法，我觉得"用力"确实不好，mental effort 的感觉体现得不明显。但是"动力"也没有太体现出这种 mental impulse。思考了很久没有特别好的译法出现。今天看到向月怡同学的查证，给了我新的思路。

向月怡：这里涉及拉邦动作分析论，该理论认为动作分析基于四大因素：身体（body）、劲力（effort）、空间（space）和身形（shape）。

Effort, or what Laban sometimes described as dynamics, is a system for understanding the more subtle characteristics about movement with respect to inner intention. The difference between punching someone in anger and reaching for a glass is slight in terms of body organization – both rely on extension of the arm. The attention to the strength of the movement, the control of the movement and the timing of the movement are very different.

Effort has four subcategories (effort factors), each of which has two opposite polarities (effort elements).

Effort Factor	Effort element (*Fighting* polarity)	Effort element (*Indulging* polarity)
Space	Direct	Indirect (flexible)
Weight	Strong	Light
Time	Sudden (quick)	Sustained
Flow	Bound	Free

Laban named the combination of the first three categories (Space, Weight, and Time) the Effort Actions, or Action Drive. The eight combinations are descriptively named Float, Punch (Thrust), Glide, Slash, Dab, Wring, Flick, and Press. The Action Efforts have been used extensively in some acting schools, including ALRA, Manchester School of Theatre, LIPA and London College of Music to train in the ability to change quickly between physical manifestations of emotion.

Flow, on the other hand, is responsible for the continuousness or ongoingness of motions. Without any Flow Effort, movement must be contained in a single initiation and action, which is why there are specific names for the Flowless Action configurations of Effort. In general it is very difficult to remove Flow from much movement, and so a full analysis of Effort will typically need to go beyond the Effort Actions.

https://en.wikipedia.org/wiki/Laban_movement_analysis#Effort

在笔者的三节单元课中，希望用"拉邦动作分析元素"来进行课程的进阶与难度的提升。德国知名舞蹈理论家、教育家、"拉邦动作分析与拉邦舞谱"的发明者鲁道夫·拉邦，认为动作分析:"是一种系统化的动作观，是透过实际参与观察，企图了解人类动作意义与结构之原理原则，其根植于四大类动作因素，包括身体(Body)、劲力(Effort)、空间(Space)和身形(Shape)。"②

http://www.doc88.com/p-5761520626129.html

为了观察多样化特性的广场舞，我们搜集了三种不同来源的广场舞舞蹈，分别为网路版、官方版以及民间版，并邀请两位拉邦动作分析专家，对153段舞蹈动作片段进行拉邦动作分析，将舞蹈动作依照空间因子、重力因子、时间因子三个维度进行分析，每个维度中有两个极端劲力元素（Effort element），当动作表现明确时，能同时满足三个维度的劲力元素，则属于行动驱使（Action Drive）。个别舞蹈动作分析后，比较三种不同来源的广场舞舞蹈动作，其中发现重力程度维度下官方版所属强烈劲力的动作多，网路版与民间版的轻柔劲力动作较多，强烈劲力动作容易让身体感受到压力，容易产生不安、焦躁的情绪。

kreader.cnki.net：基于拉邦动作分析之广场舞设计指南与体感系统开发

台湾台业艺术大学舞蹈研究生的动作分析研究课的课程简介中将"energy"翻译成"劲力"而将"effort"翻译成"动作质地"。

一、課程目標

本課程以拉邦動作分析的基本元素，引導學員了解人的身體極限。如何經由肢體與空間(space)、時間(time)、劲力(energy)的關係，尋求出動作質地的各種可能性，以及其如何影響著人的情感表達及與外界、人與人之間的溝通(relationship)。課程中將經由對動作分析基本元素之了解，訓練學員的觀察能力，因此可以熟練的活用在教學、評論、創作、表演以及每日生活動作之改善。

本課程結合表演創作以及拉邦動作分析(Laban Movement Analysis/LMA)學理，針對人類行為(Body)、動作質地(Effort)、人體朔型(Shape)、空間和諧學(Space Harmony)等LMA四大分析理論進行對人類行為之探討。本課程之創意規劃在其創作與理論之相輔相成，還有科學以藝術之相模合。舞蹈領域者可以加強其表演、創作以及教學之能力；戲劇工作者得以施展於其角色之成功模擬；學員可運用動作質地之探討以及其空間使用，重新研究動畫中模擬真人的最佳動作設計。本課程意圖跨越本校藝術人之局限，結合醫學科學之參與與增長。本課程於過去吸引了台北大學運動科學研究所學生，加上北藝大戲劇系、新媒體與音樂系研究生，經由這些非舞蹈人之參與，更增廣了本課程之多面向。

https://aaa.tnua.edu.tw/class/page.aspx?id=2437

中国台湾地区也有的论文中将effort翻译成"动作质地"（截图略）；慕课相关课程简介也将energy翻译成"劲力"。

但是从上面维基百科介绍上可知，拉班对effort的定义更接近一种动力（dynamics），因此翻译成"劲力"更贴切。相对地，下文的energy似乎没有承载与"劲力"相关的含义，因此按字面翻译成"能量"。

王：综上讨论，"劲力"是比较合适的说法，可以体现出physical and mental effort。

建议译法:我们能体会劲力与愉悦的关系。(向)

10

原文:We are aware of the connection between effort and pleasure, we are aware of the distance between our body parts, we are aware of the friction between flesh and bones, we sense the weight of our body parts, yet, our form is not shaped by gravity…

原译:我们清楚吃力和享乐之间的关系、清楚身体各部位之间的距离、清楚肉与骨的摩擦、我们感知着身体各部的重量,但,我们的体态并不由重力塑造。(于)

改译1:我们清楚努力和快乐的关系、清楚身体各部位的距离、清楚肉骨间的摩擦、我们感受着身体各部位的重量,但我们的体态并非由重力塑造(王)

改译2:我们知道用力和快乐之间的关系、身体各部位的距离、肉骨间的摩擦,我们感受到了身体各部位的重量,但我们的形态不受重力摆布。(李)

改译3:我们体会动力与愉悦的关系,我们能感受身体器官间的距离,我们觉察肉骨的摩擦,我们能感知器官的重量,但我们的身体形态不再受地心引力左右。(周)

改译4:我们体会劲力与愉悦的关系,我们能感受身体器官间的距离,我们觉察肉骨的摩擦,我们能感知器官的重量,但我们的形态并非由重力塑造。(王)

如何理解 form,见如下讨论:

周:Form: this is a word that is most commonly used to refer to movement (dance) from an abstract point of view. The 'form' of movement, also called the 'shape', would include its occupation of space, timings, body uses and such kind of elements that do not express other contents than movement itself. In this sense, the form could be understood as opposed to the content, the qualities, dynamics or any expressive and communicative feature that makes up movement.

https://www.contemporary-dance.org/dance-terms.html

In Gaga, we have a term that says "collapse into movement." It actually means that we're not shaped by gravity; we're shaped by a force that opposes gravity. The importance of collapse is to help you to measure the force that you need to oppose and play with gravity.

www.theglobeandmail.com/arts/theatre-and-performance/choreographer-ohad-naharin-on-developing-the-dance-language-gaga/article33531396/

"Gaga is about many things. It's about listening to the scope of sensation, to the weight of our body parts, to the texture, the distance between our limbs, to the floor's energy," Naharin tells me as he speaks on the phone from his home in Tel Aviv. "It's about the collapse, but the collapse that doesn't allow gravity to shape it. It allows gravity to work in horizontal forces and horizontal movement, so it's also about the sublimation of forces and the use of forces that are not only ours."

https://www.limelightmagazine.com.au/features/batshevas-dance-will-literally-drive-you-gaga/

王：我同意周老师的查证资料，但是查证资料里面有一句关键的话是：Form: this is a word that is most commonly used to refer to movement (dance) from an abstract point of view. The 'form' of movement, also called the 'shape', would include its occupation of space, timings, body uses and such kind of elements that do not express other contents than movement itself.

我的理解是，这个 form 不仅仅指身体（静态）的形态，即体型，而且是舞者在做动作时的形态，是动态的形态。

处理成"舞姿"可以，但是斟酌再三，为了尊重 Ohad 的语言风格，还是处理为"形态"。但是，这个形态是抽象的动态形态，而不是体型或身形。

李：两位都是芭蕾舞者，我本来没有发言权。但看到苏阳的资料，觉得可以用"型态"一词。"型"的搭配有"型塑""型材"，"型"的本义是用泥土做的模子。舞姿或身体的造型，也是刻意做出来的，因此，我觉得可以用"型态"。

> **建议译法**：我们能体会劲力与愉悦的关系，感受到身体器官间的距离，觉察肉骨之间的摩擦，感知器官的重量，但我们的型态并非由重力摆布。……（李）

李：语言还是简练一些。之前"我们"太多了。

11

> **原文**：... we are aware of where we hold unnecessary tension, we let go only to bring life and efficient movement to where we let go ...
> **原译**：我们清楚哪里的紧张是多余的，我们放松，是给放松之处带去生命、让动作更为高效。（于）
> **改译1**：我们清楚哪里的紧张是多余的，我们放松紧张的身体，是为了让它重获生机、动作更为高效。（王）
> **改译2**：我们知道哪里的紧张是多余的，我们放松紧张的地方，是为了让这个地方重获生命、动作更为高效。（李）

王：这里修改后我觉得有点不符合逻辑和搭配。"让这个地方重获生命"似乎说不通。我比较倾向维持原译，我理解是让紧张的身体部位重获生机。

周：efficiency of movement：

> the form of perception thresholds, afterimages, and such. Like the feelings produced by muscular tension and relaxation, these are basic and ineluctable, but they tell us nothing about the real qualities of movements. To judge such qualities we rely

on the recognized efficiency of movement, the animal ease of which Spencer spoke. But the easiest movement is not, after all, the most graceful. We appreciate movement as expressive of the mover's will. The most beautiful movement is accordingly not the most efficient but that which is eloquent of efficiency: movement clearly articulated by the mover to make its structure evident, to give it a perceptible purposiveness independent of any extraneous purpose it might have. Such movement answers to, and is a special form of, the articulate effectiveness

books.google.com: The Aesthetics of Movement

4. MOVEMENT EFFICIENCY

The Eastern definition of optimal performance contains elements such as an implicit ability to produce highly refined movements, intuitively, and seemingly automatically. Sellers-Young explains that, in the learning process of Nihonbuyo, accustoming oneself to this specific mode of sensing requires effort and concentration, but by continuing to attend to those sensations through movement, the dancer attains an **implicit sense of kinetic economy**. After this sense is achieved, the dancer reaches the state of 'no mind,' where movements arise without intention. Sellers-Young identifies an initial stage of effortful (cognitive) concentration, an intermediate stage of finding and embodying **optimal movement economy**, and a final stage of **complete automation**. In other words, the training philosophy of 'no mind' asserts that optimal performance is achieved through a process of cognition, embodiment, and automation. Here, the idea of optimal performance points to an implicit somatic awareness, refined movement efficiency, and autonomous movement generation.

Christopher Cordner, a scholar in philosophy, discusses the idea of 'graceful' movement, as a concept inseparable from this type of optimal movement performance. He mentions that the perception of grace involves the observer's recognition of the mover "being at home in the world." He explains that, **when the mover has an implicit and deeply internalised sense of the relations**

within the body and how it is situated in its space, this understanding manifests as an effortlessness or ease in movement.

http://moco17.movementcomputing.org/wp-content/uploads/2017/12/ds1-sakuta.pdf

Body awareness/finesse. If you've ever watched a professional dancer – from break dancer to ballerina – you will soon realize just how much absolute control they have over every single part of their body, from the tips of their toes to the very tops of their heads. As the saying goes, it's all in the details, and dancers don't just move an arm – they move a shoulder, an elbow, a wrist, a finger. That much control contributes greatly to the <u>efficiency of movement</u> in general.

https://www.humantwopointzero.com/the-benefits-of-dance-on-sports-performance-and-on-life-in-general-2/

> 改译3：我们知道身体什么部分太紧绷，放开是为了唤醒它，使它动时更敏捷矫健。（周）

李："矫健"的意思是强壮有力，经常用来形容步伐。"放开部位"搭配不当。

> 建议译法：我们知道身体什么部位绷得太紧，放松是为了让这个地方恢复活力，运动起来更加敏捷……（李）

12

> 原文：We are turning on the volume of listening to our body, we appreciate small gestures, we are measuring and playing with the texture of our flesh and skin, we might be silly, we can laugh at ourselves.
> 原译：我们不断提高音量、去聆听我们的身体，我们在意小幅动作，我们衡量又玩味着皮与肉的质感，我们可能犯蠢，我们可以自嘲。（于）

王：看到 appreciate 的第一反应可能是欣赏，但是这里是 to be fully conscious of / be aware of 的意思。

verb (used with object), **appreciated, appreciating.**

1. to be grateful or thankful for:

   They appreciated his thoughtfulness.

2. to value or regard highly; place a high estimate on:

   to appreciate good wine.

3. to be fully conscious of; be aware of; detect:

   to appreciate the dangers of a situation.

4. to raise in value.

周：Gesture: in the Laban language (system for analyzing and recording movement), the word gesture is used to talk about movements that do not involve carrying the weight of the whole body throughout space. A gesture would be <u>different to a transfer of weight </u>(for example, raising an arm would be a<u> gesture</u> and stepping forward would be a <u>transfer of weight</u>). Some people also use this word to talk about movements of the body or limbs that express or emphasize ideas, feelings or attitudes, in opposition to what would be a movement, considered only in an abstract way.

https://www.contemporary-dance.org/dance-terms.html

周：In a Gaga class you will often hear the phrase finding pleasure in movement mentioned. You will also hear words that are associated with it, like: smile to each other and be silly.

https://brage.bibsys.no/xmlui/bitstream/handle/11250/2491198/hogstad_masteroppgave_digitalversjon.pdf?sequence=1&isAllowed=y

In Gaga you can look strange and you can, and should, laugh. Maintaining distance to yourself is necessary. If dancers were serious about an imaginary ball traveling through their body or going into the role of a boiling pot of spaghetti and wanted to look good while doing so, the exercise would be fruitless.

https://muditalab.com/ohad-naharins-gaga-dance-2f835a897bf3

> 改译1：身体之声，用心聆听，我们揣摩细微动作，丈量肌肤之理，舞动身体之兴，我们可能愚蠢，我们可以自嘲。（王）

周：就这一句话，就能发现文体飘忽不定。可暂时处理如下：我们调大声量聆听自己的身体，我们体会肢体的小律动，我们度量并把玩着肌肤的纹理（比"肌理"节奏好），或许我们傻，但我们能自嘲。

下一段的 groove 就是最佳例子。groove 的时候必须感觉到身体上的每一个毛孔、每一根毛发。

注意文体，Gaga 是很接地气的现代舞动作语汇，不要翻译成"孔雀开屏"。

王：确实我文体把握得不够好，对 Gaga 的精髓还不了解。

> **改译 2**：我们调大声量聆听自己的身体，我们体会肢体的小律动，我们度量并把玩着肌肤的纹理，或许我们傻，但我们能自嘲。（周）
> **改译 3**：我们调大音量聆听自己的身体，我们体会肢体微小的律动，我们度量并把玩着肌肤的纹理，或许我们傻，但我们能自嘲。（李）
> **改译 4**：我们调大音量聆听自己的身体，我们体会肢体的小动作，我们度量并把玩着皮肉的纹理；我们或许像傻瓜，但我们能自嘲。（周）
> **建议译法**：我们调大音量聆听自己的身体，体会肢体的小动作，度量和把玩皮肉的纹理；我们或许像傻瓜，但我们能自嘲。（李）

李：还是感觉"我们"太多。

13

> **原文**：We connect to the sense of "plenty of time", especially when we move fast. We learn to love our sweat. We discover our passion to move and connect it to effort. We discover both the animal we are and the power of our imagination.
> **原译**：我们感受着"充分的时间"，特别是当我们的动作加速时。我们学着爱自己的汗水，我们发掘运动的热情，继而知道如何用力。我们发掘出自身动物性的同时，也发现了自己想象的力量。（于）

王：如果翻译成"充分的时间"语言并没有脱壳，中国读者恐怕也不知道啥意思。我的理解是 plenty of time 就是 enough time。

> 改译 1：我们感受到"时间在静止"，特别是在快速移动时。我们学着爱自己的汗水，我们发现舞动的激情，将它与努力相连。我们发掘自己的野性与想象力。（王）

周：Sense:

It is largely based on working with mental images that go directly to the central headquarters of the body—the nervous system. When stimulated by the images, the body can break out of motor patterns, leave the comfort zone and let go of repeatability. Effective mental images have to act on the nervous system just as bait does to a fish—attract attention, arouse appetite and provoke action. It is best to use visions that in some way are overly sharp, precise and dynamic—so that the body can experience the image. In Gaga there are images such as a snake in the spine, a ball traveling all over the body, bones moving under the skin or a body boiling like spaghetti sauce.

https://muditalab.com/ohad-naharins-gaga-dance-2f835a897bf3

所以当舞者快速移动时，要 connect to 的 sense 是 plenty of time。

plenty of time 跟 yield 或 letting go 相关。

Gaga technique was explained by Ya'ara Moses as 'as basket of tools', a language which can be applied to any form, from Cunningham to Ballet. She expressed that she sees these tools as 'keys' with which we can seek to '**unlock the treasures already inside us**'. We are using these tools to tap in **and access 'what god gave us**' rather than imposing an external standard and form onto ourselves without any consideration of what is already within. By listening to what is inherent within our physicality and emotions and allowing ourselves to become available to respond to this or other ideas such as 'stuff travelling through' with a sense of playing with plenty of time. As dance artists this can provide for us a wonderful world to explore as we move, both within improvisation and within the set form of sequences.

http://www.idocde.net/idocs/573

4.5. The Effect of Gaga

"It's hard for me to let go: I need to let go from the beginning, it allows me to be more open" (A, personal communication, March 16, 2015). A explains that for her, there is a big overlap between Gaga and life. She says that there is this active core work that she can do herself that relates to being more open and more listening. A explains that she will use her Gaga toolbox when she is stressed – if, for example, she is late for something, **she will say to herself "plenty of time"** or **think about her flesh, asking herself "am I grabbing, can I get there faster if I let go?"** She explains that sometimes she uses language, sometimes she just have to listen or feel it: "I listen to my body when I'm moving, even when I'm walking on the street is much different now than it used to be before. I think I was very turned off before". A mentions that she really struggles to do this when she is working on her computer: "It's a challenging to break that habit of cutting myself from the body because. I'm just sitting here typing I'm not paying attention. I'm not consciously directing the focus to my body." The problem that A is talking about here, is something that I will look further into in chapter 6 with the use of body image and body schema (Gallagher, 2005).

https://brage.bibsys.no/xmlui/bitstream/handle/11250/2491198/hogstad_masteroppgave_digitalversjon.pdf?sequence=1&isAllowed=y

---

改译2：我们想象着"时间还充裕",尤其在快速移动时。我们学会喜爱自己的汗水,我们发现自己热爱舞动并将它融于动力之中。我们发掘自己的野性与想象力。(周)

建议译法：我们想象着"时间还充裕",尤其在快速移动时。我们学会喜爱自己的汗水,发现舞动的激情,并把激情融于劲力。我们发掘自己的野性与想象力。(李)

14

> **原文**：We are "body builders with soft spine".
> **原译**：我们是"有着柔软脊柱的塑型者"。（于）
> **改译**：我们是"软脊柱健美家"。（王）
> **建议译法**：我们是"脊柱柔软的健美家"。（李）

李：注意节奏。

15

> **原文**：We learn to appreciate understatement and exaggeration. We become more delicate and we recognize the importance of the flow of energy and information through our body in all directions.
> **原译**：我们学着欣赏低调，亦欣赏夸张。我们愈发精致，也认识到能量与信息在体内四处流动的重要性。（于）

王：delicate 在文本语境中，应该是敏锐、敏感的意思（so fine as to be scarcely perceptible; subtle）。

> **改译1**：我们学着欣赏低调，亦欣赏夸张。我们愈发敏锐，也意识到，身体通过四向伸展所流露出的能力与信息，是多么重要。（王）
> **改译2**：我们学习欣赏低调与夸张。我们变得更细腻，也明白能量和信息通过身体传向四面八方的意义。（周）

李：这能量到底是在体内循环，还是激情四射？后面注释中有句话：
　　Grooving can also involve giving and receiving energy from a partner at a distance across the room.
　　说明是激情四射。

> **建议译法**：我们学会欣赏低调与夸张。我们变得更加细腻，也体会到能量和信息在体内四处流动的意义。（李）

16

> 原文：We learn to apply our force in an efficient way and we learn to use "other" forces.
> 原译：我们学习有效地运用力量，也学习如何借用"其他"力量。（于）
> 改译1：我们学习有效地运用力量，也学习如何借用"它力"。（王）
> 改译2：我们学会高效用力，也学会如何"借力"。（李）
> 改译3：我们学会使力时如何省力，也学会"借力"使力。（周）
> 建议译法：我们学会如何省力，也学会如何借力。（李）

17

> 原文：We discover the advantage of soft flesh and sensitive hands, we learn to connect to groove even when there is no music.
> 原译：我们发现了肉体柔软与双手灵敏的优势，我们学着随舞曲翩然起舞，即便没有伴奏。（于）

王：前后逻辑矛盾：没有伴奏，怎么还能随舞曲起舞？groove 在很多 Gaga 的视频中都有解释。Gaga 舞者对 groove 的解释不一，但是基本的意思是 dance spontaneously, with natural response。

> 改译1：我们发现柔软肉体与灵敏双手的优势，我们学习即使没有音乐也可以随心起舞。（王）
> 改译2：我们发现柔软的躯体与敏感的双手带来的优势，我们学会即使没有音乐也可以跳出节律。（李）

舞蹈知识

周：connect 在 Gaga 语汇中是很重要的部分，不可掉以轻心。

　　Grooving can also involve giving and receiving energy from a partner at a distance across the room. I posit that the ability to connect to each other's. Groove is at the heart of the empathic response that makes Gaga class so satisfying. Friedes-Galili enthused, "we laughed out loud while Grooving and then let the memory of that laughter guide our own personal dances" (Fricdes-Galili 2008a).

https://www.academia.edu/6458350/Building_Bodies_with_a_Soft_Spine._Gaga_Ohad_Naharins_invention_in_practice_its_roots_in_Feldenkrais_and_the_vision_of_a_pedagogy

What to Expect

"Connect your effort to your pleasure."

"Listen to how your skin touches the air around you."

"Connect to your floating spine."

"Be delicate with the availability to snap."

"Connect to your groove."

These are all phrases you may hear from your teacher in a Gaga class.

http://www.dancespirit.com/gaga-everywhere-2326554069.html

周：谓语动词 expect 后面的内容，都是上 Gaga 课时叫学员或舞者 connect 的情景。

Gaga is about discovering your body in a new way, at the same time gaining strength, flexibility and stamina. We also connect to things like being silly, shaking and quaking and we use expressions as thick flesh, sensitive skin, juicy joints or soft hands. These are images that help us to create actual physical reactions. By recognizing our movement habits we can also change them, and in Gaga we work with many layers at the same time.

http://www.naim.org.il/en/gaga/

The use of images is also a major part of the language in Gaga. This is a (small) list of examples from the classes I took at Suzanne Dellal Centre:

- Ropes of the arms
- Helium balloons lifting the knees
- Moving though honey
- Marionette threads holding you

- Having small weights on our body parts
- Softness in the movement
- Pulling the bone out of the flesh
- Spine like seaweed
- Traveling balls
- Floating
- Shake
- Quake
- Soft flesh

　　https://brage.bibsys.no/xmlui/bitstream/handle/11250/2491198/hogstad_masteroppgave_digitalversjon.pdf?sequence=1&isAllowed=y

Students use combinations of Gaga movements, allowing themselves free rein until they are moving without conscious thought, **sensitising the body through an awareness of** "soft flesh [and] sensitive hands" (Gaga people. dancers 2013), and by the students' connection to their inner rhythm.

　　https://www.academia.edu/6458350/Building_Bodies_with_a_Soft_Spine._Gaga_Ohad_Naharins_invention_in_practice_its_roots_in_Feldenkrais_and_the_vision_of_a_pedagogy

> **改译 3**：我们发现柔软的躯体和敏感的双手中的裨益，我们学会找身体的节律，即使没音乐。（周）
> **建议译法**：我们发现拥有柔软的躯体和敏感的双手带来的裨益，我们学会捕捉身体的节律，即使没有音乐伴奏。（傅天伊）

18　词义

In music, **groove** is the sense of propulsive rhythmic "feel" or sense of "swing". In jazz, it can be felt as a persistently repeated pattern. It can be created by the interaction of the music played by a band's rhythm section (e.g. drums, electric bass or double bass, guitar, and keyboards). Groove is a key of much popular music, and can be found in many genres, including salsa, funk, rock, fusion, and soul.

https://en.wikipedia.org/wiki/Groove_(music)

19

原文：We are aware of people in the room and we realize that we are not in the center of it all.

原译：我们具备他人在场意识，并且很清楚自己根本不是全场的中心。（于）

改译1：我们知道屋子里有其他人，也清楚自己不是人群的焦点。（王）

改译2：我们知道屋子里还有其他人，也清楚自己不是人群的中心。（李）

建议译法：我们知道屋里还有其他人，也明知自己不是人群的中心。（周）

20

原文：We become more aware of our form since we never look at ourselves in a mirror; there are no mirrors. We connect to the sense of the endlessness of possibilities.

原译：正因为我们从不去看镜中的自己，我们更了解自己的形态；那儿没有镜子。我们与可能的无尽感相联通。（于）

改译1：我们对自己的形态更为敏感，因为我们从来不照镜子；这里没有镜子。我们与无尽的可能相连。（王）

改译2：我们对自己的形态更为敏感，因为我们从来不照镜子；我们不用镜子。我们感受到无尽的可能性。（李）

改译3：我们对自己的身体形态感觉更敏锐，因为我们从来不照镜子；这里没镜子。我们畅想无尽的可能性。（周）

改译4：我们对自己的身体形态感觉更敏锐，因为我们从来不照镜子；这里没有镜子。我们畅想无尽的可能性。（傅天伊）

马尚：单从节奏考虑，删掉了"性"。

> **建议译法**：我们对自己的身体形态感觉更敏锐，因为我们从来不照镜子；这里没有镜子。我们畅想无尽的可能。（马）

21

> **原文**：Yielding is constant while we are ready to snap...
> **原译**：自我们准备起舞开始，就有源源不断的收获（于）

王：yielding 在这里不是"收获"的意思。

Invitation to Dance: Softening and Yielding

Begin with a full minute of slow and deep breathing. Let your breath bring your awareness down into your body. When thoughts come up, just let them go and return to your breath. Hold this image of "Softening and Yielding" as the gentlest of intentions, planting a seed as you prepare to step into the dance.

https://abbeyofthearts.com/blog/2013/10/27/invitation-to-dance-softening-and-yielding/

yielding 的意思就是放松身体，专注于思想，深呼吸，回到身体最自然的原点。

周：to yield 是 Gaga 身体动作语汇中的重要概念。to yield is to let go。身体 yield 了，就是抛开了习惯，关节便不会僵硬，能开发身体中许多我们忽略的可能性。跳 Gaga 时，身体总是控制和失控之间。身体 yield 了之后，因无规可寻，便能重新体察自己的认知系统，在每一个当下探索各种可能性，挑战身体的极限，将肌肉跟 feel 结合一起。Ohad 认为一贯的舞蹈方式会阻滞我们体内力量的流动，因身体没法放开而关节无法打开（比如芭蕾是端着的，一位就是一位，二位就是二位，没有 in-between）。身体打开后，舞者便能体验肢体最原始、未经雕琢，甚至怪异的部分。身心是完全融合的。snap 则相反，是一种突变，一种突然释放能量的感觉。肌肉放无可放的时候，就是 snap。舞者身体的肌肉孕育能量，绷紧后瞬间全部释放，很有爆发力。其实找个视频做一些 Gaga 动作就能找到其中感觉。

周：Yielding is constant while we are ready to snap... 可暂且处理如下：随顺是常态，但我们能随时爆发（力量）。

> **建议译法**：随顺是常态，但我们能随时爆发（力量）……（周）

22

> **原文**：We explore multi-dimensional movement, we enjoy the burning sensation in our muscles, we are aware of our explosive power and sometimes we use it.
> **原译**：我们探索多维度的移动，享受肌肉间滚烫的感觉，清楚体内的爆发力，有时候也利用这种爆发力。（于）
> **改译 1**：我们探索多维度移动，享受肌肉的灼热感，我们感受体内的爆发力，有时候也利用这种爆发力。（王）
> **改译 2**：我们探索多维度运动，享受肌肉的灼热感，我们感受体内的爆发力，有时候也利用这种爆发力。（李）
> **改译 3**：我们探索多维动作，享受肌肉灼热的感觉；我们能感受体内的爆发力，并且时而使用它。（周）
> **建议译法**：我们探索多维动作，享受肌肉灼热的感觉；我们能感受体内的爆发力，有时还会小试一下。（李）

23

周：跟前面的 yield + snap 是一个感觉。

24

> **原文**：We change our movement habits by finding new ones, we can be calm and alert at once. We become available...
> **原译**：我们发现新的动作、从而改变自己的动作习惯，而我们能够同时保持平静与警觉。我们进入状态（于）

> **改译 1**：我们通过发现新动作改变动作习惯，我们可以马上变得冷静、警觉。我们准备就绪。（王）
> **改译 2**：我们发现新动作，改变旧动作，我们可以既冷静，又警觉。我们随时作好了准备。（李）

周："Many times when I dance, I connect to feminine forces, forces that create availability to both yielding and explosiveness, to both delicacy and aggressiveness."

http://www.dancemagazine.com/ohad-says-7-best-quotes-mr-gaga-film-2307059394.html

Gaga into Performance: Harnessing the Available Body
March 24 - 28 (Monday-Friday)

https://www.facebook.com/events/384904154980296

Naharin takes dancers who have already received a solid grounding in traditional dance technique and selects those who, "have the leftover baby in their bodies — being without self-consciousness ... untamed and available" (Friedes-Galili 2012).

…

Gaga has enabled Naharin to develop articulate bodies by working with dancers who are already at a physical peak and who understand how their bodies work, within the confines of their existing training. He then looks for them to make their bodies, "*available*" (Gaga people.dancers 2013), to receive his layer of training which will free them from the chains of this early training.

https://www.academia.edu/6458350/Building_Bodies_with_a_Soft_Spine._Gaga_Ohad_Naharins_invention_in_practice_its_roots_in_Feldenkrais_and_the_vision_of_a_pedagogy

More important to Gaga than moving is making yourself available to movement. Wear comfortable clothing, give yourself lots of space and play music loud enough to create a mood but not so loud or beat-driven that it calls the shots. Many Gaga exercises rest on imagining your body is a hollow container; as creator Ohad Naharin sometimes says, "Feel the music decorate your body on the inside.

https://www.timeout.com/chicago/dance/gaga-movement-101

> **改译 3**：我们改变移动习惯以便探索新的移动方式，我们能从容又警觉。我们的身体听任使唤。（周）

傅天伊：这里是 by finding new ones，那是不是应该有一个动作的逻辑关系，是"通过探索新的移动方式来改变移动习惯"呢？

周：是。第一句的逻辑要倒过来。"我们探索新的移动方式，改变移动习惯。"

> **建议译法**：我们探索新的移动方式，改变移动习惯，我们能从容又警觉。我们的身体听任使唤。（周）

第十二单元　金融财会

Exercise 12　Global Tax Policy Post-BEPS and the Perils of the Silk Road?

翻译情景

跨国公司在不同国家经营，一些国家的税率高，一些国家的税率低。跨国公司通过一些内部操作，把利润转移到在低税率地区运营的子公司，包括空壳公司，这样就可以少缴税，对于政府来说，就意味着少收税。政府把这种现象称之为"税基侵蚀和利润转移"（Base Erosion and Profit Shifting）。

2012年，G20峰会（中国是成员）责成OECD（经济合作与发展组织，中国不是成员）采取行动，防止跨国公司把利润从高税收地区转移到低税收地区。该行动被称为"BEPS行动计划"（BEPS Action Plan或BEPS Project）。2015年G20峰会就"15项BEPS多边工具"（BEPS Multilateral Instrument）达成一致，2016年11月24日《多边工具》获得通过，2017年6月8日在巴黎签署，成为《实施税收协定相关措施以防止税基侵蚀和利润转移（BEPS）的多边公约》（The Multilateral Convention to Implement Tax Treaty Related Measures to Prevent Base Erosion and Profit Shifting），[1] 中国也是签署国之一。由于跨国公司也把大量利润从中国转移到避税天堂，导致中国政府损失大量税收，所以，中国政府积极参与制定和落实 BEPS 行动计划。

本单元节选的作者是维也纳经济和商业大学（WU）教授 Jeffery Owens。Owens 教授是国际税法专家，曾任 OECD 税收政策与管理中心（Centre for Tax Policy and Administration）主任，2012 年初退休后担任维也纳经济和商业大学全球税收政策中心主任（Vienna University Global Tax Policy Center），同时为安永会计师事务所（Ernst and Young）等企业和机构作税收政策顾问。[2] 这些背景资料都是编者查出来的。将来这些宏观资料都需要译者自己去查。

这篇文章于 2016 年 11 月发表在 Asia-Pacific Tax Bulletin 第 6 期（注意：当时《多边工具》还未获通过，所以称为 proposals）。文章摘要称：

This article addresses the implications of the OECD's BEPS proposals for investment in, and the growth of, Asian economies. The authors argue that, in the post-BEPS world, Asian countries should adopt international coordination and cooperation, expand their permanent establishment rules and broaden their interpretations of the arm's length principle to their best economic advantage, rather than unilaterally and incoherently over-implementing the new anti-BEPS weapons.

---

1 The Multilateral Convention to Implement Tax Treaty Related Measures to Prevent Base Erosion and Profit Shifting, sometime abbreviated BEPS multilateral instrument, is a multilateral convention of the Organisation for Economic Co-operation and Development to combat tax avoidance by multinational enterprises (MNEs) through prevention of Base Erosion and Profit Shifting (BEPS). The BEPS multilateral instrument was negotiated within the framework of the OECD G20 BEPS project and enables countries and jurisdictions to swiftly modify their bilateral tax treaties to implement some of the measures agreed.

https://en.wikipedia.org/wiki/Multilateral_Convention_to_Implement_Tax_Treaty_Related_Measures_to_Prevent_Base_Erosion_and_Profit_Shifting

2 https://www.prnewswire.com/news-releases/jeffrey-owens-appointed-as-senior-tax-policy-adviser-to-ernst—young-158107695.html

https://www.linkedin.com/in/jp-owens/

本单元从文章中选取了一些重点段落。为了特别训练翻译的全局意识和逻辑思维,各选段逻辑不直接相连,需要通读上下文、宏观把握选文背景与脉络以后,方可翻译。

假定自己为某个国内的国际税收咨询机构翻译这篇文章。

训练重点

本单元重点训练译者的全局意识和查证能力。请先通读全文,宏观把握全文论点、各段之间的逻辑关系、以及每段的中心思想,再调动网络资源、咨询相关专家,帮助翻译。

训练难点

本单元的训练难点是如何通过网络资源,快速了解一个领域的专业知识。这篇文章专业性非常强,如果不具备相关背景知识或者是查证能力,根本无从下手。希望大家通过本次训练,进一步巩固全局意识、查证能力和逻辑思维能力,今后遇到再专业的材料都不畏惧;同时,也希望通过本单元练习,让大家顺带学习一点预防BEPS的专业知识,为今后相关领域的翻译提供一些背景支撑。知识就是通过一次次翻译逐步积累起来的。

训练方式

本次练习分原文、翻译提示、参考译文、译者注四部分。请先尝试独立翻译。完成后再参看翻译提示,并继续查证、修改、润色,形成第二稿。然后再看参考译文和译者注。本单元是本书的最后一个单元,也最具有挑战性,希望你不畏艰难,努力完成这次练习,相信努力越多,收获就会越大!

原文 [1]

Global Tax Policy Post-BEPS[2] and the Perils of the Silk Road[3]?

Jeffery Owens[4]

...

(p.5) The reform of substantive rules[5] to curb tax avoidance[6] through BEPS[7] (hereinafter referred to as "anti-BEPS" rules) has not yet altered the broader equation of residence versus source country taxing rights[8]. In the area of transfer pricing[9], in particular, the final BEPS report appears to have fallen short of the expectations raised by many commentators and by countries such as China and India, since the United States was quick to take this off the agenda[10]. As such, if the core of transfer pricing rules remains unchanged under the arm's length principle[11], what are countries to do with the abundant information and CbCRs[12] they will receive? Will the granular information on GVCs of MNEs reveal BEPS risks and lead to grounded assessments which could not have occurred in the past[13]? Or[14] will the scrutiny of massive MNE data simply[15] reveal the complex (and still legitimate) operation of the arm's length principle of transfer pricing under the functionally separate legal entity[16] approach?

...

(p.8) Therein[17] lie some of the new perils that are expected to surface along the Silk Road. Some of the potential pitfalls that can emerge in Asia post-BEPS pertain to the risk of uncoordinated and unilateral over-implementation of what may be interpreted as anti-BEPS measures, particularly in the area of transfer pricing and tax treaty entitlement. The inadvertent enforcement of anti-avoidance or anti-abuse theories that were experimented with in the discussion drafts (and in academia) leading to the final BEPS reports, may overburden tax administrations throughout Asia, and cause a tsunami of litigation[18] with highly uncertain prospects. This may be a risky venture for tax administrations to embark on. Going "beyond arm's length" and seeking to unilaterally adopt formulary apportionment[19] results through interpretation[20] of anti-BEPS language or policies, is a danger that could hurt economies in Asia.

...

(p.9) Quite strikingly, China is now also adopting an innovative Other Method[21], the "Value Contribution Apportionment Method" (VCAM), under which "MNE profits are to be allocated across the value chain based on analysis of how value creating contributions have been made to group profits, with reference being made to assets, costs, sales and employees."[22] Note, BEPS Actions 8-10 indicate "DEMPE" (Development, Enhancement, Maintenance, Protection and Exploitation) as[23] the standard to assess value creation pertaining to intangibles, as substantive activities that would allow the recognition of intangible ownership and control over risk.[24] China is adopting a broader view on intangibles by setting out a "DEMPEP" approach[25] (which adds "promotion" to the definition of activities which entitle returns on intangibles), and expanding the interpretation of Location Specific Advantages (LSAs)[26], which would reinforce its[27] pre-BEPS view on comparability[28] particularly in respect to market premium, and lead to an ever-increasing use of the Profit Split Method (PSM)[29] post-BEPS as well as the use of the new VCAM. Both methods could be used when the Chinese authorities ascertain that local intangibles or LSAs would justify the disregard of otherwise comparable transactions or enterprises from third countries[30]; and if LSAs and market premium rise to the level of unique and valuable intangibles, a substantial portion of global profits from value chains operated by MNEs would be allocated to China.

...

(p.14) The tax burden in countries with a substantial consumer market or with substantial workforce[31] can increase if the Chinese or Indian approaches are fully adopted, and this may be perceived[1] as an adequate policy response to the BEPS concerns raised by the digital economy. Double taxation might ensue if these adjustments are effected unilaterally, whilst other countries continue to conform to the OECD Guidelines. Other jurisdictions might follow China and India which could shift taxing rights away not only from U.S. or Europe but from other Asian countries which serve as regional supply chain hubs or treasury centers for global MNEs and/or that are also capital exporters, such as Hong Kong, Singapore, the Republic of Korea and Japan.

翻译提示

1 **全局意识**
请大家针对原文和译文，分别回答 Who is talking to whom? About what? When, where and why? And how? 然后再开始翻译。

2 **全局意识：BEPS 的背景知识**
翻译前，请调查 BEPS 的来龙去脉，以及什么叫 post-BEPS。

3 **全局意识：上下文**
Silk Road 是指什么？面临什么危险？为什么用问号？

4 **全局意识：作者立场**
作者是前任 OECD 财政事务委员会主任，他对国际税收政策的历史和现状的解读，具有权威性，用词不当的可能性较小，遇到逻辑上不清楚的地方，先查证有些词是否有其他意思；另外，请通读全文，思考作者的立场是什么？他的立场与身份经历有无关系？

5 **查证能力**
substantive rules 相对于什么规则？在 BEPS 领域是指什么？

6 **查证能力**
tax avoidance 是什么意思？和 tax evasion 有什么区别？中文分别叫什么？

7 语言能力：修饰关系

through BEPS 修饰 curb 还是 avoidance？

8 查证能力

想要理解这句话，要重点查查什么是 residence country taxing rights？什么叫 source country taxing rights？broader equation 是指数学公式中的方程，还是指权利上的平衡？如果能先理解 residence country 与 source country 之间的权利分配问题，整句话的意思就容易理解得多。

9 查证能力

什么是 transfer pricing？转让定价和转让定价，哪个说法更常见或者更达意？转让定价和跨国企业避税有什么关系？

10 语言能力 / 查证能力

this 指什么？为什么美国不想谈 transfer pricing？anti-BEPS 规则损害了谁的利益？此处的材料比较少，可能需要你咨询相关专家。如果实在不明白，可以在修改以后看译文尾注相应解释。

11 语言能力 / 查证能力

什么叫 arm's length principle？原文 transfer pricing rules under the arm's length principle 建议视为一个整体理解。

12 逻辑思维 / 查证能力

CbCRs 是指什么？此处可以参考一下 BEPS 行动计划 13 提供的国际规则模板。进一步阅读，或许可以发现对现行模板中独立交易原则和公式分配法的讨论。请试着将这两种模板与双重征税问题联系在一起。

13 查证能力

"Will the granular information on GVCs of MNEs reveal BEPS risks and lead to grounded assessments which could not have occurred in the past?" 这句话主要在讲税局收到大量信息以后，怎么用的问题。建议译者调查 granular 以及两个缩写 GVCs 和 MNEs 的意思。

14 **逻辑思维**

or 的前后是什么关系？

15 **理解**

为什么用 simply？

16 **查证**

functionally separate legal entity approach 是非常复杂的概念，可以试着查查在 BEPS 行动计划 7 中有没有什么新发现。

17 **全局意识：上下文**

therein 即使不需要显化在哪里，译者也要明白指代关系。请看上文。

18 **理解**

the inadvertent enforcement of anti-avoidance or anti-abuse theories that were experimented with in the discussion drafts (and in academia) leading to the final BEPS reports, may overburden tax administrations throughout Asia, and cause a tsunami of litigation with highly uncertain prospects 这句话还是跟双重征税问题分不开。审校时注意以下问题：

1) 注意 administration 是复数，那么它应该指税局，还是税收征管工作？
2) 查查 anti-avoidance 和 anti-abuse 与兜底条款和 GAAR（General Anti-Avoidance Rule）有什么联系？
3) 这些条款给税局的工作带来什么影响？

19 **查证能力**

查查 formulary appointment 是指什么？

20 **全局意识：上下文**

这里的 interpretation 是带有主观性的。联系上下文。如果去主观解读政策的话，会带来什么样的后果呢？与本句末尾的 danger 有什么关系？

21 **指代关系**

Other Method 是指什么？能否找到中国的具体规定（中文的）？

第十二单元 · 金融财会

22 标准化
引号中的内容请还原为中文原始规定,不要翻译。

23 逻辑关系
as 是指"正如"还是"因为"?

24 查证能力
control over risk 是在 BEPS 行动计划 8—10 中非常重要的一个概念。请查查它和 substantive activities 有什么关系?

25 查证能力
这句话提到的内容也涉及 BEPS 行动计划 8—10 的 DEMPE。请查查 DEMPEP approach 具体指什么?它是否为转让定价中颇具争议的问题?

26 查证能力
请查查 LSA 具体指什么,与转让定价有什么关联?

27 指代关系
its 是指谁?

28 指代关系
查查 comparability 具体指什么?

29 查证能力
请查查 Profit Split Method (PSM) 是指什么?

30 理解
from third countries 背后是指什么?

31 指代关系
联系上下文,看看 countries with a substantial consumer market 指哪个国家? countries with substantial workforce 又是指哪个国家?

32 逻辑主语
may be perceived by whom ? 这里的逻辑主语应该是谁?

参考译文

后BEPS[1]时代全球税收政策及"一带一路"[2]的危机?[3]

杰弗里·欧文斯(Jeffery Owens)

……

通过实质性规则[4]改革,遏制基于BEPS的避税[5]行为,并未从整体上改变居民地与来源地征税权的分配问题。[6]尤其在转让定价方面,BEPS的最终报告似乎没有满足很多意见反馈方以及中印等国的期待,原因是美国很快便将这个问题从议程上拿下。[7]鉴于此,如果独立交易原则指导下的核心转让定价规则维持不变,那么各国将如何处理收到的海量信息和国别报告?[8]有关跨国企业全球价值链的这些细节信息,是会揭示BEPS风险,让各国据此对跨国企业应纳税款,作出以前无法实现的判定,[9]还是仅仅显示在采用独立实体征税法的背景下,转让定价的独立交易原则运作起来十分复杂(但仍然合法)?[10]

……

这里面就存在一些可能会在"一带一路"沿线国家出现的新风险。[11]在后BEPS时代,亚洲可能会出现一些隐患,包括缺乏协调地或单方面过度实施所谓应对BEPS的措施,尤其是在转让定价和享受税收协定待遇方面。[12]在BEPS最终报告定稿前,征求意见稿以及学术探讨中曾提出一些反避税或反滥用理论。这些理论如果不慎重考虑就加以运用,不仅会让整个亚洲的税务征管工作不堪重负,还可能产生海量诉讼案件,而这些案件的结果有相当大不确定性。[13]这对税务机关而言,可能是冒险之旅。[14]越过独立交易原则,通过解读应对BEPS的表述或政策,单方面采用公式分配法计算出的结果,可能会严重危及亚洲的经济体。[15]

……

值得注意的是,中国还在创新性地采用"其他方法",即"价值贡献分配法"。[16]按照该方法,"跨国公司在价值链上的利润分配,以分析价值创造对跨国集团利润的贡献为依据,并参考资产、成本、销售和员工等因素".[17] 请注意,BEPS 行动 8-10 将 DEMPE（开发、提升、维护、保护和应用）视为评估无形资产价值创造的标准,即用以确认无形资产所有权和风险控制权的实质活动。[18] 中国对无形资产采用了更宽泛的定义,提出 DEMPEP 分析方法［即在有权获得无形资产回报的活动定义中加入了"推广活动"(P)］,并扩大了对"地域性特殊优势"(LSAs) 这一概念的解读,[19] 这将强化中国在前 BEPS 时代有关可比性（特别是有关市场溢价）的观点,并在后 BEPS 时代更多地运用利润分割法和新的价值贡献分配法。[20] 只要中国税务机关认定采用本地无形资产或地域性特殊优势原则理由充分,就可以不适用原本的第三国可比交易或公司法法,转而采用上述两种方法；[21] 而如果地域性特殊优势和市场溢价成为独特而有价值的无形资产,跨国公司经营价值链中很大一部分利润就会分配到中国。[22]

……

如果全面采用中国或印度的做法,在拥有巨大消费市场或大量劳动力的国家,跨国企业的税负会加重,[23] 而这种结果可能被视为在税收政策层面对数字经济中 BEPS 问题的恰当回应。但如果单方面进行这些调整,而其他国家继续遵守《经合组织转让定价指南》,则可能产生双重征税。[24] 其他税收管辖区没准会仿效中国和印度,这样可能不仅会将征税权从美国或欧洲转移出去,还可能将征税权从亚洲其他一些国家或地区转移出去。这些国家或地区,比如香港、新加坡、韩国和日本,或者是全球性跨国公司区域供应链中心,或者是财资中心,同时又是/或者是资本输出地。[25]

译者注

1 全局意识
   BEPS 的背景知识

李：**Base erosion and profit shifting (BEPS)** *refers to tax avoidance strategies* that exploit gaps and mismatches in tax rules to artificially shift profits to low or no-tax locations. Under the inclusive framework, over 100 countries and jurisdictions are collaborating to implement the BEPS measures and tackle BEPS.

http://www.oecd.org/tax/beps/

POST-BEPS

The OECD BEPS project has rapidly moved to the implementation phase, leaving a fundamentally changed landscape in its wake. *This new environment requires businesses to re-evaluate their operational and financing structures, identify communications strategies and assess their tax strategy, all with the aim of developing a sustainable tax framework.*

https://webforms.ey.com/gl/en/issues/
webcast_2017-04-20-1400_navigating-in-a-post-beps-world-permanent-
establishments-in-a-post-beps-world

王：(Anti-) BEPS 计划就是反对税基侵蚀和利润转移的行动计划，该计划包括15项核心行动，聚焦三项核心原则：coherence、substance 和 transparency。

BEPS CORE PRINCIPLES

The 15 Action Items within the OECD BEPS initiative focus on three core principles: Coherence, Substance and Transparency.

- Coherence: Domestic tax systems are coherent – tax deductible payments by one person results in income inclusions by the recipient. Action Items 2—5 address international coherence in corporate income taxation to complement the standards that prevent double taxation with a new set of standards designed *to avoid double non-taxation.*
- Substance: Action Items 6 – 10 focus on aligning "tax rights" with substance. Current rules work well in many cases, but must be modified to prevent instances of BEPS. The involvement of third countries in the bilateral framework established by treaty partners puts a strain on the existing rules, in particular when done via *shell companies that have little or no economic*

substance: e.g. office space, tangible assets and employees. In the area of transfer pricing, rather than replacing the current system, The OECD BEPS initiative aims to fix the flaws, in particular with respect to returns related to over-capitalization, risk and intangible assets.

- Transparency: Because preventing BEPS requires greater transparency at many levels, Action Items 11 – 15 call for: improved data collection and analysis regarding the impact of BEPS; taxpayers' disclosure about their tax planning strategies; and less burdensome and more targeted transfer pricing documentation. These Action Items together require "Country-by-Country" (CbC) reporting, which has raised scrutiny over the information to be disclosed as well as safe-guarding of such information. Only in July, 2016, did the IRS issue final regulations regarding CbC Reporting, which will be required of all companies with world-wide revenue in excess of €750 million (approximately $850 million).

https://www.withum.com/kc/understanding-the-post-beps-world/?utm_source=Int%27l+Tax+Month+6+%7C+2016&utm_campaign=Int%27l+Tax+Month+%7C+7-15-16&utm_medium=email

李：思考发现，此处的 BEPS measures 其实是指 anti-BEPS measures。进一步观察，会发现为了行文简洁，会用 BEPS 表达多种意思：本身的意思、anti-BEPS、Anti-BEPS project 等，请大家注意分辨。

2　全局意识：上下文

王：从全文看，Silk Road 指的是 a new, two-way Silk Road，即原文中提到的 One Belt, One Road。

王：the perils of the Silk Road 是指什么？搜索 peril，在原文第八页找到以下内容，请见斜体部分。peril 意指危险，这种危险主要是对 BEPS 行动计划执行不力或执行过度造成适得其反的效果：

Therein lie some of the new perils that are expected to surface along the Silk Road. Some of the potential *pitfalls* that can emerge in Asia post-BEPS pertain to the *risk of uncoordinated and unilateral over-implementation* of what may be interpreted as anti-BEPS measures, particularly in the area of transfer pricing and tax treaty entitlement. The inadvertent enforcement of anti-avoidance or anti-abuse theories that were experimented with in the discussion drafts (and in academia) leading to the final BEPS reports, may *overburden tax administrations throughout Asia*, and cause a *tsunami* of *litigation* with highly uncertain prospects. This may be a risky venture for tax administrations to embark on. Going "beyond arm's length" and seeking to unilaterally *adopt formulary apportionment results* through interpretation of anti-BEPS language or policies, is a *danger* that could hurt economies in Asia.

The adoption of such unilateral action would not only have highly uncertain revenue results (given the complex nature of the factual and legal problems that would be at stake), but, irrespective of the outcome of the protracted litigation that would ensue, uncoordinated enforcement or unilateral aggressiveness and litigation in the area of transfer pricing would be detrimental to the operation of GVCs in Asia by U.S. and European MNEs. This could trigger potential distortions through disaggregation or fragmentation of such value chains, potentially dampening inward FDI and *Knowledge-Based Capital* (KBC) transfers into Asia. Further, such uncoordinated stance could inspire similarly unilateral and aggressive postures in other developing and emerging nations wherein Asia is itself an investor, not to mention trigger adverse responses in the developed world. *Harmful tax competition may become the new normal.*

3

原文：Global Tax Policy Post-BEPS and the Perils of the Silk Road?
原译：后 BEPS 时代全球税务政策：一带一路上的危险？

李：如果全文重点是一带一路上的危险，可以用冒号。

> **改译 1**：后 BEPS 时代全球税务政策和"一带一路"上的危险？（李）
> **改译 2**：后 BEPS 时代全球税务政策及"一带一路"的危机？（雷）
> **改译 3**：后 BEPS 时代全球税务政策危及"一带一路"政策？（雷）
> **改译 4**：后 BEPS 时代全球税务政策带来"一带一路"的瘫痪？（雷）
> **改译 5**：后 BEPS 时代全球税务政策为"一带一路"政策带来的风险（雷）

李：李延雷是北外高翻校友。长期从事国际税收方面的翻译工作，后转型为企业提供 BEPS 相关咨询服务。做本次练习时，请他作了针对性讲评。下面是李延雷的评论，来自他的讲座。

雷：关于标题的翻译，如果不了解 BEPS 的情况，可能翻译起来比较困难。以上我的四个翻译版本，从专业人士的角度看，都是可以的。这里面暗含翻译的自由度问题。自由度取决于你对**原文**专业的背景了解。了解得越多，灵活度越大。

此处的难点在于 perils of the Silk Road 到底怎么翻译。如果大家读过论文，就知道这篇论文是在讲 BEPS 这个全球意义上的反避税行动。BEPS 其实就是指 Base Erosion and Profit Shifting。翻译成中文就是"税基侵蚀和利润转移"。用中国人更能理解的话来说，就是避税问题。避税就是通过侵蚀你的税基，或者转移你的利润，减少应纳税所得额。英文这种说法讲得比较具体，中文其实就是避税的意思。但是，从严格意义上讲，避税又不能完全代表 BEPS 的内涵，所以我们在翻译的时候，还是把它处理成"税基侵蚀和利润转移"，但是简单意义上来讲，它就是一个避税问题。

在 2013 年实行 BEPS 以前，跨国公司其实钻了很多空子来避税。比如一个美国公司，在中国做生意，享受了中国的优惠待遇，获得了大笔利润，回美国还不用上税，这是一个两头通吃的行为。如果所有企业都这样的话，那美国政府就没有税收财政来源了；中国政府也是——虽然提供给跨国公司很多优待，但是没有征到税。

所以，近些年媒体的报道披露了跨国公司避税的问题，这些避税行为侵害了很多国家的利益。以 G20 为首的国家，推动 BEPS 协议，在 OECD 层面探讨如何解决跨国公司的避税行为。OECD 组织虽然不是联合国，但是它在国际影响力上远远超过联合国，特别是在很多经济、商业领域。联合国的影响力更多是政治层面。因为全世界各国都在大力推进税收征管和税法改革，所以在这种情况下，物极必反，就会做很多出格的事情。对于中国来说，做得太出格就会影响中国"一带一路"的战略，影响东西方贸易流通，甚至会影响到发展中国家产业升级换代问题。

雷：论文中作者想强调的就是危机的问题。对于完全不了解BEPS内容和背景的读者，说"危机"可以帮助读者抓住核心内容。再柔和一点，可以说"危及'一带一路'建设"。"瘫痪"是更严重的词。为什么用"瘫痪"？中文的"瘫痪"和英文的peril都有清辅音，而且表达的状况是危险的。此外，从国际税收演变角度看，翻译成"瘫痪"并不觉得过分，因为很多专业人士会有这样的担心。"危险"这个词不好，从国际咨询公司或者税收角度，用"风险"这个词更频繁一些。总之，这个标题的重点就是如何解释peril这个词。我们需要通过标题来传达文章核心意思。

宋俊阳：我批改的班所有同学都把"Silk Road"翻译成了"丝绸之路"，我给他们的批注是"讲的其实是'一带一路'。'丝绸之路'的历史气息比较浓厚，一般用于追溯起源；提到BEPS，最好还是用'一带一路'"。想问一下，Silk Road翻译为"丝绸之路"是否确实有欠妥当？当然，还有同学用了简称"丝路"。

宋俊阳：另外，几乎所有同学都把标题中的问号去掉了，他们认为标题不构成一个问句。我的想法是，翻译为"后BEPS时代全球税务政策及一带一路的危机"确实后面不应该加问号，但是这个问号又必须保留，那么能不能换一种表达方式，翻译为"后BEPS时代全球税务政策，'一带一路'隐患重重／面临何种危机？"之类的有疑问语气的标题呢？

王：问题一，翻译成"丝绸之路"没有问题。"丝绸之路"这种译法和"一带一路"的译法体现两种不同的翻译观。"丝绸之路"是较为贴近字面的翻译方法。"一带一路"是"丝绸之路经济带"和"21世纪海上丝绸之路"的简称。

而李延雷老师的翻译，尽力想要展现文字背后的实际含义与指代。因为这里的"丝绸之路"就是"一带一路",所以处理成"一带一路"更明确,也没有问题。处理成"丝路"也可以。你可以在批注框中给学生建议,告诉他们这里的"丝绸之路"实际就是指"一带一路",他们的用法不必算错。问题二,我认为这个问号需要保留。是不是"危机",作者也是在做试探性的回答。如果不加问号,语气就过于绝对化,好像危机已成既定事实。所以我想可以修改为:后 BEPS 时代全球税收政策:"一带一路"上的危机?这个译法还需要跟李老师讨论。你可以先建议学生问号不可以省略,不然语气过于绝对。

李:我同意苏阳老师的意见。

王:tax policy 我觉得还是应该处理为"税收政策"。

《税收辞海》中对"税收"一词的解释:"国家为了实现其职能,按法定标准无偿地集中一部分社会产品所形成的分配,是国家取得财政收入的一种主要形式,本质上体现为国家为主的分配关系。"《辞海》中对"纳"一字解释为"交付、致送",则"纳税"可解释为:纳税人依税法交付、致送税款。《辞海》对"征税"一词解释为"国家依税法将赋税等收取解入国库"。《税收辞海》对"税务"一词解释为"税收的事务。有广义与狭义之分。广义的税务是指:国家税收活动全部工作事务,包括国家对税收政策的研究、制定、宣传、贯彻和执行等工作;税收法律、法规、规则、决议等的建立、调节、修订、改革、完善、解释和咨询工作;税务机构的设置、领导分工,税务人员的配置、组织、教育、培训、监察等工作;税款的征收、减免、退补等工作;税务登记、纳税辅导、纳税鉴定、纳税申报、纳税检查、财务管理、发票管理和税收票证管理等工作,税务检察、违章处理、税务行政复议与诉讼等工作,税收计划、会计统计等工作;税务档案工作;国际税收谈判;国际税务关系协调;国际税收协定的签订,执行工作,税务科研、学会、刊物等工作,以及其他税务工作。狭义的税务一般指税收的征收、管理工作。"

综上,税收更强调取得国家财政收入的一种形式,而税务无论是广义还是狭义,还包括事务性工作。

比如,"上海市地方税务局"官方译法为 Shanghai Municipal Bureau of

Local Taxation。本文用的是 tax，结合全文，应该是税收政策。

李：同意这个分析。网上都是说"税收政策"。"税务"和"税收"意思上不"搭配"。

> **建议译法**：后 BEPS 时代全球税收政策及"一带一路"的危机？（李）

4

> **原文**：substantive rules

雷：从业内人士角度，substantive rules 是指跨国公司的商业活动有没有实质性，因为实质性会决定纳税多少。在一个国家的实质性活动越多，向该国纳税就越多。简而言之，substantive rules 可以理解为实质性规则。

李：延雷所表达的意思，就是下段引文中所说的 ensuring that profits are taxed where economic activities generating the profits are performed and where value is created：

Base Erosion and Profit Shifting

Developed in the context of the OECD/G20 BEPS Project, the 15 actions set out below equip governments with domestic and international instruments to address tax avoidance, *ensuring that profits are taxed where economic activities generating the profits are performed and where value is created*.

http://www.oecd.org/tax/beps/beps-actions.htm

文章中也有一句话用了 substantive activities 指企业的实质活动：

Note, BEPS Actions 8-10 indicate "DEMPE" (*Development, Enhancement, Maintenance, Protection and Exploitation*) ... as *substantive activities* that would allow the recognition of intangible ownership and control over risk.

但经过更多调查，我发现 substantive rules 虽然可以翻译为"实质性规则"，但其意义却不是关于企业实质活动的规则，而是相对于一般性规则、辅助性规则的实质性规则，就是下文所说的 substantive norms：

Nonetheless, one could identify <u>five topical groups of action items</u>. <u>First</u>, there are the more-<u>general, overarching action items</u> that represent some ongoing challenges to the international tax regime. This group includes action items one ("Address the Tax Challenges of the Digital Economy") and five ("Counter Harmful Tax Practices More Effectively, Taking into Account Transparency and Substance"). <u>A second group includes the perhaps "true" action items: **substantive norms**</u>, which had their vulnerability exposed by BEPS and which require technical revision to address these challenges. These are action items two ("Neutralise the Effects of Hybrid Mismatch Arrangements"), three ("Strengthen CFC Rules"), four ("Limit Base Erosion via Interest Deductions and Other Financial Payments"), six ("Prevent Treaty Abuse"), and seven ("Prevent the Artificial Avoidance of PE Status"). This group should include the transfer pricing regime as well, yet due to that regime's centrality to both the threat presented by BEPS and to the BEPS project itself, this Part discusses it separately in a third group that includes action items eight through 10 ("Assure that Transfer Pricing Outcomes Are in Line with Value Creation") and 13 ("Re-examine Transfer Pricing Documentation"). <u>A fourth group includes the supporting cast, a set of action items dealing with administrative and compliance issues.</u> These are action items 11 ("Establish Methodologies to Collect and Analyse Data on BEPS and the Actions to Address It"), 12 ("Require Taxpayers to Disclose Their Aggressive Tax Planning Arrangements"), and 14 ("Make Dispute Resolution Mechanisms More Effective"). Finally, this Part separately discusses action item 15 — which explores the possibility of developing a multilateral instrument — because it is the direct manifestation of the key insight of the BEPS project: promoting the necessity of a universal, collaborative international tax regime.

https://scholarship.law.ufl.edu/cgi/viewcontent.
cgi?article=1652&context= facultypub

另一篇文章中说得更清楚，reform of substantive rules 是指对国际税法实体规则的改革，相对于程序性规则改革，比如提高 Transparency，促进 Exchange of Information。下文所述 substantive law action items 就是指在实体法方面应该采取的行动：

This article focuses on the substantive tax treaty implications of the BEPS project. It begins with this introduction of the relevant context for the project. Section 2. follows with an analysis of the key substantive law action items identified by the OECD plan as affecting tax treaties. Section 3. proceeds to briefly examine the administrative action items to the extent they may affect the success of the BEPS project.

…

Note that the BEPS project deals primarily with substantive international tax norms, and in that it is different from parallel initiatives, such as the Global Forum on Transparency and Exchange of Information for Tax Purposes (Global Forum). The goal of the latter is to facilitate a one-dimensional flow of information rather than reconcile competing claims. Therefore, one should be careful not to conclude that the many successes of such forum could simply be replicated by the BEPS project. In particular, the reliance on best practices with some coordination may be very useful to facilitate administrative collaboration, but it has proven to be insufficient for the reconciliation of substantive tax claims.

https://www.ibfd.org/sites/ibfd.org/files/content/pdf/WTJ-Free-Article-March-2015-Newsletter.pdf

substantive rules 在法律领域常见的说法是"实体性规则"，意思就是"实质性规则"，相对于"程序性规则"。但既然 BEPS 业内人士说"实质性规则"意思清楚，我们不妨遵循客户建议。

5

王：要注意区分 tax avoidance 和 tax evasion。由以下材料可知，tax avoidance 是合法的，而 tax evasion 是不合法的。

Tax avoidance is the legal usage of the tax regime in a single territory to one's own advantage to reduce the amount of tax that is payable by means that are within the law.

https://en.wikipedia.org/wiki/Tax_avoidance

Tax evasion is the illegal evasion of taxes by individuals, corporations, and trusts.

https://en.wikipedia.org/wiki/Tax_evasion

解析偷税与漏税、节税、避税的区别：

1. 偷税与漏税的区别

偷税是行为人以偷逃国家税款为目的的故意行为，而漏税是纳税人并非故意未缴或少缴应纳税款，属于无意识而发生的过失行为。造成漏税的原因一般有：

（1）纳税义务人不了解或不熟悉税法规定和财务制度，或因粗心大意、工作草率而错用税率、漏报应纳税目、少计应税数量、销售金额和经营利润等。

（2）税务机关因特殊情况和税务人员失职，没有及时将税种、税率的调整变化通知到纳税义务人，致使计税有误，造成税款漏征。

（3）纳税义务人没有详细报告其经营状况，而税务人员也未按规定程序进行审核，二者都没有完全履行法定义务，双方混合过错造成漏税。漏税不是犯罪行为，对于漏税，税务机关可以在3年内追征。

2. 偷税与节税的区别

节税与偷税有天壤之别，节税是指纳税义务人在税法和其他经济法律许可的范围内，通过对其投资、经营、理财等活动的事先谋划，以达到税务负担最低化目的的一种行为，节税是行为人根据政府制定的法律设定方案进行择优选择，是合法行为。

3. 偷税与避税的区别

所谓避税，是指采用非违法手段减轻或者不履行纳税义务的行为。广义的逃税包括偷税与避税。偷税与避税虽然都是减少或者不履行纳税义务的行为，但二者之间有着本质的不同：避税是在纳税义务发生前采取各种合乎法律规定的方法，有意减轻或者免除税收负担的行为，大多数情况下是符合立法意图的，如利用经济特区的税收优惠政策在经济特区投资，有些则是钻税法不够完善的空子；偷税是发生纳税义务后，采用非法的手段减少或者不履行纳税义务，在任何情况下，偷税都是国家法律所不允许的。对于钻法律空子的避税，只能通过不断完善税收法律的方法来防止；对于偷税，则依法追究刑事责任，加强打击是减少偷税犯罪的重要手段。

https://jingyan.baidu.com/article/d8072ac4415b64ec95cefdbe.html

6

原文：The reform of substantive rules to curb tax avoidance through BEPS (hereinafter referred to as "anti-BEPS" rules) has not yet altered the broader equation of residence versus source country taxing rights.

原译：限制税基侵蚀和利润转移避税的实体性规则（下称"反BEPS"规则）经过改革，尚未改变居住国征税权与来源国征税权之间的大平衡。

改译1：通过BEPS（税基侵蚀和利润转移）项目改革反避税 实体规则（下称"反BEPS"规则）的努力，尚未改变居住国征税权与来源国征税权之间的总体平衡。（李）

李：*Income or profits which result from international activities such as cross-border investment may be taxed where the income is earned (the **source country**), or where the person who receives it is normally based (the **country of residence**).* Residence taxation of income is based on the principle that people and firms should contribute towards the public services provided for them by the country where they live, on all their income wherever it comes from. Source taxation is justified by the view that the country which provides the opportunity to generate income or profits should have the right to tax it....

Fundamentally, the treaties **strike a compromise between source and residence taxation***. Some rights to tax are given to the source, and the residence country is required to relieve double taxation either by giving a credit for such source taxes paid, or by exempting the relevant income from its taxes.*

Generally, source jurisdictions retain their right to tax active (business) income, except for short-term activities, but give up some of their right to tax passive (investment) income.

https://www.taxjustice.net/cms/upload/pdf/Source_and_residence_
taxation_-_SEP-2005.pdf

王：broader equation of 是什么意思，如何处理？上面查到的 the treaties strike a compromise between source and residence taxation 给出了查证线索，这个 equation 应该谈的就是权利的平衡问题。

equation

noun • UK /ɪˈkweɪ.ʒən/ US /ɪˈkweɪ.ʒən/

equation noun (STATEMENT)

⭐ C1 [C] **a mathematical statement in which you show that two amounts are equal using mathematical symbols:**
In the equation 3x - 3 = 15, x = 6.

> 改译 2：通过与实质性有关的税法来遏制税基侵蚀和利润转移行为（下称"应对 BEPS"的税制）的改革并未改变居民地征税权与来源地征税权的分配这个宏观 / 更大层面的问题。（雷）

雷：anti-BEPS，翻译成"应对"更地道，这是业内人士比较专业的说法。anti 这个词在英文里不一定都翻译成"反"。在论文中提到 BEPS 的概念，其实都是想表达 anti-BEPS 的概念。在实际翻译中一定要照顾读者的感受。

雷：这句话想表达的意思是，现在对实质性规则的改革，并没有改变 BEPS 背后的根本性问题。这背后还有一个更根本的问题，就是国家之间征税权分配的问题。在商业时代，跨国公司的运营是全球化运作。每个国家都有自己的税收制度，但是制度之间并不衔接。

"居民地"当中的"居民"，并不是 citizenship 的概念，而是税收概念上的居民，即你达到一定税收标准之后，你从税收意义上构成居民。反之，也有可能你是公民，但是你不需要缴纳太多的税。

  not yet altered the broader equation of residence versus source country taxing rights 实际上是讲一个天平的概念。它并不是方程的意思。比如，一家美国公司在中国卖软件，中国消费者买了它的软件。这家公司的所得或者收入来自于中国，中国就是这家公司所得的 source country。那什么是 residence country 呢？比如一家美国公司，它在美国注册，那这家公司就是美国的 resident，即美国的税收居民。美国对这份所得，也是有征税权的。所以当跨国公司有跨国经营活动的时候，征税权到底是在哪一国，就是争议的问题了。但是现有的规则是，把大部分征税权放在居民国，而不是来源国。但是对于发达国家和发展中国家来说，发达国家在全世界肯定有更多投资，很多情况下是投到发展中国家。那发展中国家如果把更多的征税权都让给居民国的话，发展中国家就无税可收了。当然，国与国之间会有很多税收协定，会对税收居民、交易行为等有更具体的规定。所以可想而知，跨国经营活动涉及很多复杂问题。

> **改译 3**：通过实体税法规则改革，遏制税基侵蚀和利润转移造成的避税行为（下称"反/应对 BEPS"的税制），并未从宏观/整体上改变居民地征税权与来源地征税权的分配问题。（李）

王：税基侵蚀和利润转移，可以理解为一种避税行为，所以是否可以考虑删去？还有，此处李延雷老师在讲座中提到，"应对"更合适一些，不一定所有 anti 都要翻译成"反"。

> **改译 4**：通过实体税法规则改革，遏制税基侵蚀和利润转移避税行为（下称"应对 BEPS"的税制），并未从整体上改变居民地与来源地征税权的分配问题。（王）

李：省略没问题。但也可以不省略，从别的角度简化，比如不翻译 BEPS，因为之前已经出现过。括号中的 anti-BEPS rules 也可以省略。因为这个简称并不常用，28 页的文章中，总共才出现两次。

> **建议译法**：通过实质性规则改革，遏制基于 BEPS 的避税行为，并未从整体上改变居民地与来源地征税权的分配问题。（李）

7

> **原文**：In the area of transfer pricing, in particular, the final BEPS report appears to have fallen short of the expectations raised by many commentators and by countries such as China and India, since the United States was quick to take this off the agenda.
>
> **原译**：特别是在转让定价方面，由于美国迅速将居住国与来源国征税权问题撤下讨论议程，因此 BEPS 最终报告似乎没有达到很多评论员以及中国和印度等国的预期。（雷）
>
> **改译 1**：特别是在转让定价方面，由于美国迅速将该议题撤下议程，BEPS 最终报告似乎没有达到很多评论家以及中国和印度等国的预期。（李）

李：纵观全文以及 BEPS 行动计划 8 至 10，转让定价是一个核心词。转让定价就是指关联方之间，利用各地区的利率和税收政策的差异，实现避税。转让定价是跨国企业避税的一种方式。

雷：this 指代 transfer pricing。什么是转让定价？转让定价就是关联方之间交易的定价。关联方就是有利益关系的两方。关联方之间的定价就叫转让定价。转让定价在国际税收领域有什么问题呢？就是转让定价的利润，更多是放在哪一方。比如说，美国有一家公司在中国卖东西。它的成本定多少，售价定多少，这些都是关联方交易中颇有争议的问题。现在 BEPS 报告类似于一个国际规则参考。甚至在欧洲很多国家，会把 BEPS 报告当做自己国家规则的一部分，参照 BEPS 税收立法，管理本国税收征管。所以，这句话的意思是，目前 BEPS 报告，并没有明确划分在居民国和来源国之间的征税权问题。为什么提到 commentators 呢？如果你知道 OECD 立法的过程的话，你就知道作者想表达的含义了。commentators 在这里也不是随便说的，它涉及很多 civil society。有一些欧洲和美国的 civil society，提倡的观点对发展中国家和正在崛起的国家来说，是非常有利的。反之，这些观点很不利于发达国家，在很多发达国家看来比较极端。中印提出的转让定价规则和传统的转让定价规则相比，还是有很大区别的。所以，以中国为首的这些国家，包括 civil society 声音是很强烈的，但是最终的报告并没有体现出他们的意愿。因为美国很快就把这些问题从日程下撤下来了。美国在 OECD 决策过程中，绝对是举足轻重的力量。

王：课后与李延雷讨论为什么 United States was quick to take this off the agenda。我们猜测，transfer pricing 背后涉及国家间的博弈，因此，有可能议题还没完全形成，就可能被撤了下来。

> 改译2：尤其在转让定价方面/领域，由于很多意见反馈方以及包括中国和印度在内的一些国家的参与大大提升了大家对相关最终报告内容的期待。但由于美国很快便将该议题从议程上拿下，最终报告（至少）从形式上来看并没有达到大家那么高的预期（的结果）。（雷）

雷：transfer pricing 一定要翻译成"转让定价"，不是"转移定价"。因为"转移定价"这种表达受日本语影响比较多。final BEPS report 不是指所有行动的最终报告，而是仅涉及转让定价的 BEPS 8—10 三项行动共享的一份报告（见 www.oecd.org/tax/beps/beps-actions.htm）。所以用的是单数 the report。appears to have fallen short of the expectations 的意思是，最终报告的基调和用词，并没有像当初讨论中那么过激。

李：延雷的修改过于自由。除非译者有充分信心和最终决定权，否则，不宜这么自由。在了解背景的前提下，口译可以这么翻译。

> 改译3：尤其在转让定价方面/领域，BEPS 的最终报告似乎没有满足很多意见反馈方以及中印等国的期待，原因是美国很快便将该议题从议程上拿下。（李）

王：还没有成为一项"议题"。

> **改译 4**：尤其在转让定价方面，BEPS 的最终报告似乎没有满足很多意见反馈方以及中印等国的期待，原因是美国很快便将该计划从议程上拿下。（王）
>
> **建议译法**：尤其在转让定价方面，BEPS 的最终报告似乎没有满足很多意见反馈方以及中印等国的期待，原因是美国很快便将这个问题从议程上拿下。（李）

8

> **原文**：As such, if the core of transfer pricing rules remains unchanged under the arm's length principle, what are countries to do with the abundant information and CbCRs they will receive?
>
> **原译**：同样，如果转让定价规则的核心在独立交易原则之下保持不变，各国接收的大量信息和国别报告对他们而言有什么用呢？

王："What am I to do?" is roughly equivalent to "What should I do about this?" where "this" is some kind of problem you have, specifics to be understood from context. It is not commonly used anymore, but will be understood by native speakers.

> **改译 1**：这样，如果独立交易原则下的核心转让定价规则保持不变，各国将如何使用收到的大量信息和国别报告？（李）

雷：transfer pricing rules under the arm's length principle 应当视为一个整体。原文把 remains unchanged 提前了，否则这句话头重脚轻。我们可以调换一下语法结构，改为：<u>if the core</u> of transfer pricing rules under the arm's length principle <u>remains unchanged</u>。这样更易于理解。

雷：转让定价的核心规则，其实就是英文中的 arm's length principle，或者独立交易原则。独立交易原则是什么概念呢？比如我们作为两个关联方，虽然我们之间有交易，但是我们不要抱在一起，以示公允。在 BEPS（BEPS

视情况理解为"反 BEPS 项目")出现之前,独立交易原则实际上是国际规则在转让定价领域最明显的体现。在 BEPS 讨论之初,各国都在讨论,是否要改变这个基石。最后的决定是维持这个基石。

这句话的意思是,如果我们还坚持独立交易原则,各个国家会如何处理、使用富余信息?CbCR 是指 country-by-country reporting。这个报告要套用 BEPS 行动计划 13 提供的国际规则模板,涉及经营上和财务上的关键数据。除了 CbCR 之外,行动计划 13 还规定要披露有关跨国公司关联交易中的一系列问题,这就是所谓 abundant information。

作者为什么要说,如果转让定价核心不变(即独立交易原则不变),要担心如何处理、使用这些富余信息呢?"What are countries to do with the abundant information and CbCRs they will receive?" 这里涉及一个背景知识。在探讨行动计划 13 时,跨国公司、咨询机构代表的问题是,现在信息模板是使用了另外一个概念,就是公式分配法(formulary apportionment approaches)。公式分配法和独立交易原则是两个并行概念。历史上,人们一直争论关联交易定价和征税权划定,到底是应该使用什么工具。有一派说用独立交易原则,有一派说用公式分配法。如果大家阅读转让定价相关材料,有一章专门讨论这两种方法的优劣。当然最后是把公式分配法毙掉了。但是,直到现在,还有很多跨国公司担心,如果一些国家税务局在拿到国别报告以后,在独立交易的原则下(或者打着独立交易的旗号),仍旧采用公式分配法去征税,那么就会出现双重征税的问题,这样他们就会损失大笔利润。

杨昉:CFA 课程中对 arm's length principle 的解释是:想象两个人在交易,中间有一臂之隔,那么这样的交易有以下三个条件:1. 信息透明,因为双方可以相互看到对方;2. 交易双方有距离,意味着关系不是特别近,非内部交易;3. 交易价格是市场承认的公允价格。所以 arm's length principle 是一个特别形象的说法。

王:商务部网站对 arms' length principle 的处理方式:

三、欧盟处罚苹果"动了美国的奶酪"。美国批评欧盟处罚苹果的做法,认为这"不公平"。美方曾警告,如果欧方执意处罚苹果,美方将以某种方式还击。美方称，欧委会正把自己变成一个"超国家的税务机构"，威胁到 OECD "税基侵蚀和利润转移项目"各方达成的"正常交易原则"共识（arm's-length principle），即一家跨国公司分布在不同国家的子机构向内部流通产品和服务所收取的价格。美国真正担心的是，由于美国税法允许延期纳税，美国企业留在海外的利润总额超过 2 万亿美元，面对这块肥肉，欧盟也想分一份。美国政策制订者们认为，只有美国联邦政府才有权在这笔巨额利润返还美国时征税。布鲁塞尔处罚苹果的决定会让美国各派政治力量搁置税法改革分歧，一致同意降低企业海外利润返还税率，以免让欧盟从中渔利。

http://www.mofcom.gov.cn/article/i/jyjl/m/201609/20160901394156.shtml

FT 中文网也将其处理为"正常交易原则"：

国际上公认的利润分配原则是"正常交易原则"（arm's-length principle）。该原则要求企业内部的跨国转让须采用竞争市场条件下形成的价格。但品牌产品或专利药不可能存在竞争市场：这就是为何上述交易对所有者来说是有利可图的。在实践中，正常交易定价是以自我作为参照。

http://www.ftchinese.com/story/001039398

王：李延雷老师在这里更倾向使用"独立交易原则"。此处大家处理成"独立交易原则"和"正常交易原则"均可。

> 改译2：在这种情况下，如果转让定价规则的核心在独立交易原则下仍然保持不变，对于将来会收到的大量信息和国别报告的内容，相关国家能将如何使用呢？（雷）

李：明确了独立交易原则和转让定价之间的关系。原则是宏观的，规则是具体的。作为补充，转让定价遵循独立交易原则，不是说企业自愿决定遵守这个原则，是税务局要求的。不这样做，要受处罚。从企业的利益来看，他们才不想遵守这个原则。他们总想通过内部定价，把利润留给税收低的地方。但尽管税务局要求很严，他们还是钻空子。这就是为什么反复强调适用独立交易原则。这里是一些资料：

Regulations on transfer pricing ensure the fairness and accuracy of transfer pricing among related entities. Regulations enforce an arm's length transaction rule that states that companies must establish pricing based on similar transactions done between unrelated parties.

Transfer Pricing Documentation

Transfer pricing is closely monitored within a company's financial reporting and requires strict documentation that is included in financial reporting documents for auditors and regulators. This documentation is closely scrutinized. If inappropriately documented, it can lead to added expenses for the company in the form of added taxation or restatement fees. These prices are closely checked for accuracy to ensure that profits are booked appropriately within arm's length pricing methods and associated taxes are paid accordingly.

https://www.investopedia.com/terms/t/transferprice.asp

近日，澳大利亚助理财政部部长大卫·布莱伯利称，谷歌公司2011年在澳大利亚的收入超过11亿澳元，但谷歌将其收入转至税率较低的爱尔兰及荷兰分公司，再转到百慕大群岛。结果是，谷歌在澳大利亚仅缴税7.4176万澳元，远低于澳大利亚企业所得税税率要求的30%。布莱伯利的言外之意就是：谷歌在澳大利亚挣大钱，却在百慕大付小费。

http://world.people.com.cn/n/2012/1128/c57507-19721439.html

像这样的例子，肯定是没有遵循所谓"独立交易原则"。

建议译法：鉴于此，如果独立交易原则指导下的核心转让定价规则维持不变，那么各国将如何处理收到的海量信息和国别报告？（李）

9

原　文：Will the granular information on GVCs of MNEs reveal BEPS risks and lead to grounded assessments which could not have occurred in the past?
原　译：有关跨国企业全球价值链的琐碎信息，是否会揭露BEPS风险，并开始为评估提供依据？（费）

王：What is granular information？

Best Answer: The opposite of "looking at it from 30,000 feet". As you delve into an analysis, people might say, "Let's get more granularity." So, *it means to get more specific detail - as compared to "getting the whole picture".*

https://answers.yahoo.com/question/index?qid=20100917020539AAGMZxr

雷：the granular information on GVCs 是指跨国公司在主体文档里面，向税局披露很多详细的经营、税务、交易信息。那这时候税局是否会简单、粗暴地判定跨国公司的经营活动和应缴纳税务呢？这里的 grounded assessment 其实就是说，这些税局可能会 ground their assessment based on such information。虽然这些信息会暴露出跨国公司一些不当行为，但是，这些不当行为不一定是跨国公司有意为之，而是历史原因。"Will the granular information on GVCs of MNEs reveal BEPS risks and lead to grounded assessments which could not have occurred in the past?" 这句话是说，税局收到大量信息以后，会怎么用的问题。

王：What is GVC? 在原报告第三页可以找到答案：

Asian growth is therefore fueled by flows of FDI, which fostered the insertion of Asian firms in highly sophisticated *global value chains (GVCs)* often managed by MNEs from developed countries (most notably from the U.S.).

王：What is MNEs？在原报告第二页的注释二中可以找到答案：

See UNCTAD WIR2015, Op. Cit. fn. 1 supra. Developing Asia became the world's largest investor in 2014, as *Multinational Enterprises (MNEs)* from the region increased their investments abroad by 29% to reach a staggering USD 432 billion (out of USD 468 billion invested by MNEs from all developing economies). In comparison, outflows from European countries were virtually unchanged at USD 316 billion in 2014, whereas outward investment by U.S. MNEs increased by 2.6% to USD 336.9 billion.

"多国企业"还是"跨国企业"？这里是一点资料：

从经济文献看，对于从事跨国生产经营活动的经济组织有许多各式各样的名称，例如：跨国公司或跨国企业（Transnational Corporations or Enterprises，简称 TNC 或 TNE）、多国公司或多国企业（Multinational Corporations or Enterprises，简称 MNC 或 MNE）、国际公司或国际企业（International Corporations）、超国家公司或企业（Supernational Corporations or Enterprises）、环球公司或企业（Global Corporations or Enterprises）等，其中使用最为普遍的是多国公司与跨国公司。1972 年 7 月 28 日，联合国经济与社会理事会通过决议，由联合国秘书长指定一个知名人士小组研究"多国公司的作用及其对发展过程，尤其是发展中国家的发展过程和国际关系的影响"，在知名人士小组 1973 年提交的题为《多国公司对发展和国际关系的影响》的报告中使用的是"多国公司"。但是在 1974 年 8 月 2 日联合国经社理事会第 57 届会议上讨论知名人士小组报告时，一些代表尤其是拉美国家代表提出，在拉美国家，"多国公司"特指那些在安第斯条约组织（The Andean Group）帮助下由该组织成员共同创立与经营的公司；而那些主要以一国为基地，从事跨国生产经营活动的公司应称为"跨国公司"。联合国经社理事会采纳了上述建议，并决定将各种名称统一为"跨国公司"，并设立政府间的跨国公司委员会和跨国公司中心，作为永久性机构。自此，联合国的有关文件与出版物都统一使用"跨国公司"名称。

http://course.shufe.edu.cn/gjmyx/dzjc/chapter9/1_1.htm

可见这些名称区分不大。但维基百科认为不同名称有些微区别。感兴趣者可以调查。

改译 1：一种可能是，各国可以史无前例地利用有关跨国企业全球价值链的具体信息，发现 BEPS 风险，并据此对这些风险进行评估。（李）
改译 2：有关跨国企业全球价值链的细节信息是否会暴露出 BEPS 风险，并导致据此作出应纳税情况的判定？（雷）
改译 3：有关跨国企业全球价值链的细节信息是否会暴露出 BEPS 风险，并导致各国据此作出跨国企业应纳税款的判定？（李）
改译 4：有关跨国企业全球价值链的细节信息，是否会暴露出 BEPS 风险，让各国据此对跨国企业应纳税款，作出以前无法实现的判定？（王）

李："暴露"不如"揭示"中性。

建议译法：有关跨国企业全球价值链的这些细节信息，是会揭示 BEPS 风险，让各国据此对跨国企业应纳税款，作出以前无法作出的判定？（李）

10

原文：Or will the scrutiny of massive MNE data simply reveal the complex (and still legitimate) operation of the arm's length principle of transfer pricing under the functionally separate legal entity approach?

原译：或者说，采用"功能上为独立实体"方法，审查大量跨国公司数据，能否彻底揭露在转让定价中复杂地（但仍合理的）独立交易原则操作情况？（雷）

改译 1：另一种可能是，各国仅仅利用大量的跨国公司数据，揭示在"功能上为独立实体"这一方法指导下，转让定价中独立交易原则复杂（但仍旧合理的）运作情况？（李）

李：前一句的 granular information 和后一句的 massive MNE data 意思相同，都可以概括为"这么多信息"。两句话的意思是：税务局利用这么多信息会发现跨国公司避税的蛛丝马迹（从而采取措施），还是只能望洋兴叹（独立交易原则操作起来水真深啊！），但什么也做不了（人家的避税操作都合法啊！）？ Simply is used for emphasizing that what you are saying is *nothing more than* what you say it is: The reason we didn't come was simply because of the rain.

李：legitimate 更多的是指合理性。所谓合法，是指符合自然法。不是制定法。

改译 2：或者也可能对跨国公司大量数据的深度审阅（反而）让人们认识到对于功能相对独立的法人实体，转让定价独立交易原则的运用仍然合法，但却十分复杂？（雷）

雷：BEPS 实际上有 15 项行动计划。其中行动计划 7 涉及常设机构问题。常设机构是一个非常复杂的概念。在常设机构概念中，有 functionally separate legal entity approach 这种方法，和转让定价有密切相关。它意思是，你的每一个法人都是独立的，各有各的功能。这是转让定价中经常采用的一种降低合规风险的手段，决定生产商是完全不承担研发失败的后果，还是承担一部分风险。虽然很多中国企业强调全产业链，但是往往很高端的企业在功能上却是割裂的，也就是从转让定价的角度，它的是 functionally separate 的。研发就是做研发，不做技术，分门别类。这句话的说的是，采取按独立实体征税的方法，规则要怎么运用的问题。因为按照单一功能，虽然很容易确定规则，但是会出现利润划分问题。

雷：税局可能会简单判定跨国公司在某国的税收。但是跨国公司的经营活动比较复杂，or 在这里表现出作者喜忧参半的意思，传达作者复杂的心情，是笔触上的小小转折。如果各国税局能分析这些具体、充足的信息，那税局是否可以更理解跨国公司，知道跨国公司的运作非常复杂，进而简单地做出判定（前面所指的 grounded assessment）。simply 改译为"反而"，但在字面上讲是"仅仅"。能否翻译成"反而"，取决于你对这句话的理解和把握。

李：我和延雷的理解有所不同。我仍然认为 or 表示两种情况取其一。两句话的意思概括起来，就是：这么多信息可能有用，也可能无用。当然，我对里面涉及的专业知识仍然一知半解，也许我的理解不对。

如果把 or 前后两句合并起来翻译，可以译为：有关跨国企业全球价值链的这些细节信息，是会揭示 BEPS 风险，提醒各国对相关风险作出之前无法做到的知情判断，还是仅仅显示会显示在采用独立实体征税法的背景下，转让定价的独立交易原则运作起来十分复杂（但仍然合法）？

> **建议译法**：或者，对跨国公司大量数据的审核，可能仅仅揭示在采用独立实体征税法的背景下，转让定价的独立交易原则运作起来十分复杂（但仍然合法）？（李）

11

> 原文：Therein lie some of the new perils that are expected to surface along the Silk Road.
> 原译：这其中的一些新危险，可能出现在一带一路沿线。（费）
> 改译：这里面就存在一些可能在"一带一路"沿线国家出现的新危险。（李）

李：therein 是指上一段叙述的各个方面，不必明确翻译出来。

雷：最早 BEPS 成员国都是发达国家。我们国家至今不是 OECD 的正式成员。从商业角度，如果不是 OECD 成员，无法参与制定很多国际规则。BEPS 项目是 OECD 携手 G20 发起的，中印等金砖国家属于 G20，所以在 BEPS 规则制定中很活跃。因为他们意识到，一定要积极参与规则制定。但是，这些国家的税收制度比较落后，在实际操作中可能存在的危机，他们却没有意识到。

> 建议译法：这里面就存在一些可能会在"一带一路"沿线国家出现的新风险。（雷）

12

> 原文：Some of the potential pitfalls that can emerge in Asia post-BEPS pertain to the risk of uncoordinated and unilateral over-implementation of what may be interpreted as anti-BEPS measures, particularly in the area of transfer pricing and tax treaty entitlement.
> 原译：在亚洲后 BEPS 时代，涉及的风险是不协调或单方面过度实施可能被解释为反 BEPS 的措施，尤其是在转让定价和税收协定待遇方面。
> 改译1：在亚洲后 BEPS 时代，一些潜在陷阱就会显露出来，包括缺乏协调或单方面过度实施所谓的反 BEPS 措施，尤其是在转让定价和税收协定待遇方面。（王）

> **改译 2**：在后 BEPS 时代，亚洲可能出现的陷阱包括缺乏协调或单方面过度实施所谓的反 BEPS 措施，尤其是在转让定价和税收条约待遇方面。（李）
>
> **改译 3**：在后 BEPS 时代，亚洲可能会出现的一些潜在误区，包括缺乏协调或单方面过度实施所谓应对 BEPS 的措施，尤其是在转让定价和税收协定待遇享受方面。（雷）
>
> **改译 4**：在后 BEPS 时代，亚洲可能会出现一些潜在误区，包括缺乏协调或单方面过度实施所谓应对 BEPS 的措施，尤其是在转让定价和享受税收协定待遇方面。（李）

王：potentail pitfalls 是否可以处理为"潜在隐患"？我觉得也不能单单理解为"误区"。"误区"是表象，作者所要强调的是误区带来的"隐患"。

> **改译 5**：在后 BEPS 时代，亚洲可能会出现一些潜在隐患，包括缺乏协调或单方面过度实施所谓应对 BEPS 的措施，尤其是在转让定价和享受税收协定待遇方面。（王）

陈西金燕：觉得"潜在"和"隐患"有些重复，查了一下 potential 和 pitfall 的英英释义如下：

potential: having or showing the capacity to become or develop into something in the future;

pitfall: a hidden or unsuspected danger or difficulty.

个人认为，译文中的"会"就可以表达 potential 的意思了，pitfall 就是"隐患"。

建议译为"在后 BEPS 时代，亚洲可能会出现一些隐患……"。

另外，如果不看原文，不太理解"缺乏协调"是什么意思。查了一下英英释义，如下：

uncoordinated: badly organized.

个人认为意思就是：没有条理、紊乱。

建议译为"包括紊乱或单方面地过度实施所谓应对 BEPS 的措施……"

王：对于第一个问题，我非常同意你的分析，确实有些重复。对于第二个问题，个人认为"紊乱"这个词不符合这篇文章的语境。我去查了一下"紊乱"的中文释义：

紊乱：1. 杂乱新陈代谢紊乱；2. 纷乱秩序紊乱

看这个释义，我认为"紊乱"更多指人身体代谢或者是国家/社会秩序混乱。我去中文语料库里做了进一步确认：

- 各种染色体的结构一旦出现一些较小的不平衡，就可能引起性功能紊乱。

青年"病态人格"种种，孙晓明，1985-5-1；
《青年一代》，青年一代杂志社

- 此在世界各国已成惯例，按中国目前社会之紊乱情形，由政府设立尤属必要。

我国师范教育之危机及其改革刍议，李淑敏，1933-12-18，
国闻周报，国闻周报社。

我理解的 uncoordinated 还是"不协调"的意思，就是各国为应对 BEPS 所采取措施之间的不协调。所以，我还是觉得原译更好些。但是我也不是特别满意目前的译法，只能说可以接受。如果有新的想法了，我们可以继续讨论。

陈西：看了你的分析和查证，我也认为"紊乱"这个词的确欠妥。

对于"uncoordinated"这个词，我还是认为译为"不协调"属于有些刻板的对应，算是背单词的后遗症。

英英释义中，uncoordinated 有两个意思：

1. badly organized：我认为具体的译法要分析不同的语境，有不同的处理方法。Mac 自带的英汉词典里译为"考虑不周"一般搭配 approach, effort, service。我认为还是比较符合原文语境的。

2. (of a person or their movements) clumsy: Mac 的英汉词典译为"笨拙的、不协调的"。一般形容的是 person, movement, action。不太符合原文语境。

当然，"协调"这个词也常用于表示"正确处理组织内外关系，为组

织正常运作创造良好的条件和环境，促进组织目标的实现。"（来自百度百科释义）

百度百科中的搭配例句有：色彩协调；各部门的发展必须互相协调；协调产销关系等。

看这些例句，还是觉得都不太适合原文的内容，总是差着那么一点。

这么分析下来，我觉得译文处理为"包括考虑不周或单方面过度实施所谓应对 BEPS 的措施……"更合适。

题外话，我觉得 coordinate 与协调的对应属于翻译腔成功入侵规范汉语的一个例子。苏阳老师的译法其实完全没问题，是我有些较真了，觉得也许有比这个简单对应更贴合原文、能更好达意的处理方法。

王：谢谢你的建议，推动我继续思考这个问题。我先去 Merriam-Webster 查了 uncoordinated 的意思：

Definition of uncoordinated: lacking coordination: not coordinated: such as
a: not able to move different parts of the body together well or easily

… I'm every bit as clumsy and uncoordinated on a virtual skateboard as I would be on a real one—Peter Cohen

b: not characterized by smoothness or regularity

… the uncoordinated twitching of a heart no longer able to beat — Jerry Adler

jerky uncoordinated movements

c: *not well organized*

我同意学姐的看法，我也认为文中 uncoordinated 是指 not well organised。但是，我对中文释义"考虑不周"有些疑问。我的理解是，"考虑不周"多指轻虑浅谋、计划不周密、不全面。使用"考虑不周"时的行为主体多为单一个人（或团体）。比如说："如有考虑不周之处，还请多多包涵"。而原文是 uncoordinated and unilateral over-implementation of what may be interpreted as anti-BEPS measures。从语法角度看，uncoordinated 修饰的是 anti-BEPS measures，意指政策不统一、不协调。这个统一、协作问题，就涉及多个行为主体之间的协调，而非仅哪一国考虑不周。进一步查证资料，也可以印证此观点：

The justification for this is straightforward: If each Member State took unilateral and uncoordinated action to fight tax avoidance, especially by taking different approaches to implementing the BEPS recommendations, the internal market would be affected by even more fragmentation and obstacles to cross-border activity. The alignment of the six measures proposed by the Commission with BEPS Actions is thus no accident: the Commission explicitly aims to prevent a "fragmentation of the internal market, which would possibly result from uncoordinated unilateral actions by Member States" with respect to the BEPS project.

http://kluwertaxblog.com/2016/02/05/the-commission-proposal-for-an-anti-beps-directive-some-preliminary-comments/

从上文可以看出，这个 uncoordinated 和 unilateral 是直接相关的，也就是一些成员国可能单边实施所谓的应对 BEPS 措施，但是却没有顾忌到与其他国家的政策、措施整合问题。我也同意学姐的看法，"不协调"确实有些欧化。但是，"不协调"这种用法目前也算是广为接受的欧化表达了。有些欧化表达已积重难返，而且说"不协调"，我想读者可以理解什么意思，所以应该是可以维持原译的；或者我想我们可以适当增译，改为：包括各国政策不统一或单方面过度实施所谓应对 BEPS 的措施……不知学姐觉得如何？

陈西：经过你的分析，我的思路也更清晰了。我之前提出这个疑问主要也是因为在批改作业的时候感觉很多同学直接用"不协调"，但似乎没有真正了解原意和背景，甚至有些用法很僵硬、不自然，并不是参考译文中的那种比较规范、可以接受的表达。我想等最后批改完毕，看情况写进批改总结中，具体举例。

我批改的这个班级只有一位同学没有用"不协调"这个表达，尝试找一个符合语境的其他表达。我个人还是觉得这种译法值得鼓励。对于另一封邮件中苏阳老师提到的对翻译风格不同的学生，我们应该给予不同的建议，我非常赞同，也学到了很多。

改译 6：在后 BEPS 时代，亚洲可能会出现一些隐患，包括缺乏协调或单方面过度实施所谓应对 BEPS 的措施，尤其是在转让定价和享受税收协定待遇方面。（陈西）

李：你们的讨论很有意义。关于 pitfall 和 potential 意思重复问题，同意大家的共识，可以省略"潜在"。但有时在翻译重要文件时，为了不给某些用户抓把柄，我们也不去较真，也会把"潜在"翻译出来。关于"协调"，同意苏阳的分析，可以继续用。"缺乏协调或单方面过度实施"之所以不顺，是因为这个短语拆分开来是"缺乏协调实施"+"单方面过度实施"。前者加一个"地"，改为"缺乏协调地实施"，就会好一些。另外，我也同意陈西所说，同样使用"协调"，有些人把它很好地嵌入了一个句子，有些人却没有做好。

建议译法：在后 BEPS 时代，亚洲可能会出现一些隐患，包括缺乏协调地或单方面过度实施所谓应对 BEPS 的措施，尤其是在转让定价和享受税收协定待遇方面。（李）

还可以改为：……包括在实施所谓应对 BEPS 的措施中缺乏协调或单方面采取过火行动，尤其是在转让定价和享受税收协定待遇方面。

13

原文：The inadvertent enforcement of anti-avoidance or anti-abuse theories that were experimented with in the discussion drafts (and in academia) leading to the final BEPS reports, may overburden tax administrations throughout Asia, and cause a tsunami of litigation with highly uncertain prospects.
原译：BEPS 最终报告的讨论草案（以及学术界）探讨了反避税理论和反滥用理论。如果这些理论执行不力，可能给整个亚洲的税务管理带来过重负担，引发诉讼潮，使前景充满不确定性。（雷）

> **改译 1**：如果实施 BEPS 最终报告的讨论稿（以及学术界）所探讨的反避税和反滥用理论，就可能无意中给整个亚洲的税务机关带来过重负担，引发结果难料的"诉讼海啸"。（李）

雷：anti-avoidance 和 anti-abuse 相当于国际税收领域的兜底条款。这个兜底条款是什么概念呢？我通过规范转让定价的制度或者其他税收制度没法合理征税时，会动用一个看穿你一切、否认你一切的做法。这个 anti-avoidance 还有一个对应术语，GAAR（General Anti-Avoidance Rule）。这一概念是指，如果一个国家认为，我现有的法律没有办法制衡跨国公司的避税行为时，就会启动应急机制或者所谓的兜底条款去征税，否认你的价值。因为税局也清楚，很多跨国公司根据税收制度漏洞制定避税策略，一些税局无法根据现有法规制衡跨国公司避税的架构，所以会制定所谓的兜底条款，即如果我认为你有问题，我就会启动这个兜底机制，去否认你的避税架构，征收我应征收的税费。

inadvertent enforcement 就是比较有深意的用法了，因为作者无法直接明说这些国家在实际操作中潜在的无形危机。中国企业正在大量走出去，如果"一带一路"沿线的国家学习中国这种比较 aggressive 的做法，可能一时得到一点收益，或者征到一点税收，但是中国企业可能在俄罗斯等国受到不公正待遇，面临更大损失。所以在跨境大规模的商业运作中，最让人担心的是税务问题。这也就是后 BEPS 时代可能面临的问题。

> **改译 2**：而对于那些在 BEPS 最终报告定稿前，在征求意见稿以及学术界探讨中出现过的（一般）反避税或反滥用理论，如果不加慎重考虑就加以运用则不仅可能让整个亚洲的税务征管工作不堪重负，而且还可能导致产生海量的（税务）诉讼案件，并且是结果有相当大不确定性的诉讼案件。（雷）

雷：这句话是指双重征税问题。如果适用各种理论，导致跨国公司多缴税，跨国公司就会和税局产生争议，这就会 overburden tax administration。

administration 并不是指税局,而是"税务征管工作",内行人一看这个词就会觉得特别顺畅。tsunami of litigation 是什么意思呢?在中国哪有税局和纳税人对簿公堂呢?但是很多发达国家是有税务法庭的。很多纳税人对税局不服,纳税人可以告税局。税务法庭可以判定,如果税局征税不合理,可以把税款退还纳税人。制度不完善,就会导致双重征税,就会有纳税人和税局对簿公堂。这种情况在 BEPS 之前是没有这么多的。为什么企业要动用这个手段?肯定是因为它有很大负担,才会启动这样的诉讼。换句话说,如果我活不下去,那就无所谓了。with highly uncertain prospects 是指国际税收领域另外一个重要概念,就是不确定性的问题。很多跨国公司最为担心的就是这个不确定性问题。因为即使对簿公堂,跨国公司也不一定可以得到希望的判决。同时,对于税局来说,影响也是消极的。因为税局需要找大量资料证明对跨国公司的判定结果。

> **改译 3**:而对于那些在 BEPS 最终报告定稿前,在征求意见稿以及学术界探讨中出现过的(一般)反避税或反滥用理论,如果不加慎重考虑就加以运用,则不仅可能让整个亚洲的税务征管工作不堪重负,而且还可能导致产生海量的(税务)诉讼案件,而这些案件的结果有相当大不确定性。(李)

王:从表达角度讲,这里句首连用这两个介词短语,是否可以考虑修改一下句式?

> **改译 4**:而在 BEPS 最终报告定稿前,对于在征求意见稿以及学术界探讨中出现过的反避税或反滥用理论,如果不慎重考虑就加以运用,不仅会让整个亚洲的税务征管工作不堪重负,还可能产生海量诉讼案件,而这些案件的结果有相当大不确定性。(王)

李:你提出的问题很好,只是改译还没有避免。

建议译法：在 BEPS 最终报告定稿前，征求意见稿以及学术探讨中曾提出一些反避税或反滥用理论。这些理论如果不慎重考虑就加以运用，不仅会让整个亚洲的税务征管工作不堪重负，还可能产生海量诉讼案件，而这些案件的结果有相当大不确定性。（李）

14

原文：This may be a risky venture for tax administrations to embark on.
原译：这对税务机关而言，可能是一场冒险之旅。（费）

王：数词是否必要？

建议译法：这对税务机关而言，可能是冒险之旅。（李）

15

原文：Going "beyond arm's length" and seeking to unilaterally adopt formulary apportionment results through interpretation of anti-BEPS language or policies, is a danger that could hurt economies in Asia.
原译：越过独立交易原则，力求通过阐释反 BEPS 的语言或政策，单方面采用公式化分配法结果计征所得税，是危险的，会损害亚洲各经济体。（费）
改译 1：超越独立交易原则，通过对反 BEPS 语言或政策的解释，单方面采用公式化分配法是危险的，会损害亚洲各经济体。（李）

雷：seeking to unilaterally adopt formulary apportionment results through interpretation of anti-BEPS language or policies，这里的 results 不是多余的词，而是有特别意思的。这个 formulary appointment 并不指具体结果，而是代表一种理念和方法，这个 results 就是指通过这种理念和方法形成的结果。

> **改译 2**：越过独立交易原则，用所谓的应对 BEPS 的说辞或政策解读来单方面采用公式分配法可能会严重危及亚洲的经济（发展）。（雷）

雷：interpretation of anti-BEPS language or policies 里 interpretation 是指要清楚说明的意思。结合上下文，interpretation 强调主观性，即税局会从它自身国家利益角度，去主观地做一些判定。比如，某些国家说，你这是 BEPS 里面涉及的内容，这种情况是不允许的，所以我们要启动 anti-abuse 和 anti-aovidance 的兜底行动。如果这种情况大量出现会怎么样呢？这里作者用的是 danger 这个词。这种伤害不仅会伤及跨国公司，也会伤害税局。兜底计划仅在无计可施的情况下才能启动，如果你频繁启动，不仅引发诉讼海啸，跨国公司也可能不在这个国家做生意了。同样地，如果别国对中国海外公司频繁启动这种兜底行动，那中国也没得利润可图了。这会影响双向的流动，对谁都不好。最后，economies 指的是经济的发展，而不是字面上对"经济"的危及。老外的意思是说，中国再这样发展下去，经济会成问题。论文开篇就讲到，双向的流动，对双方国家都是好的。但是如果滥用避税规则，穷国永远跳不出穷国的圈子。hurt 这个词很简单，但是这种伤痛是很痛很痛的。

> **改译 3**：越过独立交易原则，用所谓的应对 BEPS 的说辞或政策解读来单方面采用公式分配法可能会严重危及亚洲的经济发展。（李）

王：原文是 economies，而非 economy。

> **改译 4**：越过独立交易原则，通过解读所谓的应对 BEPS 的说辞或政策，单方面采用公式分配法，结果可能会严重危及亚洲的经济体。（王）
> **建议译法**：超越独立交易原则，通过解读应对 BEPS 的表述或政策，单方面采用公式分配法计算得出的结果，可能会严重危及亚洲的经济体。（李）

16

> **原文**：Quite strikingly, China is now also adopting an innovative Other Method, the "Value Contribution Apportionment Method" (VCAM) ...
>
> **原译**：值得注意的是，中国还在采取创新性的"其他方法"，即"价值贡献分配法"。（费）

雷：strikingly 是指吸人眼球的意思，比如 strikingly tall。所以这个词是有很深刻的含义的。字面上可以处理为"值得注意的"。那为什么人家会说 strikingly？因为中国现在采用所谓的"其他方法"，虽然叫 innovative，但是很多人都不认可。

王：如下图信息可知，中国并没有全盘采用 BEPS 提案，而是有选择地采纳：

> conducted. On October 5 2015 the OECD publicly released its 2015 Deliverables under the BEPS initiative, corresponding to the original 15 actions of the 2013 BEPS Action Plan work programme and following the 2014 Deliverables. Beyond simply implementing these deliverables, China tends to pursue a selective approach to the BEPS measures, leveraging BEPS guidance to apply a unilateral approach to key issues, a trend we already remarked upon in last year's edition of *China Looking Ahead*.
>
> That China adopts such a selective approach has been confirmed by the contents of the long-awaited public discussion draft guidance on the implementation of 'Special Tax Adjustments' (the Draft), released by China's State Administration of Taxation (SAT) on September 17 2015. The Draft explains that China will not adopt all BEPS proposals and will naturally tailor them to China's circumstances.

进一步阅读，得知 Other Method 指的是 Other Transfer Pricing Method。也就是其他转让定价方法。

> **Value contribution apportionment method**
>
> The Draft introduces the VCAM as one among the 'Other TP Methods'. Under this method MNE profits are to be allocated across the value chain based on analysis of how value creating contributions have been made to group profits, with reference being made to assets, costs, sales and number of employees. It is stated to be appropriate to use where comparability information is difficult to obtain and where, at the same time, the consolidated profit for the MNE and value creating factor contributions can be reasonably determined.

With the explicit introduction of the new VCM method, it remains to be seen whether the Chinese tax authorities will be even more inclined to dismiss potential comparables, on grounds of LSAs, local intangibles or other factors, and use the absence of comparables to push in the direction of using this new method.

In addition to VCM, the value chain analysis requested in the TP documentation local file is further evidence of SAT's ardent support for the value chain theory. Moreover, the Draft requests that, regardless of the TP method selected, the enterprise shall state its contribution to the overall profit or residual profit of the group in the local file documentation.

http://www.internationaltaxreview.com/Article/3511707/Chinas-new-transfer-pricing-guidelines-and-BEPS.html

　　这就引发一个问题：转让定价的方法都有哪些？经调查，一共有五大转让定价方法。由下方资料可知，"其他方法"即指交易净利润法和利润分割法，主要考查关联企业间待定交易所产生的利润，是以利润为基础的方法：

> ■ 转让定价就是指关联企业之间就一项关联交易进行定价，包括有形资产的购销、转让和使用、无形资产的转让和使用、融通资金以及提供劳务等。根据我国转让定价税收法律法规及《OECD转让定价指南》的规定，适用于公平交易原则的主要转让定价方法包括：可比非受控价格法，再销售价格法，成本加成法，交易净利润法，利润分割法。前三种方法属于传统交易方法，以交易价格为基础，后两种方法在《OECD 转让定价指南》中属于"其他方法"，主要考察关联企业间特定交易所产生的利润，是以利润为基础的方法。

　　由此可知，VCAM 指的应该就是利润分割法的一种。但是利润分割法的英文缩写是 PSM，所以要继续查 VCAM 是什么。查证可知，利润分割法包含两种方法：贡献利润分割法及剩余利润分割法。贡献法是《OECD 转让定价指南》所讨论的第一种具体的利润分割方法。指南对该方法的定义为：根据各关联企业所履行的职能的相对价值，并尽量参考外部市场上独立企业之间在类似情况下如何分配的做法，将从关联交易所获得的总利润在关联各方之间进行分配。剩余法对关联交易利润的分割采取两个阶段，即基本利润分割阶段和剩余利润分割阶段。在有形财产的交易或服务中，如果涉及具有价值的无形资产，那么在该交易的总利润中有一部分是可归属于有形财产或服务的基本利润，另一部分是剩余的可归属于无形资产的利润。第一阶段的分割是对可归属于有形财产交易的基本利润的分割，使足够的利润被分配给关联各方以弥补其成本并提供与其从事的基本活动相称的报酬；分割的第二阶段是对可归属于无形资产的剩余利润的分割，通常以无形资产的成本为依据。

https://wenku.baidu.com/view/a9894e5f65ce0508773213dd.html

雷：VCAM 这里面用的一些方法，就是公式分配法。所以中国是打着独立交易原则，行公式分配法之实，这是很多老外的看法，所以作者用 strikingly。利润分配为什么重要呢？跨国公司在很多地方都有经营，向跨国公司征税首先要思考这个公司有多少利润可提。对于税局，他会考虑跨国公司的利润会怎么分配。按照 VCAM 分配就是指按照对价值创造的贡献分配。比如说，一个美国的跨国公司在中国有研发中心。这个研发中心在别人眼中可能看似很重要，比如有 300 人的研发队伍，对美国集团公司非常重要。中国可能这么看。但是对于美国的集团来说，300 人研发队伍不算什么，我这边有系统架构师，搞全球突破性的研发、创发系统，而中国业务只是一小部分。这个 argument 会一致持续下去。这里面说到 value contribution，contribution 不是一个简单的概念，它还涉及 assests、costs、sales、employees，有很多细分的方法论和体系可用来证明 contribution 有多少、怎么量化。所以下文才会提到"资产、成本、销售和员工等因素"；这就回到刚才的 CbCR 国别报告。如果你做翻译都没有看过 CbCR 的话（BEPS Action Plan 行动 13 附录里面都是有的），那是不行的。里面横行、纵行都会涉及 assests 和 costs 等。老外认为，中国现在就在使用公式分配法。

> 改译：值得注意的是，中国也在创新性地采取"其他方法"，即"价值贡献分配法"。（雷）
> 建议译法：值得注意的是，中国还在创新性地采用"其他方法"，即"价值贡献分配法"。（王）

李："也"建议还原为原译的"还"。上一段说中国采取了什么措施，这一段说中国"还"采取了什么措施。如果前一段说外国采取了一项措施，这一段可以说"中国'也'采取了这项措施。"

17

原文:... under which "MNE profits are to be allocated across the value chain based on analysis of how value creating contributions have been made to group profits, with reference being made to assets, costs, sales and employees."
原译:该方法指的是通过分析价值创造因素对跨国集团利润的贡献,在价值链上分配跨国企业利润,分配时考虑资产、成本、销售和员工等因素。(费)
改译:按照该方法,跨国公司在价值链上的利润是考虑资产、成本、销售和员工等因素,按照价值创造因素对跨国集团利润的贡献来进行分配。(雷)

王:此句是直接引用。考虑到"价值贡献分配法"是中国提出的方法,我也认为可以直接引用。以下是李演演同学找到的国税总局的说法:

"价值贡献分配法通过分析价值创造因素对跨国集团利润的贡献,将其合并利润在位于不同国家的关联企业之间进行分配。分配时应当考虑与价值贡献相关的资产、成本、费用、销售收入、员工人数等某一个或者某组要素组合。"

价值贡献分配法通常适用于难以获取可比交易信息但能合理确定合并利润以及价值创造因素贡献的交易。

http://hd.chinatax.gov.cn/hudong/noticedetail.do?noticeid=577376

建议译法:按照该方法,"跨国公司在价值链上的利润分配,以分析价值创造对跨国集团利润的贡献为依据,并参考资产、成本、销售和员工等因素。"(王)

18

原文:Note, BEPS Actions 8–10 indicate "DEMPE" (Development, Enhancement, Maintenance, Protection and Exploitation) as the standard to assess value creation pertaining to intangibles, as substantive activities that would allow the recognition of intangible ownership and control over risk.

> **原译**：注意，BEPS 第 8—10 项行动计划指出，DEMPE（开发、提升、维护、保护和应用）是评价无形资产价值创造的标准，是确认无形资产所有权和风险控制的实质性活动。（费）
>
> **改译 1**：请注意，BEPS 第 8—10 项行动指出评价无形资产价值创造的标准为 DEMPE（后续开发、价值提升、维护、保护和应用），该标准是用以确认无形资产所有权和风险控制的实质性活动。（李）

李：原译意思不错。改译 1 把重心后移。请延雷确认，第二个 as 是"因为"还是"正如……"。我理解为后者。

雷：这句话容易产生误解，要再讲一下。这里的 as 不是"因为"，而是"正如"的意思，也就是说前后在概念上是很类似的。substantive 就是开头讲的实质性概念。意思是，如果你有实质性的活动，我就可以确认无形资产所有权的所在地和对风险的控制。……这个实质性的活动是指什么呢？比如说，你在中国的公司是不是就是一家皮包公司？如果你公司没有人，只有一个注册地址，或者公司人很少，就不存在 substantive activities。只有你有几十人、上百人，有正规的管理和运作，这才叫有 substantive activities。比如说一家跨国公司在中国有 300 人的研发团队，中国会认为，这家公司在中国是有实质活动的，而不是外包式、合约式的活动。中国认为，这家公司是创造无形资产的经济所有权。只要中国认定这家公司有经济所有权，你公司也承认的话，那中国就要多征税了。然后，control over risk 是在 BEPS 行动计划 8—10 中非常重要的一个概念。就是说，关于对风险的控制，以前有一个手段，就是签一个合同，说由总部承担风险，然后关联方就会说，这个风险是由总部控制的。但实际上风险控制的人员水平、能力、资源都在这家公司，这种情况下，历史上都认定，你如果签一个合同，合同说是由总部控制的，就算总部承担风险；但现在税局越来越多质疑，如果你总部只是签一个合同，什么都不干的话，控制权还是应该在我这边，而不是在总部。所以这个概念是直接跟 substantive activities 挂钩的。substantive activities 如果再做进一步分析的话，就是 DEMPE。它涉及具体的工作，不是空泛的概念。所以 as 意思就是"就像"的概念。

改译 2：请注意，BEPS 行动 8—10 将 DEMPE（开发、提升、维护、保护和应用）视为评估无形资产价值创造的标准，就像通过实质活动才能确认无形资产的所有权和风险的控制权一样。（王）

建议译法：请注意，BEPS 行动 8—10 将 DEMPE（开发、提升、维护、保护和应用）视为评估无形资产价值创造的标准，即用以确认无形资产所有权和风险控制权的实质活动。（李）

19

原文：China is adopting a broader view on intangibles by setting out a "DEMPEP" approach (which adds "promotion" to the definition of activities which entitle returns on intangibles), and expanding the interpretation of Location Specific Advantages (LSAs).

原译：中国对于无形资产采用更广阔的视角，提出 DEMPEP 分析方法（在无形资产收益权认定活动的定义中加入 P 表示"推广"），并扩大对地域性特殊优势的解释。（费）

改译 1：中国以更宏观的视角看待无形资产，提出 DEMPEP 分析方法（在无形资产收益权认定活动的定义中加入 P 表示"推广"），并扩大对地域性特殊优势的解释。（王）

改译 2：中国通过提出 DEMPEP 的分析方法（即在有权获得无形资产回报的活动定义中加入了"推广活动"（P））对无形资产采用了更宽泛的定义，并扩大了对"地域性特殊优势"（LSAs）这一概念的解读。（雷）

雷：这里提到行动计划 8-10 的 DEMPE，这个说法涉及无形资产。无形资产是跨国经营经常涉及的一个概念，也是转让定价领域颇具争议的地方。因为它是无形的，看不见摸不着。而且每一个无形资产不管有多简单、多复杂，基本上都是独一无二的。它的价值可高可低，而且跟它的成本是没有任何关系的。它的价值很难说清楚。比如说可口可乐就值 100 亿美元，但是它能不能值 101 亿呢？没有人能说清楚。世界上最好的估值专家也说不清楚。比如印度说，可口可乐在印度没有价值——尽管他们做了很多推广——但是，美国却认为可口可乐价值连城。这句话是说，国际规则中定了 DEMPE 说法，但是中国要加一个 promotion。promotion 和 enhancement 概念不是很像吗？为什么还要加一个 promotion 呢？这就涉及更深层次的问题。中国有一个成功的案例，而且是双边案例，获得了国外税局的认可，说的是中国可以多获得一块利润，因为中国在这一案例中做了很多 promotion 的工作。这个也是国外税局承认的。所以中国税局非常坚定地在国内法中加入这一条。

然后就是 LSA。如果你做一些 research，就知道这个概念也是这些年在转让定价领域非常火的一个词，但是也没有一个明确的规定，或者可操作的方法。expanding the interpretation of LSA 讲的就是跨国公司的利润在中国应该分配多少，这其实并不是那么清晰的。如果中国税局扩大对 LSA（地域性优势）的解释，但是能不能这么做，要做到什么程度，这是很有争议的。LSA 从逻辑上分为两个概念，一个是 location savings，一个是 market premium。先说 location savings，比如是指你在中国办工厂是不是比美国成本要低？当然现在也有一些争议了。但是传统概念上讲，中国税局会认为，跨国公司在中国建厂，是因为中国成本低。最早是这样，但是后来发生了很大变化。跨国公司在中国开工厂，其实不止看成本这一项。背后有很多复杂的概念，时间关系就不讲了。

再说 Market premium，比如古奇的包，在欧洲卖两万，在中国可能卖五万，中国税局会说，这是因为中国市场特殊因素造成的，因为中国人就愿意掏这么多钱买，或者中国人觉得越贵越好，故意定这么高，这个叫 market premium。这个问题还存在于生产、销售、研发等环节。

comparability 是指可比性，或者可比因素。转让定价中有一个基本概念，就是可比。比如手机最早只有一个牌子。这个手机怎么定价呢？我和你是关联方，你和他是非关联方，我和他也是非关联方，我和你的定价怎么定？我卖给你 100 块，卖给他 100 块，就 OK，这就可以，这叫一视同仁。但是如果我卖给他 100，卖给你 50，这就有问题了。但是你想想，这里的问题是这么简单吗？我跟他可能根本不做生意。他给的条件和工作和你给我的完全不一样，这价钱能一样吗？定价一样吗？这就叫可比。就是说我们做生意的时候，不要光看交易，比如我也卖给你手机了，我也卖给他手机了。这是外行人的看法。内行人的看法是,我卖给你的条件是什么,你做了什么,你投入了什么,动用了什么资产,承担了什么风险。比如说,这个东西我卖给你,卖不出去,你承担所有的风险,和我卖给你,卖不了是你的事,利润会一样吗?如果第三方的交易都有不一样的情况,为什么关联方要一样呢?这就是可比性的问题。比如某产品在中国或者巴西卖得很好,但是在美国可能不好,这个时候是否要适用 market premium 这个概念呢?也是会有争议的地方。

> **改译3**:中国通过提出 DEMPEP 的分析方法(即在有权获得无形资产回报的活动定义中加入了"推广活动"(P)),对无形资产采用了更宽泛的定义,并扩大了对"地域性特殊优势"(LSAs)这一概念的解读。(李)
> **建议译法**:中国对无形资产采用了更宽泛的定义,提出 DEMPEP 分析方法〔即在有权获得无形资产回报的活动定义中加入了"推广活动"(P)〕,并扩大了对"地域性特殊优势"(LSAs)这一概念的解读。(王)

20

> **原文**:... which would reinforce its pre-BEPS view on comparability particularly in respect to market premium, and lead to an ever-increasing use of the Profit Split Method (PSM) post-BEPS as well as the use of the new VCAM.
> **原译**:这将强化前 BEPS 时代关于可比性特别是有关市场溢价的观点,导致更多地使用后 BEPS 时代利润分割法以及新的价值贡献分配法。(费)
> **改译1**:这将强化中国前 BEPS 时代有关可比性(特别是有关市场溢价)的观点,让后 BEPS 时代中利润分割法和新的价值贡献分配法使用数量日益增加。(王)
> **改译2**:这将强化中国在 BEPS 时代之前有关可比性(特别是有关市场溢价)的观点,导致后 BEPS 时代不断扩大使用利润分割法和新的价值贡献分配法。(李)

李：……reinforce its pre-BEPS view 中 its 指代的是中国，具体来说就是中国税务机关或国税总局。国税总局考虑到本地持有无形资产的情况，不断质疑和否定基于可比企业的分析方法。

雷：因为有争议，所以会导致 lead to an ever-increasing use of the Profit Split Method (PSM) post-BEPS as well as the use of the new VCAM。利润分割法和 VCAM 的适用是有前提的，即如果现在各国有争议的话，可能会二一添作五，简单分一分得了，因为争议太多了。

> 改译3：这将强化中国在 BEPS 时代之前有关可比性（特别是有关市场溢价）的观点，导致后 BEPS 时代更多地运用利润分割法和价值贡献分配法这一新方法。（雷）

王："这一新方法"并不符合逻辑，因为有两种新方法。

> 建议译法：这将强化中国在 BEPS 时代之前有关可比性（特别是有关市场溢价）的观点，并在后 BEPS 时代更多地运用利润分割法和新的价值贡献分配法。（王）

21

> 原文：Both methods could be used when the Chinese authorities ascertain that local intangibles or LSAs would justify the disregard of otherwise comparable transactions or enterprises from third countries...
>
> 原译：使用这两种方法的前提是，中国当局确定地方无形资产或地域性特殊优势可以不考虑第三国可比交易或企业
>
> 改译1：使用这两种方法的前提是，中国当局确定，地方无形资产或地域性特殊优势为可比性因素，不必考虑第三国可比交易或可比企业。（王）
>
> 改译2：使用这两种方法的条件是：中国当局认定存在地方无形资产或地域性特殊优势，因此不必考虑第三国可比交易或可比企业。（李）
>
> 改译3：只要中国税务机关认定本地无形资产或地域性特殊优势的存在可以提供理由放弃使用其他第三国的可比交易或公司，就有权使用这两种方法。（雷）

雷：disregard of otherwise comparable transactions or enterprises from third countries 背后是在讲另外一个比较常见的定价方法，那个定价方法会比较多使用 comparable transactions 或 enterprises。所以他说，应用这种 LSA、利润分割法或 VCAM，会抛弃本来（otherwise）可比的交易和企业。因为要评定跨国公司的利润和税收，需要找到可比的交易或中国企业。但这些可比交易和企业在关联交易中是很稀有的；而且严格意义上说，中国企业欠债太多，还达不到跨国公司的经营水平（业务功能分类水平），所以跨国公司在中国的业务和中国公司相比，没有可比性。利润水平不合理，这个时候就采用第三国的企业作对比，比如拿日本、韩国、欧洲相关企业做对比。

> **建议译法**：只要中国税务机关认定采用本地无形资产或地域性特殊优势原则理由充分，就可以不适用原本的第三国可比交易或公司法法，转而采用上述两种方法。（李）

22

> **原文**：... and if LSAs and market premium rise to the level of unique and valuable intangibles, a substantial portion of global profits from value chains operated by MNEs would be allocated to China.
>
> **原译**：而且，如果地域性特殊优势和市场溢价达到独特且有价值的无形资产水平，跨国企业运营的价值链上相当一部分全球利润将分配到中国。（费）
>
> **改译 1**：而如果地域性特殊优势和市场溢价达到独特而有价值的无形资产的程度，跨国公司经营价值链中相当比例的利润就会被分配到中国来。（雷）

雷：and if LSAs and market premium rise to the level of unique and valuable intangibles 的意思是，不是有无形资产，就能获得更高的利润；这种无形资产必须是 unique 的，而且要有重要价值。intangibles 不是简单的会计用语，而是更复杂的概念。unique 和 valuable 从国际规则角度，也有大段的论述，用更复杂的类别、概念解析。这里的意思是如果 LSA 和市场溢价达到这种水平的话，那就意味着，一个跨国公司大量的利润要放在中国了。

建议译法：而如果地域性特殊优势和市场溢价成为独特而有价值的无形资产，跨国公司经营价值链中很大一部分利润就会分配到中国。（王）

李：另外注意，根据前文注释资料，LSAs（包括 market premium）不属于无形资产，但这里说中国认为是无形资产。

23

原文：The tax burden in countries with a substantial consumer market or with substantial workforce can increase if the Chinese or Indian approaches are fully adopted...
原译：如果中国或印度的方法得到充分采用，那么拥有巨大消费者市场或大量劳动力的国家税务负担会加重。（佚名）
改译 1：如果全面采用中国或印度的做法，对于拥有巨大消费市场或大量劳动力的国家来说，税务负担会加重。（王）

王：countries with a substantial consumer market 指中国。上文说过：**China**, for example, tends to view the exploitation of its **consumer market** through a Chinese permanent establishment as representative of an intangible asset which is unique and valuable to an entire global firm...while pursuing the application of profit split approaches with indicators geared towards "market intangibles". This stance can be viewed as an approximation to **global formulary apportionment with predominance of the sales factor**.

王：countries with substantial workforce 指印度。上文说过：The Indian position on "location savings" and supply-side advantages, on the other hand, can recapture synergetic gains associated with **an assembled workforce** and require increased profit mark-ups under one-sided transfer pricing methods, or even view the **activities of skilled labor based in India as indicative of unique and valuable contributions justifying the use of a global profit split**.

> **改译 2**：如果全面采用中国或印度的做法，在拥有巨大消费市场或大量劳动力的国家，跨国企业的税务负担会加重。（李）

雷：如果刚才大家认真听了，就会知道中国和印度的 other innovative method 可以让中印多征税。但是如果中国和印度说，我们有巨大的消费市场和劳动力，我们有 LSA，所以跨国公司就应该多交税，跨国公司就会说：如果在其他国家做生意，人家不会管我要额外的利润，你们（中、印）征税，会加重我们的税负。"税负"是一个常见的概念。"税收负担"也 OK 啦，但是翻译成"税负"的话，内行人听起来更顺一些。

> **建议译法**：如果全面采用中国或印度的做法，在拥有巨大消费市场或大量劳动力的国家，跨国企业的税负会加重。（雷）

24

> **原 译**：... and this may be perceived as an adequate policy response to the BEPS concerns raised by the digital economy. Double taxation might ensue if these adjustments are effected unilaterally, whilst other countries continue to conform to the OECD Guidelines.
> **原译**：而且，这在政策上充分回应了数字经济下的 BEPS 关切。如果单方面实施这些调整，而其他国家继续遵守经合组织准则，则可能产生双重征税。（佚名）
> **改译 1**：可能有人认为中印的做法是在政策上对数字经济下 BEPS 关切的适当回应，但如果单方面实施这些调整，而其他国家继续遵守经合组织准则，则可能产生双重征税。（李）

李：may be perceived by whom？这里的逻辑主语应该是中国和印度。也就是说，中、印认为这个做法是合理的，但实际可能会造成税局过重的负担。may 是"可能"，不是"可以"。如果用可以，就表示作者赞同。但作者其实不赞同；作者只是说，中印两国可能认为这种做法不错。

> **改译 2：** 而这种结果可能会被视为在税收政策层面对数字经济下 BEPS 问题的恰当回应。但如果单方面进行这些调整，而其他国家继续遵守《经合组织转让定价指南》，则可能因此/随之产生双重征税。（雷）

雷： 为什么 and 翻译成"而"呢？如果你理解背景，又熟读原文的话，就知道这里表达的是，你（中、印）在这么做，但你还认为是理所当然的。double taxation 的意思并不是从跨国公司角度来讲，而是从政府的角度。比如从中国和印度政府的角度看，会觉得我对你有很大贡献，你为什么不多交税呢？这个 concerns raised by the digital economy 是指什么？这就涉及 BEPS 行动计划 1 里面的核心内容。这个 1 讲的就是在现在所谓的数字经济时代，很多跨境行为是可以远程操作的。比如说一家美国公司在另外一个国家有很多的人，但是它在这个国家交税非常少。因为美国说，你这些人对我的公司来说都是辅助性的，做的工作也是简单的，所以不应该交那么多税。但是，从政府的角度，认为这是不合理的。那政策上怎么应对呢？政府认为如果你的人员达到一定规模，我就有权征你的税。你就必须按水平交税。这样我不仅响应了 LSA 的理念，我还回应了对数字经济下 BEPS 的关切。但是从跨国公司角度讲，这样征税可能是不合理的。所以在政府眼中，是 adequate policy response 的东西，对于跨国公司来说，会觉得是和主流规则不相符的规定。因为跨国公司觉得，虽然在你们国家的人多，但是不产生实质经营内容，或者贡献和技术含量不大。如果你总是这样要求的话，那不好意思，我不在你这儿做生意了。这两派都有自己的论点。这个争论是永无止境的。另外，these adjustments 是指涉及 consumer market 或者 substantial workforce 的调整。如果中、印单边去 effect 或者实施（这些规则）的话，而别的国家反而继续遵守 OECD Guidelines，会出现什么情况？那首先倒霉的就是跨国公司。因为，这对跨国公司来说是无中生有、双重征税。

> **建议译法：** 而这种结果可能被视为在税收政策层面对数字经济中 BEPS 问题的恰当回应。但如果单方面进行这些调整，而其他国家继续遵守《经合组织转让定价指南》，则可能产生双重征税。（王）

25

> 原文：Other jurisdictions might follow China and India which could shift taxing rights away not only from U.S. or Europe but from other Asian countries which serve as regional supply chain hubs or treasury centers for global MNEs and/or that are also capital exporters, such as Hong Kong, Singapore, the Republic of Korea and Japan.
>
> 原译：其他辖区会仿效中国和印度，这样不仅可能将征税权从美国或欧洲转移，还可能将征税权从其他亚洲国家或地区转移，这些国家或地区可能是全球跨国公司区域供应链中心或财务中心，也可能是资本输出地，比如香港、新加坡、韩国和日本。（佚名）
>
> 改译：其他税收管辖区／国家或地区可能／没准／也许会仿效中国和印度，这样可能不仅会将征税权从美国或欧洲转移出去，还可能将征税权从亚洲其他的一些国家或地区转移出去。这些国家或地区，比如香港、新加坡、韩国和日本，或者是作为全球性跨国公司区域供应链中心，或者是财资中心，或者是资本输出地／国／出资地。（雷）

雷：OECD Guidelines 是转让定价领域专门的一本手册和书。jurisdiction 并不仅仅包含国家。在税收上，香港就属于一个 jurisdiction，因为它有独立的财政大权。所以税收上的 tax jurisdiction 就是指有独立征税权和征管权的国家或地区。所以比较专业的翻译就是"其他税收管辖区"。这是比较固定的一个翻法。内行都知道你在说什么。对于稍微外行一点的人就说，"有独立税收管辖权的国家或地区"。或者再通俗一点，没有必要强调独立管辖权，实际就是国家或地区啦，也能表达基本的意思。所以你要考虑翻译的对象。might 我给出了几种译法。直译可以翻译为"可能"，但是其实更接近"没准"（比较口语化）或者"也许"（用词比较折中）。所以最后一句讲的是，如果这种情况出现的话，那么采用这些规则的国家（中、印）有机会把征税权从美国、欧洲那边转移到自己的国家。而且很有可能把所谓的征税权从别的国家转移过来。这里涉及一个非常简单，但是很大的背景。其他的亚洲国家就是最后说的香港、新加坡、韩国和日本。这些国家除了日本是 capital exporters 之外，另外那些国家都承担前面所说的职能，即 regional supply chain hubs or treasury centers for global MNEs。因为香港、新加坡都是在税收筹划里面比较重要的财资中心。这个财资中心 treasury centers 其实是一个特殊的概念，跨国公司在经营的时候，都会把很多东西拎出来。其实财资中心就是管理跨国公司现金流的重要中心。所以这种地方有很多投资、外汇风险，就类似跨国公司的小银行。这些小银行会在新加坡和香港，因为这些地方有人员、有政策。作者的意思是说，如果中、印继续这么搞的话，不仅会流失大量跨国公司，连新加坡等财资中心的利润也会搞走。

李：and/or 译为"同时又是 / 或者是"吧，再严谨一些。

> **建议译法**：其他税收管辖区没准会仿效中国和印度，这样可能不仅会将征税权从美国或欧洲转移出去，还可能将征税权从亚洲其他一些国家或地区转移出去。这些国家或地区，比如香港、新加坡、韩国和日本，或者是全球性跨国公司区域供应链中心，或者是财资中心，同时又是 / 或者是资本输出地。（李）